Crawford Kirkwood.
27 Wilson St.

April 16th, 1945.   Girvan.

From Painting] [*by Wm. Hole, R.S.A.*

The Mission of St Columba to the Picts.

A Short History of Scotland

by

P. Hume Brown, M.A., LL.D.

*Late Fraser Professor of Ancient (Scottish) History and Palæography
University of Edinburgh ; and Historiographer-Royal
for Scotland*

Oliver and Boyd Ltd.
Edinburgh: Tweeddale Court
London: 98 Great Russell Street, W.C.1

THE Publishers desire to thank the Trustees of the Scottish National Portrait Gallery for kind permission to reproduce in their *History of Scotland* the important series of historical mural decorations, painted by the eminent Scottish artist, Mr Wm. Hole, R.S.A.; and also the Plans and Works Committee of the Edinburgh Town Council for their courtesy in allowing them to include reproductions of several historical paintings by Mr Hole, which are in their possession.

In connection with the preparation of the blocks, they have pleasure in acknowledging Mr Hole's kindness in placing certain negatives at their disposal.

Their thanks are also due to Mr Tom Scott, A.R.S.A., and several other gentlemen, to the Society of Antiquaries of Scotland and other institutions for their kindness in granting permission to reproduce illustrations of articles of archæological and historical interest in their possession; and, lastly, to Messrs James Maclehose & Sons, Glasgow, for the privilege of utilising certain of the illustrations which appear in their *Scottish History and Life*.

PRINTED IN GREAT BRITAIN BY
OLIVER AND BOYD LTD., EDINBURGH

CONTENTS

LIST OF ILLUSTRATIONS

ix

HISTORY OF SCOTLAND

1. THE EARLIEST DWELLERS IN SCOTLAND

HOW did there come to be a country called Scotland and a people called the Scottish people? When we look at a map of Scotland, we see that it is made up of the mainland and a great number of islands lying near it. The mainland stretches from the Pentland Firth in the north to the Cheviot Hills and the Solway Firth in the south. But why does Scotland end at the Cheviot Hills, and how is it that the Hebrides, or Western Islands, and the Orkney and Shetland Islands belong to it? Why are the mainland and all the islands called by the one name of Scotland? Then there are two different languages spoken in Scotland. The Highlanders speak Gaelic, the Lowlanders speak English, and yet both Highlanders and Lowlanders are known as Scotsmen. How did they come to be called by this one name though they speak different languages, and differ from each other in many other ways? It is to answer these questions that this book has been written, and we have to go a long way back to answer them.

The land we now call Scotland was not always

Stone Hammers.

known by that name, and the people who lived in it were not always called Scots. There was, indeed, a

Arrow-heads of Flint.

time when neither the land nor its people had a name to themselves. For Scotland, like all other countries, was once inhabited by people who were not civilised, but were merely savages or barbarians. As these people did not write books, how do we know that they once lived in Scotland?

One day, in the year 1894, some workmen were quarrying stones in the side of a cliff oppo-

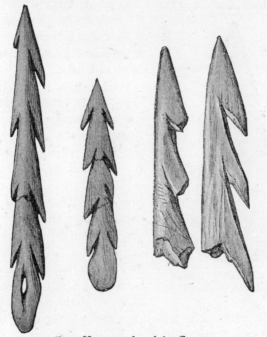

Bone Harpoons found in Caves.

site the Bay of Oban, in Argyleshire. On digging into the cliff, they came to a cave twenty-five feet long and more than sixteen feet wide, and in the cave they found things which showed that men must once have lived in it. There

A

were heads of hammers made of stone, and many tools and implements made of horn, such as harpoons, chisels, borers, and pins. The skulls of human beings were also found, and the bones of animals which had been killed and eaten by the cave-dwellers, who must, therefore, have been clever hunters and fishers. At what time these men lived nobody can say, but it must have been more than a thousand years before the birth of Christ.

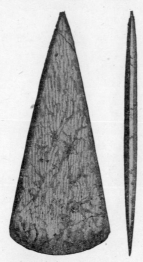

Polished Axe of Greenish Quartz, from Berwickshire.

And not only in Argyleshire but in other parts of the country, things have been found that must have been made by men's hands in those far-off times. For instance, on the Carse of Stirling, quite near to the town of that name, there was found the skeleton of a whale, and on its skull was the head of an axe made of a deer's horn, which must have been used by some one when the whale was cast ashore. And, indeed, near the same place the skeletons of no fewer than twelve other whales have been found, which shows that in those times the sea must have come much farther in than it does now. In the Carse of Stirling, also, there have been found great heaps of shells— oyster-shells, mussel-shells, and others—with fireplaces beside them. This proves that the people who once lived there fed on shellfish, which they roasted in the fire. Then in different parts of the country, in deep bogs and in the beds of rivers, canoes have been dug up, which were made by hollowing out trees with fire. We learn from this that the men to whom they belonged were able to sail on lakes and rivers, and even some distance on the sea.

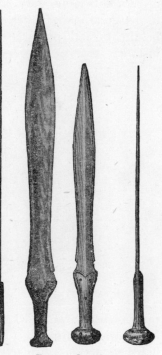

Now, when we look at the things that have been found in different parts of the country, we see that those early dwellers in Scotland did not stand still, but became more and more civilised in their ways of living. We know this from the tools and ornaments they made, which were very different at different times. In the farthest back times they made their

Bronze Swords.

tools and other things of stone or bone or horn, and often they fashioned them so skilfully that we cannot understand how they were made.

The time when men made tools of stone is called the Stone Age; but a day came when a great step forward was taken. They learned to make bronze, which is got from the melting and mixing of copper and tin, and is much harder than either of these metals. Of course, they did not stop all at once using stone, but they began to use bronze more and more, and became very skilful in making things with it. A great many articles of bronze have been found in ditches and peat-bogs and other places. For instance, bronze daggers have been dug up, and

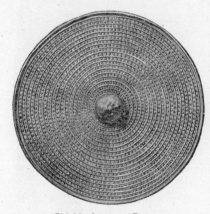

Shield of beaten Bronze.

razors, spear-heads, sickles for cutting corn, shields, and even trumpets. Ornaments, too, such as bracelets, necklaces, finger-rings, ear-rings, and crowns, show that the people of the Bronze Age, as it is called, were not always thinking of fighting, but also took pleasure in looking at beautiful things. It is very interesting also to know that the men of the Bronze Age understood the use of gold, for a great many gold ornaments have been found which were made by their hands.

Then another step forward was taken; iron began to be used instead of bronze, though, of course, bronze was only given up by degrees. The use of iron instead of bronze made a great change in the way of making weapons, tools, and ornaments, as these had now to be hammered out instead of being cast in moulds. Many articles belonging to the Iron Age have been found in different parts of Scotland. For example, out of a loch in Kirkcudbrightshire there was once taken a large pot of bronze, in which were found tools and implements

 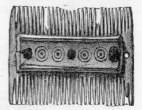

Combs made of Bone.

such as axe-heads, hammers, saws, and nails, all made of iron. In the Bronze Age we saw that ornaments were made of gold, but in the Iron Age silver ornaments were much more used. The chief thing to be remembered about the Iron Age is, however, that it was the time just before books began to be written. And, indeed, in the Iron Age, in some countries, men knew the alphabet and began to write, though whether this was the case in Scotland we cannot tell.

Before we have done speaking of the Prehistoric Times, as they are called, there is one other thing that must not be forgotten, and that is, the way in which

the people buried their dead. It is curious that
the tombs where the dead were buried have lasted
longer than the houses they inhabited when they
were living. In different parts of the country there
are still to be seen great circles of tall unhewn stones,
though sometimes most of the stones have fallen.
Inside these circles there are great heaps of stones,
called cairns, and when the stones are removed it is

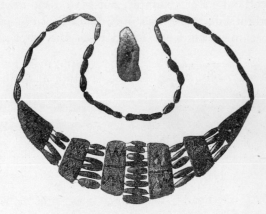

Jet Necklace found in Ross-shire.

found that people have been buried there. Now,
it is interesting to know that these tombs were
differently made at different periods, and this enables
us to tell whether those who were buried in them
lived during the Stone Age or the Bronze Age or
the Iron Age.

In the tombs of the later Stone Age there are
usually chambers where the dead were buried, whereas
in the tombs of the early Bronze Age only a few such
chambers are found, and none in those of the Iron

Age. Sometimes the bodies were buried whole, as bones found in the tombs show, but usually they were burned. In the tombs of the Bronze Age beautiful urns made of clay are found, in which the ashes of the dead had been put. It is strange to discover that in the graves are also found the heads of arrows, of spears, and of axes, and ornaments such as beads, necklaces, and ear-rings. Some of these ornaments are very precious too. What could these people have meant by putting such things in tombs, that could be of no use to the dead? Was it because they expected the dead some day to rise

Section of Chambered Cairn, Argyleshire.

from the grave, and use their weapons and ornaments, just as they had done before they died? Or was it only to show how much they honoured and loved those who had passed away? To these questions we cannot be sure that we have the right answer.

What has been told in this chapter is learned from the different things that have been found above the ground and below it, all over the country. But after this we have books also to tell us what we should like to know; and so the new time is called the Historic Age, to mark it off from the Prehistoric Times of which we have been speaking.

2. THE COMING OF THE ROMANS—JULIUS AGRICOLA. A.D. 80 TO A.D. 86

The first book written about Scotland was not by a writer who was born in that country, but by a Roman, called Tacitus. The name of his book is *The Life of Julius Agricola*, and it is written in Latin. Agricola was the father-in-law of Tacitus, and was a great Roman general. He was the first man who tried to conquer the country lying to the north of the Cheviot Hills and the Solway Firth.

But how did Agricola come to lead his soldiers to a land so far distant from his own? It happened in this way. Rome was at first only a small village, but it grew to be a great town, and then its people began to conquer the country lying near it. Soon they conquered the whole of Italy, and in course of time all the lands round the Mediterranean Sea. Then the famous Roman general, Julius Cæsar, one of the greatest men who ever lived, conquered France, or Gaul, as it was then named, and it was this conquest of Gaul that in the end brought the Romans to Scotland. The people in what we now call England, but which the Romans named South Britain, gave help to the people of Gaul in fighting the Romans, and so the Romans found it necessary to conquer them also. Then having subdued South Britain, they were forced to lead their armies into North Britain, as the North Britons often made war on the South Britons. Thus we see how Agricola had come all the way from Italy, and led his soldiers into Scotland.

It was in the year A.D. 80, more than eighteen hundred years ago, that Agricola, at the head of his army, entered North Britain to subdue it, as South Britain by this time had already been conquered. In some ways his task was difficult, and in other ways it was made easy for him. His great

Roman Iron Helmet with Face Mask.

difficulty was the want of good roads along which he could lead his army from one place to another. Almost the whole country was then taken up with forests, and deep bogs, or great stretches of water. There were only patches of ground here and there on which crops were grown. Often, therefore, when the army was toiling through these difficult places the enemy would suddenly appear and fall upon the soldiers, when they were perhaps tired out with a long day's march.

But, on the other hand, the North Britons were not nearly a match for the Romans at fighting. In the first place, the Romans were far better armed. Most of them, though not all, wore metal helmets on their heads, and had armour on their breasts and thighs. In their left hands they carried large shields, and in their right hands they had short, strong swords with sharp points, with which they pierced the bodies of their enemies.

The Britons also had weapons made of iron or bronze, but their shields were too small to defend them. Their swords too had not sharp points like those of the Romans, and were too long to be easily used when they fought close together. Then the Romans were all trained soldiers, and had been taught to obey their officers, and to fight exactly as they were told. But what made Agricola's task easiest was that the Britons did not all unite and make one great army under one general. The reason of this was that the Britons were not really one nation, but were divided into a great many tribes, each having a chief of its own. These tribes were often at war with each other, so that instead of having to fight all the Britons at once, Agricola fought with one tribe after another, and so was able to gain easier victories.

We do not know exactly into what parts of North Britain Agricola first led his army, though it may be found out some day. It is pretty certain, however, that he came in by the east and not by the west side of the country, and we know quite well how he set about trying to subdue it. What he did was to conquer one tribe after another, and then build forts, in which he put soldiers to defend them.

In this way, after two years' fighting, he conquered all the tribes to the south of the Firths of Forth and Clyde, and compelled them to obey him.

But the most difficult part of the country still remained to be conquered—the country of the Highland hills, which was inhabited by a people called the Caledonians. These were tall men with red hair, and were the bravest fighters of all the Britons. Before trying to conquer the Caledonians, however, Agricola made a long row of forts from the Firth of Forth to the

Roman Foot-Soldier with Standard.

Firth of Clyde, to prevent them from coming down into the Lowlands, which he had already subdued. At last, in the fourth year after he had come to North Britain, he led his army into Caledonia, but as he marched into the wild country, some of his officers became so frightened that they advised him to return.

And they had good reason to be frightened. One night the Caledonians fell upon one of Agricola's camps, killed the sentinels, and would have gained the victory, had not Agricola sent soldiers from another camp and driven them off. The Caledonians, however, were not cast down by their defeat, and went on fighting as before, till the coming of winter compelled Agricola to march back to the Lowlands.

Roman Horse-Soldier.

But Agricola was determined to conquer the Caledonians, and next summer he again led his army into their country. The Caledonians knew that he would return, and they prepared to defend themselves and their homes. Many of the tribes joined together and put themselves under a leader, called Calgácus,* the first hero in Scottish history who has a name. The women and children were sent away into safe places, and every man who could fight, old or young, took up arms to defend his country. At length, the two armies came in sight of each other at a place called

* *Calgácus* and *Graupius* are now accepted as more probable forms than *Gálgacus* and *Grampius*.

Mons Graupius, though where that place was we shall probably never find out.

Then was fought the first battle on Scottish ground of which the story has come down to us. The way the Caledonians fought was to throw their darts from a distance, and then rush in and try to break the ranks of the enemy. But, as we have seen, they did not fight well close at hand, because their shields were too small, and their swords had not sharp points like those of the Romans. Agricola knew this, and what he did was to pick some of his best men and make them get into close grips with the Caledonians, who, though they fought as bravely as men can fight, at last gave way and fled into the neighbouring forests. This was the last great battle that Agricola fought in North Britain, for he was now called back to Rome, from which he never returned.

---

3. THE ROMANS IN NORTH BRITAIN— THEIR DEPARTURE.   A.D. 86 TO A.D. 412

When Agricola left North Britain, he thought he had completely subdued the part of it south of the Firths of Forth and Clyde, but he was greatly mistaken. As we saw, he had made a row of forts to keep the Caledonians from coming down into the Lowlands, but, as soon as he was gone, they broke through the forts just as if they had not been there. Then, about forty years after Agricola had left, there came another great Roman to Britain,—an

emperor this time, and not merely a general.   This
was the Emperor Hadrian, whose chief delight was to
travel through all the lands over which he ruled.
But when Hadrian came into North Britain, he saw
that Agricola's row of forts was useless.   He therefore
returned south, and built a wall of turf between the
river Tyne and the Solway Firth, so that it looked as
if he had left the whole of North Britain to itself.   But
this did not make things any better, as the North

Britons broke through Hadrian's wall and made war
on the South Britons, who were now living peacefully
under the government of the Romans.

But it shows how determined the Romans were to
conquer the North Britons that, about twenty years
after Hadrian had left, another Roman army was
sent into their country.   The Roman emperor then
reigning was called Antoninus, and was one of the
best and greatest men who ever ruled any people.
Antoninus, however, did not come himself, but sent

one of his generals, called Lollius Úrbicus. We know hardly anything of what Úrbicus did in the way of fighting, but he must have conquered all the tribes south of the Firths of Forth and Clyde, just as Agricola had done. We know this, because he built a wall in the same place as Agricola's row of forts, that is, between the Firths of Forth and Clyde.

Now this wall is a very wonderful piece of work, and shows that the Romans had quite made up their minds to keep a hold of North Britain. To this day many parts of it are still standing, and in going from Edinburgh to Glasgow by the railway you can see a piece of it at Greenhill Station. It begins at Carriden, on the Firth of Forth, and ends at Old Kilpatrick, on the river Clyde, and is more than thirty miles long. It is made in this way.

First of all, there is a foundation of stone, and on this foundation sods of turf are neatly laid. It is about twelve feet high, and about fourteen feet thick at the bottom. Besides the wall there was a deep ditch on the north side of it, so that if the Caledonians tried to get into the Lowland country they would first have to leap into the ditch and then climb the wall. On the south side of it there was a broad road along which the soldiers could march from one part of the wall to another, and at every two miles there was a fort from which watch could be kept for the enemy night and day.

This wonderful piece of work is called the Wall of Antoninus, because it was by his order that it was made. The country people, however, had another name for it; they called it Grahame's or Grime's

Dyke, which means the Devil's Dyke, and they gave it this name because they thought that it could hardly have been made by the hands of men.

Strange to say, not even this great wall kept the brave Caledonians out of the Lowlands; and, besides the Caledonians, another tribe, called the Mæatæ, began to give the Romans trouble. Indeed, things became so bad in North Britain, that at last another Roman Emperor thought that he must come himself and try to subdue the country completely. This was the Emperor Severus, who was his own general and had already fought in a great many wars. So in the year A.D. 208, more than a hundred years after Agricola had first come to North Britain, Severus led a great army into the country of the Caledonians. He was not in a very fit state to undertake such an expedition. He was now an old man, and so ill with the gout that he could neither walk nor ride, but had to be carried on a litter.

This time the Caledonians did not do as they had done when Agricola came against them. They did not come out and fight Severus in a great battle. What they did was to follow his army wherever it went, and, whenever they got the chance, to fall upon it suddenly and to slay any soldiers who had fallen behind. But Severus was a very cautious general, and, before leading his army forward, he cut down the forests that stood in his way, and made bridges across the rivers, so that his soldiers should have good roads to march along. So he went on farther and farther till, it is said, he reached the Moray Firth, which was much farther north than any Roman had yet gone. Then Severus thought he had

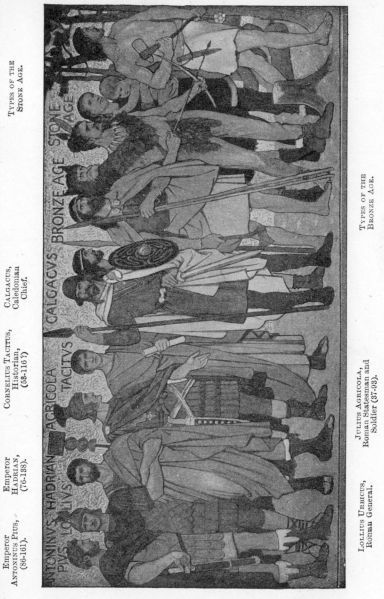

Emperor ANTONINUS PIUS, (86-161).

Emperor HADRIAN, (76-188).

CORNELIUS TACITUS, Historian, (58-116?).

CALGACUS, Caledonian Chief.

TYPES OF THE STONE AGE.

JULIUS AGRICOLA, Roman Statesman and Soldier (37-93).

TYPES OF THE BRONZE AGE.

LOLLIUS URBICUS, Roman General.

gone far enough, and led his army back to the
Lowlands, always followed by the Caledonians, who
seem never to have left him alone.

And what was the result of this long and
dangerous journey? It is said, though it is difficult
to believe it, that from first to last fifty thousand of
his soldiers were killed; and after all he had not
thoroughly subdued his enemies, the Caledonians.
Indeed, Severus had hardly got back to South
Britain, when they and the other tribe, called the
Mæatæ, began to give as much trouble as ever, and,
as this great general died at York three years after he
had left North Britain, all his labour had been in vain.
It should be said that Severus did one other thing
which shows how anxious the Romans were to keep
hold of Britain. He caused a wall to be built at the
same place as Hadrian's, that is, between the river
Tyne and the Solway Firth. This wall was made of
stone, and parts of it can still be seen. If, as people
now usually think, this wall was really made by
Severus, it would look as if he had given up North
Britain and thought only of keeping South Britain
safe.

We see how hard the Romans had found it to
conquer North Britain, and even to keep hold of the
parts of it which they did subdue. No doubt the
chief reasons for this were the bravery of its people,
and the difficulty of getting from one part of the
country to another, on account of the mountains and
forests, and bogs and waters, with which it was
covered. But there was another reason still: the
Romans had to carry on so many wars in other
countries that they could not spare a sufficient

number of soldiers to conquer North Britain once
for all.

And, indeed, there came a time when they found
it difficult to keep hold even of South Britain,
for a number of enemies began to attack it all at
once. The Scots from Ireland came in their ships
and invaded the west coast; a people in North
Britain, called the Picts, attacked it from the north;
and the Saxons from Germany, who were one day
to conquer the whole of South Britain, plundered the
east coast. And at last a time came when the
Romans had no soldiers to spare, for the city of
Rome itself was attacked by a barbarian tribe,
and plundered by its leader, Alaric, in the year
410; and two years afterwards the Roman legions
left both North and South Britain for ever, and the
native inhabitants were left to live by themselves.

The Romans had been coming and going to
North Britain for more than three hundred years
—as long a time as from now back to the reign of
Mary, Queen of Scots. What is there to show
that they were so long a time in our country?
When the Romans completely conquered any land,
as they did South Britain and Gaul, this was what
happened. The native people of the country learned
to speak the Latin language, to wear Roman clothes,
and in every way to become just like Romans. The
conquerors also taught them to build Roman houses,
and towns grew up containing temples for the
worship of the gods, courts of justice, and even
theatres and schools. This was what took place in
South Britain and Gaul, but it was not the case in
North Britain. All that the Romans were able to do

in North Britain was to defend their forts, and keep
them from being taken by the enemy, so that when
they left the country it was almost as if they had
never been there.

But even if we did not read about it in books,
there are still things to be seen in Scotland which
tell us how long a time the Romans were there and
how hard they tried to conquer it.   There is that
great Wall of Antoninus, parts of which we can still
see ; and there are roads in different parts of the
country which are still called Roman Roads, and are
used even to the present day.   Here and there, also,
both north and south of the river Forth, there are the
remains of the forts which they made, and in which,
when they are dug up, many things are found which
the Romans used when they lived in them.   But, as
we have heard so much of these forts, let us see what
they were like, and let us take one which has been
dug up, and which we know best from a book that
has been written about it.

This fort is called the Bar Hill Fort, because it
stands on one of what are called the Bar Hills.
These hills are about a mile to the north-west of Croy
Station, which you pass on the railway between
Glasgow and Edinburgh.   Of course, when the
Romans made a fort, they had to see that it was in
a right place.   There must be water near it ; it must
be easily got at from the other forts ; and it must be
on a spot which it would be easy to defend against
the enemy.   Suppose we had paid a visit to the Bar
Hill Fort when the Romans were there, what should
we have seen ?

First we should have come to a high wall or rampart made of turf, and about twelve feet thick. The wall was built in the form of a square, and had a gate on each side. At the four corners of the wall and at each side of the gates there was a wooden tower, and in all these towers there were catapults, or machines for throwing large stones at the enemy. If we had entered by one of the gates, we should have seen that on three sides there were two deep ditches, while on the fourth side there was only one ditch, because it was thought that on that side only one was needed. We now see what a strong place a Roman fort was, and how difficult it must have been for the enemy to break into it.

And now let us see what it was like inside. First of all, we should have seen that a Roman fort was a large place, for this Bar Hill Fort took up nearly three acres ; that is to say, it was as big as a fair-sized field. Looking round us, we should have seen that the fort inside looked like a little town. A number of streets ran through it so that the soldiers could pass from one part of it to another, and there were a great many buildings, which served for different uses. In the middle was what was called the Prætorium, which was made of stone and had a roof of red tiles, and which was the headquarters of the regiment. Then there were the barracks made of wood, with thatched roofs, where the soldiers lived ; and there were workshops, baths, a storehouse, and places into which the refuse of the fort was put.

Now it was only soldiers who were allowed to live in the fort ; what then was done with their wives and children, for many of the Roman soldiers had wives and children ? It must be remembered that

the Romans lived a great number of years in these
forts, and that they were really their homes. Outside the fort a little village was built, in which
the wives and children lived, as well as old

Woman's Boot (Roman), found near Melrose.

soldiers who were no longer able to fight, and
traders who sold the things that were needed both
in the village and in the fort. Of course, if the
enemy ever came against them, then the people in

Man's Shoe (Roman), found near Melrose.

the village could be taken into the fort, where they
would be safer.

As we should expect, when the Bar Hill Fort was
dug up, a great many things were found which the

Romans had used when they lived in it. Pots and tubs made of clay were discovered, pieces of glass that had been used for bottles and windows, a chariot wheel and other wheels, boots and shoes, barrels, children's playthings, and, what is most interesting of all, stones with Latin inscriptions on them. It will be seen, therefore, that the Romans lived in their forts just as they did at home, and that they had everything around them that they needed.

There is one thing more which must not be forgotten before this chapter is finished. Just about the time the Romans left, there was living in the land one whose name and work are remembered to this day. This was St Ninian, who, as far as we know, was the first to preach the Christian religion in Scotland. Ninian was born on the shores of the Solway Firth about the year A.D. 350, and, as his father was a Christian, he was baptized when he was a child. When he grew up he went to Rome to be better taught, for Rome was now a Christian and not a pagan city, and on his return he made his home near the town of Whithorn, in Wigtownshire. The rest of his life Ninian spent in preaching the gospel to the people who lived to the south of the river Forth, and at his own home he built a church which was called *Candida Casa*, the Latin for White House, because it was built of light-coloured stone and not of wood. Ninian was the first man who laboured in Scotland in the cause of religion of whom we know anything, and his name will never be forgotten. In different parts of the country there are wells, called St Ninian's Wells, to which sick people were taken, because it was thought that Ninian had blessed the water; and at the present day there are still many churches which bear his name.

---

4. THE BEGINNINGS OF SCOTLAND.
449-844

After the Romans left North Britain, it is a long time—nearly a hundred and fifty years—before we hear of it again, and the reason is that there are no books to tell us what was happening in the country. When we next read about it in books, however, we find that a great change had taken place. When Agricola came to North Britain, there were as many as seventeen tribes in the land, each with a chief of its own, who had nothing to do with each other except when they went to war among themselves. Now, however, instead of seventeen tribes we find only four great kingdoms, each governed by its own king. This was a great step forward, as it showed that the whole of North Britain might one day become one kingdom with one king to rule over it. We have now to see who those four peoples were, as it is from them that there came to be a country called Scotland, and it is from them that most Scotsmen of the present day are descended.

The largest of the four kingdoms was one which took in all the country from the river Forth to the Pentland Firth, and was inhabited by a people known as Picts, to whom the Romans gave this name because they painted their bodies when they went to war—the Latin word *pictus* meaning *painted*. We cannot tell where these Picts came from or even what language they spoke. They were divided

Map showing Four Peoples.

into the northern and southern Picts, but one king ruled over them both; and we shall presently hear of a Pictish king who did a thing which has made his name to be remembered. This Pictish kingdom lasted for several hundred years, but we shall see that it came to an end in a strange way, and that of all the four peoples of whom we are speaking, the Picts are the only people whose name went out of use, and is now only read of in books.

The name of the second people we cannot forget, because it is from them that Scotland got its name, and it is owing to them that there came to be a country called Scotland, and a nation known as the Scottish nation. The "Scots" was the name of the second people, and fortunately we happen to know more about them than about the Picts. First of all, we know that they came from the country which we now call Ireland, but which then and for long afterwards was called, not Ireland, but Scotia or Scotland, so that Irishmen were Scotsmen before ourselves. Then we know what language they spoke; it was the same as the Highlanders now speak, though, of course, it has changed a great deal during the hundreds of years since the ancient Scots spoke it. We know also the name they gave to the part of North Britain in which they settled; it was called Dalriada, after the part of Ireland from which they came, and was what we now call Argyleshire and the islands near it. And, lastly, we know that the Scots were not pagans like the other three peoples, but Christians, for in Ireland, from which they came, Christianity was known before it was known in North Britain. Dalriada was the smallest of all the kingdoms, yet it was from it that the first kings came who ruled over the whole of Scotland.

The name of the third people can easily be remembered, because it is a name which is still given to both Scotsmen and Englishmen. They were called Britons, and the part of the country they inhabited was chiefly the valley of the river Clyde. When the Romans first came to our island, these Britons were the chief inhabitants whom they found there, and this was why they named the island Britannia, or Britain. In course of time, however, the Britons had been driven into the west, both in South and North Britain, so that now they were not so strong and numerous as they had once been. They belonged to the same race as the Scots, that is, they were Celts; but the language they spoke was not like that of the Highlanders, but like that of the people of Wales, who are also Celts. The place where their king lived was called Alcluyd, which was afterwards named Dunbarton, or the "fortress of the Britons," and their country was known as Strathclyde, because it lay chiefly in the valley of the river Clyde. The Britons must not have been so brave in war as the other three peoples; at least, they were usually beaten when they fought, which they often had to do, with the fourth people who have now to be mentioned.

These last people were called Angles, and their name, also, cannot be forgotten, as *Angles* is just *English*, and *England* is simply *Angle-land*. The Angles came from the banks of the river Elbe, in Germany, and settled along the east coast of Britain under different leaders. It is only with one of these leaders, however, that we have to do. His name was Ida, and in the year 547 he became king of a kingdom which was called Bernicia, or the "country of the braes," which reached from the river Tees in England to the Firth of Forth in Scotland. These Angles were a very warlike people, and were constantly trying to conquer all their neighbours, and especially the Britons of Strathclyde, whom they hated and never left in peace. At one time, indeed, it seemed as if the Angles and not the Scots were to give the first kings to the whole of North Britain, and if that had happened, there would not have been a country named Scotland and a nation called Scotsmen, but only England and Englishmen. As for the language the Angles spoke, their name tells us that it was the same as we speak to-day, though many words have been changed and added since they spoke it. We have, therefore, this strange thing—that Scotsmen get their name from the Scots, who spoke Gaelic, and their language gets its name from the Angles, who came from the banks of the Elbe. How this happened, we shall see before long.

5. ST COLUMBA, ST MUNGO AND ST CUTHBERT

How did these four peoples, the Picts, the Scots, the Britons, and the Angles, come to be one nation, and how did the whole country come to be called Scotland? This is what we have now to try to understand. In the times of which we are speaking, men went to war with each other much more readily than we do now. Kings were always quarrelling with one another as to where their lands began and ended, and there was only one way of settling the quarrel, and that was by fighting. Now, as there were four kings in North Britain, each was afraid that his neighbour would become too strong and try to conquer all the others, and so sometimes two and even three kings would unite and make war on a third or fourth king of whom they were afraid. The result was that the four kings were almost constantly at war among themselves, until at last one became stronger than all the others, and made himself ruler over the whole country.

But there were other things besides fighting that helped to make the four kingdoms into one, and one thing that helped a great deal was that in course of time all the people of North Britain, as we must still call Scotland, came to be of one religion—namely, Christianity. As long as one people was pagan and another Christian, they looked on each other as enemies, and could never live together under one ruler. It was not only the fighting kings, therefore, but the peaceful missionaries who preached the gospel, that helped to make the country that came to be called Scotland. We do not know the names of all the missionaries who helped in this work, but there is one who did more than all the rest, and whose name will be remembered as long as Scotland lasts —St Columba.

The first thing we have to remember about Columba is that he was not born in North Britain, but in Ireland, or Scotia, as it was then called. He is said to have belonged to the royal family; but, whether this is true or not, he was at least a great man in his own country, and was known as a great preacher who had set up many churches and monas-

teries for the teaching of Christianity.   It was in the
year 563, when he was forty-two years old, that
Columba landed, along with twelve companions, on
the little island of Iona, which was to be his home
for the rest of his life.   We know what this home
was like, because a life of Columba was written by
one who lived there after him, and who had spoken
to those who knew Columba himself.   First of all,
there was a little church, made of wood and clay,
and not of stone like that of St Ninian.   Then quite
near it were the houses, or rather huts, also made of
wood and clay, in which the brethren lived—that of
Columba being at a little distance from the rest.
Round them all was a high wall made of turf, which
would both shelter them from storms and keep
them apart from other people who might be living
on the island.   Those who dwelt in the monastery, as
it was called, were divided into three classes, who had
each different duties to perform.   One class conducted the religious services of the community,
another class was in training to become ministers
of the gospel, and the third and largest class did all
the work that had to be done with the hands.

After Columba had been two years in Iona, he
undertook a long journey, and it is with this journey
we have chiefly to do in a history of Scotland.
Along with some of his brethren from the monastery,
he went to the king of the Picts, whose name was
Brude, to try to persuade him and his people to
give up being pagans and to become Christians.   As
King Brude lived near where the town of Inverness
now stands, they would be able to sail almost the
whole way, first through the sea and then through

the lochs that are now joined by the Caledonian canal.

At first, it seemed as if Columba was not to succeed in his errand, for when he arrived at Brude's palace, which would be only a building of wood with a great wall round it, he found the gates closed against him. Then, we are told, a wonderful thing happened; Columba made the sign of the Cross, and the gates opened of themselves. Brude was so astonished at this that he listened to what Columba had to say, and the result was that he agreed to become a Christian, and, as the people then did just what their kings did, his subjects became Christians also. This is the story that is told of how the Picts were converted; but no doubt there must have been other reasons why Brude and his people changed their religion, and the chief reason was perhaps that Columba was a man whose words and whose appearance made people think that he was sent by God. At all events, the Picts soon became a Christian nation, and Columba and others of his brethren travelled often through their country, preaching and building churches wherever they went. Now that both the Picts and the Scots of Dalriada were Christians, they both considered Iona the chief place of their religion, just as the Jews did Jerusalem. Iona, indeed, came to be looked on as a holy spot, and for a long time to come, Scottish and even Norwegian kings, when they died, were brought to be buried there.

At the same time as Columba, there lived in North Britain another great missionary, of whom, however, we do not know so much that can be true. His name was Kentigern, which is said to mean "chief lord," but he is better known by his other name, Mungo, which is thought to mean "dearest friend," or "dear and lovable." Many wonderful things are told of St Mungo which we cannot believe, but it is true that he spent a great part of his life in preaching the gospel to the Britons of Strathclyde. As Iona was the chief home of Columba, so Glasgow was the principal centre

Tombs of the Kings, Iona.   [*Photo by Valentine.*

of Mungo, and to this day Glasgow is often styled "the city of St Mungo," and its cathedral is called "the Cathedral of St Mungo."

Of all the peoples in North Britain only the Angles of Bernicia were now pagans; but about forty years after Columba's death, a missionary, named Aidan, was sent from Iona to preach the Christian religion to them also. It was another missionary, however, who did most to spread the gospel in Bernicia, or Lothian, for by this name Bernicia now begins to be called, and his name became better known even than the names of St Columba and St Mungo. This was St Cuthbert, who is called the "Apostle of Lothian," because he did more than any one else to make the people of that country Christians.

We do not know where Cuthbert was born, but the story is told that one night, when he was watching his sheep (for he began by being a shepherd) among the Lammermoor Hills, he saw a company of angels come down from heaven, and then return carrying with them the soul of Aidan, the missionary who had first preached to the Angles. We cannot, of course, believe all the stories that are told of the devoted men who gave their lives to teaching Christianity in those far-off times. We cannot believe, for example, that St Ninian made a bed of leeks grow up in a few hours, or that St Columba raised a man from the dead, or made a stone swim. So we cannot believe that St Cuthbert really saw the soul of Aidan and the angels bearing it up to heaven. But we do know that he went up and down the country of Lothian, sometimes on horseback and sometimes on foot, trying to persuade the people to give up their pagan worship and become Christians. And so successful were his labours that, when he died, it was believed long afterwards that miracles took place at his tomb. A piece of cloth, which he is said to have used in the services of the Church, was made into a flag or standard, and it was thought that the army which had it was sure to win the victory. More than eight hundred years after his death, the Scots believed that the English won the battle of

VIKINGS.

St Cuthbert
(635?-687).

St Columba
(521-597).

Brude,
Pictish King.

Rederech Hael,
British King.

St Ninian
(360?-432).

Kenneth
Macalpine.

Adaman,
Columba's Biographer
(—704).

St Aidan,
(—651).

St Kentigern, or
St Mungo
(518?-603).

Druid
or
British Priest

Theodosius
Roman
General.

Flodden, because they had the standard of St Cuthbert. To this day, many churches are named after this saint; as, for instance, the church of St Cuthbert in Edinburgh.

Before we finish this chapter, there is one thing more that has to be mentioned, and it is very important. At the time of which we are speaking, there were two Christian Churches in the West of Europe. There was the Irish Church, of which we have heard so much, and to which St Columba and St Aidan belonged; and there was the Roman Church, of which the Pope, or bishop of Rome, was the head. The Irish Church was different in some things from the Church of Rome. It had nothing to do with the Pope, and its missionaries went on their preaching journeys without being commanded by him. The two Churches also had different opinions on two things which do not seem very important to us, but which they thought very important. The clergy of the Irish Church shaved their heads in one way, and the Roman clergy in another; and there was also a quarrel between them as to the exact date of Easter, that is, the day when Christ rose from the dead. Now the question came to be, which of the two Churches was to have the upper hand in Britain and Ireland. The Roman Church was far stronger than the Irish, because many countries on the Continent, such as Italy, France, and Germany, belonged to it, as well as a large part of England. What happened, therefore, was that the Roman Church gained the victory; and not long after the death of St Cuthbert the Irish Church came to an end in North Britain, and even in Iona, and the Roman Church took its place.

C

We cannot help being sorry that the Irish Church, which had done so much good and to which such men as Columba and Aidan had belonged, thus came to an end ; but, on the whole, it was well for Scotland that it did. By becoming a part of the Roman Church, Scotland came into touch with the other Christian countries, and it learned from them a great deal which it could not have learned had it remained a part of the Irish Church. How much it learned we shall see further on, and why it is important to remember that the Roman Church took the place of the Irish Church.

---

6. THE FOUR KINGDOMS UNITED

KENNETH MACALPIN (844-860).   MALCOLM II. (1005-1034)

The Picts, the Scots, the Angles, and the Britons were now all of one religion, so that it was made easier for one king to become ruler over the whole of North Britain. At first, it looked as if the king of the Angles was to be this ruler. For a long time the kings of the Angles were the strongest, and compelled all the other kings to obey them ; but at last a king of the Picts, called Brude, determined no longer to submit to the Angles, and collected a great army to fight them. The king of the Angles at that time was Ecgfrith, and he also raised an army and marched all the way from Lothian to a place then known as Nectan's Mere, but now called Dunnichen, in Forfarshire. There was fought, in the year 685, one of the most important battles in the whole history of Scotland. Ecgfrith was defeated, and he himself and almost all his army were slain. After this battle the Angles grew weaker and weaker, and now there was no danger that their king would become ruler over the whole country. The reason why this battle is so important is that, if Ecgfrith had won the victory, it is likely that there never would have been a country called Scotland and a nation called the Scottish nation; for if the Angles had become the masters, the whole country would have been named Angle-land or England, and its people would have been Angles or English.

At last, in the year 844, an event happened which we cannot explain, because there are no books to tell us about it. A king of the Scots of Dalriada, named Kenneth MacAlpin, that is, Kenneth, son of Alpin, became king of the Picts as well as king of the Scots. There was now only one king to the north of the river Forth and the Firth of Clyde, and soon we hear no more of the Picts and Pictland, but only of Scots and Scotia. So now there were only three kings in North Britain instead of four, and the question was, which of the three that were left would prove to be the strongest.

As Kenneth MacAlpin now ruled over two peoples instead of one, he was more powerful than either the king of the Britons or the king of the Angles. We are not surprised, therefore, that Kenneth set his mind on conquering the Angles and winning their land. No fewer than six times did he lead an army into Lothian to subdue it; and we are told that he burned Dunbar and Melrose, which shows that there were places then that had these

names. But Kenneth was never able to conquer
the Angles completely, and, when he died, he was still
only king of Scotia. The kings who came after him,
however, were as keen as he was to become rulers of
Lothian, and for nearly two hundred years one king
after another tried to subdue it.

The king of Scotia who at last succeeded in
conquering Lothian, was Malcolm II., who reigned
from the year 1005 to the year 1034. It was in the
year 1018, a date not to be forgotten, that Malcolm
collected an army of his Scots; an army so large,
we are told, that it could not be counted. Leading it
across the river Forth, he marched through the
whole of Lothian till he came to a place called
Carham, on the banks of the Tweed, where Lothian
ended. At this time the Angles, whom Malcolm
had come to conquer, ruled over all the country from
the river Tees to the river Forth. When the
Angles heard that Malcolm was coming against
them with his great host, they were filled with
terror. A short while before he came, a comet had
appeared in the sky and shone for thirty days.
Now, in those times and for long afterwards, when
a comet was seen, men believed that something
dreadful was going to happen, and when the Angles
were told that Malcolm was coming against them,
they thought this was what the comet meant. And
their fears proved to be right, for in the battle that
was fought the Angles were defeated, and almost
every full-grown man who lived between the Tees
and the Tweed was killed; so that there was hardly
a man left to defend their country.

A story is told of a bishop who lived at the time,

which shows what a terrible blow their defeat at Carham was to the Angles. "Wretched me!" he is said to have exclaimed, "who have served as a bishop in these times. Have I lived to such old age to see this overwhelming disaster? The land will never again be what it was. O St Cuthbert! if I have ever done what pleased thee, may the remainder of my life be short." And the poor bishop's prayer was answered, for, a few days later, he took ill with a mortal disease and died.

The battle of Carham is not so well known as the battle of Bannockburn, of which everybody has heard; but in many ways it is the more important of the two, from what happened after it. The Angles were no longer able to stand against King Malcolm, as they had lost almost all their fighting men in the battle, and the result was that Malcolm became ruler of Lothian as well as of Scotia. But what this meant was that Scotland was not to end at the river Forth, but at the river Tweed. Now, if the Angles had gained the victory at Carham, Lothian would have remained part of England, which would then have reached to the river Forth, and Scotland would only have had the Highlands to the north of that river.

But still another fortunate event happened during the reign of Malcolm. In the very year (1018) in which he won the battle of Carham, the king of the Britons of Strathclyde, or Cumbria, as it was now called, died, and left no heir to succeed him. But there had been several marriages between the families of the kings of the Scots and the kings of the Britons, and thus it happened that the nearest heir to the throne of Cumbria was King Malcolm, or, at least, his grandson Duncan. And so, at last, after so many hundred years, one king became master of the whole of North Britain from the Tweed to the Pentland Firth. For some time to come, however, the name of Scotia was given only to the land north of the Forth ; but afterwards, as we know, the name came to be applied to the whole country which is now called Scotland.

7. THE HOMES OF THE NORTH BRITONS

We have seen how North Britain came to be one country ruled by one king ; let us now see what kind of homes the North Britons lived in after the Romans left, till the time of Malcolm II. We know very little of these homes from books, but, as parts of them are still standing, we know pretty well how they were made.

These houses are not all of the same kind, which shows that the people of North Britain did not all live in the same way. For instance, there is a kind of house which is mostly found in the country where the Britons of Strathclyde lived.   These houses are called Lake-Dwellings, because they are built not on land but in lakes, at a little distance from the shore.   This is how these Lake-Dwellings, or *Crannogs*, as they are named in Scotland, were made.   If there happened to be an island or several islands in the lake, the houses were built on these, and were, of course, almost all made of wood.   If there did not happen to be an island, then an island was made by sinking stones and logs of wood to the bottom till they rose above the surface of the water.   Then, that the people who lived in the dwellings might be able to get to the shore, canoes were kept, or a causeway was made which could be destroyed when it was necessary.   In the year 1863, when Loch Dowalton, in Wigtownshire, was drained, nine of these islands were discovered which had been made by men's hands, and in them

Lake-Dwelling (restored).

were found a number of things that had been used by those who had lived there.   There was a hearth-stone, and also the bones of oxen, pigs, and sheep which had been the food of the Lake-Dwellers. There were also found an iron axe, the heads of hammers, beads of glass and amber, a bit of a leather shoe, and a sauce-pan of bronze, which must have been made by Roman hands, as it had the owner's name stamped on it in Latin.   And near the islands were several canoes, each made of a single tree, by hollowing it out.

Why did these people make their houses in lakes and not on the dry land, where it would have been so much easier to build them? It was to be safe from their enemies, who would not be able to take them by surprise, and who would have to use canoes to reach the islands, and canoes cannot be made in a moment. We do not know when these Lake-Dwellings were first made, but from the articles made of iron found in them we know that their inhabitants must have belonged to the Iron Age. People must also have dwelt in them after the Romans left North Britain, because, as we have seen, things made by the Romans are found in them. What we now think, though we cannot be quite sure, is that the Britons of Strathclyde lived in the Lake-Dwellings to be as safe as possible from their enemies, the Angles, who were constantly making war on them.

A very different kind of home from the Lake-Dwellings is one that is chiefly found to the north of the river Forth, though a few are also found to the south of it. These houses are called Brochs or Pictish Towers (because the Picts were supposed to have lived in them), and are high, round castles, with very thick walls. It is very likely, indeed, that those who made these Brochs only used them when they were attacked by their enemies, and that they had other houses in which they usually dwelt. In the Orkney and Shetland Islands, and in the counties of Caithness, Sutherland, and Ross, there are the ruins of more than three hundred of them. They were chiefly built near the banks of rivers, lochs, and the shores of the sea, which means that the people who dwelt in them lived chiefly on the fish they caught. In a little island among the Shetlands, called Mousa, there is one of these Brochs, of which so much is left standing that we can see how they were made.

Broch of Mousa, Shetland. [Photo by Valentine.

Though the top is broken off, it is forty feet high, that is, higher than a two-storey house. It is built of stones laid on each other, but without lime to hold them together, and the walls are about sixteen feet thick. There is only one door, and when you go inside you find a staircase which leads up to six floors or galleries; and when the building was whole there must have been still more. In such a place a great number of people could live together, and it would have been hard indeed, at a time when there were no cannons, for an enemy to break into it. From the things that have been found in the Brochs, we can see that the people who lived in them belonged to the Iron Age, like those who lived in the Lake-Dwellings. They must have known how to grow corn, and how to spin and weave; they had lamps and utensils for cooking; they had ornaments such as beads and bracelets; and altogether they must have been able to live very comfortably, when they were not troubled by their enemies.

There is still another kind of dwelling in which the North Britons must have lived after the Romans left the country. These are what are called Earth-houses, or Picts' houses, because the Picts were supposed to have lived in them. Sometimes in ploughing fields, the plough has come against a flat stone, which looked as if it had been placed there by the hands of men, and when the ground was dug up one of these Earth-houses was found. A narrow hole leads into a winding passage, which grows wider and wider till you come to a chamber, with the walls and the floor and the roof all flagged with flat stones. Sometimes there are two or three chambers, and sometimes there are as many as forty houses together, so that there must have been quite a village made up of them. On the surface of the ground near them, there have also been found the remains of what have been dwelling-houses and folds for cattle, and it is thought that the people may have lived in the underground dwellings in winter and in those above ground in the summer. Just as in the case of the Lake-Dwellings and the Brochs, things have been found in the Earth-houses which show that people lived in them after the time of the Romans, and that they knew the use of iron, and grew corn, and reared sheep and cattle.

These, then, were the homes in which our fore-fathers lived for a long time after the Romans left the country, and the way these houses were built shows that the people who dwelt in them were not mere savages.   But we know also that they could not only build strong and comfortable houses, but that they could make beautiful things which any workman of the present day would be proud of.   For example, there have been found such things as shields, sword-sheaths, mirrors, bracelets, and other ornaments, usually made of bronze, but sometimes of silver or gold, and all beautifully decorated with figures, and some of them painted red, yellow, blue, and green.   Such things as these were made while the people were still pagan ; but when they became Christian they began to fashion new things, such as bells, crosses, and ornaments, for the churches, with such wonderful patterns on them, that the most skilful artist now could not make them better.

But there was another kind of art, quite as wonderful, which must not be forgotten.   In Ireland, those who lived in the monasteries were very fond of writing books and painting pictures in them, and this they could do more beautifully than the monks of any other country.   When the Irish missionaries came to North Britain, therefore, they brought this art with

Illustration from Book of Deer.

them ; and we are told that, when St Columba was in Iona, he spent a great deal of his time in copying religious books. Only one book of this kind has come down to us, but who wrote it we cannot tell. It is called the Book of Deer, from the village of Deer, in Aberdeenshire, where one of Columba's monasteries was set up, and it is supposed to have been written in the ninth century, that is, the century in which Kenneth MacAlpin lived. Besides other things, it contains the Gospel of St John and portions of the other three Gospels, beautifully written in Latin, and with pictures or illuminations, as they are called, in different colours.

8. THE ENEMIES OF THE KINGS OF SCOTLAND

We have now finished the first part of the history of the Scottish people, which tells how there came to be a kingdom of Scotland ruled over by one king. The question now was—Would this kingdom hold together, and would all the people agree to live under one ruler ? We shall see that very often it seemed as if the kingdom would break up, and that there would again be several kings instead of one. The reason of this was that the king of Scotland had so many enemies to fight against, that it was very difficult for him to overcome them all. First he had diffi-culties within his own kingdom, and, if we think for a moment, we can easily understand how this was. The people over whom he ruled spoke different languages; those to the north of the Forth spoke Gaelic, those in Strathclyde or Cumbria spoke a language like the Welsh, though not quite the same, and those in Lothian spoke English. Then these different peoples had long been enemies, and had often fought against each other. In those days, also, men did not go from one part of the country to another as they do now, but remained all their lives where they were born; so that there could be no mixing of the different peoples by marrying or making friends with each other.

How could a Scot from the north of the Forth go and make his home in Lothian, when the people living there could not speak his language? Indeed, it was just the people of Scotia and the people of Lothian who came to hate each other most bitterly, and we shall soon see why this was so, and how it was that this hatred between them made it so difficult for one king to rule over them both.

But the kings of Scotland had still another danger to fight against within their own kingdom. There was a part of the country called Moray, much larger than the present county of Moray, in which there lived a family who claimed that the crown of Scotland belonged to them and not to the family that possessed it. For fully two hundred years the descendants of this family kept trying to win the crown for themselves. Almost every time a new king came to the throne, they rose in rebellion, and very often there were more rebellions than one in the course of a single reign. These "mormaers" of Moray, or earls of Moray, as they came to be called, were, therefore, a thorn in the side of the kings of Scotland, as they could never be sure when a new rebellion would break out.

Besides these enemies within their kingdom, the kings of Scotland had two enemies without, against whom they had often to fight—the Northmen and the English.

The Northmen were people who came from Norway, Sweden, and Denmark, and their chief business was to sail to places where they could find anything to plunder, and then land from their ships and carry off everything on which they could lay their hands. They were the boldest sailors in the world, and so fond of fighting that they would sometimes fight among themselves for amusement. The ships in which they sailed were called galleys, and were shaped like dragons, with a dragon's head for the bow and its tail for the stern. To make their ships go as fast as possible they had twenty and even thirty oars on each side, and they had also a square sail with stripes of red, white, and blue. At first when the Northmen began to come, they only landed for a short time till they had got all they wanted, and then sailed away, carrying with them not only property, but men and women and children, whom they sold as slaves. They were so little afraid of long voyages, that they sailed along the coasts of France and Spain, and even into the Mediterranean Sea, landing to burn and plunder wherever they found a convenient place. It was in summer, when the sea is quietest, that they went on their expeditions, and then the people who lived on the coasts never knew when they might come; and so great was the fear of them, that in the churches there was a prayer said in these words: "God save us from the Northmen."

Before the period we have now come to, these terrible vikings, as they were called, had already paid

Viking Ship.

several visits to Scotland. Among other places, they had landed at Iona; and, as they were heathens and cared nothing for the sacred things of Christians, they carried off everything they thought of any value, destroying the rest, and killing many of the monks. But a time came when the Northmen were not content with merely landing and sailing away with booty. They now tried to conquer lands and to settle in them; and so, about the year 890, long before Scotland had become one kingdom, a king of Norway, called Harold the Fair-haired, came with a great fleet and conquered the Orkneys and the Shetlands and the Western Isles. Not long afterwards, the Northmen got possession of Caithness and Sutherland, so that the whole of Scotland did not belong to its king. It will now be seen what dangerous enemies the Northmen were to the kings of Scotland, who could never be the real masters of their kingdom till they got rid of them.

The other enemy of the kings of Scots was even more to be feared than the Northmen. This enemy was England. Just like North Britain, South Britain had for a long time been broken up into a number of kingdoms, but now South Britain also was ruled over by one king. Now, therefore, there were two great kingdoms in the whole of Britain, one to the north of the river Tweed, and the other to the south of it. Would they agree to live peacefully side by side with the Tweed between them? We know that they did not live peacefully together. On the contrary, they went on quarrelling and fighting with each other for more than five hundred years, till at last, in the year 1603, James VI. of Scotland became king over both countries.

And why was it that they could not agree to be friends? The truth is that both countries were equally to blame. The kings of the Scots thought that the

D

three northern counties of England—Northumberland, Durham, and Cumberland—belonged to them, and we shall see that one Scottish king after another tried to conquer them, and sometimes succeeded. On the other hand, the kings of England claimed that Lothian and even the whole of Scotland belonged to them, and that the kings of Scots were their vassals, that is, that they were bound to obey them.

We see, therefore, why the two countries came to be constantly at war with each other ; but as Scotland was much the smaller of the two, and its kings had so many enemies in their own kingdom, there was a great danger that the country of the Scots would be the one that would be conquered in the end. For hundreds of years, indeed, Scotland had to fight in order to be a free country, and in doing so she had to spend so much money and blood that it kept her people poor, though it also made them brave, and hardy, and stubborn.

In this second part of our history, then, we have to see how the kings of Scots held their kingdom together, now fighting one enemy and now another, and all the time trying to make their subjects in Highlands and Lowlands more and more obedient to their commands.

---

9. LOTHIAN AGAINST SCOTIA

Kings :—DUNCAN (1034-1040).   MACBETH (1040-1057).
MALCOLM III. (CANMORE) (1057-1093)

Duncan and Macbeth, the two kings who came after Malcolm II., would hardly be remembered if Shakespeare had not written about them in his play called *Macbeth*. The story told in the play is this. Once when Macbeth and his friend Banquo were going across a moor near Forres, in the county of Elgin, they met three witches, who told Macbeth that he would one day become king of Scotland. Macbeth could not get this out of his mind; and to win the crown, he murdered King Duncan in his bed. Then Macbeth was king for a short while, when Malcolm, Duncan's son, came against him with an army made up of Scots and English, and defeated and slew him; and so got his father's crown. Shakespeare got this story from a Scottish writer, but we know that it is not all true.

What really happened was this. Duncan was quite young when he came to the throne, and not an old man as Shakespeare makes him, and he was not a strong king like his grandfather, Malcolm II. Now, it has just been mentioned that there was a family in Moray that claimed the right to the crown, and Macbeth was the head of this family. So Macbeth rose in rebellion against Duncan, and a battle was fought near Elgin, in which Duncan was defeated and killed. Macbeth in this way became king of Scotland, though not of the whole of it, like Malcolm II.

Macbeth reigned for seventeen years, and seems to have made a good king. At least, we know that he was very generous to the Church, as he gave lands to it, and even went on a pilgrimage to Rome, which other kings did in those times, and distributed money among the poor. At last, however, as Shakespeare tells us, Duncan's son Malcolm came against him with an army of Scots and English, and defeated and slew

him, at a place called Lumphanan, in Aberdeenshire.
The chief thing to be remembered about the reigns
of Duncan and Macbeth is that the family of Moray
were such dangerous enemies to the kings of Scots;
and many of Duncan's successors were to find this as
well as himself.

Malcolm III., called Canmore, which means Big-
head, is the first king whom we can really be said to
know, and his reign is one of the most important in
the history of Scotland. A new state of things began
during his reign which, in the end, was to make it
quite a different country from what it had been,
and it is easy to understand how this happened.
During the time that Macbeth reigned, Malcolm, of
course, could not live in Scotland, as his life would
not have been safe. For fifteen years he lived in England, and learned to speak English, and to like the
English people and their ways. Besides, it was with
the help of the English that he had gained his throne,
so that he was bound to be grateful to Edward the
Confessor, the king of England at whose court he
had lived. The result of all this was that Malcolm
liked the people of Lothian, who spoke English,
better than the people of the north, who spoke Gaelic,
and he paid more attention to Lothian than to Scotia,
though Scotia was the home of his ancestors. Thus
there came to be jealousy and hatred between the
two peoples, and we shall see that, during Malcolm's
reign and long after, this was the cause of great
trouble in the kingdom.

Malcolm seems, like most kings of that time, to
have liked fighting better than anything else; at
least, whenever we hear of him, he is usually at war

with some enemy. In the very beginning of his reign the men of Moray as usual rose against him, but he soon put them down, and only at one other time did they give him any trouble. But the chief enemy against whom he fought was the people of the north of England, for, as has already been said, the kings of Scots believed that the north part of England belonged to their kingdom. No fewer than five times did he lead an army into that part of England to try to conquer it, but he never succeeded. But though he did not conquer it, the people who lived there would not be likely to forget his visits. In those days, when kings made war, what they did was to burn houses and even churches, to slay or carry off all the cattle and sheep, and to kill almost every human being who came in their way; and this was what Malcolm did all the five times that he led his army into England. In one of these invasions it was said that "old men and women were slaughtered like swine for the banquet," and that so many people were carried off as slaves that there was not a house in Scotland in which one of them was not to be found.

But Malcolm did not have it all his own way, and the people of Lothian had to suffer for his love of war. At the beginning of Malcolm's reign, it was still the old English kings who ruled in England: first Edward the Confessor, and then Harold. But in the year 1066, when Malcolm had reigned nine years, William the Norman conquered England, and he was not a person to be trifled with. Six years after William became king of England, he came against Scotland with both an army and a fleet, and marched through Lothian, where, however, " he found nothing to reward his pains."

Then, as Malcolm had not an army strong enough to fight him, he crossed the river Forth and came to Abernethy, which was one of Malcolm's chief towns; and there the two kings met and made a treaty, in which Malcolm agreed to be William's " man," that is, to submit to him as his king. But it was the Conqueror's son, William Rufus, from whom Malcolm had to suffer most; for Rufus not only invaded Scotland but conquered Cumberland, which, as part of Strathclyde, belonged to the kings of Scotland. So, after all his fighting, Malcolm gained nothing in the end, since he did not win Northumberland and Durham, and lost Cumberland. This was the beginning of the wars between the kings of England and the kings of Scotland, which were to go on for so many hundred years, and in which now one king was to win and now another.

But we have still to mention the most important event that happened in the reign of Malcolm. When William the Norman conquered England, the heir of the old kings, called Edgar the Atheling, had to flee from the country. When Malcolm had to flee from Macbeth, he had found a home at the court of Edward the Confessor, and so now the Atheling came to find a home in Scotland, and brought with him his mother and two sisters, one of whom was called Margaret. Not very long afterwards, Malcolm married Margaret, and this marriage brought about a great change in Scotland. In the first place, all the descendants of Malcolm who became kings of Scots were half English in blood. And not only

The Landing of St Margaret at Queensferry, A.D. 1068.

were they half English in blood, but they were English in their ways, and liked English laws and customs better than the old Scottish ones. Since this was the case, these new kings came to think Lothian, where the people spoke English, more important than the country to the north, where Gaelic was spoken. We can easily understand, therefore, how the people of the north came to dislike their half-English kings, for after all it was they who had given a king to Scotland and who had conquered Lothian, and they thought that they and not the English-speaking people of Lothian should be most liked and favoured by their kings.

And now, let us see how Margaret herself tried to change things in the country to which she had come as a stranger. We know a good deal more about her than about her husband Malcolm, as a book was written about her by one who knew her. One thing this book tells us is that Malcolm was so fond of her that he used to kiss the books which she read, but which he was not able to read himself. This being the case, she had a great influence over him, and got her own way in most things. First, then, Margaret made great changes in the king's court. Up to this time the king's servants had only been common people, but now persons of high rank became his attendants, just as was now the case in the courts of other kings, where great nobles looked after the king's clothes, his food, his wines, his horses, his game in the forests, and other things.

Margaret also made the people about the court dress more grandly than they had done before, so that, we are told, the whole place shone with the gay clothes that were worn. Before she came, only common dishes had been used at the king's table, but now they were made of gold and silver; or, at least, the writer tells us, if they were not really of gold and silver, they were gilt to look like them. In this way, then, Margaret made the court of King Malcolm just like the courts of the kings of England and France, and of other countries. And not only at the court, but among the people she made great changes. She made the merchants who traded with foreign countries bring home clothes of bright colours and also ornaments, so that, as the people were now dressed, they looked " like a new kind of creatures."

It was in the Church, however, that Margaret made the greatest changes. She, of course, belonged to the Church of Rome, as did all the kings and queens of the West of Europe; but few of them were so pious and devoted as she was. At certain times of the year, she and Malcolm every morning washed the feet of six beggars; then nine little orphans were brought, to whom she gave food with her own hand ; and afterwards, along with the king, she did the same thing to three hundred beggars. But what Margaret wished above all was that the clergy of Scotland should all do as the Church of Rome commanded. Now, all the clergy of Scotland, as we have seen, did belong to the Church of Rome, but those to the north of the Forth believed many things of which that Church did not approve. So, to make them do and believe what she thought right, she got Malcolm to bring them together that she might show them where they were wrong. As she could not speak Gaelic, Malcolm had to explain what she said, and we are told that they agreed to make the changes which she wished; and indeed, if they had not, Malcolm, we are also told, would have compelled them to do so. In making all these changes, both in the court and in the Church, Margaret did not please the Scots of the north, who thought that she was trying to do away with their laws and customs and bring in

Photo by Wilson.

Malcolm Canmore's Window, Dunfermline Abbey.

English ones, and we shall see how they showed their dislike of her when she and Malcolm died. Among the English-speaking people of Lothian, however, she was loved and almost worshipped, and down to the Reformation, when Scotland became a Protestant country, if a great victory was gained, it used to be said that it was owing to the prayers of St Margaret.

We have now only to tell what was the end of Malcolm and his queen, for the end came to both almost at the same time. In the year 1091, Malcolm made up his mind to invade England for the fifth time. Margaret was then lying very ill in the Castle of Edinburgh, and she prayed him not to go, but Malcolm would not listen to her. He marched with his army till he came to the banks of the river Alne, in Northumberland. Here, when he was not expecting them, the English came upon him and completely defeated his army, Malcolm himself and his eldest son being slain in the battle. Malcolm's body was taken in a cart to Tynemouth, a place near at hand, and there it lay for twenty years, when it was brought to Dunfermline Abbey, which had been built by him and his wife. On the fourth day after the battle, his son Edgar, who had escaped, came to his mother's bedside with the terrible news, and immediately afterwards she died.

10. SCOTLAND AGAIN DIVIDED

DONALD BANE	1093-1094
DUNCAN II.	1094-1094
DONALD BANE AND EDMUND	1094-1097
EDGAR	1097-1107
ALEXANDER I.	1107-1124

The sons of Margaret were still with the dead body of their mother, when the Castle of Edinburgh, in which it lay, was suddenly surrounded by a number of armed men. Their leader was a brother of Malcolm, called Donald Bane, who had come to try to take his nephews prisoners, that he might himself become king. Though Donald was Malcolm's brother, he had not liked his English ways, but wished the Scots of the North to be the chief people in the kingdom, so that the Scots were glad to help him to win the crown. He did not succeed, however, in catching his prey. A thick mist came on, and in the darkness Margaret's sons, carrying her dead body, escaped from the castle by a back gate, and got safely to Dunfermline, where they buried her in the Abbey. But it shows how displeased the people of the North were with the changes that had been made by Malcolm and Margaret, that their sons dared not for fear of their lives remain in Scotland, but had to flee to England for safety.

So Donald Bane now became king, but he did not reign long. Malcolm Canmore had a son called Duncan, who was not the son of Margaret, however, but of Malcolm's first wife ; and this Duncan thought he had a better right to the throne than Donald. Now Duncan had been given to William the Conqueror by Malcolm as a pledge that he would keep the treaty which had been made between them at Abernethy. Duncan, therefore, lived at the English court, and became quite like a Norman. This being the case, William Rufus became his friend, and let him have an army of English and Normans to go to fight against Donald Bane and win the crown of Scotland for himself.

And Duncan did succeed in beating Donald and did become king, but he, also, reigned only for a short time ; indeed, only for six months. No fewer than three enemies rose against him, one of whom was Donald Bane himself, and the second was another son of Malcolm and Margaret, who was called Edmund, and was said to be the only bad son of his mother. A great battle was fought at a place called Mondynes, in Kincardineshire, in which Duncan was defeated and slain; and to this day a large stone is still standing which is said to mark the spot where he fell. So now Edmund and Donald Bane divided the kingdom between them, and reigned for three years. None of these kings that have been mentioned—Donald Bane, Duncan, and Edmund—would be worth remembering, but when so many of them reigned in such a short time it shows in what an unsettled state Scotland still was, and how easily it might have been broken up, had a strong king not arisen to hold it together. Such a king was not to come now, but he was to come soon.

William Rufus did not like the way things were going in Scotland; what he wanted was a king of Scotland who would be his friend and also his "man," and we have seen what that meant. But neither Edmund nor Donald Bane was friendly to the English, as it was owing to the people of Scotia that they had been made kings. What Rufus did, therefore, was this: he gave an army to Edgar, the son of Margaret who had brought her the news of his father's death. As Edgar marched north with his army, it is said that St Cuthbert, the great missionary of Lothian, appeared to him in the night and said, "Fear not, my son, for God has been pleased to give thee the kingdom." And Edgar did gain a complete victory over Donald Bane and Edmund, and took them both captive, and kept them in prison for the rest of their lives.

Edgar reigned for nine years over both Scotia and Lothian, but he was not quite a free king. If it had not been for William Rufus he would never have won the crown, so that he had to take care that he did not offend him. Edgar was not fond of fighting as his father Malcolm had been ; but, on the contrary, was so fond of living at peace with everybody, that he was called Edgar the Peaceable. One thing that happened during his reign shows that he would not go to war if he could help it.

We have seen how the king of Norway, Harold the Fair-haired, conquered all the Western Islands and set a Norwegian ruler over them. But in the days of King Edgar the people of these islands rose in rebellion against the Norwegians, and slew both them and their chief. The king of Norway at this time was Magnus Barefoot, and when he heard of what the islanders had done, he determined that he would teach them a lesson. So with a great fleet of ships and an army aboard them, he first sailed to the Orkneys, and set his son to rule over them. Then he went to the Western Islands, and, as the islanders were not strong enough to fight him, he burned all their houses, killed every person who had not retired to a place of safety, and carried off as much plunder as he could.

But Magnus did not stop at the Western Islands ; he sailed on to the Isle of Man and the Isle of Anglesea, and conquered them also. And then, on his way home, he sent a message to Edgar to tell him that the Western Islands belonged to Norway, and not to Scotland. If Edgar had been like his father Malcolm, he would rather have gone to war with Magnus than have agreed to this, as the kings of Scotland always claimed that the islands belonged to them, though the Norwegians had conquered them. But Edgar did not wish to fight, and the two kings made a treaty by which Magnus did a very clever trick. The bargain was that Magnus was to have all the islands to the west, between which and the mainland a ship could sail. And what did Magnus do? He went aboard a ship and had it dragged over the land from East Loch Tarbert to West Loch Tarbert, and so by the bargain got possession of the peninsula of Cantyre as well as of all the Western Islands! In this way these islands were completely lost to the kingdom of Scotland, and more than a hundred years were to pass before another king of Scots won them back.

Before Edgar died, he is said to have made an arrangement which shows that he must have thought that one king could not rule over the whole of Scotland. His next eldest brother, named Alexander, was to reign over the land to the north of the Forth, with the title of king; and his youngest brother, David, was to be set over Strathclyde and Lothian, but to be under Alexander, and not to be called king. And this was what actually happened, for Alexander I., who succeeded Edgar as king, gave most of his attention to the country that was still called Scotia, while David ruled almost like a king in Strathclyde and the part of Cumbria to the north of the Solway. It was lucky for Scotland that this arrangement did not last long, as then there would have been no Scotland such as there is at the present day. For this is what would have taken place. The

English would have conquered Lothian, and so England's northern boundary would have been, not the river Tweed as it is now, but the river Forth. And very likely the English would have conquered Scotia also in course of time, and then the whole of the land from the English Channel to the Pentland Firth would have been called England, and there would have been no Scotland at all. It was a lucky day for Scotland, therefore, when, at the death of Alexander I., there arose a king who was strong enough and wise enough to rule the whole country and to hold it firmly together. The great king who did this was David I., the brother of Alexander, and the youngest son of Malcolm Canmore and Margaret, and it is of his long and happy reign we have now to read.

---

11. A GREAT KING

DAVID I. (1124-1153)

The reign of David I. is one of the most important in the whole history of Scotland. Indeed, there is only one other reign that is so important, and that is the reign of Queen Mary. What makes Mary's reign so important is that it was then that Scotland became a Protestant country, and this made such a great change that its people became like another nation. In David's reign Scotland did not change its religion ; on the contrary, owing to what David did, it became more Catholic than ever. But what makes David's reign remembered is that he did two great things. First, he in the end overcame all his enemies both within and without, and so made himself a real king over the whole of his kingdom. And the second thing he did was to make Scotland what it continued to be till the time of the Reformation. Let us first see, then, how David conquered all his enemies and made himself a real king.

The first thing to be remembered about him is that he had lived a long time in England before he became king, for when he was still a boy he had been taken there to escape from his uncle, Donald Bane. So, living at the court of the Norman king of England, he became more a Norman than a Scot. He learned to speak French like the Normans, he made friends among the Norman nobles, and he came to like the way the Norman kings governed and to wish to be a king such as they were. And still another thing is to be remembered about David : he married an English wife, called Matilda, who was the daughter of an earl of Northumberland, and we shall soon see what this marriage meant. As for David's character, those who wrote about him at the time could not find words strong enough to praise him. They called him, for instance, " the comforter of the sorrowing, the father of the fatherless, and the friend of the widow," and " the best of all his kin." David had his faults like other people, but it is best that men should be remembered for their good qualities and not for their bad ones.

David had not been long king when, as usual, the family of Moray rose against him, and so strong were they that it took him five years to conquer them. Indeed, he was not able to put them down with the

E

help of his own subjects, and he had to seek assistance outside of his own kingdom. And where did he
find this assistance? Among the Norman lords with
whom he had made friends before he became king.
A lord in Yorkshire, who owned a great deal of land,
gathered a number of other lords and came to Carlisle,
from which they meant to go to the help of David. But
they did not need to come. When the men of Moray
heard that these mail-clad warriors were marching
against them, they sent to David to say that they
were willing to submit to him, and they gave up their
leader Malcolm as a prisoner. Then, to make sure that
the Moray men would not trouble him any more, he
took their lands from many of them and gave them to
Normans, who would be on his side if ever war
should arise again. All through his reign David
continued to give lands to Normans. No doubt this
was because they were such good fighters, and would
always be ready to help him if the people of Scotia
and other parts of the country should rebel against
him.

The other great enemy of David was England, and
for nearly five years he was almost constantly at war
with that country. The cause of this war was that
David, like his father Malcolm, thought that the
counties of Northumberland and Durham belonged
to Scotland and not to England. And David had a
stronger reason for thinking this than his father had,
because his wife Matilda was the daughter of the
earl to whom these counties had once belonged, and
so they should by right belong to her. Now, it
happened that, during David's reign, England was in
such a state that she was not so able to defend herself

as in the days of William the Conqueror and William Rufus. The reason was this. Before Henry I., the last king of England, died, he had said that he wished his daughter Maud or Matilda to succeed him. But, as soon as Henry was dead, Stephen, Earl of Blois, got himself made king, though he had sworn to Henry that he would not. The result was that some of the English took the side of Maud and some took the side of Stephen, and there was war between them for many years. This being the state of things in England, therefore, David had a better chance if he went to war with that country.

And David found a good excuse for invading England, because Maud was his niece, and he could say that he wished to put her on the throne, which was hers by right. So with this excuse he twice led an army into England against Stephen, and the second time he had to fight one of the greatest battles the Scots ever fought. The army which David led was perhaps the largest that had ever been seen in Scotland. There were men in it from Galloway, from Lothian, from Scotia, and even from the Western Islands and the Orkneys. So terrible indeed did David's host appear, that a writer who lived at the time says that "he came as if he meant to conquer the whole of England." Through the counties of Northumberland and Durham he marched, carrying all before him, but when he entered Yorkshire he was brought to a stop.

The Archbishop of York, a very old man, said that it was a disgrace that they should allow their country to be conquered without striking a blow in its defence, and he put such a spirit into the barons and the people of Yorkshire that an army was collected to fight the Scottish king. In the midst of their army they placed the mast of a ship, and put on the top of it a cross and the banners of three saints, and a consecrated wafer which was supposed to be the body of Christ. It was from this that the battle got its name of the "Battle of the Standard," by which it is better known than by the place where it was fought, which is called Northallerton. Then, to make the army fight more bravely, the archbishop gave it his blessing, and presented it also with the banner of St Peter, the patron saint of York, so that everyone might know that he was fighting for his religion as well as for his home.

David made a great mistake in the way he arranged his army before the battle. The men from Galloway claimed that they had the right to fight in the front ranks, but, as they had no armour to protect them, they were not a match for the mail-clad Norman knights. David knew this quite well, but he let the Galloway men have their way, and they began the fighting. They fought for two hours as bravely as men could fight, but, when their last chief had been killed, they began to yield. What did most damage to the Scots was the arrows of the English bowmen—those arrows which in many a battle afterwards the Scots were to know to their cost. Then, while it was still uncertain which side was to win, an Englishman held aloft a bloody head, and the Scots, thinking it was the head of their king, began to lose heart and to flee from the field. Another unlucky thing also happened to the Scots. Prince Henry, David's son, beat the English against whom he fought, but he pursued

them so far that he did not return in time to help the
rest of the Scottish army. So the end was that the
Scots were completely defeated, and 12,000 of them
were left dead on the field of battle.

But, though David had been thus so completely
defeated, he did not leave England, but only went as
far north as Carlisle with the rest of his army.
Indeed, King Stephen had so much to do in fighting
against the friends of Maud, that he was glad to make
a treaty with David which would keep him out of
England. And by this treaty (1139) David got nearly
all he wanted. He did not get both the counties
of Durham and Northumberland, but he got the
second, and a good deal of land in other parts of
England besides. This was the end of David's wars
with England, so that both over the men of Moray
and over the English he had been victorious.

But the greatest trial of David's life came to him
when he was near his end. His only son and heir,
Prince Henry, died, and was mourned not only by
his father but by all who knew him, as he promised
to be one of the best kings that Scotland ever
had. The year after his death David himself
took ill at Carlisle, where he was then staying, and he
passed away so quietly that his attendants did not
notice his end. He died, we are told by one who was
then living, "at daybreak, when the sun with his
rays of light was dispelling the darkness," and he was
found "with his two hands joined together on his
breast, and raised to heaven."

12. THE FEUDAL SYSTEM

We have seen in the last chapter how David overcame all his enemies and made Scotland one kingdom again, as it had been under Malcolm Canmore, and we have now to see what changes he made in the country. These changes had begun to be made in the time of Malcolm, but it was David who carried them out completely. What he really did was just to make Scotland like other countries, such as England, France, and Germany. And it is to be remembered that until the time of the Reformation, and even longer, Scotland remained very much the same as he left it.

The first thing of which every nation has to think is to make itself safe against its enemies, for, if the people of any country do not feel themselves safe, they cannot live in comfort or make any progress. At the present day we have what is called a standing army, which is kept up by the taxes paid by the people. But in the times of which we are speaking there were no standing armies. How, then, did a country make itself safe against any enemy who might wish to conquer it? It was in this way.

When a king was strong enough, he was the master of all the land in his kingdom, and what he did was to give larger or smaller parts of it to those whom he could trust, or who had done him any service. Now, those to whom he gave the land did not pay rent for it, but they took an oath that they would serve him and be faithful to him. And their great service was to assist him when he went to war with any of his enemies.

From Painting by Wm. Hole, R.S.A.]

The Good Deeds of King David I.

When the king went to war, therefore, he sent word
to all his vassals, as they were called, who were bound
to come with all their men, fully armed and with all
the food they needed, and attend their lord the king
for thirty or forty days, though after that time he
could not compel them to stay with him. In this
way, then, the king could at any time collect an
army; that is, if the vassals were willing to obey
him, which was not always the case either in Scotland
or other countries.

The chief people in the country, then, were the
king and the vassals who held great portions of land
from him, and who were called the greater barons or
lords, with the title of earl. But these great vassals had
also vassals under them, to whom they gave land, and
who had to do for them what they themselves did for
the king—that is, to assist them when they went to
war. Then under these sub-vassals there were two
other classes. There was the class called free
tenants, who rented land from some greater or
smaller baron and paid him a rent either in money,
or, what was the usual way, with what was produced
on the land—grain, or cattle, or sheep, or poultry, or
other things. Lowest of all was the class called serfs,
who were just slaves, who could be bought and sold
like cattle, and who were not allowed to leave the land
on which they were born nor to marry without their
lord's permission.

Now, we see that the important thing for David
and kings like him was that the great nobles or
barons should be faithful to him, for, if two or three
were to join together and rise against him, they
might be stronger than the king himself. The men

to whom David chiefly gave lands were Normans from England, because he could depend upon them, and because they were the best soldiers of the time.

For example, he gave the land of Annandale to an ancestor of Robert Bruce, and he gave Renfrewshire to an ancestor of the Stewarts, who afterwards came to be the kings of Scotland. And how did David get the lands to give them? We saw how he did in the case of the land of Moray. The men dwelling there had rebelled against him, so he took their lands from many of them and gave them to Normans who had done him some service.

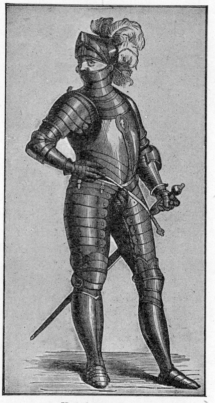

Knight on Foot.

And in other parts of the country he did the same thing, so that most of the land came to belong to Normans who had come from England.

And he not only gave the Normans most of the

land, but he also gave them the chief offices about the court. It was only the very greatest nobles who got these offices, which it was considered a great honour to hold. The chief of these great officials were : the Constable, who commanded the army when the king was not present ; the Chamberlain, who looked after the king's accounts ; the Seneschal, who managed the royal household ; the Marshal, who commanded the horse soldiers in the army ; and the Chancellor, who was the king's chief adviser, and who kept the great seal with which the king sealed all his important letters.

Now, we have seen how the king could raise an army when he needed it, and the next question is, Where did he find the money to pay all the expenses of keeping up his court? At the present day the royal family is kept up by money which the country has to pay in taxes, but this was not the way in which courts were kept up in the time of King David, and long afterwards. When the people were taxed then—at least in Scotland—it was not to pay the king's own expenses, but for some other purpose, such as to pay a ransom for him if he were taken prisoner.

First of all, the king had lands of his own, from which he got grain and cattle and sheep and poultry to feed his household. Then from the towns which were called Royal Burghs he received an annual sum of money, because they were built on his land, and because he gave them certain privileges of trade which the other towns did not possess. On all the goods sent to foreign countries, also, the merchants had to pay a tax, and this came to a considerable sum every year.   The great barons, too, besides serving him in war, had to pay money to him on certain occasions.   If he was taken prisoner, they had to help to pay his ransom, and when his son was made a knight or when his daughter got married, they had also to pay certain sums according to the extent of their lands.   Also, at any time, the king, if he chose, could go with all his servants, and live in their castles ; though, of course, he could not do this for long, as otherwise he would have eaten them up.   Lastly, when fines were taken from criminals who were tried in the king's courts, these fines went into the king's pockets.   In all these ways, then, the kings could get the means of keeping themselves and their households, though most of them spent more money than they could afford.

What has been just described is called the Feudal System, and it was this state of things that now existed in Scotland and other countries, and which continued to exist for many hundred years.

----

13. HOW PEOPLE LIVED UNDER THE FEUDAL SYSTEM

We have seen that under the Feudal System there were three classes of people, the greater and lesser barons, the free tenants, and the serfs in the country ; and now let us see how these different classes lived— leaving out the towns, of which something will be said in another place.   First, let us take the barons, as they were the most important class.

When the vassal received land from the king, he went into his presence, fell on his knees, and put his hands in those of the king, who then kissed him on the mouth. At the same time he took an oath that he would be the king's faithful vassal all his life.

Let us now follow him to the lands which he has got from the king. If there was not a castle already on the lands, he would at once set about building one. At first these castles had been built of wood, but by King David's time, they were usually built of stone. The chief thing thought of in building them was that they should be so strong that they could not easily be taken by an enemy. They were, therefore, built in some place which made it difficult for an enemy to attack them—such as a hill, or the middle of a lake or even of a bog. The walls were made so thick that, except with cannons, which did not exist in those days, they could not be broken down. For windows, which at this time had no glass, they had small holes from which stones could be thrown and arrows shot. Round the castle there was a high, thick wall, and outside the wall there was a deep and broad moat or ditch, over which was the draw-bridge, which could be raised or let down, so as to keep people out or let them in. Near the castle there was a hamlet, where the people lived who worked the ground from which the lord got food for himself and his household.

In this castle, then, the baron lived with his family and his retainers, that is, the armed men who were kept by him, and who were ready either to defend the castle or ride out with him against any enemy. At time of meals, everybody, both the lord and his family and the retainers, sat down at one table in the great hall of the castle; those of higher rank sitting at the upper end, and those of lower rank at the other.

And how did the great lord spend his time? First, he had business to attend to. When the king needed him in war or required his advice, he had to put himself at the head of his retainers and march to wherever the king happened to be. Every baron, also, had a court on his land in which criminals were tried, and he had the right of "pit and gallows"; which means, that he could hang men and drown women when they were found guilty of crimes that deserved death. Usually, however, the baron had an officer, called a bailie, who tried the persons who were brought before the court.

The great lord, therefore, had not much business to look after, and so he had to fill up his time with amusements. His chief amusement was hunting, and in those days hunting was much more exciting than it is now, as there were wolves and wild boars to be killed, and not merely foxes, and hares, and rabbits. In addition to hunting there was hawking, in which the ladies also took part—the sport being to see a falcon fly above a heron and then swoop down and kill it. But there could not be hunting and hawking at all times of the year, and so the baron must often have found it difficult to know how to fill in the day. A writer who lived in those times gives this list of the amusements of a feudal baron : hunting, fishing, fencing, jousting, chess-playing, bear-baiting, receiving guests, talking with ladies, holding his court, keeping himself warm, and watching the snow fall.

But the great amusement of those times was the tournament or tourney. As fighting was the chief thing about which the barons thought, to be brave

Knight on Horseback.

and skilful fighters was their great ambition. So their very play was a kind of war, and sometimes the play was very much in earnest. A king or some great baron would send out heralds through the country, and even into other countries, to say that on a certain day he would hold a tournament. Then as many knights as wished to show off their skill and courage would come to the place appointed. Sometimes the tourneys lasted several days, when many champions came, and it must have been a gay sight all the time it lasted. The fighting took place in what were called the *lists*—a long, broad piece of level ground, enclosed by barriers, to prevent people from getting inside. All around were the tents and pavilions of the great persons who had come to see the sight, and of the champions who were to take part in the tourney. On the tents and on trees were hung the standards and the shields of the combatants, so that everybody might know who they were.

For the chief people, of whom many were ladies, there were raised seats from which the lists could easily be seen. At the one end of the lists were the challengers, and at the other end those who were to fight them. All the champions were armed just as in time of war; they were covered from head to foot in mail; in their left hands they carried their shields, and in their right long lances, and a sword or a battle-axe hung at their sides. Usually the fighting took place on horseback. With their lances at rest, they galloped at full speed against each other, and each tried to unseat his opponent. If the one unhorsed got to his feet, his enemy leapt from his horse, and then they fought with their swords or battle-axes. Usually both the lances and swords were blunted, so that there might not be so much danger; but if the champions happened to be enemies, they fought with sharp swords and lances, just as in war, and in that case they were often wounded or slain. When the tourney was over, a lady, who had been chosen as "the lady of the tournament," gave the prize to the champion who had shown himself the bravest and most skilful fighter, and at night there was a great feast, to which the combatants and the chief people were invited.

The times of which we are speaking are called "the days of chivalry." To understand what this means, let us look at the way in which the son of a lord was brought up and educated. When he was a boy of ten or twelve, he was first sent to be a page to some great lady, so that he might learn how to be courteous, that is, to learn the manners of courts. Then he was put under some lord, whom he had to attend at table, carving his food and doing him other such services. When he grew older he became a squire; that is, he looked after the weapons of his master, and followed him to the wars and defended him in the time of battle. But his great ambition was to become a knight, and to gain this honour he had to show that he was brave and true, and skilful in using his weapons. Being made a knight was a very solemn thing, and the candidate, as he was called, had to go through a kind of religious service. He had to fast and to bathe, which meant that he was to be pure in mind as well as clean in body; he had to confess his sins to a priest, and watch all night in a church. When all this had been done, a sword was bound to his side and gold spurs put on his feet. Then he knelt down before the person who was to make him a knight, who gave him a blow on the cheek or on the shoulder, and said, "Be thou a good and faithful knight." And, last of all, the new knight took an oath that he would defend the weak and helpless, and never do anything that was mean or dishonourable. This, then, is what was meant by chivalry—skill and bravery in war; gentleness towards the weak, especially women; and hatred of what was not fair and just.

The free tenants lived a very different life from that of the barons. They are called free, because they were not slaves like the serfs, but could remove when they pleased from the lands of one lord to those of another. As was said, they rented a piece of ground from some lord, and paid him with sheep or cattle, or poultry or grain, or other things that the land produced. At certain times of the year, also, as, for instance, at seed-time and harvest, he and the men he employed had to work on the lord's own farm. Then he had to have all his corn ground at his lord's mill, and had to give him a certain quantity of it for having it ground. When the lord went to war, the tenant had to go with him, and provide his own weapons and his food. The free tenant, therefore, was not so free after all, and it must have been hard work for him to provide for himself and his family. But the lot of the serf was far worse. He and his family were all slaves, and could be sold at any time. Not only the lords but even the clergy had slaves. Very often the serfs tried to run away, but there were laws that ordered them to be sent back to their masters wherever they were found.

We have seen that every baron had a court, where persons accused of any crime were tried and punished. But the ways of trying whether persons were guilty or not were very different from ours. One way was this: if you wished to prove yourself

F

innocent, you got a number of persons living in the neighbourhood to take an oath that you were not guilty, and if they did so, you were then allowed to go free. This way of trying accused persons was called *compurgation*. But there were other ways that were more curious. To prove that you were innocent, you plunged your naked hand and arm into boiling water

Combat between Knights on Foot.

or took hold of red-hot iron, and, if the skin were healed within a certain time, you were supposed not to have committed the crime with which you were charged. This was known as *trial by ordeal*. But the strangest way of all was this: if anyone accused you of a crime, you could challenge him to fight a duel, and if you conquered, you were thought to be innocent, but if you were beaten, you were judged guilty. This seems a strange way of deciding whether a person was guilty or not, but it did not seem strange to the people of those times, as they believed that God would never allow an innocent person to be punished. In course of time, however, men found that innocent persons were sometimes punished instead of the guilty, and even in the time of David they had begun to think that trial by compurgation, or by the ordeal of fire or by combat, was not the right way to find out whether a crime had been committed or not.

14. WHAT DAVID DID FOR THE CHURCH

What David did for the Church is better remembered than what he did in bringing in the Feudal System, and for a very good reason. In many parts of the country we can still see the ruins of the great monasteries which he built as homes for the clergy. Here is a list of those monasteries, the ruins of which are still to be seen after nearly seven hundred years—Kelso, Dryburgh (where Sir Walter Scott is buried), Melrose, Newbattle, Dundrennan, Kynloss, Cambuskenneth, Holyrood, and Jedburgh. Those who live near where the ruins of any of these monasteries are will see what splendid buildings they must have been when they were newly built.

Now what David did for the Church was even more important for Scotland than his bringing in the Feudal System. Let us see how this was the case. We know already that, even before the time of Malcolm Canmore and Margaret, the Church of

Dryburgh Abbey.

Rome had become the Church of the whole of Scotland. We have seen, also, that Margaret did all she could to make the Scottish clergy do and believe exactly what the Church of Rome commanded, and that she and Malcolm together had built the Abbey of Dunfermline, where both of them were buried. And Margaret's sons were as eager about the Church as she was. Both Edgar and Alexander gave rich gifts to it, and they took a great interest in the clergy. But it was David, the last of her sons who reigned, that was the kindest friend of all to the Church. He gave it so much money and land, indeed, that James I., who lived three hundred years after him, called him a "sore saint to the crown"; which means that David was so pious that he made the kings of Scotland poor by giving away so much to the Church.

In the Church of Rome, just as is the case to-day, there were two kinds of clergy. There were the *regular clergy*, who lived in the monasteries, and there were the *secular clergy*, who went about the world just as Protestant ministers do. We have seen what a feudal castle was like, and now let us look at a monastery, and see how those living in it spent their time.

The first thing we should have come to in approaching it was a high and strong wall, just like that round a castle, for in those days and long afterwards not even religious buildings were safe in time of war. If we had entered by one of the gateways through the wall, we should have gone into the outer courtyard, where there were buildings we should hardly have expected to find there. There were workshops for

tradesmen, a granary for storing grain, and store-
houses where all kinds of tools and implements were
kept. Then we should have come to another wall,
though not so strong as the outer one, and, passing

A Monk.

through its gateway, we should have entered what
were called the cloisters, where only the monks were
allowed to walk. On one side of the cloisters were
the rooms where the monks lived. There was the
refectory where they took their meals, the kitchen, the
cells where they slept, the infirmary for the sick, and

the scriptorium or library where they read and wrote books. But the most important building of all was the church, which had beautiful carving all over it both inside and outside, with painted windows, and contained many precious things given by people for the good of their souls.

And how did those who lived in the monasteries spend their time? Their first duty, of course, was to perform the religious services for which the monastery had been built, and every day the monks took turns in going through these services, which lasted from early morning till late at night. But besides these brethren who attended to the religious services there were the lay brethren, who had to do the work of the monastery. The inmates required to be fed and clothed, so some of the lay brethren had to serve as cooks and tailors. Constant repairs too were necessary in such a large building, which made it needful that many had to become good workmen. Near the monastery there was a large garden, where some of the monks grew vegetables and fruits.

The monasteries had also farms close by, on which crops were grown and sheep and cattle reared, to supply the brethren with food and clothing. The farm-work was done by the serfs, for, as we have seen, the Church also had serfs, who were looked after by lay brothers from the monastery. And besides this farm there were other farms, which were rented out to tenants who paid for them with part of the crops they grew, and the cattle and sheep and poultry which they reared. Then in different parts of the country, the monastery had a great deal of land which was given to it by the king or the nobles. On this land the monks reared great numbers of sheep, and sent their wool to foreign countries in exchange for things which could not be got at home. If there was coal on the land, they worked the coal; and if the lands were near the sea, they made salt from the water and sent it also to foreign countries.

It will be seen, therefore, that monasteries were busy places, and we can understand how they did much good to the country in many ways. The monks were the best gardeners, the best farmers, the best road-makers, the best bridge-makers; and their lands were better tilled than the lands of the barons. The great good they did was to cultivate land which had been a wilderness before, and they showed the people how this was done. All the larger monasteries had what were called guest-houses, or apartments where travellers received food and lodging for the night. There were also shelters for beggars and the poor, who were always sure of getting refreshment at the monasteries; though this had the bad result that it encouraged people to beg, and in Scotland, just as in other countries, there came to be so many beggars that they were the terror of all the country.

We have now seen how the regular clergy lived and spent their lives, but what about the secular clergy? Their way of living was very different. The heads of the monasteries were called abbots or priors, but the chief men of the secular clergy were the bishops, which means overseers. Before King David's time there were only four bishops, but David added five more. The bishops lived in the chief towns, such as St Andrews, Glasgow, and Dunkeld, and they had charge of parts of the country which were called their dioceses. What they had to do

A Monk in his Study.

was to see that there was a sufficient number of churches in their dioceses, and that the clergy connected with these churches did their duty properly.

In this way, then, the country came to be covered with churches where the people could be taught the Christian religion. And it should be said that in connection both with the churches and with the monasteries there were schools where children were taught to read and to sing, though in those days it was mostly those who wished to be monks or priests who attended these schools.

And how were the churches and the clergy kept up? It was in this way. Rich people gave money or land to have the churches built and to pay for the expenses connected with them, and the people who attended the churches were expected to pay a tithe, that is, a tenth part, of their incomes, besides little sums at funerals and baptisms, and also for offerings to the altar. Usually, however, as there was very little money in the country at that time, the people paid in such things as formed the chief part of their own property.

From this account of what David did for the Church, it will be seen that it was even more important than what he did in bringing in the Feudal System. In the first place, the Church helped to make all the people of Scotland feel that they belonged to one nation, as they all believed in the same religion. Then the Church taught that peace and quietness were better than war, a lesson which was very much needed in those times when, as we have seen, fighting was the chief delight of the feudal barons and all those connected with them. The Church also looked after the poor, and, as the clergy were almost the only persons who were educated, they were the teachers as well as the preachers. Some of the clergy, indeed, did not act up to what the Church taught, and were quite as quarrelsome as the barons ; but the best of them tried to do as much good as they could, and for this we should be grateful to them.

---

15. THE ENGLISH COUNTIES LOST, AND ARGYLE CONQUERED

MALCOLM IV. (THE MAIDEN)	.	(1153-1165).
WILLIAM THE LION.	. .	(1165-1214).
ALEXANDER II.	. .	(1214-1249).

The reigns of the kings who came immediately after David were not so important as his, and there is not much to be said about them. A few events happened during these reigns, however, which have to be kept in mind, as otherwise we should not understand some things that took place afterwards. We have seen how King David made Scotland one kingdom again, and compelled the people in all parts of the country to obey him ; so that when he fought the Battle of the Standard he had men under him from north and south, and east and west. But the people of Scotland were not yet content to live under one king, and we are now to see that many of them tried again and again to set up other kings, so that often it seemed as if the kingdom were going to break up once more and become what it had been after the death of Malcolm Canmore. In this chapter we shall speak of no fewer than three reigns—only noticing what is important in each of them, for in this book it is with

Scotland and its people more than with kings that we have to do.

The first king to reign after David was Malcolm IV., his grandson, for, as we have seen, Prince Henry, Malcolm's father, who would have been king, died before he came to the throne. Malcolm was only twelve years old when he began to reign, and though he lived till he was twenty-four years old, he always looked so young that he was called Malcolm the Maiden. Now, Malcolm being such a young king, his enemies at once tried to take advantage of him. First of all, the men of Moray rose in rebellion against him, just as they had done against the kings who had reigned before him. But with the help of his Norman nobles Malcolm was too strong for them, and he not only defeated them, but took their leader prisoner, and kept him in Roxburgh Castle for the rest of his life. But Malcolm had trouble with others besides the men of Moray.

For instance, once when Malcolm was staying in the town of Perth no fewer than six earls, at the head of an army, surrounded the town and tried to get him into their hands. Luckily, however, some of the clergy made peace between the king and the earls, who agreed to break up their army. But no sooner was this danger past than a rebellion broke out in another part of the country, and this time in Galloway. The men of Galloway, it must be remembered, did not speak English like the men of Lothian, but Celtic, and they continued to speak that language for nearly six hundred years after this time. They had also laws of their own, and they hated the Norman barons to whom David had given lands in their country. So they now rose in rebellion against Malcolm, and he had to lead an army no fewer than three times against them before they were subdued. It will now be seen that, in spite of all that David had done, it was still very difficult for one king to rule over the whole of Scotland.

But Malcolm's greatest enemy was the king of England, and he was not so successful against him as against his enemies at home. We saw that, in the reign of David, parts of the northern counties of England were in his hands, but this of course could not be pleasant for an English king. And it happened that at this time a king was reigning in England who was very well able to look after himself. This king was Henry II., a very clever ruler, but who was not too particular how he got what he wanted. Henry had taken an oath to David that he would not try to gain back the Northern Counties; but when he saw Scotland ruled by a boy like Malcolm, he thought this was a good opportunity for breaking his word. He therefore told Malcolm that if he did not give back the counties, he must be his enemy.

What could Malcolm do? He had so many enemies at home that he could not go to war with England, and, besides, certain of his own advisers told him that to give the counties back was the wisest step he could take. So, rather than go to war, he let Henry have the counties, and Scotland never got them back again. This is the most important event of Malcolm's reign, and it was a very important one both for England and Scotland. For, had these counties continued to belong to Scotland, she might have become a stronger country than England, and, in that case, the history of Englishmen and Scotsmen would have been different. Only one thing more may be said about Malcolm. Like his grandfather David, he was very generous to the Church. So much was this the case, that a certain St Godrich, who lived at that time, said that Malcolm and Thomas Becket were more pleasing to God than any other men between the Alps and the North—though we may wonder how the saint came to know this.

The next king who reigned was Malcolm's brother, who is known as William the Lion. He got the name of "the Lion" in this way. In the times of the crusades thousands of warriors went from all the countries in the West of Europe to the Holy Land, to recover the sepulchre where Christ was buried. But, as they were clothed in mail from head to foot, they could not recognise each other. So they put emblems on their shields and standards by which they might be known. Some took animals as their emblems or *arms*, as they came to be called, some took plants, and some shells, and almost any kind of object that would serve to distinguish the shield. The King of France had lilies as his arms, the King of England three lions or leopards, and William a lion, and thus he got the name of William the *Lion*. And this emblem suited him, for during his reign of forty-nine years, the longest in Scottish history, he was almost constantly fighting with one enemy or another.

There is only one event, however, in William's long reign that deserves to be particularly remembered, and it is not a very pleasant one for Scotsmen to think of. William, being a warlike king, determined to try to recover the English counties which his

brother Malcolm had lost.   And it so happened that
he found an excuse for invading England for this
purpose.   The eldest son of Henry II. had rebelled
against his own father, and William agreed to help
him on condition that he received these counties and
other lands in England besides.

At the head of a great army, therefore, William
crossed the Border in the year 1174, and began to

Alnwick Castle.   [*Photo by Valentine.*

besiege the town of Alnwick.   But the barons of Yorkshire determined to stop him, and they marched north
with the intention of giving him battle.   There
happened to be a thick fog as they drew near to
Alnwick, so William did not see them approaching,
but, just as they reached the town, the fog cleared off
and there they saw William and a little band of knights
amusing themselves in tilting under the walls.   The
greater part of William's army had been scattered

through the country, so that he had very few men with him. But, though his enemies were so much more numerous, William did not think of fleeing. " Now it will be seen who is a true knight," he cried, and rushed to the fight. His horse immediately fell mortally wounded, and, before he could get free from the saddle, he was taken. Many of his followers, seeing their king a captive, gave themselves up also.

The King of Scotland was a prisoner, and the prisoner of a king who would not let him easily off. With his feet tied under the body of the horse on which he rode, William was led into the presence of Henry, who was overjoyed to see his enemy in this plight. To make sure that he would not escape, Henry took him across the English Channel to Normandy, and put him in chains in the castle of Falaise. Then, a month or two afterwards, Henry agreed to let him go free on one condition, but it was a hard one : William was to acknowledge Henry as the lord of all Scotland, and to reign only as a vassal king.

Thus, at length, Henry had succeeded in doing what so many English kings before him had tried to do : he had made Scotland a part of England. For fifteen years Scotland was in this position ; but at last Henry died, and a new king came to the throne, namely, Richard Cœur-de-Lion. From the moment that Richard became king he had set his heart on one thing, and that was to go on a crusade to the Holy Land. Now, to carry out this wish, he required a large sum of money, so he proposed to William that he would let him be a free king again if he would pay ten thousand marks. In this way, then,

Scotland once more became an independent kingdom,
just as it had been before the treaty of Falaise.
There is only one thing more that need be said
about the reign of William. Nearly throughout
the whole of it there were rebellions in different
parts of the country. We know very little of
these rebellions, but the end of them all was that
William got the upper hand, so that when he died in
the year 1214, he left Scotland to his successor as a
united kingdom.

The king who succeeded William was his son,
Alexander II., and to Alexander's reign also belongs
one event which should be remembered. This event,
however, was not a disgraceful one like the treaty of
Falaise, but, on the contrary, it helped to make the
Scottish kings stronger than they had been before.
The country called Argyle had always belonged to
the kings of Scots; indeed, as we saw long ago, it
was from Dalriada, the old name for Argyle, that the
Scots first came. But though the people of Argyle
were the subjects of the kings of Scots, they had
never been very obedient to them, and had often
fought on the side of their enemies. But Argyle lay
so far out of the way and was so difficult to reach
with an army, that no king of Scots had as yet succeeded in completely conquering them, and this was
what Alexander determined to do.

In the year 1221, therefore, Alexander collected an
army, composed of men from Galloway and Lothian;
and, as the easiest way of reaching Argyle, he prepared a fleet to sail from the Firth of Clyde. But it
was late in the autumn before he was ready to start,
and he had not sailed far when a great storm arose

G

which nearly wrecked his fleet, and he had to return to the port of Glasgow without having reached Argyle. But Alexander was determined to subdue Argyle, and next year, as soon as the winter was over, he marched his army into that country. As the different lords and chiefs did not unite against him, he had not much difficulty in conquering them, and soon he was master of the whole district. And now he did exactly what King David had done in the case of Moray. He let those who had been friendly to him keep their lands, but from those who had been his enemies he took their lands and gave them to followers of his own whom he could trust. In this way, then, the people of another part of Scotland were brought to obey the king as they had never done before.

There were rebellions in Alexander's reign just as in the reigns of his predecessors, but Alexander was so strong a king that he had not much difficulty in putting them down. Here is a story which shows what wild and savage things could be done at this time, and which shows that the bishops were not always good friends with the people. There was a bishop of Caithness, called Adam, who was so greedy that he made those who lived in his diocese pay double of what they ought to have paid to support the Church. The people grumbled at this, and at last, on a Sunday in the year 1222, three hundred of them made their way into his house. The Earl of Caithness lived close by, and some of the bishop's servants ran to him and told him in what danger the bishop was; but all that the earl said was, "If the bishop is afraid, let him come to me." The bishop had good reason to be afraid, for the angry crowd seized him, beat him, stripped him, and then carried him to his kitchen fire and roasted him alive.

When this news was brought to Alexander, he was just about to start for England, but he put off his journey, collected an army, and at once marched to Caithness. As there was no army to fight against him, he soon got the chief criminals into his hands, and put them to death with such fearful cruelties as might well have frightened other persons from roasting bishops. As for the Earl of Caithness, Alexander took a great part of his lands from him ; and, as this same earl was burned some years afterwards in his own house, people said that this was his punishment for not having saved the bishop.

A short time before his death, Alexander was trying to carry out a great enterprise which he had long thought of. This plan was nothing less than to try to win back the Hebrides from the king of Norway. It will be remembered that in the year 1102, during the reign of King Edgar, Magnus Barefoot, the king of Norway, had conquered these islands, which had been lost to Scotland ever since. But it was very important for Scotland that the Hebrides should not belong to another king, as they were a convenient place for all her enemies to take shelter in.

Alexander first tried to persuade Hakon, who was then king of Norway, that the islands really belonged to Scotland and not to Norway ; but, of course, Hakon would not listen to this. Then Alexander offered to buy them, but Hakon told him that " he was not in want of money." But Alexander was determined to have the islands, so he collected a fleet, and sailed to conquer them. On the voyage, however, he became very ill, and, when he reached the bay of Oban, he had to be put ashore on the island of Kerrera, where he died ; and the people of the neighbourhood said that his death was a punishment for doing an unjust action in trying to conquer the islands from the king of Norway. But we shall see that the king who came after Alexander did conquer the islands, and the people of Scotland, at least, did not think that this was wrong.

---

16. CONQUEST OF THE HEBRIDES

ALEXANDER III. (1249-1286)

Alexander III., the son of Alexander II., was only eight years old when he became king, and an old Scottish writer has told us exactly how he was crowned. The ceremony took place at Scone, which had long been the most important place to the north of the Forth. In the presence of a great number of the nobles and the clergy, the young king was led to the cross, which stood in the graveyard of the church, and there he was placed on the throne; and this throne has a strange history. It was called *Lia Fail*, which means in Gaelic *the Stone of Destiny*, because it was thought that no one could reign in Scotland except he had sat on it when he was crowned, and that so long as this stone was in Scotland the Scots would possess the land. It was believed that it was the stone which had been Jacob's pillow when he saw the angels at Bethel, and that it was brought to Scotland by Scota, daughter of Pharaoh, king of

Egypt, from whom Scotland was supposed to have got its name.

This wonderful stone was afterwards carried off by Edward I., and it is now in Westminster Abbey, and to this day our kings sit upon it when they are crowned. Alexander, then, sat down on this stone, which was covered with silken cloth woven with gold, and after the bishop of St Andrews had consecrated him, all the great nobles who were present strewed their garments under his feet, as was done when Christ entered Jerusalem. This should have ended the ceremony, but suddenly a Highland bard rushed forward, fell on his knees before the

Coronation Chair, with the Stone of Destiny beneath the Seat.

king, and told him in Gaelic the names of all his ancestors back to Scota, the daughter of Pharaoh!

As Alexander was only eight years old, regents had to be appointed to govern the country till he grew to be a man. But the question was—Who were to be the regents? The great nobles could not agree among themselves, and now one party of them got the upper hand and now another, and so it was that, till Alexander came to the age of twenty-one and was able to rule himself, the country was never at rest. When Alexander did begin to rule, however, he soon showed that he was one of the best kings who ever reigned in Scotland. During his reign there were none of those rebellions of which we have heard so often, and there was so little war of any kind that he was called " the peaceable king." But there was one enemy who came against him who might have done much harm to Scotland, and the story of how this enemy was beaten and what happened afterwards is one of the best known in the history of Scotland.

We have seen how Alexander II. had died just as he was about to try to retake the Western Islands from Norway. Now from the time that Alexander III. began to rule for himself, he made up his mind that he would accomplish what his father had failed to do. Just as his father had done, he began by trying to make a bargain with Hakon, for it was still the same Hakon who was king of Norway ; but Hakon would not hear of any bargain. Then one of Alexander's nobles, the Earl of Ross, began to make war on the chiefs of the islands, who sent to Hakon to ask for his assistance. Hakon determined that he would come to their help, and teach such a lesson to the King of Scots as he would not soon forget. By and by the news came that Hakon was preparing a fleet which was to be larger than any fleet that had ever sailed from Norway. When this news came, not only the people of Scotland but the people of England also were frightened, for the days of the terrible vikings were not yet forgotten.

In the month of July 1263, Hakon set sail from Norway on his voyage to punish the King of Scots. He had more than a hundred vessels, and aboard them were the men who were to do the fighting, if Alexander was not too frightened to fight. Hakon's own galley was made of solid oak, with a gilded dragon at the bow and the stern, and in it were the bravest warriors of Norway. He first sailed to the Orkneys, where the fleet anchored for a short time, and, while it was there, a thing happened which made the Norwegians fear that the expedition would not have a good end. At full mid-day the sun was suddenly darkened, and nothing of it was seen but a narrow rim. Astronomers tell us that on the 5th of August 1263 there was an eclipse of the sun, and it was this eclipse of the sun that terrified the Norwegians. But Hakon continued his voyage, and sailed down through the Western Islands, many chiefs joining him with their ships on the way, and at last he came to anchor in the bay of Lamlash, in the island of Arran.

King Alexander had not been idle all this time. He had not a fleet large enough to fight Hakon on the sea, but he did what he could to prevent his kingdom from being invaded. He fortified the castles near the sea, he sent out ships to watch the Norwegians, and he collected an army which he brought to Ayr, as it was near Ayr that he expected Hakon to land. Alexander, however, had a plan in his mind which he now tried to carry out. It was now well on in the month of September, and at that time of the year, as we know, great storms usually arise. But if one of these storms should come on, it would

From Painting by Wm. Hole, R.S.A.]

Battle of Largs, A.D. 1263—the Attack of the Scots.

Battle of Largs—the Fight at Sea.

do more damage to Hakon's fleet than any amount of fighting. So what Alexander did was to keep Hakon waiting as long as he could before there should be any fighting. He pretended that he wished to make a treaty, and sent some barefooted friars to Hakon with this message, and the friars kept coming and going between the two kings. In this way day after day passed, and at last the very thing happened which Alexander had wished.

On the 1st of October a terrible storm arose, which lasted for two days. So violent was this tempest, indeed, that the Norwegians believed that it had been raised by Scottish witches; but the Scots thought that it was St Margaret who had caused it, to save them from the Norwegians. The result was that many of Hakon's ships foundered at sea, or were wrecked on the shore near the town of Largs, in Ayrshire. Then the people of the neighbourhood fell upon the shipwrecked Norwegians, and carried off such things as had been saved from the wrecks.

Next morning Hakon brought help to those who had been wrecked, but by this time a small army of Scots, of whom about 1500 were horsemen in armour, had come to the spot. A battle then took place, and, though the Norwegians fought as bravely as they always fought, they were driven back to the boats which had been sent to take them off. Among the Scottish knights who pursued them was one called Sir Piers Curie, who was arrayed in beautifully gilded armour, and wore a belt embroidered with jewels. The Norwegians, when they were driven to the shore, had formed into a circle to defend themselves better against their enemies, and as Sir Piers rode round the circle, a Norwegian captain suddenly stepped out and with one stroke of his sword cut off his thigh. Sir Piers dropped dead from his saddle, and the Norwegian stooped down and stripped him of his shining belt. Then the fighting began again, and at last most of the Norwegians got into the boats and were rowed to the fleet. But Hakon had no longer the heart to go on with the war. Besides the great number of his ships that had been lost, many of those that were left were so damaged as to be of little use, and his men were no longer so ready to fight after all their misfortunes. So Hakon sailed back for Norway by the same way he had come. But Hakon was never to reach Norway. He stopped on the way, at Kirkwall, in the Orkneys, and there he took ill and died. " At midnight (on the 15th of December)," says the old Norwegian writer who tells the story of Hakon's expedition, "at midnight, Almighty God called King Hakon out of this mortal life."

After the defeat and death of Hakon, Alexander had little difficulty in subduing the Western Islands, and three years afterwards he made a bargain with Hakon's successor, King Eric, by which Eric agreed to give the islands to Scotland. The bargain was that the Scots should pay 4000 marks at once, and 100 marks every succeeding year for all time coming. So at last the Hebrides had become a part of Scotland, and they were never again taken from her. But a long time had still to pass before the Orkney and Shetland Islands also came to form part of the kingdom of Scotland.

The last years of Alexander's reign were made sad

and gloomy both for him and for his people. All his children, one after another, died before him. His daughter, Margaret, who had married Eric, king of Norway, left an infant daughter as the only heir to succeed to the throne. If this infant died, nobody could say who should reign, and it was very likely that war would arise between the different persons who might wish to wear the crown. During the winter of the years 1285 and 1286, people had a feeling that something dreadful was going to happen to the country. At Christmas there was thunder and lightning, which is very unusual, and meteors often blazed in the sky, and in those days this was thought to mean that some great calamity was about to befall.

[*Photo by Valentine.*

Alexander III.'s Monument, near Kinghorn.

And a great calamity did happen. On the 19th of March 1286, Alexander held a council in the castle of Edinburgh. It was late before the council broke up, and the day was stormy, but Alexander had made up his mind to return that night to Kinghorn, in Fife, where his queen was staying. So he mounted his horse, and, along with his attendants, he rode to Queensferry. By the time they had crossed the ferry, the night was so dark that the riders could not see each other. As they rode on, their guides lost the way, and they had to let their horses find it for themselves. At last they came near Kinghorn, when suddenly the king's attendants were startled by a noise. On riding up, they found that the king's horse had stumbled over a cliff, and at the bottom of the cliff lay the lifeless body of Alexander.

The day of Alexander's death was one of the saddest that has ever come to Scotland, for, as we shall see, it was followed by troubles and misfortunes which would not have happened if he had lived and left a son like himself. And for many a day to come the people looked back to the time of " good King Alexander," when there was peace and love in the land, and when there was " abundance of ale and bread, of wine and wassail cake, and of sports and mirth."

---

17. AN OLD SCOTTISH TOWN

Between the days of St Columba and the days of Alexander III., seven hundred years had come and gone, and great changes had taken place in Scotland during that time. In the days of Columba there were four kings, who had nothing to do with each

other, except when they went to war, which was
very often. Four hundred years passed, and then
one king, Malcolm II., became ruler over the whole
country. But, though there was now only one king,
it was a long time before he could make all his
subjects obey him, and we have seen that during all
the kings' reigns from that of Malcolm Canmore to
that of Alexander III., there were constant rebellions
which they often found it very difficult to put down.
Alexander III., indeed, was the first king who was
not troubled by rebellions, and who really made
himself obeyed by all his subjects. Scotland, therefore, was never happier or more prosperous than it
was during his reign. Now, it was in the towns
that this happiness and prosperity was seen most,
and so it is time that we should know what a town
was like in those days, and how their inhabitants
lived and went about their business. We have
already read how the barons, and the clergy, and
the free tenants, and the serfs lived in the country ;
but the life of the town people was very different
from theirs.

In the first place, how did there come to be towns?
There were two things that caused people to
come together, and in course of time to make up
a town. The first was that by living together they
made themselves safer against their enemies, and the
second was that by living together they could supply
each other's wants better, as some people could follow
one trade and some another. Now, it is curious that
just about the same time—during the reign of Malcolm
Canmore—towns began to appear all over the West
of Europe. In Scotland, too, at that time towns

must have been beginning, for we saw that Margaret got Scottish merchants to bring things home from foreign countries. The places where towns were built were usually near the castles of kings or barons, or near some monastery or great church, where the inhabitants could defend themselves from their enemies. Generally, also, they were built near the sea, or beside some river that flowed into the sea, so that trade might be carried on with foreign countries.

Now, in Scotland there came to be three kinds of towns or burghs—Royal Burghs, Burghs of Regality, and Burghs of Barony. The Royal Burghs were so called because they were built on the land of the king, to whom they had to pay rent, and who in return gave them certain privileges which the other burghs did not have. For instance, they were allowed to trade through the whole country and also with foreign countries, which the other burghs were not allowed to do. The Burghs of Regality and the Burghs of Barony had not the king over them, but some baron or abbot or bishop, and so they were not so important as the king's burghs. It is a Royal Burgh, therefore, we must look at, if we wish to know what the best kind of town was like in the times of Alexander, and, indeed, in times long after those of Alexander.

Suppose, then, that we were paying a visit to one of these Royal Burghs. Before we came to it we should have known that we were approaching a town, for at some distance from it we would have seen cattle and sheep browsing on the town *common*, the pasture-land that belonged to the town. For every morning the town-herd blew his horn to let his beasts know that it was time to go to pasture, and they knew the sound at once. Going still nearer the town, we come to the *town acres*. These were little fields round the town, and in the times when there were few people in the towns, each of the inhabitants had a field of his own. And now we come to the burgh itself, but we should not have got into it so easily as into a town nowadays. All round it there was a deep ditch, and on the other side of the ditch a great stockade or paling, which it would be difficult to get over.

The only way of entering the town, indeed, was through one of the gates which opened into it. But at each of the gates there was a keeper, to whom you had to explain who you were and what brought you there, before he allowed you to enter. If he was not satisfied, he would have you taken to the magistrate, who might order you to be put in the town prison, which was usually only a deep hole in the ground. The reason why all this care was taken with strangers, and why there was a ditch and a stockade round the town, was, of course, because the inhabitants were always in fear lest some enemy should get into the town and plunder it. At a later time than the reign of Alexander, a stone dyke was made round the town instead of a stockade; but in Scotland there were never great walls with towers such as there were on the Continent.

If it was the early morning when we entered the town, we might perhaps have seen a man going through the street beating a drum or playing some other musical instrument. This was to waken the town folk and let them know that it was time to begin the day's labours, for in those days there were neither watches

ALEXANDER III.   WILLIAM THE LION   DAVID I.,   MARGARET, Sister of   MACBETH,   DUNCAN I.
(1241-1286).   (1143-1214).   "The Sore Saint"   Edgar the Atheling   Mormaer of Moray   (——-1040).
   (1084-1153).   (1047-1093).   (——-1057).

THOMAS,   ALEXANDER II.   MALCOLM, the Maiden   ALEXANDER I.   MALCOLM CANMORE   GRUACH,
the Rhymer.   (1198-1249).   (1141-1165).   (1078-1124).   (——-1093).   Wife of Macbeth.

H

nor clocks. And we must remember that a town in those days was a very small place, and more like what we nowadays call a village than a town. The first thing that would have struck us as we looked around would have been that the town was a very dirty place. There would be great midden-heaps everywhere, for these were only removed on the Sunday mornings, and not always then.

The streets, of course, were not paved, and there were great ruts in them and often deep holes, so that you were in danger of breaking your neck if you did not pick your steps carefully. Then everywhere we should have seen pigsties built beside the houses and in the open street, and pigs running about just as dogs do now, but only far more of them. These pigs were a great nuisance in the town, as they often got among people's feet, and caused serious accidents, especially in the case of children and old folk. A law was made that no pig was to go about the streets except it were led by a rope, but this law was not obeyed, and the pigs continued to run about just as they pleased.

If we took a walk through the town, we might find that it was made up of one main street, called the Hiegait or High Street, with a great number of wynds or closes on both sides of it. In the time of Alexander III. most of the houses were built of wood, so that there was always great danger of fire. People were forbidden to carry lights not properly covered, from one house to another; and it was ordered that there should be ladders kept to reach the tops of the houses should a fire break out. Even in the main street the houses were not built in an

H

even line as they must be built now, but many of them jutted into the street and almost blocked the way. As for the shops, they were not at all like what we now call shops, but wooden erections called *booths*, which jutted into the street, so that the passers-by could see everything in them that was for sale.

The largest building in the town was the parish church, in which many other things went on besides religious services. For instance, the magistrates used to meet in the church to do the business of the town, and traders and merchants to make their bargains. Round the church was the churchyard, which must have been a very disreputable place. Swine, goats, cattle, sheep, and horses browsed among the graves, and very often the refuse of the town was thrown into it. In the middle of the town was the town cross, which had at first been placed there to show that they were Christian people who dwelt round it. In course of time, however, the cross was put to many uses. It was from the cross that the town-crier proclaimed the laws of the burgh and of the kingdom. If anyone broke the laws of the town, he was made to stand at the cross with a paper crown on his head so that everybody who passed might see him. And, as often as not, the wool merchants and the cloth makers used the cross for drying their wool and cloth upon.

This was what the town was like during the day, but what was it like at night? We should not have seen, because it was almost in total darkness. The magistrates constantly made laws commanding the booth-keepers to keep lights in their booths, but the laws were hardly ever obeyed. If any person went out at night, he had to carry what was called a bowet or lantern, and if he did not, he was put in the netherhole, or prison of the town. What did the people do when there was so little light either in the streets or in their houses? Most of them went to bed when it became dark, and remained there till the sun rose, when they could see to begin their daily work. And, indeed, there was a law that forbade

Great Seal of Alexander III.

tradesmen to do work at night, because they could not then see to do it well.

This is not a very pleasant picture of an old Scottish town, but the towns in other countries were not much better. In those days people had not the same notions about neatness and cleanliness that we have; but we shall see that the inhabitants of those towns, which we should think were wretched places to dwell in, lived busy and industrious lives, were good craftsmen and traders and merchants, and had comforts and pleasures and amusements of their own.

18. THE DWELLERS IN THE TOWNS

We have just seen what an old Scottish town was like, and now let us see how the town people lived and went about their daily business. And it is to be remembered that long after the time of Alexander III. they lived almost exactly in the same way. The dwellers in the towns were divided into two classes, called freemen and unfreemen. The freemen were also called *burgesses*, and they were the only persons who had all the privileges which the king gave to his Royal Burghs. Before a man could become a burgess he had to pay a sum of money, and he had to possess armour and weapons so that he should be ready to fight the enemies of the king if he were called upon. He had also to take his turn in watching and guarding the burgh, and this went on always, as the town was never sure when it might be attacked by some enemy.

Altogether, the duties of the burgess were so heavy that he often wished he had never become one. Still, he was much better off than the unfreemen, who had a very hard time of it, and who did not at all like the burgesses, with whom they were constantly quarrelling. An unfreeman could not keep a shop or booth, he could not follow any trade, he could not be an artisan or craftsman. And what must have been very disagreeable, on market-days in the town he had to stand on the opposite side of the street from the freeman, to show that he was an unfreeman. So it will be seen that the unfreemen were what the Bible calls " hewers of wood and drawers of water," that is, they had to do all the hardest work in the town and got very little for it.   Of course, the unfreemen were not slaves, and they could leave the town when they pleased, but they would have been no better off wherever they went.

But the freemen or burgesses were also divided into two classes, who did not live very happily together.   The one class was made up of the merchants and the other of the craftsmen.   The merchants were the great people of the town, and they wished to have all the power in their own hands. To keep themselves apart from the craftsmen they had a *guild* or society, to which nobody but a merchant could belong.   Indeed, if any merchant took up a craft, he had to leave the guild and was looked down upon by all the other merchants.   Now, there were a great many craftsmen of different kinds in the towns, and they did not like the merchants to have it all their own way and to carry their heads so high.   But, as the craftsmen were a very important class of people, something more should be mentioned of them.

As was just said, there were many different kinds of craftsmen.   There were smiths, armourers, shoemakers, butchers, potters, saddlers, glovers, bonnet-makers, dyers, masons, tailors, and others. Each craft had a different dress, which nobody else was allowed to wear.   If a poor unfreeman put on the dress of any craft, he was treated like the jackdaw who appeared among the peacocks in peacock's feathers.   Each craft lived in a separate part of the town, and so to-day we have streets called Candle-maker Row and Potterrow, which means that candle-makers and potters lived in that part of the town. Every craft had a flag of its own, and a patron-saint to whom they gave offerings and for whom they kept an altar in the church. To see that the members of the craft did their work properly, an officer, called a deacon, was chosen, who could punish anyone who broke the rules of the craft.

To get into a craft you had to become an apprentice to a master, and bind yourself to serve him for a number of years. The apprentice lived in the house of his master, who gave him food and clothes, and could flog him if he misbehaved. When the boys of Paris became apprentices, they made a bargain that their master's wife should not be allowed to beat them. When the apprentice had finished his time of service, he was shut up in a room by himself, and had to make a boot or a saddle or a coat of mail, according to his trade, which had to be examined by the deacon of the trade. If the article were well made, then the apprentice became a journeyman, but, if it were not well made, he had to serve for some time longer. With all these craftsmen at work in different parts of it, the town must have been a busy place, and, indeed, rather a lively one, as every now and then there were quarrels between the craftsmen and the merchants as to which of them should have the power in managing the business of the town.

And how was the business of the town managed? In a very different way from what is the case now. Every year a town council was chosen, and at first only merchants could be councillors, but in course of time craftsmen also were chosen. The councillors did many things which seem very strange to us nowadays. For instance, they fixed the prices of everything that was sold in the town, so that a shoemaker, or a glover, or a butcher could not charge what he liked for his goods. And they not only fixed the prices of things, but they had to see that all the things that were sold were good. To make sure that this was the case, officials were appointed to look after the tradespeople and the craftsmen. There were ale-tasters who went into the breweries and tasted the ale before it was sold, to make sure that it was good ; and so with bread and flesh, and boots and gloves, and everything that was made and sold in the town. Then the councillors had to see that no one broke the laws of the town. The unfreemen frequently gave them a great deal of trouble by selling or making things which they were not allowed to do.

The great events in the life of the town were the markets that were held every week and the fairs that were held every year, and the councillors had to look after these also. On the morning of the market-day, the people in the country round about brought into the town whatever they had to sell, but before they got in they had to pay a tax at the gates. Then their goods were taken to the town cross, where the officials examined them and fixed the prices at which they were to be sold. Before the market began, a bell was rung, and all the sellers had to be in their right places. But what seems curious to us is that the unfreemen were not allowed to buy before the freemen had got what they wanted.

It was the fair, however, that made the greatest stir

in the town, for then traders and merchants came in crowds from long distances, and brought things which were not to be had in the town itself. The magistrates had then a busy time of it, as they had to see that " the peace of the fair " was kept. To try and punish those who broke the peace of the fair, a court was held which had a curious name. It was called the " Court of the Piepoudres," or the " Court of the Dusty-feet," the dusty-feet being the traders who had come from a distance to sell their wares.

Another business of the magistrates was to look after the beggars and sick people, of whom there were always a great number. In every town there was a class of people of whom we know nothing nowadays, but who are still known in Eastern countries. These were the lepers, of whom there were then very many in every country, owing to the dirty habits of the people. As the disease of leprosy was then thought to be very infectious, the lepers were not allowed to live in the town, and a hospital had to be built some distance off, where they might be shut up. Edinburgh, for instance, had a hospital at Liberton, which just means Lepertown. The lepers were only allowed to come into the town on certain days and to stand at certain places, where they received alms from the passers-by, and the rule was that bad butcher-meat, which other people could not eat, was given to them. Of course they were not allowed into the church, but sometimes a hole was made in the wall through which they could see the altar, and the priest going through the service.

From this account of an old Scottish town and its inhabitants we may think that it could not have been very pleasant to live in those days.   Perhaps, however, people lived just as happily then as now.   At all events, they had far more holidays than we have, for besides the Sundays there were as many as fifty Saints' Days, on which they were not allowed to do any work.   On these idle days there were all sorts of amusements, of which something will have to be said farther on.   Then in Alexander III.'s reign, at least, the most of the people had plenty to eat and drink.   The poorer people drank ale, and ate oatmeal and pease porridge, and we have seen that the magistrates of the burghs took care that both the ale and the bread should be good.   As for the richer people, they could even afford to buy luxuries that were brought from other countries, for among the things sold in the town booths were pepper, ginger, almonds, rice, figs, raisins, and wines.   But we have now come to a time in the history of Scotland when the people had other things to think of than amusements, for they had to fight for the independence of their country.

---

19. SCOTLAND WITHOUT A KING.
1286-1292

When Alexander III. died, the heir to the throne was his grand-daughter Margaret, who was only about three years old.   She is called the "Maid of Norway," because she was born in Norway, and was the daughter of Eric, king of that country, who had married Margaret, the daughter of Alexander.   The first thing that had to be done on the death of

Alexander was to choose guardians to govern the country till she grew up, and so six guardians were chosen, three to rule to the north of the river Forth, and three to the south of it. This was not a good arrangement, as so many guardians were sure to quarrel among themselves. It was the only thing that could be done, however, as they would not agree to have one guardian over the whole country.

Now, what everybody must have been wondering was—if the Maid of Norway should die, who would then be the right person to be king? There was one person who was already thinking that he was the right person, and that was Robert Bruce, lord of Annandale, the grandfather of the great king, Robert Bruce, who won the battle of Bannockburn. There were two reasons why Bruce thought that he should be king. He was the son of the second daughter of David, the brother of William the Lion, and, besides, Alexander II., before Alexander III. was born, had wished him to be king. But, as the other great lords in the country did not wish him to be king, he tried to gain the crown for himself. He got all his friends round him at his castle of Turnberry, in Ayrshire, and collected an army and made war for nearly two years. But he did not succeed in his end, for the people believed that the Maid of Norway, the grand-daughter of " good king Alexander," was their rightful queen.

And what did King Eric think of what was going on in Scotland? He knew that it would be a proud day for Norway when his daughter grew up to be a woman, for she would be queen not only of Norway, but also of Scotland and of those

Western Islands which had been taken from King Hakon. But what if some Scottish baron should make himself king of Scotland before she grew up? This was what Eric was afraid of, and he now took a step to make sure that it would not happen. He sent a message to Edward I., king of England, to ask him to do something to prevent anyone else from getting the Scottish crown except the lawful heir, the Maid of Norway. Now, he could not have asked anyone who would be more ready to help him than Edward, who had a plan of his own about Scotland. This plan was, in some way or other, to make Scotland a part of England, so that there should be one king over both countries. Edward was glad, therefore, to receive Eric's message, as it gave him a chance of interfering in the affairs of Scotland.

What Edward did was to ask the six guardians to send some persons to England, who might meet Eric's messengers and come to an agreement about the young queen. So the guardians sent four commissioners to Salisbury, in England, where they met Edward and the commissioners of Eric. The arrangement that was come to was this. Margaret was only to be sent to Scotland if there was peace in the country, and she was not to be allowed to marry without the consent of her father, and without the approval of Edward.

And now we see what was in Edward's mind. The year after the meeting at Salisbury, he let it be known that he wanted Margaret to marry his own son Edward. Now, if this marriage had taken place, it would have brought about all that King Edward wished, for when his son grew up he would have been king both of England and Scotland, and so the two countries would have been peacefully joined together. However, both the guardians and King Eric were quite willing that the marriage should take place, and in the year 1290 a treaty of marriage was made at Birgham, a place in South Berwickshire, on the borders of the two countries. Now the Scots were quite aware that there was a great risk that the marriage might end in Scotland becoming a part of England, and they took care that the treaty should prevent this from happening. But all these plans came to nothing; the marriage never took place, and the danger to Scotland was to arise in another way.

Not long after the marriage had been all arranged, Margaret sailed from Norway to come to Scotland, but she was never to see the country of which she was the queen. On the way the ship stopped at the Orkney Islands, and there she died. But her father wished to make sure that the story of her death was true, so he had her body taken home to Norway, when he saw for himself that it was indeed the body of his own child. And it was well that this was done, for a year after the death of King Eric, a woman from Germany came to Norway and said that she was Margaret, Queen of Scots. But people knew that the real Margaret was dead, and both the woman and her husband were put to death.

All Scotland was in sorrow for the death of the child-queen, because no one knew what would happen next. A king must now be chosen, and who was he to be? No fewer than thirteen persons came forward, each claiming that he was the rightful heir. And who was to decide the matter? There was no one in Scotland who had the right to say who should be king, and the great barons in the country were so divided among themselves that they would never have agreed to choose one. As the only way out of the difficulty, the Scottish barons and clergy decided that Edward I. should be asked to settle who was to be their king. Edward consented to be the judge, but he made a hard bargain beforehand. All the claimants, that is, those who claimed to be the lawful heirs to the Scottish throne, had to admit that Edward was lord of Scotland, and had a right to say who should be king under him; and as a guarantee that they would keep their word, all the castles of Scotland were put into Edward's hands.

In the hall of the castle of Berwick, on the 17th of November 1292, Edward at last settled who was to be king. Of the thirteen claimants only eight were present, and of these eight only three had really good claims, so that it was between these three that Edward had to decide. One of these three we already know—Robert Bruce, who was the son of the second daughter of David, Earl of Huntingdon, the brother of William the Lion. The other two were John Balliol, grandson of the eldest daughter of David, Earl of Huntingdon, and John Hastings, grandson of the third daughter of the same earl. What Edward decided was that, as Balliol was descended from the *eldest* daughter of the Earl of Huntingdon, he had the best right to the Scottish crown, and so John Balliol became king of Scotland. But he was not a free king, for the day after the " award," as it was called, he had to do homage to the king of England as his lord and master.

20. A USELESS KING

JOHN BALLIOL (1292-1296)

The Scots did not think much of the king whom
Edward had given them.   They called him the
"Toom Tabard"—*toom* being the Scotch word for
empty, and a *tabard* a coat worn by heralds, so
that what the nickname meant was that Balliol
was called king, but was not really one.   And the
reign of Balliol, which lasted only four years, showed
that the Scots were right.   He was never really his
own master ; first, because many of the nobles would
not obey him ; and secondly, because Edward would
never leave him in peace.   For what Edward wished
Balliol never to forget was that he, Edward, was his
lord and master.   When any Scotsman could not get
what he wanted from Balliol, he went to Edward
with his complaint, and Edward took his side.   At
last there came a time when Balliol and his friends
could bear this no longer.

In the year 1294 Edward wanted to go to war with
France, but he had great difficulty in getting money
and soldiers, as his subjects in England had been
taxed so much already that they did not wish to pay
any more.   So once again he called Balliol to London
and told him that he must raise both money and
soldiers in Scotland, and then come with his chief
barons and go with him to France.

Now the Scots never liked paying taxes even to
their own kings.   Instead of doing what Edward told
him, therefore, Balliol held a Council at Scone to ask

its advice, and the Council advised him to take a step which really meant that he was to go to war with Edward. First of all, every Englishman who was then in Scotland was to be sent out of the country, so that it should be governed by none but Scotsmen. Then next year (1295) Balliol, with the advice of his Council, did something still bolder. He made a treaty with France, which was Edward's enemy, and by this treaty it was arranged that France and Scotland should help each other against England, which was the enemy of both of them. Now this treaty is very important in the history of Scotland, because it was the beginning of what is called the Franco-Scottish Alliance, of which we hear so much in these days. From this time till the reign of Queen Mary the French and the Scots often made treaties with each other, and, when they did so, it was always to make themselves stronger against England, which was anxious to conquer both France and Scotland.

The year after the French treaty, the Scots made Edward still more angry than he already was. Just as in the old days of Malcolm Canmore and David, they invaded Northumberland and Cumberland and plundered the inhabitants. But Edward was not a king to be trifled with, and he determined that he would make Balliol repent of what he had done. With a great army, therefore, he came against Berwick-on-Tweed, which was then a Scottish town, and one of the richest either in Scotland or in England. But Berwick had a wall round it and a strong castle, and its inhabitants thought they could prevent Edward from taking their town. So when he summoned them to surrender, they refused, and the fighting began.

The English had both a fleet and an army, but the people of Berwick burned three of their ships and compelled the others to keep at a distance. If Edward was to conquer the town, therefore, he would have to break through the wall. In those days, generals fought in the armies which they commanded, and Edward, to encourage his men, led them on. Mounted on his horse, which was called Bayard, he was the first to leap the wall. Then his soldiers broke in after him, and a terrible slaughter began. Men and women, old and young, were put to death, and so many were slain that it is said that for two days the blood ran like a river down the streets of the town.

But the taking of Berwick was only the beginning of what Edward intended to do against Scotland. He had come to punish Balliol and to take his kingdom from him. While he was still at Berwick, he got news that the castle of Dunbar, which had been in possession of the English, had been betrayed into the hands of the Scots. On hearing this, he at once sent the Earl of Surrey with an army to retake it, and a battle was fought at Dunbar in which the Scots were completely beaten, and no fewer than three earls taken, besides four barons and many knights.

This was not a good beginning for John Balliol; but, if all the nobles of Scotland had gathered round him, he might still have beaten Edward, for when a whole country rises against an enemy it is very difficult to conquer. But this was exactly what the Scottish nobles did not do, and many of them even took sides with Edward against their own king; and among those who did so was Robert Bruce, the

EDWARD
BALLIOL
(——-1367).

Sir WILLIAM DOUGLAS,
Knight
of Liddesdale.

Sir THOMAS RANDOLPH,
Earl of Moray
(——-1332).

ROBERT BRUCE
(1274-1329).

Sir WILLIAM
WALLACE
(1274?-1305).

EDWARD I.
OF ENGLAND
(1239-1307).

ROBERT DE BRUCE
(1210-1295).

Sir ANDREW MORAY,
of Bothwell
(Guardian).

DAVID II.
(1324-1371).

Sir JAMES DOUGLAS,
"The Black Douglas,"
(1286-1330).

COUNTESS OF
BUCHAN.

JOHN BALLIOL
(1249-1315).

MARGARET,
Maid of Norway
(1283-1290).

son of the claimant Bruce, and the father of the great Robert Bruce. Why, we ask, did these Scottish nobles fight against their own king? The reason was that many of them had lands both in England and in Scotland, and, if Edward should be victorious, they would lose their lands in both countries. And we shall see that this was very unfortunate for Scotland in the time coming, for the Scottish nobles were so divided in their minds, that now they fought on one side and now on the other.

As there was no great Scottish army to fight him, Edward had not much trouble in subduing the country. He led his army to Edinburgh, and, though the Castle was a very strong place, he took it after only ten days' siege. Then he went on to Stirling, where there was nobody to fight against him; and at last he came to Perth, where he made a great feast and there were great rejoicings. But by this time the unhappy Balliol saw that it was useless to try to resist any longer, and he sent a very penitent message to Edward to tell him that he was willing to submit and make peace.

When a vassal submitted to his lord whom he had offended, he had to go through a very humbling ceremony, and this Balliol had now to do. In the churchyard of Stracathro, in Kincardineshire, he appeared before the Bishop of Durham, for Edward himself would not condescend to come. He was dressed only in his shirt and drawers— for so an offending vassal had to come into the presence of his lord—and in his hand he held a white wand, which he gave to the bishop as a sign that he surrendered the kingdom of Scotland to the

I

English king.   And so John Balliol's reign came to
this disgraceful end, for Edward at once sent him a
prisoner to England.   After three years Balliol was
allowed to go to France, and on his journey thither
a curious event happened.   In those days, just as
now, people's luggage was examined when they
went from one country to another, and among
Balliol's luggage were found the royal crown and seal
of Scotland, a number of gold and silver cups, and a

Great Seal of John Balliol.

sum of money.   When this was told to Edward, he
ordered that the seal should be brought to himself;
that the crown should be offered at the shrine of St
Thomas Becket, the martyr, at Canterbury ; and that
Balliol should be allowed to keep the cups, and also
the money, to pay his travelling expenses.

As there was now no king in Scotland to fight
against him, it was easy for Edward to subdue the
whole country.   To make certain, however, that there
should be no rebellion against him, he led his army
to Elgin, and then back to Berwick.   It is said that

Robert Bruce, of whom we have just heard, asked Edward to make him king, as he was the next heir after Balliol. But Edward turned sharply upon him and said, "Do you think I have nothing to do but conquer kingdoms for you?"

To show that Scotland was no longer to be a kingdom, Edward ordered that the Stone of Destiny, on which the kings of Scots had been crowned, should be taken to England; and, besides the Stone, the Holy Rood or Cross of St Margaret, and all the documents or papers that might show that Scotland had once been an independent kingdom. Last of all, Edward made those who had land in Scotland sign their names, or have them signed, in a list, to show that they recognised him as their king, and, if their names were not entered in the list, their land was to be taken from them. This list of names is called the "Ragman's Roll," and, as the names have been printed in a book, we can still read them. There are about two thousand names altogether, and they are the names of the chief families who then lived in Scotland. Among them is one name which was to become one of the most famous in the history of Scotland—the name of Robert Bruce, soon to be the deliverer of his country.

Scotland being now completely subdued, as Edward thought, he had to arrange how it should be governed. As he could not be sure that the Scottish nobles would be faithful to him, he determined that Englishmen should govern it. So the Earl of Surrey, who had gained the battle of Dunbar, was appointed Guardian of the whole kingdom;

Hugh de Cressingham, a churchman, was made
Treasurer, and had to look after the money; and
William Ormsby was made Justiciary, and had to
see that all who broke the laws were tried and
punished. So we are now to think of Scotland as
completely in the hands of the English. It was
Englishmen who raised the taxes; it was Englishmen
who tried those who broke the law. All the chief
castles had English soldiers in them, and these
soldiers were kept by the money and the goods of
Scotsmen. If food for men or horses were wanted,
it was taken from the Scots, who were sometimes
paid and sometimes not. We can imagine, therefore,
how angry all Scotsmen must have been to see
Englishmen everywhere, behaving as if they were
lords and masters. But Edward was greatly mistaken when he thought that he had completely
subdued Scotland, for he had not long been home in
England, when Scotland's most famous hero arose to
fight for his country.

----

21. WILLIAM WALLACE.   1296-1305

The hero who arose was William Wallace, whose
name will be remembered as long as Scotland lasts.
And this hero was not a king or a great baron, but
a simple gentleman with very little land of his own,
if indeed he had any at all. He was the son of Sir
Malcolm Wallace, who owned lands at Elderslie, near
the town of Paisley, in Renfrewshire. When a great
man dies nowadays, a book is written about him which

[Photo by Valentine.

Statue of Sir William Wallace.

tells the story of his life from the day of his birth to the day of his death. But this was not the case in the times when Wallace lived, so that we do not know nearly so much of him as we should like to know. However, Wallace was not forgotten by his countrymen after his death, and parents used to tell their children all the stories they had heard about him. Nearly two hundred years after he was dead, a poet called Blind Harry used to go about the country telling these stories to all who would listen to them, and they were afterwards put into a book called "The Life of that Noble Champion of Scotland, Sir William Wallace, Knight." The stories told by Blind Harry are not all quite true, but even when they are not true, they show how much Wallace was thought of by his countrymen.

When we read of great men we always like to know what they looked like, and Blind Harry tells us how Wallace looked. He was very tall and strong; and in those days, when generals fought along with their men, it was necessary that they should be strong as well as brave. He had piercing eyes, fair hair, and there was the mark of a wound on the left side of his chin; and he always looked serious, and even sad.

As there were Englishmen everywhere in the country, Wallace could not avoid meeting them, and stories are told which show that he more than once had quarrels with them. For instance, he was one day coming home from fishing near Ayr, when he met some Englishmen who wanted to take all the fish he had caught, from the boy who was carrying them. Wallace said he would let them have some of the fish, but the Englishmen insisted on having them all, and at last they came to blows. The only weapon Wallace had was his fishing-rod, but he struck down one of the Englishmen with the butt-end of it, and, getting hold of his sword, he put the others to flight, and so saved his fish.

Another story told by Blind Harry explains how Wallace came at last to rise against the English. One day, in the town of Lanark, where Wallace was living with his wife, he and his friend, the good Sir John Graham, were walking through the streets, followed by their attendants. They were all gaily dressed in green, and an Englishman began to mock at their finery. A crowd of English gathered round them, and one of them touched Wallace's sword, which was then thought a great insult. Out flashed the sword, and the Englishman was killed on the spot. Then more English soldiers came, with the governor of the garrison at their head. Wallace and his friends fought on till they reached his house, when his wife opened the door, and they all escaped through the house into a wood not far off. Then, as Blind Harry tells the story, the governor, whose name was Hazelrig, did a horrible thing. He burned Wallace's house and killed his wife. Wallace was told what had happened, and that very night he collected a band of men, and made his way into Hazelrig's house and slew him in his bedroom. Then a great fight took place in the streets, and the end of it was that Wallace and his men became masters of the town.

Blind Harry tells another terrible story which he must have heard from people in the country, but we may hope that it is not all true. The story is that the English governor of Ayr invited a number of Scottish nobles and gentry to meet him in a great building called the Barns of Ayr. From the beams that held up the roof he hung ropes with nooses at their lower ends, and, as the people who came were let in two by two, they were all hanged one after another. Wallace also had been invited, but luckily he came late, and a woman met him and told him what was being done. He determined to take a terrible revenge. He got the woman to mark with chalk all the doors of the houses in Ayr where Englishmen lived. In the middle of the night, his men came into the town and tied all the handles with ropes, and after this was done they set fire to the houses, which were made of wood. Not an Englishman escaped, for those who got out of the houses were killed by Wallace's men, who were waiting for them outside. And this is the frightful tale which was known in the country as the "Barns of Ayr."

But if Wallace had only done deeds like these, he would not have been remembered as he is to-day. What really made him a great man was that from the very first he tried to free his country, and that he, though only a simple gentleman, succeeded in doing this for a time. For we must remember that he was not a king or a great noble, who could gather an army round him when he so desired. How, then, did he succeed in doing what he did? It was in this way. First of all, he got a number of brave men round him, who hated the English as much as he did. Then, wherever there was a castle or a small town, in which there were not too many English for his small band to fight with, he tried to drive the English out of it. In this way, he took castles and towns all over the country. And, then, other brave Scotsmen, seeing what he had done, tried to do the same thing, and so within a year after King Edward had left Scotland, it looked as if the English might soon be driven altogether out of the country.

At last, Wallace collected such a great army that he was able to besiege Dundee, which was held by

Old Bridge of Forth.

[Photo by Valentine.

(The ancient stone bridge, where the battle was fought, crossed the river higher up. No trace of it is now in existence.)

the English, and was one of the largest towns in Scotland. And now the Earl of Surrey, the English Guardian, and Cressingham, the Treasurer, thought it was time that Wallace should be stopped, or the English would soon have to leave Scotland. So they led a great army to Stirling, which was still in the hands of the English. When Wallace heard of this, he at once brought his army from Dundee to the banks of the river Forth, on the opposite side from Stirling. The way that Wallace placed his army showed that he was a great general. If the English attacked him, they would have to cross the river first, and, if he were beaten, he could escape north into the Highlands. On the other hand, the way the English behaved showed that they had no great general among them. Before fighting, however, the English general sent two friars to Wallace to ask him to submit. But the answer of Wallace was: "Go back and tell your masters that we did not come here to ask for peace, but to fight for our freedom. Let them come on, and they will find us ready to fight them."

Now the only way the English could cross the river was by a stone bridge on which only two men could walk abreast. The Earl of Surrey was told that there was a ford not far off through which his men could wade across, and he would have liked to do this; but the Treasurer Cressingham, who was a churchman and knew nothing of war, said that they were wasting both time and money, and that they should attack the Scots at once.

So two by two the English began to cross the bridge, a brave knight, Sir Marmaduke Twenge, leading the way. Wallace waited till a considerable number of them had crossed, and then he bade his spearmen rush in upon them and seize the end of the bridge, so that the English army was cut into two portions. The English knight, Sir

Marmaduke, charged against the Scots, but his men soon turned their backs. Then some one told him that he might save his life by swimming his horse across the river. "I will not drown myself to please any man," he answered, and he cut his way back to the bridge and got to the other side in safety.

Only very few of the English who had crossed the bridge escaped, most of them being slain or drowned. Among those who were killed was Cressingham, and the Scots hated him so much for his pride and cruelty, that they took the skin off his body and kept pieces of it—a thing which was sometimes done in those days in other countries besides Scotland.

The day of the victory of Stirling Bridge, as it is called, was the proudest day in Wallace's life. The Earl of Surrey was so completely beaten in the battle, that he and his army fled to England, and left a great deal of booty, which fell into the hands of Wallace and his men. Then, as there was no longer an English army in the land, Wallace was soon able to drive the English out of all the towns and castles, so that Scotland was once more made a free country. A short time after the battle of Stirling Bridge, also, Wallace did a thing which shows that he thought of other things besides fighting. He caused a letter to be written to the cities of Lübeck and Hamburg, in Germany, to tell them that Scotland was now a free country, and that it was ready to trade with them just as it had done in the days before it had been conquered by King Edward.

Wallace was now so strong, indeed, that he deter-

The Battle of Stirling Bridge, A.D. 1297.

mined that he would pay Edward back for all the harm he had done to Scotland. At this time there was a great famine in Scotland, so that many of the people could hardly get food to eat. So, with as large an army as he could collect, Wallace invaded Northumberland and Cumberland, as so many kings of Scots had done before him. The English writers who tell the story of this invasion say that Wallace and his army did many cruel things. They not only burned villages and carried off plunder, but put many innocent people to death. But, even if all these stories were true, it was just what the English had done in Scotland, and, indeed, it was the way in which all wars were carried on in those days.

And what was the great King Edward doing while all this was going on in Scotland? He was in Flanders fighting against the French, but the moment he heard the news, he sent orders for a great army to be collected in England. No sooner did he get home, than he put himself at the head of his troops and marched into Scotland. That he might have plenty of provisions for his soldiers, he ordered a fleet of ships to come with him and keep close into the shore. But the fleet was kept back for a long time, so that the army began to suffer for want of food. Now, when Wallace knew that the English were coming, he did what was usually done when the English invaded Scotland. He ordered all the people to hide themselves in out-of-the-way places and to take all their goods and provisions with them. So as Edward marched further and further into the country, he and his men began to be in great straits. And what made things worse was that the Welsh and English soldiers in his army quarrelled and even fought with each other.

All this time, too, Edward did not know where Wallace and his army were, so that it looked as if he would have to march back to England without having seen the enemy. At last, when he had got as far as Kirkliston, two Scottish nobles sent a boy to tell him that he would find Wallace and his army at Falkirk. Edward was delighted that he was to find his enemy at last, and marched to Linlithgow, on the way to Falkirk. During the night, when he was encamped at Linlithgow, he was injured by a kick from his horse, but the next morning he was as ready to fight as if nothing had happened. It was on the 22nd of July, in the year 1298, that Edward at last saw before him the enemy whom he had sought so long.

After Wallace had returned from his invasion of England, he had been chosen Guardian of Scotland; but though he was Guardian, most of the nobles did not obey him, and either took the side of Edward or did not fight at all. The result of this was that he could collect but a small army, and had only one man against three Englishmen. When Edward came in sight of Wallace's army, this was how he found it arranged. There were four separate bodies of men arranged in circles, which were then called *schiltrons*. These men were armed with long spears, and when they fought, the front rank knelt down on one knee so that the rank behind could point its spears over the shoulders of those who were kneeling. When all the spears were thrust out, the circle looked like a wood of spears, and was very

difficult for an enemy to break through.   Between
these schiltrons were placed archers, mostly men
from the forests of Selkirk and Ettrick, who were
armed with bows and short swords; and behind
the schiltrons were the horse-soldiers, of whom, however, Wallace had not nearly so many as the English.

Before the fight began Wallace said to his men,
"I have brought you to the ring; now show how
you can hop."   And most of them, but not all,
hopped, that is, fought as bravely as men can fight.
Those who did not fight well were the horse-soldiers,
for when they were attacked by the English they
fled almost without striking a blow, and it was
believed that this was because there were traitors
among them.   The English horse-soldiers with their
lances couched then rode against the Scottish bowmen who were on foot and had only their short
swords to fight with, which were not of much use
against horse and man clothed in mail.   But they did
not flee like the horse-soldiers; they fought where
they stood till almost every one of them was slain;
and, when the battle was over, the English admired
their tall and strong bodies as they lay dead on the
field.

But though both the Scottish bowmen and cavalry
were defeated, the spearmen in the schiltrons still
stood firm.   Again and again the English knights
rode against them and tried to break the ring, but
it was like riding against a rock.   But what the
mounted knights could not do, the English archers
did.   From a safe distance they poured their arrows
among the Scots, who could do nothing against them,
and so many of them were slain that a gap was at

last made, and then the English knights were able
to rush in. Fortunately, just behind the Scots was
a forest called the Tor Wood, and Wallace was able
to save part of his army by retreating to it.

After the battle of Falkirk we know very little of
what Wallace did. He gave up being Guardian, as
he had no longer an army at his back. But we do
know that to the end he went on fighting against
the English, and that he would never give in to
say that Edward was king of Scotland. Edward
knew that Wallace was his greatest enemy, and he
determined to get him into his hands. A large sum
of money was offered to any one who would bring
him alive or dead, and at last the day came when
he was taken. We do not know exactly how it
happened, but the story is that a servant of Sir
John Menteith told his master where Wallace was
living, and that Sir John sent men to seize him.

Now a prisoner, Wallace was at once carried off to
London, and, of course, he could expect no mercy
from Edward. He was condemned as a traitor,
though he could not be called a traitor as he had
never called Edward his king, and he was condemned
to die a traitor's death, which was the most shameful
of all deaths. For the punishment of a traitor was,
to be hanged and then beheaded, and his body dis-
embowelled and quartered. And this was the death
that Wallace died. His head was placed on a pole
on London Bridge, where the heads of English
traitors were put, and the other parts of his body
were sent to Newcastle, Berwick, Stirling, and Perth,
so that as many people as possible might see what
had been his end, and be terrified from following his

example.   But his example has never been forgotten by his fellow-countrymen, and, though it is now more than six hundred years since his death, they still remember and honour him as the greatest hero of their nation.

---

22. THE ADVENTURES OF BRUCE.   1306-1313

Now that Wallace was dead, it looked as if Edward would have it all his own way in Scotland. The whole country was conquered; English soldiers were in all the chief castles and towns, and it was Englishmen who managed everything.   But Edward was soon to find that Scotland would never submit to be governed by an English king.   Before Wallace had been a year dead, another hero arose who was to be more successful than Wallace in freeing his country.   This hero was not a simple gentleman like Wallace, but a great noble, who claimed that the crown of Scotland was his by right.   We have heard his name already; it was Robert Bruce, the grandson of that Robert Bruce who had tried to get himself made king after the death of Alexander III.   At this time Bruce was only a little more than thirty years of age, and was one of the strongest and bravest men in all Scotland, and he was to show that he was not only brave and strong, but was also a wise man and a skilful general.   As he was both Earl of Carrick and Lord of Annandale, he owned a great deal of land and had a great many followers, though when he began to fight against the English, his lands were, of course, taken from him.

Now, there was another great Scottish noble who also claimed a right to the throne, and this was Sir John Comyn, whom people called the "Red Comyn." Bruce and Comyn were not good friends. One day, when there was a great meeting at Peebles, the two had a fierce quarrel, and Comyn took Bruce by the throat, and they had to be separated by those who were standing by. However, as they both wished Scotland to be free from the English, they made a bargain with each other. Bruce said to Comyn, "If you will help me to get the crown, I will give you my lands ; or, if you like, I will help you to get the crown, if you give me your lands." Then Comyn said that he would take Bruce's lands and help him to become king. Comyn, however, did not keep his word, but told King Edward of the bargain that he and Bruce had made. Some time afterwards, Bruce and Comyn met in a church in Dumfries, and Bruce accused Comyn of breaking his promise. Then a quarrel arose between them, and Bruce stabbed Comyn with his dagger. Outside the church there were two of Bruce's friends, called Lindesay and Kirkpatrick, and when Bruce ran out, and told them that he was afraid he had killed Comyn, Kirkpatrick said, " I mak sikkar," that is, " I will make sure." The two friends, rushing into the church, killed the wounded man outright.

Whether this story is all true we cannot tell, but at any rate Bruce had killed Comyn, and killed him in a church—which was thought to make the crime much worse. It was indeed a bad beginning for Bruce to have made in his attempt to win the crown. Not only was Edward enraged against him, but the

Pope was so angry because the crime had been committed in a church, that he excommunicated Bruce, which was a terrible thing to happen to any one in those days, as it meant that every man's hand was against him, as it was against Ishmael in the Bible.

However, Bruce could not turn back now, and he was determined to do his best to win the kingdom which, he thought, was his by right. So in less than two months he had himself crowned at Scone, which, as we know, was the place where all the kings of Scots had been crowned. But the coronation was a poor spectacle compared with that of Alexander III. The Stone of Destiny, on which previous Scottish kings had sat, had been carried off by Edward, and we know that the crown had been taken away by John Balliol. Instead of the real crown, therefore, Bruce had to be content with a coronet which was got to supply its place. The right person to put the crown on his head was the Earl of Fife, but he was a friend of Edward, and so his sister, the Countess of Buchan, had to take his place. And of all the great people of Scotland, only four bishops and four earls were present to see the most famous of all the kings of Scots raised to the throne.

Bruce was now king, but he was only a king in name, for his kingdom was in the hands of the English, and almost all the great Scottish nobles were his enemies. If he was ever to be a real king, therefore, he must first win his kingdom, and that could only be done by hard fighting. But at first he was not lucky in the battles he fought. One day he and his little army were in the Wood of Methven, near Perth. As they were not expect-

ing an enemy, some of his men were busy cooking, and others were scattered over the country.

[Photo by Valentine.

Statue of Bruce, at Stirling, looking towards Bannockburn.

Suddenly a cry arose that the English were upon
them, and the Scots had no time to form their ranks.
However, those of them who were brought together

fought as long as they could.   Three times the king was dismounted from his horse, and once he was nearly taken.   At last the Scots were compelled to retreat, leaving some of their chief men prisoners in the hands of the English.   But the question was where were they to retreat to, since almost every town and castle was in the hands of their enemies.

For a month or two they wandered up and down the highlands of Perthshire, sleeping in the open air, and living on the game they killed and the fish they caught.   Then another misfortune happened.   Bruce had led his men into a narrow glen between Perthshire and Argyleshire.   Now this part of the country belonged to the Lord of Lorn, who was a relative of the Red Comyn whom Bruce had slain.   When he heard that Bruce was in his country, therefore, he determined that he would have his revenge, so he came upon the king when he was in the narrow glen, where there was no room for his knights to ride, and completely defeated him.

For the second time Bruce had been defeated, and now he was worse off than ever.   There was hardly a place in Scotland where he would be safe, and Edward had offered a sum of money to any one who would either kill him or take him prisoner. There was nothing for it, therefore, but to leave Scotland for a time, so he and a few of his friends went to the island of Rathlin, on the coast of Ireland, where they remained all the winter.   This was not a very cheerful beginning for one who had hoped to win a kingdom.   And still worse things happened than these two defeats : his wife and child and his two sisters were taken prisoners, as were also three of his brothers—all the three being put to death by Edward's orders.

But Bruce was not the man to lose heart because there were dangers and difficulties in his way, and as soon as the spring of the next year came, he determined to make another trial to win his kingdom. In the month of February 1307, just about a year after he had been crowned, some of his men took the castle of Brodick, in the island of Arran, from the

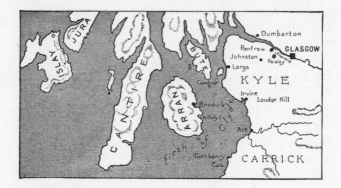

English, and to this castle Bruce now came. Opposite to Arran, and not far off, is the coast of Ayrshire, and on this coast is Turnberry Castle, which belonged to Bruce, but which was then in the hands of the English. As Bruce had friends near the castle, he thought that this would be a good place where he might land with his men.

So this arrangement was made. A countryman who lived near the castle was to kindle a fire when he thought it would be safe for Bruce and his men to land. The fire was kindled, and Bruce sailed in the middle of the night to the place. But, when he reached the shore, the countryman met him and told him that it was not he who had kindled it. Then Bruce was for sailing back again, but his brother Edward, who was always for fighting, said, " I will not go back ; I will either free Scotland or die." So Bruce determined to remain. He had too few men to be

[*Photo by Valentine.*

Ruins of Turnberry Castle.

able to take his castle from the English, but near the castle a number of English were living, so he at once fell upon them and defeated them, and got all the horses and silver-plate which belonged to the English commander, who held the castle.

And now Bruce had begun the work which was to end in his becoming a real king of Scotland, and not a king in name only. Many a year, however, had to pass before that happened, and he was to fight many battles and to have many wonderful adventures. Just as Blind Harry has told the story of Wallace, so another poet, named Barbour, has told the story of Bruce in a poem called "The Brus"—which, however, is truer than the story of Harry. There are two men of whom Barbour tells a great deal in his poem as well as of Bruce, and these men are Bruce's nephew, Sir Thomas Randolph, and the good Sir James Douglas. Next to Bruce himself, Douglas was the greatest hero among the Scots. He was very strong and brave, and because he had a very dark complexion he was called the "Black Douglas." He was gentle among his friends, but like a lion in battle; and he was always in good spirits, and kept his followers cheerful even when everything was going against them. By and by he became such a terror to the English, that mothers used to repeat this rhyme to their children :—

> "Hush thee, hush thee, do not fret thee,
> The Black Douglas will not get thee!"

Here is the story of one bold deed done by Douglas. Not long after Bruce landed at Turnberry, Douglas thought he would like to punish the English who held his father's castle in Douglasdale, in Lanarkshire. So one night he went in disguise to the house of a faithful servant, called Thomas Dickson, who lived near the castle. He told Dickson what he had come for, and some other faithful men were also told, and it was arranged what was to be done. On the holiday called Palm Sunday, all the English soldiers came to church, and Douglas and his men were also there. In the middle of the service, Douglas dropped his cloak and drew his sword, and shouted, "A Douglas! A Douglas!" This was the signal that had been agreed upon, and at once the Scots fell upon the English, who were taken by surprise and were all slain; though, unfortunately, as Douglas had given the signal too soon, the faithful Dickson was also killed. Then the Scots went to the castle, where there were only the porter and the cook, who had prepared a good dinner for the English soldiers when they should return. Of course, the Scots ate the dinner, and when they had eaten their fill, they ran all the wine out of the barrels, and made a great heap of all the provisions in the castle, and set fire to it. The Scots, who were fond of giving nicknames, called this the "Douglas Larder." And now let us return to Bruce.

As the English were almost everywhere, and Bruce had not an army to fight them, he had to keep out of the way for a time lest he should be taken prisoner. It was in his own part of the country, called Carrick, in the south of Ayrshire, and in Galloway that he now went about with his followers, hiding in woods and caves, and wherever he could find a safe place. Aymer de Valence, Earl of Pembroke, the same English general who had defeated him at Methven Wood, came with an army in search of him, and the men of Galloway, who hated Bruce because he had killed the Red Comyn, helped him in his search. Many were the narrow escapes Bruce had from being taken or slain, and the poet Barbour has told of some of them.

Here, for example, is one of Bruce's adventures. A near kinsman of his own took money from the

English, and promised to bring Bruce dead or alive.
So one day the traitor and his two grown-up sons
came upon Bruce when he had only a boy with him
to carry his bow and arrows. Bruce told the boy to
stand at a distance, so that if he were slain, he might
run and tell Douglas, who would avenge him. Then
the three men came on, but Bruce, who had his bow
in his hand, shot the father in the eye before he got
near him. The two sons then rushed upon him, and
one of them struck at Bruce with his battle-axe, but
he missed his blow and stumbled, and in a moment
a slash from Bruce's great sword stretched him lifeless
on the ground. There was only one foe left now, and
there were few men who were a match for Bruce in
single combat. It was with a spear that the last son
attacked him, but with one stroke of his sword Bruce
cut off the head of the spear, and, before his enemy
had time to draw his sword, he was a dead man.

Another story told by Barbour is this. A chief
of the men of Galloway, called M'Dougal, who was also
related to the Red Comyn, determined to take or slay
Bruce because he had killed the Comyn. It was told
to Bruce that on a certain night M'Dougal and his
Galloway men were coming against him, and, as he
had not a sufficient number of followers to fight them in
the open field, he took his men to the bank of a swift
and deep river, which the enemy would have to cross
before they could reach him. Then, as it was night,
he sent his companions to sleep a little distance off,
and he himself with only two followers sat down by
the bank to watch. After a time he heard the deep
bay of a dog; it was the bloodhound which was leading the enemy on his track.

Now, at the part of the river where Bruce was, there was a ford or shallow place, but it was so narrow that only one man could cross at a time, and the bank behind the king was very steep. So, as his armour would protect him from arrows, he thought that with his spear he would be able to kill each enemy who tried to cross and climb the bank, and that there was no need to call his men to help him. One behind the other the enemy's horsemen began to cross the ford. When the first one reached the bank where Bruce stood, Bruce with one thrust of his spear killed the rider and with a second thrust killed the horse. As there was deep water both above and below the narrow ford, the horsemen who came after the one who was slain had no room to move forward, and they all got mixed up and could not use their weapons. Right and left Bruce thrust with his spear, and without receiving a wound he slew several of his foes, while others were carried away by the river and drowned. Then the Galloway men thought they had had enough of fighting, and drew back; and so a single man had beaten a whole troop.

These stories show that Bruce was a brave and skilful knight, but he had to be more than a brave knight to gain his kingdom; he had to be a great general as well, and a great general he showed himself to be. About two months after he had landed at Turnberry, he was at Loudon Hill, in Ayrshire, at the head of a small army which he had collected, when his old enemy, Aymer de Valence, came against him. The English had more men than the Scots; but Bruce, just as he afterwards did at Bannockburn, chose his ground so skilfully, that he was able to beat off the enemy's horsemen and win the battle. This was the first victory he had gained, and the people of Scotland began to see that he might some day deliver their country from the English.

And not long after the battle of Loudon Hill, an event happened which was luckier for Bruce than his victory. Edward, the great king of England, died. When Edward heard that Bruce had once more risen against him, he was furious with rage, and led a great army against him, but he died at a place called Burgh-on-the-Sands, just on the borders of England and Scotland. It is said, though we cannot be sure that the story is true, that before his death he ordered the bones to be taken from his body and carried at the head of his army. Whether the story is true or not, we know that he could not help hating the Scots, who had given him so much trouble, and whom he had never been able to conquer completely. He called himself the "Hammer of the Scots," and he had indeed hammered them hard, but his son was to find that he had not hammered them enough. Now this son was not a man like his father, but was one of the weakest and most foolish kings that ever ruled over England. Bruce knew what kind of a man he was, and he once said that he was more afraid of the bones of Edward I. than of the living Edward II.

The death of the great Edward made Bruce's work far easier, as Edward II. had no sooner become king than he began to quarrel with his own subjects, and had no time to think of Scotland. And Bruce did not remain idle. He gained one victory after another over the English, and drove them out of the towns and castles which they still held.

The way in which Edinburgh Castle was taken will show how determined Bruce's followers were to free their country. The leader this time was not Douglas, but Bruce's nephew, Sir Thomas Randolph, who

[*Photo by Valentine.*

Edinburgh Castle.

after Douglas was the boldest knight among the Scots. A gentleman, called Francis, came to Randolph and told him that he could show him a way of climbing into the castle. So one dark night Randolph came with thirty men to the bottom of the castle rock, each of them having a ladder. They then began to climb the rock, Francis going first. When they had climbed a good way up, one of the English sentinels suddenly called out, " Aha ! I see you well," and threw a stone over the wall, which luckily went over the heads of the climbers. They thought, of course, that they had been found out, but they lay quite still, and no more stones were thrown, for the sentinel had only been jesting with his comrades. So after a while Randolph and his men began to climb again, till they came to the castle wall. Then each man put his ladder to the wall, and got safely over it. But the English were either asleep, or those who were awake had not their weapons, so that Randolph and his men had an easy victory, and the chief castle in Scotland was won.

At the end of seven years after Bruce had landed at Turnberry, almost every place in Scotland was taken from the English except Stirling Castle, and that castle was now besieged by Bruce's brother Edward. It was Edward, as we saw, who persuaded Bruce not to sail away when he was cheated by the kindling of the beacon, and now he did as bold a thing. He made a bargain with the English commander of the castle, whose name was Sir Philip Mowbray, that the Scots should get the castle, if within a year King Edward did not send an army to fight for it. When Bruce heard of this bargain, he was not pleased, as he could not raise nearly such a large army as the English. But his brother's answer was, " Let the King of England bring all the men he has ; we will fight them and more." " Be it so," was Bruce's answer, " we will abide the battle like men." It was a rash bargain that Edward Bruce had made, but it was to end in the most famous day in the history of Scotland.

23. THE BATTLE OF BANNOCKBURN.   1314

The King of England was to come and fight for Stirling Castle not later than Midsummer Day ; that is, the 24th of June. And he kept his word, for, the very day before, he and his army came to the place where Bruce was waiting for them.   As Stirling Castle was the place for which the two armies were to fight, Bruce had chosen his ground not far from the castle, so that the English would have to fight him before they could reach it.   So, on the long summer evening of the 23rd of June, Bruce and his men saw the English host draw near them.   And a splendid sight it must have been.   Edward's army was the largest that a king of England had ever led. It was said that he had one hundred thousand men, of whom forty thousand were horsemen.   It was, indeed, what the Bible calls an army, terrible with banners ; and many of Bruce's men, as they saw it come on, must have wondered if they could ever hope to win the victory over such a mighty host.

Though Scotland was now a united country, Bruce could not, of course, raise such a great army as Edward, since England had far more inhabitants than Scotland.   Indeed, though Bruce did his best to raise a strong army, he had only about half the number of men who followed Edward, so that in the battle that was to be fought, there would be two Englishmen against every Scotsman.   However, the Scots had this great advantage, that their king was a great general while the King of England was not.

And before the battle, Bruce showed how skilful he was by the way he arranged his men.

The place where he arranged them was on the banks of the little stream called the Bannock Burn, and about three miles to the south of Stirling Castle. On one side of his army was the stream which the English would have to cross before they could make their attack, and in other places there were bogs which lay between the two armies. And where there was firm ground between them, Bruce took care that it should not be easy for the English to ride over.

He dug pits, and then covered them with turf so that they should not be seen, and all over the ground he put steel spikes, called calthrops, which would lame the English horses, and break the ranks of the cavalry when they charged. In this way, therefore, the English knights were prevented from riding all at once upon the Scots, as they would have done had the ground between the two armies been perfectly smooth and open.

Calthrop from Bannockburn.

Bruce divided his army into four parts, the largest part being made up of the footmen with long spears. He had only a very few horse-soldiers, but we shall see what a good use he made of them. He had also some archers, though not nearly so many nor so skilful as the English, for the Scots never cared for archery, and always liked best to fight with their spears and axes. When the English came up, it was too late to fight that day, and so both armies lay in sight of each other waiting for the morrow's battle.

But in the evening two things happened which must have put heart into the Scots for the coming fight.

An English lord, named Clifford, rode at the head of three hundred horsemen in the direction of Stirling Castle, to carry assistance to it. Now Bruce had told Randolph that this should be prevented, and when he saw Clifford riding to Stirling, he turned to Randolph and said, " Randolph, a rose has fallen from your chaplet," meaning that he had failed in his duty. But Randolph at once put himself at the head of a troop of foot-soldiers, armed with spears, and caught Clifford on the way. At first it seemed as if Randolph were to be beaten, and Douglas asked leave of Bruce to go to his assistance. Bruce refused his permission; but Douglas could not bear to see his friend defeated and perhaps slain, and in spite of Bruce's refusal he rode off at the head of his men to give help. Before he reached the place of fighting, however, the English were seen to flee, and then he ordered his men to return, so that Randolph might have all the honour of the victory.

This was one event that was lucky for the Scots, and the other was this. During the evening, Bruce was riding in front of his army on a pony, and had only a battle-axe in his hand. An English knight, named Sir Henry de Bohun, knew him by the gold coronet he wore on his helmet, and thought that, if he could slay him, he would both put an end to the war and win great glory for himself. So, on his great war-horse, and with his lance couched, he rode full speed upon Bruce. Just as he drew near, however, Bruce made his pony turn aside, and avoided the thrust of the lance. Then in an instant he rose in

L

his stirrups to his full height, and with one blow of his battle-axe on De Bohun's helmet felled him to the ground. The Scottish leaders who were near Bruce blamed him for risking his life when so much

Bruce and De Bohun.

depended upon him, but he only said, "I have broken my good battle-axe."

As soon as the sun rose next morning, the two armies prepared for battle. Before it began, the Scots went down on their knees to pray, and when King Edward saw this, he said to an English lord near him, "See, they are kneeling to ask for pardon." "Yes," was the answer, "they are asking pardon, but from God, and not from us. Yon men

Bruce directing the Fight at Bannockburn.

will conquer or die." Then the fight began, the
English knights riding against the Scottish spearmen, who were all on foot; and this was the
fiercest part of the battle.   At the very beginning the
English archers bent their bows and sent their
arrows among the Scots as thick as snowflakes.
Had this gone on long, the same thing would have
happened as had taken place at Falkirk, when
Wallace's spearmen were shot down by the English
arrows, and the battle was lost.

But Bruce had thought of this beforehand : at his
command the Scottish mounted men rode against

the English archers, who
were, of course, all on
foot.   Their bows were
of no use in a close
fight, and soon they were
either slain or put to
flight.   For hours the
battle went on, but, as

Battle-Axe found at Bannockburn.

we know, the English were not on ground where
they could fight their best.   Their horses had not
room to move about, so that they got mixed up
among each other.   Then the boggy ground and the
steel spikes prevented the horsemen from riding
quickly, and when a horse-soldier is brought to a
standstill in a crowd, a soldier on foot armed with
a spear is more than a match for him, as he can
kill the horse, and slay the rider before the latter can
free himself from his stirrups.   And this was what
happened to thousands of the English horsemen.
When their horses were slain, they were either
trampled to death or pierced by a Scottish spear.

And so the battle raged, till a thing happened
that decided which side was to win.   From a hill near
at hand, afterwards called the Gillies' Hill, what looked
like another Scottish army was seen to descend.   It
was only the servants or gillies who attended on
Bruce's camp, and a number of men who lived in the
neighbourhood, but, as they came in a body and with
banners flying, the English thought they were really
another army, and then they lost heart and began to

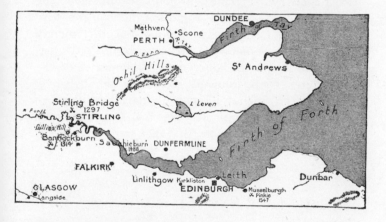

give way.   When the Scottish spearmen saw this, they
fought all the harder, and soon the enemy was fleeing
in all directions.   When King Edward saw that the
battle was lost, he at first rode to Stirling Castle,
thinking that he would be safe there; but Sir Philip
Mowbray, the commander of the Castle, told him
that by the bargain he had made with Edward
Bruce he would have to surrender it the next day.
So there was nothing for it but that the beaten king
should try to reach his own kingdom if he could.

And a narrow escape he had, for Douglas rode after
him as far as Dunbar, a distance of sixty miles, when
Edward got into a boat and sailed to Berwick, where
he was safe.

This was the greatest victory that the Scots ever
gained, and the English thought it was such a
disgrace to themselves that they said it was a
punishment for their sins. So much booty fell into
the hands of the Scots, that it made Scotland a
richer country. Precious garments, jewels, and plate,
which Edward and his knights had brought with
them, were all taken; and many of the chief men of
the English were made prisoners, and had to pay great
sums of money to be allowed to go home. But the
chief thing to be remembered about the battle of
Bannockburn is that it made Scotland again a free
country, and that it made Scotsmen feel more than
ever they had done before, that they were one people
and one nation.

---

24. THE LAST DAYS OF BRUCE.   1314-1329

The English were now completely driven out of
Scotland, but there was still one thing more to be
done; the King of England must be compelled to
admit that the King of Scots was as free a king as
himself, and this was what Bruce spent the rest of his
life in trying to bring about. At first he tried by
peaceful means to get Edward II. to admit that Scotland was a free kingdom, but Edward would not agree
to this, and so there was nothing for it but to go on with
the war against England which had already lasted so

long. But things were very different now from what
they had been in the days of Edward I.; it was now
the Scots who made war on England, and not the
English who made war on Scotland.

Bruce wished to teach Edward that he could
do a great deal of harm to England if Edward
would not have him for a friend. The first thing
that Bruce did against England after the battle
of Bannockburn was, not to invade England but to
invade Ireland. Ireland belonged to England, but
the Irish people did not like the English, and were
always rebelling against them. So when the Irish
heard how the Scots had defeated the English at
Bannockburn, they sent a message to Edward Bruce
to say that if he would come and drive the English
out of Ireland they would make him their king. Now,
as it would be a great loss to the English if they were
driven out of Ireland, Bruce allowed his brother to
collect a Scottish army and to go to Ireland and try
to win the crown. A short time afterwards, Bruce
himself went with more men to Ireland to help his
brother; and a story is told of him while he was there
which should not be forgotten, as it shows that he
was a true knight, and had a tender heart.

One morning the English came upon him and his
men, and he was just about to retreat, as the enemy
was too strong for him to fight them, when a loud
scream was heard. It was a poor woman who was ill,
and who was afraid that she would fall into the hands of
the enemy if she were left behind. When Bruce was
told this, he said that he would never leave a defence-
less woman to perish, and, instead of retreating, as he
had intended, he ordered his men to remain and

face the enemy. But when the English commander saw the Scots ready to fight him, he thought that Bruce must have received assistance, as he was too good a general to fight if he did not hope to win ; and so no battle took place. In the end, Edward Bruce was made king of Ireland ; but he was king for little more than two years, as he was killed in battle with the English. However, this invasion of Ireland by the Scots showed Edward what dangerous enemies the Scots could be, and this was exactly what Bruce had wished to teach him.

Hilt of Bruce's Sword.

But it was by invasions of England that Bruce did most harm to that country. No fewer than six times did a Scottish army cross the Border and carry off booty. Twice they defeated the English in battle, but their greatest success was taking Berwick-on-Tweed, which Edward I. had won from Scotland when he made war on John Balliol. Let us see what the Scots did when they made these invasions, or raids, as they were called. In the year 1327, two years before Bruce died, one of the greatest of these raids took place, and a French writer who lived not very long after has told the story of it. By this time Edward II. was no longer king, as his subjects had put him in prison, where he was afterwards murdered, and he had been succeeded by his son, Edward III., who was a boy of about fifteen years old.

The leaders of this raid were Bruce's two most skilful leaders—Sir Thomas Randolph, now Earl of Moray, and Sir James Douglas. Before leading their army into England, they sent a message to the young king Edward to tell him that they were coming to fight him. So Edward collected a great army, and marched north to fight the Scots as soon as he should meet them. But the Scots had not nearly such a large army as Edward, and they took their own way of fighting. Most of the men in the Scottish army rode on small ponies, which were very hardy and active, and could go a long distance without being tired out. Now, when an English army came against the Scots, it brought with it a great quantity of baggage and provisions, which prevented it from moving quickly from one place to another. But the Scots had hardly any baggage, and as for provisions, that was a very simple affair with them. Each man carried a bag of oatmeal, and a girdie on which to cook it into cakes, and with his cakes and a drink of water he had all that he needed. When the Scots were in England, however, they had better fare, for they killed the English cattle and roasted them on the fire in their own skins. An army like this, therefore, could move quickly from one place to another, while the English could only march slowly after it.

Instead of fighting the English in an open battle, then, the Scots went up and down the counties of Northumberland and Durham, burning the villages and carrying off such things as they thought were of any value. Sometimes Edward was within a few miles of them, but whenever he tried to get nearer them they slipped away. At last he thought he had caught them. The Scots were south of the river Tyne, and Edward placed his army at a ford which they would have to cross to get back to their own country. For eight days Edward lay there, and very uncomfortable days they were. It rained constantly, and his men had to cut down branches from the trees to shelter themselves; the damp wood would not burn, so that they could not kindle fires; provisions began to run short, and the horses had to eat the leaves of the trees. Still no Scots appeared, and at last, as his men began to mutiny, Edward had to leave the ford and march on again in search of the enemy. Four days afterwards, an English squire, called Thomas Rokeby, rode into his camp and told him that he could take him to where the Scots were. Edward was so delighted with the news that he made Rokeby a knight, and at once gave orders that his army should march against the Scots.

Edward found the Scots on the top of a hill on the banks of the river Wear, which he would have to cross before he could reach them. As the river was deep, and full of great stones, it would have been dangerous for him to cross, so he sent a message to Douglas and Randolph to ask them to come and fight on a fair field. But Douglas and Randolph were far too skilful leaders to do such a thing, and they sent back word that Edward might come and fight them where they were. And now the English were as badly off as they had been at the ford. They had to sleep among the rocks and stones; they had no fuel to make fires, and they had no forage for their horses; and all the time the Scots were safe on the hill with plenty to eat and plenty of firewood. On the fourth morning the Scots were not to be seen; they had moved to another hill, four miles off, where they were safer than before, as they had the river in front and a wood and a marsh behind them.

So once more the English had to trudge after them; and now they thought that the Scots could not escape, and that they would be starved and compelled to surrender. But the very night the English arrived before the camp of the Scots, Douglas with 500 horsemen came suddenly upon them when most of them were asleep, and made his way into King Edward's tent, and would have taken him prisoner, if his attendants had not defended him and given him time to escape.

At last, after some days, the Scots did begin to be in want of provisions, and thought it was time for them to be going home. So one morning when the English awoke, no Scots were to be seen. In the middle of the night they had covered the marsh behind them with the branches of trees, and got safely across, and by the time the English found they had gone, they were five miles on the way back to Scotland. Of course, it was useless for Edward to pursue them, as he could never have overtaken them; and so, after being nearly three months in England, the Scots got home to their own country with as much booty as they could carry.

At last the event happened which Bruce had been fighting for since the battle of Bannockburn. The English king and his councillors came to see that it was best for themselves that they should be friends with the Scots, and they agreed to make a treaty. So, in the year 1328, a treaty was made at

Northampton which gave Bruce all that he wanted, as King Edward agreed to recognise Scotland as a free kingdom, and Bruce as free a king as himself. And to make the bargain surer, Bruce's son, David, who was to succeed him on the throne, was married to Johanna, King Edward's sister, and so the two countries, which had been so long at war with each other, were at last at peace.

Dunfermline Abbey.

Bruce lived only a year after the treaty of Northampton, but it is pleasant to think that he did live to see that treaty made, as it was the reward of all his labours. He died at Cardross, in Dunbartonshire, where he had lived for some time; but he was buried in the Abbey Church of Dunfermline, where a marble monument brought from Paris was put over his grave. In course of time the roof of the church fell in, and the monument was so broken and covered with stones that nobody could tell where it stood. But in the year 1821, nearly a hundred years ago, when workmen were repairing the church, they found pieces of the monument, and on digging underneath, they came upon the skeleton of Bruce. Many people, high and low, came to look upon all that remained of the most famous king who had ever reigned in Scotland, one whose name will never be forgotten as long as there is a Scottish nation.

Just before he died, Bruce asked for a thing to be done which turned out not to be for the good of Scotland. In those days, kings and nobles thought it a right thing to end their days by fighting against the Saracens, who were Mohammedans and enemies of the Christian religion. Bruce would have liked to do this, but during his last years he was so busy at home that he could not carry out his wish. So, before he died, he desired that his heart should be taken out of his body, and that Sir James Douglas should carry it with him, and go to fight against the Saracens.

And Douglas obeyed his king's wish. He enclosed the Bruce's heart in a silver casket, and hung it round his neck, and with a band of Scottish men he went to fight against the Saracens in Spain.* But Douglas did not, of course, know how the Saracens fought, and in a great battle against them, in which they were put to flight, he followed them too far and he and his men were surrounded. Then taking the silver casket from his neck, he flung it

* A contemporary Papal Bull informs us that Douglas did not intend to go to Palestine, as has been for so long popularly believed, but only to fight against the Saracens in Spain.

before him, saying, "Pass first in fight, as thou wert
wont to do; Douglas will follow thee or die." So
saying, he rushed upon the enemy, and fell pierced
with many wounds. But, after the battle, the silver

[*Photo by Valentine.*

Melrose Abbey, in which Bruce's heart was deposited.

casket was found under his body, as if his last
thought had been that it should be safe, and it was
brought home to Scotland and buried in the Abbey
of Melrose. Douglas's body was also brought home
and buried in his own church, near the castle of his

fathers; but a day was soon coming to Scotland when his strong arm was to be sadly missed.

The reign of Bruce had been chiefly taken up with fighting, as the one great thing he had to do was to free Scotland from the English. And even when he was not actually fighting, he was always thinking how after his death Scotland could be made safe against all her enemies. There was one thing on which he had set his mind, and that was that Scotland should have a fleet to fight at sea as well as trained soldiers to fight on land. Now in those days it was very necessary that a country should have a fleet, and for this reason. A great many pirates, belonging to every country, were constantly sailing the seas, and what they did was to seize and rob every vessel they met, and to take the passengers prisoners and not give them up till they paid a large sum of money. If a Scottish ship sailed to any foreign seaport, there was great risk that it would be taken by pirates on the voyage, and all its goods robbed, and its crew and passengers made prisoners.

It was to fight these pirates, therefore, as well as the ships of other nations, that Bruce wished that Scotland should have a fleet, so he took a great interest in the building of ships, and had a number of large galleys made by different people, especially by those in the Western Islands, who were, of course, most at home on the sea.

But it was even more important that the Scots should be trained fighters on land than that they should have a fleet at sea. Bruce knew quite well that, though Scotland and England were now at peace, the time might come when they would again

be at war, and that it was necessary that every Scotsman should know how to fight and use his weapons.
To make sure of this, therefore, he passed several
laws, of which these are some. Once every year,
there was to be what was called a wapinchaw, that
is, a weapon-showing, which was just like what we
call a review. All the grown-up men, from the age
of sixteen to sixty, were to come to an appointed
place near where they lived, and bring their weapons
with them, and show that they knew how to use
them. Other two laws were, that every man who had
property worth £10 must have a suit of armour, and
that every man who had money enough to buy a
cow must have a spear and a bow and twenty-four
arrows. These laws, however, were not always
obeyed, and in spite of the law about bows and
arrows, the Scots never became such good archers
as the yeomen of England, as they were to know to
their cost in many a battle that was yet to be fought.

And now we have come to the end of the War of
Independence, as it is called, which had lasted for
more than thirty years. What good and evil had
this long war done to Scotland? It had certainly
done much evil. Thousands of Scotsmen had been
slain in the many battles that had been fought;
towns and villages and the estates of the nobles and
gentry had been burnt and plundered; traders and
craftsmen and the labourers in the fields had often
been kept from their work; and so at the end of the
war Scotland was far poorer than it had been in the
peaceful days of Alexander III. Still the long war
had done one good and very important thing,
and it was this. In their fight to free their country

From Painting by Wm. Hole, R.S.A.]

King Robert the Bruce granting a Charter to the Citizens of Edinburgh.

M

from the English, the Scots had been taught to feel, as they had never done before, that they were one people. No Scottish man, or boy, or woman could ever forget the deeds of Wallace and Bruce, and

Seal and Coins of Robert the Bruce.

Douglas and Randolph, and when the stories of these deeds were told by the fireside, as they were for many a long day afterwards, father and son felt that they had a country to fight for, and that it was their duty to defend it against all its enemies.

25. TWO KINGS IN SCOTLAND

David II. (1329-1371)

It was a great misfortune for Scotland that time after time, when a king died, there was only a child to succeed him. And this happened when Bruce died, for his son, David II., was only five years old when he became king. However, Bruce had taken care that the country should be well governed till his son grew up, and had appointed his old friend, Randolph, Earl of Moray, to be Guardian of Scotland, as the man whom he could trust best to rule the country wisely. But, as we shall see, Scotland was not to have Randolph long as its wise ruler.

Though David became king on his father's death, in the year 1329, about a year and a half passed before he was crowned; and something took place at his coronation which had never taken place before. David was the first king of Scots to be anointed. Now, in those days a king was not thought to be a real king unless he had been anointed, and the English used to say that the kings of Scots were not kings at all, as none of them had been anointed like their own kings. But Bruce, who seems to have thought of everything, had thought of this also, and he asked the Pope that his son might be anointed when he became king. The Pope agreed to Bruce's request, and he sent the holy oil to Scotland, though the Scots had to pay 12,000 gold florins for it.

When a king was anointed, this was what was done. The chief bishop in the land, who in Scotland was the Bishop of St Andrews, brought the vessel containing the oil which the Pope had blessed, and sprinkled it on nine parts of the king's body—on his head, his breast, his shoulders, his arm-pits, under his elbows, and on the palms of his hands. After he had been sprinkled with the holy oil, the king was supposed to become the "Lord's Anointed," like the kings of whom we read in the Bible. But we shall see that

David, in spite of his anointing, turned out to be a very poor king and a very unworthy son of his father, and that his reign was to be a very unhappy one for Scotland.

Only a few months after David had been crowned, Edward III. of England thought that, since there was only a child reigning in Scotland, this was a good opportunity for trying to make himself master of that country, as his grandfather, Edward I., had tried to do, and he set about it very cleverly. Edward Balliol, the son of poor John Balliol, wished to become king of Scots, and King Edward agreed to assist him, if, when he became king, he would be his vassal. So the bargain was made, and Balliol invaded Scotland at the head of an army. But an unfortunate thing happened for the Scots : Randolph, the Guardian, died at Musselburgh, just when he had collected an army to fight Balliol when he should come. Then another Guardian had to be chosen, and the man who was chosen, Donald, Earl of Mar, soon showed that he was not fit to fill Randolph's place. Only a week and three days after he was made Guardian, he allowed his army to be surprised by Balliol and completely beaten, at Dupplin Moor, near Perth, he himself being among those who were slain. What happened next was that Balliol had himself crowned king at Scone ; so that there were now two kings in Scotland, and all the labours of Bruce seemed to have been useless. However, Balliol had not long been king, when one night, while he and his army were at Annan, he was surprised by the Scots, and he had to flee half-dressed across the Border to Carlisle.

The next year, Balliol again came against Scotland with an army of Englishmen and some Scottish barons who wished him to be king. The first thing he tried to do was to take the town of Berwick, which Bruce had won back to Scotland. The Guardian of Scotland was now Sir Archibald Douglas, the fourth Guardian since David's reign began, and, of course, he wished to prevent Balliol from taking Berwick. So, having collected an army, he marched into Northumberland, thinking that Balliol would leave Berwick and follow him. But Balliol did not leave Berwick, and there was nothing for it but that Douglas should fight if the town was to be saved. Douglas, therefore, led his army to Halidon Hill, which is quite near Berwick, and Balliol and Edward III., who was now with him, were there to meet him.

And now happened one of the greatest defeats that the Scots ever suffered from the English, and all owing to their not having a good leader. The Scots were on one hill and the English on another, and between the two armies was a marsh, which would have to be crossed before the battle could be fought. Before the battle began, a Scotsman with a huge black dog challenged any Englishman to fight, and an English knight did accept the challenge, and slew both him and his dog. Then the Scots did what a leader like Bruce or Douglas would never have permitted them to do. They left the hill and began to wade through the marsh to attack the enemy, and, while they were floundering through it, they were exposed to the English arrows, which slew hundreds of them and almost blinded those who still struggled on. Then they had to climb the hill on which the English army was posted, and now the English men-at-arms fell upon them and, of course, had an easy victory. The Guardian himself was slain, and several earls, as well as a great number of knights and common soldiers.

After the battle of Halidon Hill, there was hardly a great man left to fight for King David, and Scotland was now just where it had been when Bruce began his wars against the English. Balliol and Edward III. divided Scotland between them, Edward getting Lothian and Balliol the rest of the kingdom. So as David's supporters were afraid that he might be taken prisoner, they sent him and his queen, Johanna, to France, where they knew he would be safe.

But it was soon seen that the examples of Bruce and Wallace were not forgotten. Sir Andrew Moray of Bothwell was chosen Guardian for King David, and he showed that he was a brave and skilful leader. For six years he went on fighting against the English, just as Wallace and Bruce had done. And during these years a very fortunate thing happened for Scotland. Edward III. wished to be king of a greater kingdom than Scotland, namely, France. So, in the year 1337, Edward declared war against France, and began between these two countries the war which is called the "Hundred Years' War," because there was hardly peace between them for a whole century.

Now this was very lucky for Scotland, as not only Edward, but several kings of England who came after him, led armies against France, and so had not so many men to fight against Scotland. And this was

what took place now, for since Edward needed all the
soldiers he had to make war on the King of France,
Balliol was left to fight for himself.   Soon he was
driven out of Scotland ; and, as the country was now
safe, David and his queen were brought home from
France, where they had been for seven years.

As David was now about eighteen years old, there
was no longer need of a Guardian, and he began to
rule for himself.   And a foolish and weak ruler he
proved to be.   There are only two things he did
which are worth remembering, and both of them
show that he was a very different man from his
father.   In the year 1346, five years after he came
home, he led a great army into England.   Of course,
his father had often sent armies into England, but it
was the way David behaved that showed how little fit
he was to be a ruler and a general.

The English and Scottish armies met at Neville's
Cross, close to the town of Durham.   Just before the
battle, one of David's most skilful soldiers, Sir John de
Grahame, came to him and asked that he might have a
number of horse-soldiers to attack the English archers,
as Bruce had arranged at Bannockburn.   David would
not listen to him, and it turned out exactly as
Grahame expected.   When the battle began, the
English archers from a safe distance shot their
deadly arrows among the Scots, whose ranks very
soon got confused.   But the truth is that, if David
had been a prudent general, he would not have fought
at all, as his army was posted on ground where
there was no room for them to fight their best.
And what was the result?   The Scots were completely defeated, and David himself was taken

prisoner, though he fought bravely, and knocked out two of the knight's teeth who took him.

For eleven years David was a prisoner in the hands of the English, and, when King Edward did at last let him return home, it was only after a very hard bargain. The Scots were to pay 100,000 marks for the ransom of their king, which was a very large sum for a poor country like Scotland in those days. Of course, they were not able to raise it all at once, and it was agreed that they should pay 10,000 marks every year till the whole debt was discharged, which would take ten years. And who paid the money? Everybody who had any money to spare. The clergy, the nobles, the merchants in the towns, and the farmers in the country, all had to contribute towards a tax which was to go into King Edward's pocket, and all owing to their king's folly. It was very hard to have to go on paying this tax year after year, and indeed it was not settled in ten years, or even in David's lifetime, and in the next reign the tax was still raised for a dead king's ransom; and the end of it was that the whole ransom was never paid !

And when the Scots did get their king home, did he prove himself worth the money? We can safely say that he did not. He did not make the country happy and prosperous, for he seemed always to be thinking of his own pleasures rather than of the welfare of his people. For instance, he was constantly paying visits to the English court, as he had come to like the English during his long imprisonment. His subjects did not approve of this, and, besides, these visits cost a great deal of money which would have been better spent in helping to pay his ransom. Then there were several rebellions of his nobles against him, which kept the country in an unsettled state, and which would not have taken place had he been a king like his father.

But the worst thing to be told against David is this. He made a treaty with Edward III., by which, if he died without leaving a male heir to the throne, Edward was to succeed him as king of Scotland! But when David asked his Parliament to agree to this, it told him that it would never consent to such a bargain, and that he was never to mention it again. And this David was the son of the king who had spent the best years of his life and the best blood of his subjects to free Scotland from the rule of an English king. When David died in 1371, therefore, there could be no such lamentations as there had been at the death of his father.

There were two calamities that happened during David's reign which were remembered long afterwards, and talked about at Scottish firesides. One was the coming of the Great Plague or Pestilence, in the years 1349 and 1350. This plague was one of the greatest calamities that ever came upon the human race. It is said to have begun in China, and it gradually spread westwards till it reached all the countries of Europe. It was one of the most horrible diseases of which man can die. The body became covered with boils and black spots, and so it was called the "Black Death." Almost all who were seized with this terrible plague died after only two days' illness. It raged through town and country, and in some places hardly any one was left alive. The dead could not be buried in the usual way, and great pits were dug, into which the bodies were thrown all together.

It was in the year 1348 that the plague came to England, but it was so long in coming to Scotland that the Scots thought that they were saved from it, and they called it the "foul death of the English." But it did come to them at last, and as many died of it in Scotland as in other countries. When one of their armies was at Selkirk, it broke out, and it is said that 5000 men perished. Then those who went home carried the infection with them, and before the pestilence ceased a third of the people of Scotland had perished.

The other event of David's reign that was long remembered was what was called " The Burnt Candlemas." Candlemas Day is the 2nd of February, and is so called because on that day people used to go to church in a procession, carrying candles, and " The Burnt Candlemas " happened in the year 1356. Just about that time Edward Balliol gave up all thoughts of ever being king of Scotland, and went to the King of England, who was then at Berwick with a great army, to tell him this. But Edward III. was as determined as ever to be master of Scotland, so he made Balliol give him the Scottish crown and a sod of earth, which meant that the whole land of Scotland was to belong to him. Then Edward sent out commands to all the chief men in Scotland that they should come and acknowledge him as their king. David had not yet returned from England, and the chief man in the country was the Earl of Douglas, who managed things very cleverly. He pretended that he and the other chief men in the country would do what Edward commanded them; but what he wanted was really time to prepare for the invasion which Edward had threatened. Now, it is said that when Bruce was dying, he gave a piece of advice which came to be called "Good King Robert's Testament." The advice was this. When the English invaded Scotland, the Scots were never to fight them in open battle, but to get out of the way and take all needful goods and provisions with them, and destroy what they could not carry.

Douglas accordingly laid the country waste with fire, and when Edward began to march through Scotland, not a single person was to be seen, and neither food for his men nor forage for his horses was anywhere to be found. He had ordered a fleet to come with provisions, but day after day passed and no fleet appeared. Then the bread his army had brought began to fail, and for fifteen days his men had nothing to drink but water, and the English soldiers were always in the habit of drinking ale.

However, he still marched on till he came to Haddington, where he destroyed a church which was so beautiful that it was called the "Lamp of the Lothians." Then he marched to Edinburgh, but, when he got there, he saw that, if every man in his army was not to perish, he must return to England as fast as he could. But, on his march home, the Scots were constantly on the watch for him. Out of the woods and from corners among the hills, they would suddenly fall upon his weary soldiers, slay many of them, and then disappear. Once, in a wood near Melrose, Edward himself was nearly taken prisoner, but at last he and his army reached the Border and arrived at Carlisle. And this is what the Scots for many a day afterwards called "The Burnt Candlemas," as all the burning took place about the time of that festival.

During the reign of David there had been as much fighting as during the times of Wallace and Bruce, and we can hardly help asking whether the people in other countries did not live more peacefully. And the answer is that they did not. England, as we have seen, was as often at war as Scotland, and it was the same in Germany, France, Spain, and Italy, where the inhabitants were constantly fighting either with themselves or with the people of some other country. We are not to be surprised, therefore, if the history of Scotland in those times is so much taken up with wars and battles. In course of time the kings and peoples of all countries came to see that peace was better than war, but, so long as the feudal system remained, and every man had to fight when he was told, there could be little peace in any land.

26. FRENCH VISITORS—BATTLE OF OTTERBURN

ROBERT II. (1371-1390)

As David II. left no child to succeed him on the throne, his nephew, Robert the Steward, as the nearest heir, was made king after him, and he was the first king of the House of Stewart, which was to reign in Scotland for more than three hundred years. The real name of Robert was Fitzalan, and one of his ancestors had come to Scotland in the reign of David I. Now David gave this Fitzalan a great deal of land in Scotland, and also made him High Steward, so that he and his descendants became great Scottish nobles. Robert, who now became king, was the seventh person in his family who had held the office of Steward, and so it was that he and his descendants came to be called Stewart, which was the old Scots spelling of Steward. And how he came to be nephew of David II. was that he was the son of Marjory Bruce, daughter of the great Bruce by his first wife, David being the son of Bruce's second wife.

Robert II. was not a great king, but everybody spoke well of him, and a writer who lived at the time says that no man could have a tenderer heart than he had. Another writer who saw him says that he was a tall, good-natured looking man, and that his eyes were so bloodshot that they looked as if " they were lined with scarlet"; and so his subjects, who gave nicknames to most of their kings, called him " King Blearie." But this was not the kind of king who was needed in those fighting times, and, indeed, during the whole of his reign, it was not Robert but nobles like the Earl of Douglas who took the lead in everything.

One of the first things to be done after Robert became king, was the making of a new treaty with France, by which the two countries bound themselves to defend each other against England. And this treaty was very necessary, as the kings of England always hoped that some day they would be able to conquer both Scotland and France. All through

Robert's reign there were constant wars on the Borders between the English and the Scots, and now one side was victorious and now the other. At last the King of France thought that he ought to send help to his allies, the Scots, and, in the year 1384, there came to Scotland a band of 2000 Frenchmen, who brought with them 1500 suits of armour and a large sum of money.

The story of their stay in Scotland is told by a French writer who lived at that time, and whose book Sir Walter Scott used to delight in when he was a boy, and, indeed, when he grew to be a man. In this book the writer tells of all the fights and adventures of the knights of all countries, and he tells his stories so well that, as we read them, we almost feel as if we were living at the time he wrote. Now this author, whose name was Froissart, had been in Scotland himself during the reign of David II., and he tells us some interesting things about the country.

When he travelled he rode on horseback, with a portmanteau on his saddle and a greyhound following him. He went as far north as "wild Scotland," as he calls the Highlands, and stayed for some time at Stirling. He does not say anything about Stirling, but he says that Edinburgh in those days had only about 400 houses ; so that it would have only between one and two thousand inhabitants, and therefore was merely a village and not a town. He also says that the country people did not mind much when the English burned their houses, as they could build them again in a few days with five or six poles, with branches of trees to cover them. He mentions another thing which seems very curious to us nowadays : the Scots had no iron to shoe horses, and no leather to make harness or saddles or bridles, and they had to get all these things sent across the sea from Flanders.

We should have expected that the Scots would be delighted when they heard that the French had come to help them against the English, but it was quite the contrary. "What brought them here?" they said; "can we not fight the English without their help? We don't understand their language, and they don't understand ours. They will eat us all up, and do more harm to us than the English themselves. Let them be told that we don't want them, and let them go back to their own country."

And, when the French did come, they were no better pleased than the Scots. They expected to find as fine houses and soft beds as in France, and these things, of course, they did not find in Scotland. So they began to grumble at their leader, who was Sir John de Vienne, and a great man in France. "What has brought us here?" they said. "Our fathers and mothers told us we should find hard beds and poor lodgings in Scotland, and they were right."

So the French and the Scots, who had made so many treaties with each other, did not get on well together. But what angered the French most was the way the Scots fought against the English. They had expected that there would be great battles, in which they would win honour and glory as brave and skilful soldiers. But we know that this was not the Scottish way of fighting. What the Scots did now was this. The Earl of Douglas and other Scottish leaders collected an army, and, along with the French, invaded England, plundering everywhere as usual. Then a great English army under the King of England, Richard II. (for Edward III. was dead), came against them.

And now the French expected there would be a great battle. But the Scottish leaders knew quite well that their army was not nearly so strong as that of the English, and instead of fighting they retreated to their own country, and, following Bruce's advice, ordered the inhabitants to get out of the way and remove all food for horses and men. So when Richard led his army into Scotland, he found nothing but a wilderness, though he did a great deal of mischief by burning the abbeys of Melrose and Dryburgh, and even the town of Edinburgh. The French were, of course, amazed that the Scots allowed their country to be treated in this way without trying to defend it. But the Scottish leaders showed them that they knew what they were doing. As soon as Richard had led his army back to England, a Scottish army entered Cumberland, and, as there was no one to oppose them, they came home with as much plunder as every man could carry. And so in the end the French saw that the Scottish way of fighting the English was the best after all.

When the war was over, the French wished to be gone from Scotland as soon as possible, but they discovered that this was not so easy to be done. In France the nobles had the right to ride through the crops of their farmers just as they pleased, and they thought that they could do the same in Scotland, but they found they were mistaken. When their servants went out to take such provisions as they

wanted, just as they did at home, the farmers and
their men fell upon them and beat them, and slew
more than a hundred of them altogether. So when
Sir John de Vienne told the Scottish leaders that
he wished to take his men home, he was informed
that they would not be allowed to go till all the
damage they had done was paid for. At last Sir
John said he would pay for the damage himself, and
then he and his knights were permitted to go. But
they went away with a very bad opinion of the Scots,
and even wished that the King of France would make
peace with England, and come with an army and
utterly destroy Scotland and its people. French
soldiers came more than once to Scotland after this,
but it was always found that they and the Scots
could not agree, and that they were best friends
when they remained at a distance from each other.

Froissart tells us of another event that happened
during the reign of Robert II. which must not be
forgotten. Of course it was a battle, as it is almost
only of battles that Froissart writes ; but of this
particular battle he says that he knew of none in
which both sides fought more bravely. This great
fight, which took place between the Scots and the
English, came about in this way. The Earl of Fife
and the Earl of Douglas, the two chief nobles in
Scotland, determined to lead a great army into
England in revenge for the invasion of Richard, of
which we have just read. When they came to the
Border, they divided their army, and arranged that
the Earl of Fife with the greater part of it should
enter England by the west side, and Douglas with
the other part should enter by the east. So Douglas

N

with his men invaded Northumberland, burning and
plundering wherever he went. In a fight that took
place, Douglas captured the pennon of Lord Percy,
the son of the Earl of Northumberland, who was of
such a fiery temper that he got the name of Hotspur.
Douglas told Percy that he would carry the pennon
home and fix it on his castle of Dalkeith. "That
you will not," said Percy. "You will have to come
and take it, then," answered Douglas.

Then Douglas marched towards Scotland, but, as
he wished to give Percy a chance of getting back
his pennon, he stopped at Otterburn, about twenty
miles from the Border. Night had come on the
second day he was there, when the cry arose in the
camp of the Scots that the English were at hand.
As had been arranged beforehand, the Scots left
their camp and moved to a place close by, where they
had better ground for fighting.

It was a beautiful moonlight evening in autumn,
so that the two armies could easily see each other.
At once the battle was joined, and as it was a
hand-to-hand fight with swords and axes, the two
enemies were so mixed up that the English archers
could not shoot for fear of slaying their own men.
The English were nearly three to one, and they
began to press the Scots backwards, when Douglas
with his two-handed axe hewed his way among the
enemy and cheered his men on.

At last he fell pierced by three lances. His
cousin, Sir John Sinclair, knelt over him and
asked how he was. "Ill," said Douglas, "but few
of my ancestors have died in their beds. Raise my
banner, call my war-cry, and let neither friend

nor foe know that I am fallen." His banner was
raised, and the cry, " A Douglas ! A Douglas ! " rang
over the field, and the Scots won the day. Percy
and many other English knights were taken prisoner,
and the dead Douglas was carried home and buried
in the Abbey of Melrose, and over his tomb was
hung the banner that had won the fight. This
is the famous battle of Otterburn, or Chevy Chase,
as it is called in an English ballad which makes the
English win the day.

All this time we have heard nothing of King
Robert, and the reason is that he was an old man,
and weak both in body and mind. He tried his
best to make peace with England and keep the
nobles quiet at home, but it was of no use, as the
Scots had to defend their country against the English,
and therefore had to be constantly fighting. As
for the nobles, we shall see that it was very difficult
to make them live at peace with one another. In the
last year of his reign Robert became so feeble that
his third son, the Earl of Fife, was made Guardian
of the kingdom, and of this Earl of Fife we shall
hear more presently.

---

27. THE WOLF OF BADENOCH--THE CLAN FIGHT AT PERTH

ROBERT III. (1390-1406)

The king that succeeded Robert II. was his eldest
son, John, who took the name of Robert III. The
reason why his name was changed was that John
was thought to be an unlucky name for a king, as

several kings of that name had been very unfortunate, such as John Balliol; John, King of France; and John, King of Bohemia. Robert III. was quite old when he came to the throne; and, like his father, he was gentle, and fond of peace. If he had lived in peaceful times he would have made a good king, but it was a king like Bruce that was needed in Scotland in those days—a king who could make himself feared as well as loved.

There were two things that had to be done for Scotland, if there was to be a country called Scotland, and a people called the Scottish people. The first thing was, that England must not be allowed to conquer the country, for the English kings never gave up the hope that some day they would be able to do this. For instance, during the reign of Robert III., Henry IV. led a great army into Scotland and besieged the castle of Edinburgh. This was the last time that a king of England came himself at the head of an army against Scotland, but many a time afterwards the English kings sent armies against the Scots though they did not lead them themselves.

The other thing the kings of Scots had to try to do was to prevent their great nobles from becoming so powerful as almost to be like kings themselves. In other countries besides Scotland, the nobles had so much land and had so many fighting men to follow them that they were quite as rich and powerful as the kings, and often rebelled against them; and we shall see that this happened more than once in Scotland, though not in Robert's reign. Then the nobles not only sometimes rebelled against the king, but they often fought and quarrelled with each other;

and this, of course, kept the country in a very unsettled state. In the first year of Robert's reign we have an example of the kind of thing that could be done when there was not a king strong enough to prevent it.

In the district of Badenoch, in Inverness-shire, there then lived a person who was known as the "Wolf of

[*Photo by Valentine.*

Loch-an-eilan—Castle of the Wolf of Badenoch.

Badenoch," and he well deserved the name. His home was a strong castle, built on a little island in Loch-an-eilan, with mountains all around ; and the ruins of his castle are still to be seen. The Wolf did many savage deeds, but we need only mention one. Not far off from the Wolf's castle were the lands belonging to the Bishop of Moray, and the Wolf, quite wrongfully, robbed the bishop of some of these lands. The bishop then excommunicated him, which, as we saw in the case of Bruce when he slew the Red Comyn, was considered a dreadful thing in those days. The Wolf soon showed how little he cared for the excommunication.

He collected a band of caterans, that is, Highland robbers, and marched to the bishop's cathedral at Elgin, which was one of the most beautiful buildings in all Scotland. Then he led his men into the cathedral, who seized all the cups and vestments of the clergy, and afterwards set fire to the sacred building. The bishop complained to King Robert of what the Wolf had done; but it shows how little power the king had, that he could not punish him as he deserved, for all the punishment the Wolf had to suffer was to stand at the door and at the altar of a church at Perth, to show that he was sorry for what he had done. And who was this Wolf of Badenoch? He was the king's own brother, Alexander, Earl of Buchan. Such a story as this shows that a strong king, and not one like Robert, was needed to rule Scotland, if it was ever to become a peaceful country.

There was one part of their kingdom which the kings of Scots found it very difficult to keep in order, and that was the Highlands. And we can easily see the reason of this. First of all, the mountains and woods, and rivers and lochs, with which the Highlands are taken up, made it almost impossible for the king to reach those who broke the law. Then the people who lived in the Highland country were all divided into clans, each with a chief of its own, which were constantly quarrelling and fighting with each other. In such a country towns could not grow up as they did in the Lowlands, and there was, of course, very little ground on which crops could be grown.

The result was that the Highlanders lived a very different kind of life from the Lowlanders. Instead of growing crops, they reared cattle on the hillsides, which they killed and ate, and they got their food also by hunting and fishing. But, as they had plenty of time to spare, and food was often scarce with them, we are not surprised that they often took to robbing their neighbours, and especially the Lowlanders who lived near them. Very often when the corn was cut and standing in the fields, a band of them would descend from the hills at night and plunder as much of it as they could carry. Just as often it would be cattle they would drive off; and, indeed, the Lowland farmers who lived near the Highlands never knew when some of the caterans, as they were called, would pay them one of these visits. And so difficult was it to put a stop to these *creaghs*, as the Highlanders called them, that they went on for more than three hundred years after the times of which we are speaking.

In the reign of Robert III. a strange thing happened between two of the Highland clans. We are not quite sure what clans these were, but they are usually called the Clan Chattan and the Clan Kay. Whoever they were, they had a fierce quarrel with each other, and it was agreed that thirty men from each clan should meet and fight out their quarrel. So it was arranged that on a certain day the sixty champions should come to the North Inch of Perth, on the banks of the river Tay, armed with bows, swords, knives, and axes. When the day arrived, thousands of people came to see the fight, King Robert himself being among those present.

Just before the battle began, it was found that a man was missing from the side of the Clan Chattan; but his place was taken by a smith in Perth, called Henry Gow, or Hal o' the Wynd, who must have been very fond of fighting. Then the battle began, and so furiously did both sides fight that all the men of the Clan Kay were slain, and only eleven of the Clan Chattan survived, though all of them were badly wounded. And this was the way in which a quarrel was settled in those times, and the king and his advisers could not help themselves, as they had not the power to punish those who had broken the law.

During the whole of Robert III.'s reign he had only the name of king. When he came to the throne, indeed, his brother Robert, Earl of Fife, remained Guardian of the kingdom just as if there was no king to rule. The Earl of Fife was a different person from his brother Robert. He was quite a match for any of the nobles, and knew how to manage them so that he should be the chief man in the country. He was also liked by the people, as he took care not to raise taxes—which the Scots never liked to pay. For about eight years he remained Guardian, and then some of the nobles thought that Robert's eldest son and heir, David, Earl of Carrick, should be made Guardian instead of him, as he was to be the next king. So in the year 1399, the Earl of Carrick, then just twenty-one years old, became Guardian in the name of his father. Just a little before this change took place, the Earl of Fife was made Duke of Albany, and the Earl of Carrick was made Duke of Rothesay, and these are the first dukes that were made in Scotland.

Now, the Duke of Albany, who was very ambitious, did not like losing the office of Guardian which he had held so long, and he and the Duke of Rothesay became bitter enemies. Unfortunately the young duke began to behave in such a way as to show that he was not fit to rule the country. He lived with bad companions, and he and they did things which made people say that it was a disgrace and a misfortune that he should be Guardian of the kingdom. So the office was taken from him, with the consent of his own father, and given back to Albany. A short time afterwards an event happened of which we do not know the whole story, and perhaps never will know.

Albany and Rothesay were now worse enemies than ever. One day Rothesay and a few of his attendants were riding to St Andrews, intending to take possession of the castle of that town. On the way, however, Rothesay was made prisoner by Albany and taken to Falkland Castle, and there a short time afterwards he died. Now, as Albany and Rothesay were known to be enemies, the story went about that the young prince had been starved to death by his uncle. Whether this was true or not we cannot tell, and it is quite possible that the prince, who had lived a wild life, may have died a natural death. If Albany was not guilty, it was certainly unfortunate that his nephew died while he was his prisoner, as everybody knew that they had long been enemies, and that Albany must be glad that the prince was now out of the way.

Before King Robert died, another great misfortune happened to him. After the death of the Duke of Rothesay, he had only one son left, a boy called James,

Photo by Wilson.

The Tower of London, from the Thames.

to succeed him on the throne. Now, when James was twelve years old, his father determined to send him to France, perhaps because he thought he would be safer there than at home. But to get to France the sea had to be crossed, and we know that in those days a voyage by sea was very dangerous, both from the storms that might arise and from the pirates who were everywhere. However, every care was taken that the young prince should arrive safely in France, and his ship sailed from North Berwick.   It had only got the length of Flamborough Head, in Yorkshire, however, when an English merchant vessel took it prisoner, and the prince was sent to London, to Henry IV., the English king, who put him in the Tower, and not for eighteen years was he allowed to return to his native country.   When the news was told to his poor old father, it broke his heart, and only a few weeks afterwards he died, no doubt thinking that his lost son would never sit on the throne of his fathers.

---

28. BURNING OF JAMES RESBY—BATTLE OF HARLAW — REGENCY OF THE DUKES OF ALBANY. 1406-1424

On the death of Robert III., his son James was declared king though he was a prisoner in England, but as some one was needed to rule the country, his uncle Robert, Duke of Albany, was made Governor of the kingdom.   The Scottish writers who lived then say that he made a good ruler, and was popular both with the people and with the nobles.   He pleased the people because he did not impose taxes, as he was very rich himself and did not need money.   He knew, also, as we have heard, how to manage the nobles and to make them his friends.   For instance, a short time after he became Governor, he got Archibald, Earl of Douglas, brought home from England, where he had been a prisoner, and ever afterwards Douglas was his friend ; and

Douglas, it is to be remembered, was after Albany himself the greatest man in Scotland.

There were no great battles fought with the English during the rule of Albany, though, of course, there was as usual a good deal of fighting on the Borders. Once Albany led a great army to invade England, but he did not carry out his plan, and his great army did so little, that the Scots gave his expedition the name of the "Foul Raid," by which they meant that it was rather disgraceful that with such a great host he had not gained some victories over the English. This is another example of how the Scots found nicknames for things and persons they did not like.

There were three events that happened while Albany was Governor, each of which is important in its own way. The first of these events was something quite new in Scotland. About this time, in many countries, people were beginning to ask whether all that the Church of Rome taught was true. For instance, John Wycliffe in England now began to teach doctrines of which that Church did not approve, and he had many followers in England, who came to be called Lollards, though all of them did not believe exactly what Wycliffe taught.

Now, one of these Lollards, named James Resby, came to Scotland and began to preach his doctrines in different parts of the country, and many people, we are told, listened to him gladly. Among the things he taught was that the Pope was not what the Church believed him to be, and that no one should be Pope who did not lead a holy life. But both in England and Scotland laws had been passed which ordered that anyone who taught such doctrines as these should be put to death. So Resby had not preached very long before he was made a prisoner, and tried for heresy, that is, for teaching false doctrines, and burned at Perth in the year 1407. He was the first person in Scotland to be put to death for his religion. His teaching was not forgotten after his death, and in some parts of the country there must have been many persons who continued to believe what he had preached to them.

The second event was a battle, and it is one of the best-known battles in the history of Scotland. It was not fought between Scots and English, however, but between Highlanders and Lowlanders; and Sir Walter Scott thought that it decided which of the two were to have the chief power in Scotland. The battle came about in this way. The Lord of the Isles, that is, of the Western Islands or Hebrides, whose name was Donald, was very anxious to get the earldom of Ross, which he said belonged to his wife. Now the Duke of Albany would not allow this, for two reasons. First, if Donald had got the earldom, it would have made him too powerful; and, secondly, Albany thought that his own son, John, Earl of Buchan, had a better right to the earldom than the Lord of the Isles. Albany, therefore, gave the earldom to his son. But the Lord of the Isles was determined that he would have it, and so he collected an army of islanders and then came to the mainland, where he was joined by many Highland chiefs at the head of their clans.

Having now got this great army, Donald led it against the town of Aberdeen, promising that, if the town were taken, his followers would get a great deal of plunder. Luckily there was a man in Aberdeenshire who knew far more about fighting than Donald, and was a more skilful leader. And who was this leader? He was the son of the terrible Wolf of Badenoch, of whom we have just read, and was now the Earl of Mar, which is a district in Aberdeenshire. This Earl of Mar got an army together, partly of gentlemen with their followers, and partly of townsmen from Aberdeen, for in those days, as we have seen, every townsman had weapons and was ready to serve as a soldier.

The two armies met at a place called Harlaw, not very far from Aberdeen, and then began one of the bloodiest battles ever fought on Scottish ground. The Highlanders had ten times as many men as the Lowlanders, but many of Mar's men were clad in armour while the Highlanders were not. Mar, like a skilful leader, put his steel-clad men in the front rank, where the fighting would be fiercest. Then the Highlanders and the Islesmen came on as they usually did with frightful yells, but Mar's steel-clad men stood firm with their spears thrust out and their battle-axes raised. The way the Highlanders fought was to stab the horses of the knights with their dirks, and then they had the riders at their mercy. But though they could not break the ranks of the Lowlanders, they had so many more men that they were able to surround them. And so the battle went on through the whole day, till night came and put an end to it.

Mar and his men that were left—and very few of them were left—remained on the field, and

when the next morning came, the Lord of the
Isles and his army were not to be seen. So
many were slain in the fight that it was called
" Red Harlaw," and the battle was remembered for
many a day. Ballads were written about it, and
long afterwards, and as far away as Haddingtonshire,
the boys at school used to play at the battle of Harlaw,
one side being the Highlanders and the other the
Lowlanders.

The third great event that happened during
Albany's rule shows that there were persons in
Scotland who were thinking of other things besides
wars and battles. In the year 1413 the university
of St Andrews, the oldest university in Scotland,
made a beginning. We have seen that there were
schools at the cathedrals and abbeys and also in
some of the towns, where both boys and girls could
be taught. But, if the scholars wished to follow up
their studies after they left school, there was no
place in Scotland to which they could go to be
taught. So what these scholars did was to go to
the universities in France, and especially to the university of Paris, which was the most famous in all
Europe.

During the reign of Bruce, in the year 1326, a
college had been set up in Paris by the Bishop of
Moray, in which Scottish scholars might live and be
taught; but now it was thought that the time had
come for Scotland to have a university of its own.
So the Bishop of St Andrews, whose name was Henry
Wardlaw, asked permission of the Pope to set up a
university in that town, for in those days a university
could not be started without the Pope's consent

The Pope gave his consent, and the day that the messenger arrived was kept as a grand holiday in St Andrews. After the religious services were over, the bells of the town were rung, all the musicians played on their instruments, and at night bonfires were kindled in the streets, and dancing and feasting followed. The poet Milton says that "peace hath her victories no less renowned than war," and the beginning of the university of St Andrews was one of the victories of peace.

All this time the young King of Scots was a prisoner in England, and along with him as a prisoner was Albany's own son, Murdoch. In the year 1416, however, Murdoch was set free, being exchanged for the Earl of Northumberland, who had been taken prisoner by the Scots. Four years afterwards the Duke of Albany died, after having ruled Scotland for nearly fifty years, and his son Murdoch became Governor after him. But Murdoch was not a man like his father, and was quite unfit to govern the country. Many of the nobles rebelled against him, and his own sons gave him more trouble than anyone else. At last, the English agreed that they would allow King James to return home if the Scots would pay a ransom for him. They did not call it a ransom, however, but a bill for their expenses in keeping and educating him. And a pretty big bill it was, for it amounted to £40,000, which in those days was a much larger sum than it is at present. This was the third ransom the Scots had to pay for a king, as William the Lion, David II., and James had all been taken prisoners by the English.

29. THE KING AGAINST THE NOBLES

JAMES I. (1406-1437)

James I. is one of the best known of all our kings. His long imprisonment in England would itself make him remembered; but during his reign events happened which help to fix it in our minds. Even if James had not been a king, people would have thought him a remarkable man. He was very strong in body, and was one of the best wrestlers, runners, archers, and riders in Scotland; and, as we know, this was a great advantage to a king in those days. And he was not only good at all kinds of sports, but he was also both clever and learned. He played on several musical instruments; he was skilful in drawing and painting; and he liked making things with his own hands such as workmen make. He was also a poet, and he wrote a poem which we can still read at the present day. It is called the "King's Quair," that is the "King's Book," and in it he tells how he fell in love with the English lady whom he married and brought to Scotland with him—Lady Joan Beaufort, daughter of the Earl of Somerset. In his poem he calls her a "milk-white dove," but she was one day to show that she was not quite so gentle as a dove. This, then, was the kind of king who was now to rule Scotland, and a hard task was before him.

As we have just seen, the country had become very unruly and unsettled under Albany's son, Duke Murdoch. Now James had made up his mind that,

O

James I. watching Lady Joan Beaufort from his Prison Window.

when he became king, all his subjects, high and low, would have to obey him. Soon after he came back to Scotland, he said one day, " If God grants me life, I will make the key keep the castle, and the bracken-bush the cow," meaning that he would make every-body safe under the law. But, if this were to come to pass, there was one thing that would have to be done, and that was to teach the nobles that, if they broke the law, they would suffer for it. And, indeed, the whole of James's reign was taken up with trying to teach the nobles this lesson.

To teach the nobles their lesson, he began with the family of the Duke of Albany. Of course, James could not love that family, as they had kept his father and grandfather from ruling ; and he probably thought the Duke of Albany had really starved his brother David to death, and had even been the cause of himself being taken prisoner by the English. He may also have feared that Duke Murdoch and his brothers might one day try to get the chief power in the country, just as their father had done. One of the first things he did, therefore, was to put Duke Murdoch's eldest son in prison, and soon afterwards he did the same thing with the Earl of Lennox, the father of Murdoch's wife.

Next year, James took a still bolder step ; he im-prisoned Duke Murdoch himself, his wife, and another son. Now, while they were in prison, another son of Murdoch did a thing which must have made James angrier than ever with the whole family of Albany. This third son collected a band of men, attacked the town of Dunbarton, and set it on fire after slaying thirty-two persons, among whom was the Keeper of Dunbarton Castle. And now James determined that Murdoch and his family would trouble him no longer. He caused Murdoch and his two sons, who were prisoners, and the Earl of Lennox to be brought to trial, though what they were tried for we cannot tell. Of course, as James wished it, they were all condemned to death. So in the year 1425, the year after James had returned, all the four were executed on the Heading Hill at Stirling Castle. No king of Scotland had ever done a deed like this before, and it must have shown the nobles that James was not a ruler to be trifled with.

The family of Albany being now sufficiently punished, James next set his mind to make the Highlanders and Islanders obey him, and this was the hardest task of all. The first thing he did was to summon a Parliament to meet him at Inverness, and to order the chiefs of the Highlands and Islands to come to it. A great number of them did come, and among them Alexander, the Lord of the Isles, who was the son of Donald of Harlaw. But when they came, they found they had been led into a trap, for James at once ordered that forty of them, including the Lord of the Isles, should be made prisoners. Some of the most dangerous of them were put to death, but Alexander and most of the others were allowed to go free after a short imprisonment. This was not fair play on James's part, as the chiefs had not expected that they would be made prisoners when they came to attend the Parliament. And, besides, it was not a wise thing to do, because after this the chiefs and nobles could not trust him.

Of course, the Lord of the Isles was very angry at the way in which James had treated himself and his friends, and two years afterwards he raised a great host and burned the town of Inverness to the ground, in revenge for what had happened there. Then James marched against him with an army, and they came in sight of each other in the district of Lochaber, in Inverness-shire. But before the battle began, many of Alexander's men deserted him because they were afraid to fight against the king, and so James gained an easy victory.

After the battle, Alexander did a thing which made James very angry. He sent a message to James offering to make peace, just as if he had been a king himself, but James told him that he must come and submit himself to his mercy. And a short time afterwards Alexander had to do this in a very humble manner. One day, when James and his nobles were worshipping in Holyrood Church, a wild figure, clothed only in his shirt and drawers, was seen to enter. It was Alexander, the great Lord of the Isles, who had come to ask James's pardon. Going up to James, he fell on his knees before him and held out his naked sword with the point in his own hand, to show that James might slay him if he pleased. James did not order him to be put to death, however, but sent him to prison, though he afterwards set him free and restored his lands to him.

It will now be seen what kind of work James had to do "to make the key keep the castle, and the bracken-bush the cow." And here are two stories which show how sternly he could act when he thought it necessary. Once a great noble struck another noble in the face in James's presence. James at once ordered him to be seized, and commanded him to lay his hand on the table. Then he told the noble who had received the blow to draw his sword and cut off the hand that had struck him.

The punishment was cruel, but another story shows what cruel things could be done in those times. A Highland robber had stolen her two cows from a poor woman, who accused him of the theft, and said she would not take off her shoes before she had told the king. Then the ruffian caused her shoes to be taken off, and two horse shoes to be nailed on her feet. In spite of this she did go to the king and told her story, and showed the wounds which the nails had made. James at once ordered that the man should be caught, and soon afterwards he was caught; and this was his punishment. He was dressed in a linen shirt, and on the shirt was painted a picture showing what he had done to the woman. Then after he had been taken through the streets in this dress, he was dragged at a horse's tail to the gallows, and there hanged.

These stories show that James was determined that the law should be obeyed in every part of his kingdom. But he was also anxious that the clergy should do their duty in works of charity and in teaching the people. This, however, they were not doing as they ought to have done, and James wrote a letter to the heads of the monasteries, to warn them what would happen if they did not do their duty more carefully; in this letter he said that, though the monasteries were very rich, they did not help the poor so much as they ought, and that the people were

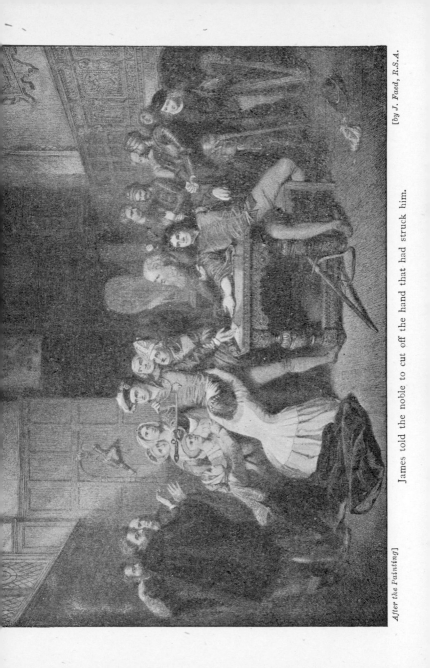

James told the noble to cut off the hand that had struck him.

beginning to lose respect for the monks. He also said that, if they went on as they were doing, the people would rise against them and take their riches from them, as indeed they afterwards did at the Reformation. However, he told the abbots that, if they and the monks would mend their lives, he would defend them against all their enemies.

And James showed in different ways that he was really a friend of the Church. For instance, he built a beautiful monastery at Perth, which must have cost a great deal of labour and money, and which was afterwards completely destroyed at the time of the Reformation. He also showed that he hated heretics, or those who taught doctrines contrary to the doctrines of the Church. We have seen how, in the times of the Duke of Albany, James Resby was burned as a heretic, and now in the reign of James there came another teacher to Scotland, who was also found to be a heretic. His name was Paul Craw or Crawar, and he came all the way from Bohemia, where the doctrines of Wycliffe were believed by many people. Crawar was a very skilful doctor, and he went about healing the sick, but he also taught the doctrines he had learned in Bohemia, which were very different from what the Church taught. When the chiefs of the Scottish clergy heard of this, they were both frightened and angry, and they caused Crawar to be imprisoned and tried. As he did not deny what he had taught, he was condemned to be burned, like Resby before him; and it was with James's consent that this was done. So there were already signs that a day might come when the Church of Rome would be put an end to in Scotland, as was afterwards to happen, though not for more than a hundred years.

And now we come to the sad ending of the poet-king's reign. He had made many enemies in trying to make the laws obeyed, and he had not always acted wisely and justly. He had wrongfully taken the lands of several nobles, so that no noble could be sure that his lands also might not be taken from him. But there was one man whom he had made his chief enemy, and a very dangerous enemy he was. This was Sir Robert Graham, whom James had put in prison in the very first year of his reign. Afterwards, also, James had unjustly taken the lands of a nephew of Graham's, and then Graham vowed that he would have his revenge. And a day came when he had the chance of taking it.

In the year 1436, James wished to spend his Christmas at Perth, so with his attendants he set out from Holyrood for that town. When he came to the Water of Leith, just outside Edinburgh, a High-land woman met him and told him that, if he crossed the Firth of Forth, he would never return. However, he went on, and came to the Blackfriars' monastery in Perth, where he was to stay. Now Graham had heard of his coming, and made his plans to slay him. James's chamberlain, Sir Robert Stewart, whose duty it was to look after the house in which the king stayed, was a friend of Graham, and made everything ready for him and his band to get into the house at night. He laid planks across the moat or deep ditch that surrounded the monastery, and he spoilt the locks of all the doors, so that they could not be locked.

James and his courtiers and ladies had spent a merry evening, when about midnight a noise was heard and the light of torches was seen outside. Fearing that it might be enemies in search of him, James seized a pair of tongs, tore up a plank in the floor, and leapt into a vault which was below the room. There were only ladies with him when the noise was heard, and one of them, called Catherine Douglas, is said to have barred the door of the room with her arm. Presently Graham came at the head of his band, and burst the door open, breaking the lady's arm. No king was to be found, and the conspirators were so angry at missing him that they insulted the queen, and one of them even struck her. Then they searched all the house, but still they could not find the king. At last they came back to the room where they had expected to find him, and now one of them saw the place where the plank had been torn up. When James had let himself down into the vault, he had expected to find a hole in the wall by which he could escape outside, but only a day or two before the hole had been built up, because in playing tennis the balls went into it.

As there was no means of escape, James must fight for his life; and bravely he fought for it. First one murderer leapt down, but, though James had no weapons, he threw him to the ground; and a second he also overcame. Then his great enemy, Sir Robert Graham, descended with his drawn sword. Wounded and weary with his struggles, James begged for mercy. "You had no mercy on others," was the answer, "and you will have no mercy from me," and he thrust his sword into the king's body, and his two comrades finished the bloody deed.

The murderers did not long escape punishment. The queen, the " milk-white dove," as James had called her, never rested till the chief of them were taken. And frightful were the tortures they had to suffer, so that even the people of that time were horrified. Graham was nailed naked to a tree and then dragged through the streets; his body was torn with pincers, his son was tortured and beheaded before him, and at length he himself was put to death, declaring to the last that he had done a just deed in slaying a tyrant. Such was the end of the reign of James I., one of the best of Scottish kings, though we cannot say that he always acted wisely and justly.

30. HOW SCOTLAND WAS GOVERNED

From the story of James's reign it looks as if a king of Scotland could do very much as he pleased in his kingdom. James had put to death many of his greatest nobles, and taken their lands from others. He placed the chiefs of the Highlands and Islands in prison, and kept them there without having them tried. Did he do all this without consulting anybody, and just because he wished it? When a king can do just as he pleases, he is called an absolute ruler. But a king of Scots was not a ruler of this kind, and he had to obey laws just as his subjects had. Let us see how it was that a Scottish king could not have everything his own way in his kingdom.

First, he had a Council to advise him in governing the country. It was quite necessary that he should have such a Council, for how could one man know what had to be done for the good of all his subjects? Of course, it was only the chief men in the land, the great nobles and the bishops and abbots, who were taken into this Council, and of these only a few of the greatest and wisest. This Council came to be called the king's Secret or Privy Council, because everything that was talked of in it was supposed to be a great secret. When anything important was to be done, the king asked his Council to meet him, and then the whole business was gone through, and it was decided what was the wisest thing to be done. Sometimes it happened that the Council was not of the same opinion as the king, and what did he do then? He might take his own way, but this was a dangerous thing to do, as the men in the Council had great power in the country, and, if they all joined together, it was made very difficult for the king to have his way carried out. What really happened was this. If the king was very determined, as James I. was, then he made the Council do as he wished; but, if he were a weak king, like Robert II. or Robert III., it was the Council that made him do as it wished. So it will be seen that the King of Scots was not free to do as he pleased, so long as his Council would not let him have everything he wanted.

But there was another Council besides the Secret Council with which the king had to do before he could have his own way. This was the National Council, and it got this name for two reasons. First, it

was not only the great nobles and clergy who sat in
it, but men of other classes in the nation, namely, the
smaller lords or barons, and the country gentlemen,
and the burgesses of the towns. And the second
reason why it was called the National Council was that
everything that went on in it was done in public and
not in private, as was the case with the Secret Council.
But the national assembly is better known by the
other name by which it came to be called—namely,
the Parliament.

The first national assembly which called itself a
Parliament, was the one which John Balliol held at
Scone in the year 1292. The first *real* Scottish
Parliament that ever met, however, was one that
Robert Bruce held in Cambuskenneth Abbey, near
Stirling, in the year 1326. And why do we call it a
real Parliament? Because it was the first Parliament,
as far as we know, in which burgesses from the
towns were present. And why did Bruce have the
burgesses to sit in the National Council? Because
he wanted money, and the towns had to pay some of
it, and he thought it right that, as the burgesses had
to do this, they ought to be in the Council as well as
the clergy and the nobles, who also had to pay. So
from this time onwards the burgesses too had the
right to sit in Parliament, though they did not always
do so.

Now, all the great barons and all the high clergy
had the right to sit in the Parliament, and could
come to its meetings when they chose. But there
were not so very many of them, and they did not all
come. But suppose that all the smaller barons and
all the burgesses had come to where the Parliament

met, there would have been no chamber big enough to hold them all. So, of course, another arrangement had to be made, and in James I.'s reign this was what was agreed upon. In each shire or county, the smaller barons chose two " wise men," as they were called, and instead of all going to the Parliament, they sent these wise men to speak for them. And the smaller barons were very glad of this arrangement, as in those days it cost a great deal of time and money to go from one part of the country to another. The same thing was done by the burgesses. Instead of all going to the Parliament, the burgesses of the royal burghs chose a few from among themselves and sent them in their place. But, although these arrangements were made, it was not till long afterwards that they were really carried out.

The Scottish Parliament was in many ways very different from the English Parliament. For one thing, in the Scottish Parliament all the different classes—the great barons, the clergy, the smaller barons, and the burgesses—sat in one room ; and in the English Parliament the lords and the commons had each a room to themselves, just as they have at the present day. When the Scottish Parliament met, this was what happened. All those who were present agreed as to what laws were to be passed, and then a number of men were chosen, who were called a committee, who had to see that the laws were written out and made known to the people so that they might be obeyed. And how were they made known in those days when there were no newspapers and when printing was not invented ? It was in this way. The town-crier in every town stood at the

town cross and read the laws aloud, so that no one
might be able to say that he had not heard of them.
And one interesting thing should not be forgotten.
In James I.'s reign, the laws began to be written in
the Scottish language, whereas before they had always
been written in Latin.

But the important thing is—How did the Parliament
and the king get on together ? Which of the two was
the stronger ? Was it the king or the Parliament that
had the greater power in the country ? The answer
is that it was just the same with the Parliament as
with the Secret Council. If the king was liked by
the people and was very determined, then he could
make the Parliament do very much as he liked. On
the other hand, if the king was not liked and was a
weak ruler, then the Parliament was the stronger of
the two. For instance, David II., as we have seen,
was a weak king, and so in his reign the Parliament
had a great deal of power. James I., however, must
have got on very well with his Parliaments, as during
his reign, which lasted thirteen years, he held no
fewer than thirteen Parliaments, which shows that
they must have been willing to do what he wished,
as otherwise he would not have called them. However, even James did not have all his own way with
his Parliaments. Once, for example, Sir Robert
Graham, who afterwards slew him, stood up and told
him to his face that he was a bad king and a tyrant,
and he even dared to ask those who were present to
make the king a prisoner.

We now see why a king of Scots could not have
things all his own way. He had to take care that he
did not offend his Secret Council, and he could not pass

any laws without the consent of his Parliament. But what he had most of all to fear was that his nobles would rise against him, for they were so powerful that, if a few of them joined together, he would be in great danger of losing his crown. And we shall see that this happened more than once to the kings that came after James I.

---

31. ABOUT THE PEOPLE AND THE COUNTRY

Having seen how Scotland was governed, let us now look at the people and the country. In James I.'s reign there came a foreigner to Scotland, who wrote about what he saw there. This time, however, the visitor was not a Frenchman, but an Italian. His name was Æneas Sylvius, and he afterwards became Pope, so that he was a very important person. On his voyage to Scotland his ship was nearly wrecked, and during the storm he vowed a vow that from wherever he landed he would walk barefooted to the nearest church to give thanks to God for having saved him from drowning. When he landed, he found that the nearest church was at Whitekirk, six miles from North Berwick. So, as it was winter at the time, he had to trudge these six miles with bare feet on the frozen ground, and the result was that he caught such a cold that he had rheumatism for the rest of his life. Now this adventure could not have put him in a very good humour with Scotland, and so, perhaps, what he says about it is rather ill-natured.

Here are some of the things which he tells us.

He went to see King James, whom he describes as a robust-looking man, but very fat. As for the palaces in which the King of Scots lived, he says that they were not so well furnished as the houses of rich merchants in Germany. What he thought very strange was that the towns had no walls round them, which all the towns on the Continent had. He also thought it odd that the houses in the towns were built of stone without lime. The houses in the country, he says, were built of turf, and the poorer ones had the hide of an ox hung up instead of a door. The common people were very poor, but at the same time they ate more meat and fish than was good for them; though bread was so scarce that it was looked on as a dainty. One thing astonished him very much, and that was that the people burned stones instead of wood. Of course, the stone was coal, which Æneas seems never to have seen in other countries. At the church doors he noticed many beggars, who went away with glad faces when these stones were put into their hands.

These are some of the things that Æneas tells us about Scotland, but we must remember that he came from Italy, which was a rich and beautiful country, so that he could not help thinking that Scotland was a poor place compared with it, as indeed it was.

But we know a good deal more about Scotland in the reign of James I. than Æneas Sylvius tells us, and this we learn from the laws James passed. For example, we know that there must then have been a great many wolves in the country, though Æneas says there were none. Every baron in the kingdom was commanded to kill all the wolves'

P

whelps he could find, and to give twopence to anyone who brought a whelp's head to him.   Four times every year, also, the baron was to have a great wolf hunt; and all his farmers with their servants were to join him in the hunt, and, if they did not, they had to give a sheep to the baron as a fine.   This proves that there must have been many wolves in the land, or such a law would not have been passed.

There must also have been great numbers of crows in Scotland in those days, as a very curious law shows us.   Every landlord was commanded to kill the young crows every year, as, when they grew up, they did so much damage to the crops.   If the landlord did not obey this law, then the tree in which the crows had built their nests was to be taken from him by the king.   If the landlord liked, however, he could fell the tree and pay a fine of five shillings. Such a law as this could never be passed nowadays, but in those days it was thought to be quite right that such laws should be made.

There were laws about buying and selling which seem very strange to us.   No one was allowed to send a horse to any foreign country unless it were more than three years old.   No one could buy cloth or any other goods from an Englishman who came to Scotland, and no Englishman was allowed to sell anything in Scotland unless he got special permission.   Another law declared that no one was to send any gold or silver out of the country.   What was the meaning of those laws which seem so odd to us? It was that people then thought that the country would soon be ruined if the people bought things made in other countries, and that, if money went out of the country, it would never come back again. For a long time afterwards people in other countries besides Scotland believed this, and the result was that trade could not grow nor the people become rich.

However, even in those days, there must have been well-to-do people in Scotland, as another law shows us. By this law it was commanded that no one except a lord or a knight was to wear silk or furs, or to have pearls or any kind of trimming on his clothes. In the towns no persons except the magistrates and their wives were to wear furs. The farmers also were told that they were not to wear coloured clothes, but plain ones made at home. Now when such laws were made, it means that many people must have had money to spare, and that they spent it on fine clothes, and dressed themselves above their station. For in those days it was thought right that all classes of the people should each have a dress of its own, so that it might be known at once whether a man was a lord or a knight, or a magistrate, or a craftsman, or a farmer.

There was one thing about which the kings and the Parliament were very anxious, and about which many laws were made, and that was that every Scotsman should be trained to fight. So the law was that every man from the age of sixteen to sixty should possess weapons according to his rank. To make sure that every one had these weapons, there were to be four meetings, or wapinschaws, each year, to which all the men in town and country were to come, and, if they did not have the right weapons, they were to be fined.

What should we think nowadays if a boy or a man were fined fourpence every time he played at football? Yet such a law was really passed by James and his Parliament, and for the following reason. It was the English archers, as we know, that had gained so many victories over the Scots, and so it was very necessary that the Scots should try to become as good archers as the English. Laws were therefore passed which forbade playing at football, as being of no use, and which ordered that near every parish church there should be a target and a shooting-ground. On every holiday (and, as we have seen, there were about sixty holidays in the year), every male person, from twelve years old, was to shoot at least three arrows at the mark ; and if he did not, he was to give a sheep as a fine. In spite of these laws, however, the Scots never became good archers, and they always preferred to fight with lances and axes.

There was a class of people who gave a great deal of trouble in Scotland and in other countries at this time, and, indeed, for a long while afterwards. These were the beggars, who in those days did not go about alone but in great bands, so that they were a terror to everybody. It was not safe to travel about the country by yourself, for if you met one of these gangs they would take everything you had, and perhaps ill-use you besides. Some of the beggars were quite well off, and actually rode on horseback ; so that the old rhyme is really true :

> " Hark, hark, the dogs do bark ;
>   The beggars are coming to town ;
>   Some in rags and some on nags,
>   And one in a velvet gown."

A gang of these beggars would often come to the house of a clergyman or a farmer, where they thought they would get plenty to eat, and compel the owner of the house to give them a night's lodging. There were great numbers of them in all the towns, and, when the king and his courtiers travelled, they would often be surrounded by beggars crying for alms.

In almost every reign laws were passed to put down these troublesome and dangerous beggars, but these laws never seemed to do any good. Every person between the ages of fourteen and seventy was forbidden to beg, and, if he were caught doing so, his cheek was to be burned with a red-hot iron, and he was then to be banished from the country. Before any one was allowed to beg he had to get a licence, and to wear a badge on his clothes to show that he was a lawful beggar. And even stricter laws than these were

Beggar's Badge.

passed, but they were never really carried out, and so the number of beggars went on increasing rather than getting fewer.

Another law passed in James's reign shows how different the country was then from what it is now. Every agricultural labourer, if he was not rich enough to buy an ox to plough (for in those days it was oxen that drew the plough and not horses), had to dig up a piece of ground seven feet long and six feet broad on every working day. And why was such a law made? It was because a great deal of land which might have been used for growing crops was not cultivated, but was left to itself, and so was of no use to the people who lived on it. So by such a law as this, more ground came to be cultivated, and more food was got for the people.

From all these laws we see how differently people then lived from the way in which we do now. But there is one thing that must not be forgotten about these laws: they were very seldom carried out. And it was the same in other countries besides Scotland; and the reason is, that the persons who should have enforced them and punished those who broke them, either had not the power to do so or had other things to attend to. However, even when the laws were not obeyed, they at least showed what was the right thing to be done; and no doubt many people did obey them.

32. AN UNRULY KINGDOM

James II. (1437-1460)

James II. was only six years old when his father was murdered; so that a long time must pass before he would be able to rule the country himself. And who was to rule it till then? There was no uncle like the Duke of Albany to act as king till James grew up, and there was no other man in the country strong enough to make all Scotsmen in Highlands and Lowlands obey him. There was, of course, the king's mother; but a woman could not govern such a country as Scotland was in those days. As there was neither a grown-up king, nor any one

From Painting]

The Coronation of James II. in Holyrood Chapel.

[By Wm. Hole, R.S.A.

to take his place, there was no peace in the land for many years to come; and the barons, great and small, did very much as they pleased, making war on each other and even against the king's authority.

It was at Perth that James I. had been slain, and the queen was so afraid to remain there, that soon afterwards she went with her son to Edinburgh Castle, where she thought she would be safe from her enemies. Then, as the young king could not be crowned at Scone, which was the usual place, he was crowned in the chapel of Holyrood; and Archibald, Earl of Douglas, was made his lieutenant, that is, he was to take the king's place till he grew up. But this Earl of Douglas was not a man like his ancestor, the Good Sir James, and was of very little use in enforcing the laws.

When the queen came to Edinburgh Castle with her son, she thought that they would be quite safe there, but she was mistaken. The governor of the castle was Sir William Crichton, who had been a great friend of James I., but who now showed that he thought more of his own interest than of the interest of James's son. What he really wished was to be the first man in the kingdom; and now that he had the young king in his power he determined to keep him, as whoever had the king in his hands would have the chief authority. So he let the queen know that she and her son were his prisoners, and would have to do as he pleased. But the queen was a very clever woman, and she managed to escape to Stirling Castle along with James. There is a story told of how she contrived to escape, but we are not sure that it is true. According to this story, she asked Crichton for leave to go on a pilgrimage to a certain church to pray for her son, and she also asked leave to take two boxes with her for her luggage. Crichton gave her permission; and what she did was to put her

Stirling Castle.   [*Photo by Valentine.*

luggage in one box and James in the other, and so escaped.

However, when the queen went to Stirling Castle, she found she had only gone into another lion's den. The governor of that castle was Sir Alexander Livingstone, and he was just as anxious as Crichton to be the chief man in the kingdom. So before long the queen was again told that she was a prisoner, and that she and the king must do as Livingstone bade them. Of course, Crichton was very angry at all this, but for a time he and Livingstone pretended to be friends, and divided the power between them. Crichton was not satisfied with this, however, and he determined to get the king into his hands once more, and he managed this very cleverly.

Crichton was told that James was in the habit of hunting in the Park at Stirling every morning; so one day, having learned that Livingstone was away at Perth, he rode at the head of a band of his men to Stirling. It was dark when he arrived there, and he hid himself and his band among the bushes in the Park and waited till the morning. When the morning came, sure enough James appeared with his attendants to hunt, and they were immediately surrounded by Crichton and his men. Crichton pretended that he had only come to free him from his enemies; but, of course, James had to ride back with him to Edinburgh whether he would or not.

Livingstone and Crichton still pretended to be friends, and they had one enemy whom they both wished to get rid of. This enemy was another Earl of Douglas, for the earl who had been made king's lieutenant had died. The new earl, whose name was William, was only eighteen years old; but he had already shown himself so bold and haughty, that he had made himself feared both by Crichton and by Livingstone. They therefore determined to get him into their power, and this was the plan they adopted. They invited him and his only brother and another relative to Edinburgh Castle, and at first pretended to be very friendly with him.

One day at dinner, however, Livingstone and Crichton suddenly began to accuse Douglas of being a traitor to his king. There is a story, though we are not sure that it is true, that a bull's head had been set on the table, which meant in Scotland that some one present was to be put to death. At any rate, all the three—Douglas, his brother, and the other relative—were seized and bound and shut up in the castle. The young king, who had become very fond of Douglas, is said to have tried to prevent his being seized, but no attention was paid to him. Then all the three were tried for treason, but the trial was a mere pretence, and they were found guilty and were beheaded in the back court of the castle. To this cruel deed the people gave a nickname; they called it the "Black Dinner," and these rhymes were made about it :—

> "Edinburgh Castle, toune and towre,
>   God grant thou sink for sin !
> And that even for the black dinoir
>   Earl Douglas gat therein."

Livingstone and Crichton had got rid of one Douglas, but another soon arose who was to be one of the greatest of all his family. This was not the next earl, however, who was called James the Gross or the Fat, but the one who came after him, whose name was William. What this earl did was to make friends with Livingstone against Crichton, and then both together they carried on war against him. The country was now in a worse state than ever, and in many parts of the kingdom there was constant plundering and fighting. One story will be sufficient to show what things were done at this time when there was no one strong enough to rule the kingdom.

There was one man in the country who was very

anxious that all Scotsmen should live at peace with each other. This was James Kennedy, Bishop of St Andrews, and a nephew of James I., whose beautiful tomb is still to be seen in the College Church of St Andrews. Now Kennedy was afraid that Douglas would soon become so powerful in the country that he would really be its king. So he made friends with Crichton, and these two set themselves up against Douglas and Livingstone. But, as we shall see, this for a time only made matters worse.

One of Douglas's friends was the Earl of Crawford, who was one of the most powerful nobles to the north of the river Forth, and who showed that he feared neither God nor man. Now, as Crawford was the friend of Douglas, he was bound to be the enemy of Bishop Kennedy. So along with Livingstone he led an army into the bishop's diocese, burned many farms and villages, and carried away many persons as captives. The bishop, being a churchman, could not pay Crawford back by doing the same thing to his lands, but there was one thing a churchman could do, and that Kennedy now did. He pronounced the curse of the Church upon the earl, which meant that in this world and the next he would be under the wrath of God. Everyone was forbidden to speak to him or give him food or lodging, and whoever did so would also come under the curse. The earl paid no heed to the bishop, and he went on living just as he had always done. But just a year afterwards, Crawford was killed in a fight that took place at Arbroath, and then people said that this was the result of his plundering and burning in the bishop's lands, and also of the bishop's curse.

33. THE KING AND THE DOUGLASES

JAMES II. (1437-1460)

When such things were done in the land, it was full time that there should be a king who would compel the greatest nobles to live in peace and obey the law. And at last James grew old enough to govern the kingdom himself. When the Earl of Crawford was slain, James was about sixteen years of age, and three years afterwards he married Mary of Gueldres, in Holland. From this time he began to show what kind of king he was.

James was not so clever and learned as his father, but he knew better how to manage the nobles, though, as we shall see, he had a great fight with one of them. When he led his armies to war, he made the soldiers very fond of him by his way of talking with them, and by his living just like themselves. There is one thing told of him which shows how bold and free he was. In those times kings and other great people never tasted food or drink until it had been tasted by some one else, to make sure that it had not been poisoned. But James took whatever was offered to him by any of his soldiers without asking anyone to taste it before him. Of course, he had a nickname, like most Scottish kings; as he had a red birth-mark on his face, his subjects called him the "Fiery Face."

One of the first things James did when he began to rule for himself showed his subjects that they had now a king who was not to be trifled with. As we have just seen, the Livingstones had joined with the Earl of Crawford in laying waste Bishop Kennedy's lands. Quite suddenly, James caused all the chief persons of the Livingstone family to be thrown into prison, and soon afterwards to be brought to trial. All their lands were taken from them, the father was kept in prison, and two of his sons were put to death. Thus at one stroke James had got rid of some of his enemies ; but he had still the greatest enemy of all to deal with, and he was not to be got rid of so easily as the Livingstones.

This enemy was that same Earl of Douglas of whom Bishop Kennedy was afraid that he would become more powerful than a subject should be in any kingdom. The reason why Douglas had so much power was that he owned so many lands, and had so many followers when he chose to go to war. He owned both Galloway and Annandale, so that he was master of a great part of the south of Scotland. Two of his brothers were also earls, and they, of course, joined with him against his enemies. Then he had made friends with other nobles in different parts of the country, who had promised to stand by him if the king should make war on him, and, as we shall see, it was this that James feared most of all.

And not only were the Douglases very powerful, they were also liked and admired by the people. The reason of this was that in those fighting times they were the bravest in war. They had led armies against the English oftener than had the kings of Scots themselves, and had gained more victories over them. Just about this time, for example, a brother of the Earl of Douglas defeated the English at Gretna, on the Borders, and took three of their leaders prisoners. For all these reasons, then, the Douglases were so powerful that it was a common saying in the country that no one dared touch a Douglas or a Douglas's man.

James and Douglas knew quite well that they must fight it out to settle which was the stronger, and so both began to make ready for war. Douglas made a league with the Earl of Ross and the new Earl of Crawford, called Earl Beardie on account of his long beard, and also the Tiger Earl, because he was so fierce and cruel; and he began to raise his own men, to be prepared if the king should come against him. Hardly any of his men dared refuse to obey him, though they knew it was against the law. One of them, however, was bold enough to disobey him, and here is the story of what happened.

Maclellan (for that was the name of this bold person) was at once imprisoned by Douglas's command. When James heard of this he was both angry and sorry, as Maclellan was a great favourite of his. So he wrote a letter to Douglas, ordering him to set his prisoner free ; and, to make sure that Douglas would get the letter, he gave it to Sir Patrick Gray, who was Maclellan's uncle. When Douglas saw Gray arrive, he knew at once on what errand he had come, and he gave orders that Maclellan should be beheaded. However, he received Gray as if he were glad to see him. "I was just going to begin dinner," he said, "so let us dine together, and open the king's letter afterwards."

When dinner was over, Douglas opened the letter, and after he had read it, he said, "The king has sent me a nice letter, but I am sorry I cannot obey his commands." Then he led Gray out to the castle green, and there was the head of Maclellan lying

beside the block where he had been executed.
"There is your nephew," said Douglas, "but unfortunately without his head; however, you can do with
his body what you please." Gray did not dare to
say a word, as he knew that Douglas could have him
put to death in a moment. So he quietly mounted
his horse, but, when he had got safely across the
drawbridge, he turned round and shook his mailed
hand at Douglas, and told him that he was a traitor
and a disgrace to knighthood, and that he would
make him repent some day of what he had done to
Maclellan. Douglas at once ordered his men to
pursue him, and they followed him almost to the
gates of Edinburgh, but, as Gray was mounted on a
swift horse, he escaped his pursuers.

Gray had not to wait long before he had his
revenge on Douglas for his nephew's death. Before
James went to war with Douglas he tried to come
to an agreement with him. He invited Douglas to
visit him at the castle of Stirling, and sent him a
safe-conduct, that is, a letter in which he promised
that Douglas would be safe as long as he was with
him. So Douglas came to the castle, and James
received him just as if he had been his friend. After
supper next day, however, James took Douglas aside
and asked him to break his bond with the Earls of
Ross and Crawford. Douglas answered that he
would not break the bond. "False traitor," James
exclaimed, "if you will not break it, this will," and
he stabbed him in the neck with a knife. Then Sir
Patrick Gray, who was standing by, felled the
wounded man to the ground with his axe, and others
who were near even stabbed his dead body.

Sir William Crichton.   Sir Alexander Livingston.   Joanna Beaufort, Queen of James I.   Robert III (1340-1406).   John Barbour, Poet-Archdeacon (1316?-1395).   Robert II., First of Stewart Kings (1316-1390).

James II. (1430-1460).   James I. (1394-1437).   Donald, Lord of the Isles (defeated at Harlaw).   David, Earl of Carrick, First Duke of Rothesay.   Earl of Fife, First Duke of Albany.   Earl of Douglas (slain at Otterburn).

Q

The murder of Douglas was a foolish as well as a wicked action, as James was soon to learn. The murdered earl was succeeded by his younger brother, James, who was to prove himself quite as dangerous as any of his family. Little more than a month after the death of his brother, the new earl rode into Stirling at the head of 600 men, though the king and his lords were then in the castle, which showed how little he cared for the royal authority. The safe-conduct which James had given to the dead earl was dragged at a horse's tail to mark how shameful it was for James to have broken his word. Then the town was plundered and burned before James's very eyes, and he had no power to prevent it. Douglas also "put the king to the horn," which was the greatest insult that could have been done to him. In Scotland, when any one refused to obey the law, an official went to the town cross of the place where he lived and blew three blasts on a horn, which meant that the person was now an outlaw, that is, that he was no longer protected by the law. So, when Douglas put James to the horn, it meant that he did not consider him his king, and that all his subjects were free to make war on him whenever they pleased.

The question now came to be—Was the king or Douglas to have the upper hand in the country? The quarrel between them went on for more than three years. Now they tried to live at peace, and now they were at war. Douglas even sought help from the English against his own king; but the English were then fighting against each other, and could not do much to assist him. At last the army

Q

of the king defeated the three brothers of Douglas at a place called Arkinholm, which no longer exists, but which was where the town of Langholm now stands. One of the brothers was killed in the battle, the second was taken prisoner and executed, and the third brother had to flee to England, where the earl

Ruins of Roxburgh Castle.

himself then was. Not long afterwards, the Parliament passed an Act which put an end to the power of the Douglases. Their lands were taken from them, some of them being kept by the king and others given to his friends. As for Douglas and his two brothers who were still living, they were declared to be traitors, so that, if ever they were taken prisoners, they would at once be put to death. This was the end of the Black Douglases, and a melancholy end it was for a family which had the Good Sir James for one of its ancestors.

James II. reigned for five years longer, but he had no more trouble with his nobles. Who among them, indeed, would have dared to rise against him when he had overcome the greatest of them all? But James made himself liked by his nobles, as he showed himself a kind as well as a strong king. He was able, therefore, to prevent them from fighting against each other; but, on the other hand, he was also able to lead them against Scotland's old enemies, the English. There were two places that belonged to Scotland which the English still held—Berwick-on-Tweed and the castle of Roxburgh—and James wished to gain back both of them.

In the year 1460, therefore, James led an army to besiege Roxburgh Castle. To break down its walls he had brought cannons with him, and this is the first time we hear of cannons being used in Scotland, though they had been used for some time in other countries. James was very proud of his cannons and took a great interest in them, though, of course, they were not to be compared with those that are made nowadays. They were not made all of one piece, but of iron bars with iron hoops round them, the hoops being fixed with wedges of oak.

On a Sunday morning, James was watching one of these cannons being fired, when it burst, and one piece of it killed James, and another piece killed the Earl of Angus, who was standing beside him. T⌢

this day the place is shown in the grounds of Floors Castle, near Kelso, where the king fell. As James was a very popular king, there was great sorrow at his death, but the chief men in his army were determined that his wishes should be carried out, and they went on with the siege of the castle. They did succeed in taking it, and its walls were so completely destroyed that only a few ruins now show the place where it stood.

From the story of the reigns of James II. and of other Scottish kings in those times, we are apt to think that Scotland must have been a much worse country to live in than any other. Battles and murders are the chief events we read of. But the truth is that things were not much better in other countries. France was a richer and more civilised kingdom than Scotland, but here are a few things that took place in France about the time of which we are speaking. Many French nobles invited the King of England to come with an army to France to fight against their own king, and this, we have seen, was just what the Earl of Douglas did. Two French princes stabbed their enemies, just as James II. stabbed Douglas. A certain French duke had his own brother murdered, and a certain count starved his son to death in a dungeon. Another noble murdered his own wife, and still another stole little children and put them to a slow death for his own pleasure. In France, also, the common people were not so well off as in Scotland. They had not so much food to eat, and they were far more cruelly treated by the nobles.

We see, therefore, that as bad as things may have

James III. presented to the nobles by his mother at the Siege of
Roxburgh, A.D. 1460.

been in Scotland, they were even worse in a great country like France. If a poor Scottish farmer had had the choice, he would certainly have preferred to live in his own country rather than in one where the nobles trampled down his crops whenever and wherever they pleased.

---

34. SCOTLAND AND THE LORD OF THE ISLES

JAMES III. (1460-1488)

Once more Scotland had a boy as its king, for James III. was only ten years old when his father was killed at Kelso. But the curious thing is that the country was better off while James remained a boy than when he came to rule for himself. At first the chief power was in the hands of Bishop Kennedy, of whom we have already read, and who did his best to rule the country for its good. In the first years of James's reign, however, Scotland passed through a great danger, from which Kennedy and his friends saved it. This danger was that the country would be divided into two, of which the Lowlands would be one part, and the Highlands and the Western Islands the other. The great danger arose in this way.

At this time the Wars of the Roses were going on in England, one side fighting for the House of Lancaster and the other for the House of York. Now Bishop Kennedy and his friends did all they could to support the side of the Lancastrians, and when the Lancastrian king, Henry VI., was driven from the throne, he came to Scotland to escape from his enemies. But when the Yorkist Edward IV. became king, he wished to pay Scotland back for the help it had given to the House of Lancaster, and there were two men who were very willing to assist him to do this. The one was the Earl of Douglas, who had been driven out of Scotland by James II., and who had never given up trying to get back the lands which James had taken from him. The other person who was ready to help Edward against Scotland was John, Lord of the Isles and Earl of Ross. This Lord of the Isles had been quite friendly with James II., but, like all the Lords of the Isles, he wished to be an independent king and not to be under the King of Scots, and this was the reason why he was willing to assist Edward against the Scots.

It was the traitor Earl of Douglas who carried out Edward's plan. He took a message from Edward to the Lord of the Isles, the result of which was that a treaty was agreed upon by all the three, which, if it had been carried out, would have put an end to Scotland as an independent kingdom. By this treaty all Scotland to the north of the Forth was to be given to the Lord of the Isles and to a kinsman of his, called Donald Balloch, and Douglas was to get back all the lands that had been taken from him by James II. As for King Edward, he was to be the lord of all Scotland, and both Douglas and the Lord of the Isles were to be his vassals.

Of course, this treaty could not be carried out without making war on Scotland, and the arrangement was that the Lord of the Isles should raise a rebellion in the North, while Douglas should invade the South with an English army. So a few months after the treaty was made, John of the Isles took the title of king, and began to behave just as if he had been one. His son, called Angus Og, led a band of his men against the town of Inverness, and made himself master of it. Then he proclaimed his father king, and ordered all the people of the Northern Counties to pay their taxes to him, and not to the King of Scots.

Luckily for Scotland, however, it was not till the next year that Douglas was able to do his part, and, as he was defeated by a Scottish army, Edward's plan for making himself king of Scotland did not succeed. But John of the Isles still continued to be a dangerous enemy of Scotland. He behaved just as if he were a king, and paid no attention to any orders that were sent to him. Some years afterwards, however, he was at last taught that the King of Scots was too strong for him. No fewer than four earls with their followers were sent against him, and he was compelled to ask for the king's mercy. His life was spared, and he was allowed to remain Lord of the Isles, but the earldom of Ross was taken from him, and became part of the lands of the king. But we shall see that even after this the Lords of the Isles still continued to give trouble to the kings of Scots.

It was chiefly owing to Bishop Kennedy that Scotland had been saved from its great danger. But Kennedy was now an old man, and he died in the year 1465—that is, five years after the beginning of

James III.'s reign. All the people were sorry at his death, as there was no one so wise as he to fill his place. He had been very rich, but he had made a good use of his riches. He gave many gifts to the churches, but what he is best remembered for is the College of St Salvator, which he built for the University of St Andrews, and which exists till the present day. Another thing he did was to have a ship made, which is said to have been the largest that had ever been built. A few years after his death this ship was wrecked on the coast of Northumberland, and many of those on board were drowned.

It was not long before the wise bishop was sorely missed. Only a few months after his death three men made a bargain with each other which was to do much mischief in the country. These three persons were Gilbert, Lord Kennedy, a brother of Bishop Kennedy, Robert, Lord Fleming, and Sir Alexander Boyd. The bargain they made with each other was that Kennedy and Boyd were to have possession of the king, and that Fleming was in some way to be made a rich man. Now, as these three barons had many powerful friends, they were quite able to carry out the plans they had laid, and they were not long in doing so.

A few months after their bargain had been made, there was a great meeting at Linlithgow, at which the king and his chief officers were present. Then Boyd and Fleming got up a hunting-party, and during the hunt they seized the king and bore him off to Edinburgh Castle against his will. Now that the conspirators had the king in their power, they took care to enrich themselves. They pretended, however, to act according to the laws. They held a Parliament in Edinburgh Castle, and Lord Boyd, the head of the Boyd family, fell at the king's feet, clasped his knees, and asked him if he had been brought to Edinburgh against his will. What could the poor king say but that he had come of his own free will?

And now for a time the Boyds and their friends had it all their own way in the country. Lord Boyd was made guardian of the king and his two brothers, and all the royal fortresses were put into his hands. A great many lands were given to his family, and the Boyds became almost as powerful as the Douglases had been. But it was Lord Boyd's eldest son, Thomas, who became their greatest man. This Thomas was one of the cleverest men then living in Scotland; he was one of the best knights of the time, and he knew how to make himself pleasant to everybody. It is no wonder, therefore, that he became so great a person in the country. He was first made Earl of Arran, and then he was married to the king's sister, the Princess Mary. But the pride of the Boyds was soon to have a fall. They had, of course, made many enemies, who were angry at seeing them with so much wealth and power in their hands. And now we have to tell how the Boyds fell as quickly as they had risen.

King James was now about eighteen years old, and his councillors began to think that it was time that he should be married. They did find a queen for him, and a queen that brought a handsome gift to Scotland. It will be remembered that, when

Alexander III. conquered the Western Islands from King Hakon of Norway, it was agreed that Scotland should pay a sum of money every year for them. But since the time of James I. the money had not been paid, and now Christian, King of Norway, who was also King of Denmark and Sweden, began to grumble and to say that the money must be paid or the islands given back. How did James's councillors get out of the difficulty? They sent Thomas Boyd, Earl of Arran, to Christian to propose that his daughter Margaret, who was only twelve years of age, should marry the King of Scots. Christian was delighted with the proposal, and, as he had not money to pay his daughter's dowry, he gave the Orkney and Shetland Islands instead; and so at last all the islands round the Scottish coasts had come to be a part of the kingdom of Scotland.

But what has all this to do with the family of the Boyds? We have just seen that Thomas Boyd, Earl of Arran, had been sent to Denmark to propose the marriage between James and Margaret. But he was also sent there a second time to bring the bride to Scotland. Now, while he was away in Denmark, the enemies of the Boyds (and there were many of them) laid a plot to have him taken prisoner when he returned, and then to have him and others of his family put to death. However, Arran's wife, the Princess Mary, heard of the plot, and, when his ship arrived at Leith, she went secretly aboard and warned him of his danger, and both sailed to Denmark, where he was safe from his enemies. But there were two of the Boyds still in their hands—Arran's father, Lord Boyd, and his uncle, Sir Alexander

Boyd. Both were charged with being traitors to the king, and were condemned to death; but only Alexander was executed, as Lord Boyd escaped to England. As all their lands were taken from the Boyds, their greatness had lasted only for about three years. This was another lesson to the nobles that in the end the king would prove too strong for any of them. Yet we are now to see that the nobles never defied the king's power so much as they did during the remainder of James's reign.

35. THE NOBLES AGAINST THE KING

JAMES III. (1460-1488)

James III. was now old enough to rule for himself, but he was not the kind of king that Scotland needed in those times. He liked peace better than war, and was fonder of music in churches than of the sound of the trumpet in battle. He did not like the nobles, whose chief delight was fighting, and the persons he chose to be his friends were men of humble rank who were clever in doing things which he admired.

The man he honoured most was one Cochrane, an architect, whom he afterwards made Earl of Mar; and among his other favourites were Roger, a musician; Hommyle, the king's tailor; and Leonard, a smith. The nobles, of course, thought it a disgrace that a king should make friends with persons of such low rank; and there can be no doubt that James was foolish in spending so much time with these men instead of trying to make friends with the nobles, and to manage them as his father James II. had done. From the time that James began to reign for himself, indeed, there was never peace between him and his nobles, and this meant that there could be no peace in the country.

James's first great quarrel was with his own brothers, the Duke of Albany and the Earl of Mar.

Craigmillar Castle.

We do not know how the quarrel began, but James must have had some reason to be afraid of them. People at the time believed that an astrologer had predicted that in Scotland a lion should be killed by its own whelps, and James thought this meant that he would be slain by his near relatives. At all events, for some reason or other, James imprisoned the Earl of Mar in Craigmillar Castle, and the Duke of Albany in the castle of Edinburgh. Unfortunately, Mar died while he was a prisoner, and people said that he had been put to death by James, which was probably not true. As for the Duke of Albany, he escaped from his prison by killing his jailers, and letting himself down the castle rock with a rope which his friends had secretly sent to him (1479).

But James's greatest quarrel was with his nobles, who said that he was letting his kingdom go to ruin. They accused him of two things which they said were doing a great deal of harm in the country. First, he spent too much money on his favourites, and followed their advice rather than that of his nobles; and, secondly, he mixed brass and lead in the silver money and made it pass as pure silver. It should be said, however, that the kings of other countries did the same thing with their money, though it was a very wrong thing to do, as in the long run it spoilt the trade of the country.

At last (1482) the nobles got a chance of showing how angry they were both with the king and with his favourites. James declared war against England, and came with his army to the town of Lauder. Most of the great nobles were present, and they determined to carry out the plan which had been long in their minds. So they met in the church of Lauder to consider what was to be done with the favourites. Then Lord Gray told them the fable of the mice and the cat. The mice, Lord Gray told them, thought that it would be a good thing if a bell were hung on the cat's neck, as then they would know when he was near at hand; but the question was, what mouse would be bold enough to hang the bell on the neck of their enemy.   So the question for the nobles was, which of them would dare to face the king, and tell him what they wanted.   Up rose Archibald, Earl of Angus, and said that he would "bell the cat," and ever afterwards he was called Archibald, Bell-the-Cat.

Just at this moment a loud knock was heard at the church door.   The door was opened, and Cochrane, the king's chief favourite, entered, gaily dressed in a riding suit of black velvet, with a gold chain round his neck and a bugle-horn ornamented with gold at his side.   Bell-the-Cat snatched the chain from his neck, and another baron took away his bugle.   "Is this jest or earnest?" asked Cochrane.   "It is real earnest, as you will find," was the answer. Then a number of the nobles went to the king's own tent, dragged out the other favourites, and bore them and Cochrane to the bridge of the town.   Now the poor wretches saw what was to be their end.   The

Two-handed Sword of Archibald, Bell-the-Cat. (Length, 8 ft.)

ropes of tents and the halters of horses were tied round their necks (though Cochrane asked that a silken cord might be tied round his, as he was an earl), and all of them were hanged over the bridge.

The king was now a prisoner, and the nobles, instead of marching against the English, led him to Edinburgh Castle, where they put him under the charge of his uncle, the Earl of Athol.   As there was no Scottish army to fight them, the English marched into Scotland through the town of Berwick, which ever afterwards belonged to England. Along with the English came the king's brother, the Duke of Albany, who had been driven into exile, and who was anxious to get back his lands. Then a peace was made between the Scots and the English, and Albany got back all his lands and honours. For a short time James and his brother seemed to be great friends, and they slept in the same bed. But they never really liked each other, and at last James managed to get Albany again driven out of the country, to which he never returned. In the next reign, as we shall see, Albany's son was to be a great man in Scotland.

After the death of James's favourites at Lauder Bridge, he and his nobles did not become better friends. James chose other favourites to whom he gave lands and honours, which were sometimes taken from nobles whom he feared or disliked. At last (1488) a number of the nobles rose against him, and determined that they would make his son king instead of him. This son, who was afterwards James IV., was only fifteen years old and was guarded in the castle of Stirling, but the rebel nobles persuaded his guardian to put him in their hands. So, at the head of their army, and with the young prince in their ranks, they marched against their king, who had also collected an army with the help of the nobles who were still faithful to him.

The two armies met at Sauchieburn, about a mile from Bannockburn. That it might bring good luck to him, James had armed himself with Bruce's sword, and he was mounted on a horse which was said to be

JAMES V. (1513-1542).

JAMES IV. (1473-1513).

WM. DUNBAR, Poet (1462?-1530?).

ROBERT COCHRANE, Architect, (——1482).

JAMES III. (1451-1488).

JAMES KENNEDY, Bishop of St Andrews, Nephew of James I.

DAVID BEATON, Cardinal and Primate (1494-1546).

GAVIN DOUGLAS, Poet-Bishop (1474-1522).

MARGARET TUDOR, Daughter of Henry VII. (1489-1541).

ARCHIBALD DOUGLAS, "Bell-the-Cat" (1449-1514).

DUKE OF ALBANY, Brother of James III.

MARGARET OF DENMARK, Wife of James III.

SIR ALEXANDER BOYD.

the swiftest in Scotland. But James was neither a skilful general nor a valiant knight, and the battle had hardly begun when he galloped from the field, perhaps because his fiery horse ran off with him, as he was not a good rider. He had not ridden far before he was thrown from the saddle. It is said that his horse shied at a pitcher which a woman dropped beside a mill-dam as she ran away in terror. James, in a fainting-fit from his fall, was carried into the mill by the people who were about, and, when he came to his senses, he was asked who he was. " I was your king this morning," he said; and the miller's wife rushed out and called, " A priest for the king, a priest for the king!" " I am a priest," said a man who was passing, and he went into the mill and bent over the king. " Is your wound mortal?" he asked. " No," answered the king, " but I wish to confess my sins and to receive pardon." " This will give you pardon," said the stranger, and he stabbed the king to the heart.

Such was the sad end of James III., who, if he had lived in more peaceful times, might have been a king both liked and respected by his subjects. But he was not a ruler fitted to govern such a country as Scotland then was. How far right was on the side of James or on that of his rebel nobles, we cannot say. There is one thing, however, that we should keep in mind. At that time the kings of other countries were trying to make themselves absolute rulers; that is, they wished to make both nobles and people obey them without question. And kings of Scotland like James I., James II., and James III., and other kings after them, tried to make themselves kings like

R

those of other countries. When the Scottish nobles sought to prevent this, therefore, they were doing a good work, though to us who live in peaceful times their way of doing it seems rough and cruel.

---

36. END OF THE LORD OF THE ISLES—A ROYAL MARRIAGE

James IV. (1488-1513)

At the time when James IV. became king, a great change was taking place in the countries of Europe. What are called the Middle Ages were coming to an end, and Modern Times were beginning.

First of all, there was a great change in the ways of fighting. In the Middle Ages a knight, clad in armour and mounted on horseback, was a match for many men on foot, who were not so well armed as he was. But when gunpowder was invented, the knight's armour did not protect him against cannon balls and gun shots, and so the soldiers who fought on foot with guns and cannons were more useful in battles than mounted knights with their lances. The result of this was that the Feudal System came to an end by degrees. Now, when kings went to war with each other, they preferred to have trained soldiers from any country where they could get them, to whom they paid money as long as they needed them. In Scotland, however, the Feudal System lasted longer than in most countries, as its kings were not able to put down the great nobles as other kings did.

Another invention made a great change in many ways: namely, the invention of the art of printing. Before books were printed, they had all to be written, and, as the writing had to be very carefully done, it took a long time to copy out a book. For example, it took about two years to write out the Bible. The result was that it was only very rich people who could afford to buy books. When books began to be printed, however, they became cheaper and cheaper, and many people were able to buy and read them who had not done so before. In this way, men were taught to think for themselves about many things, such as religion, for instance, and they were no longer content to go on just as their fathers had done, but wished to improve themselves and their ways of living. Printing was brought into England in the year 1477, but it was not till thirty years afterwards (in 1507) that the first book was printed in Scotland.

There was another thing that helped to put new thoughts into men's minds. It was found that the world was a much bigger place than had been supposed. In the year 1492, Columbus sailed across the Atlantic Ocean and discovered the West Indies; in 1497, Vasco da Gama, a Portuguese, sailed round the Cape of Good Hope, and found out a new way to India; and in 1499, Sebastian Cabot, a Venetian merchant, sailed from Bristol and discovered North America. When it was known that there was another continent beyond the ocean, kings and their subjects began to desire to have a share in its riches, and there was rivalry between them as to who should get most. It was not till long after the reign of James IV., however, that Scotland possessed land in America, the reason being that she was not rich enough to build so many ships as countries like England and Spain.

James IV. was the right kind of king to rule at a time when such changes were taking place. He was in every way a different man from his father. He was about the medium size, and very strong in body, and everybody knew him by his long beard, for men did not usually wear beards in those days. He was very fond of all manly sports. He liked nothing better than hunting and hawking; and it is told of him that he would go into a blacksmith's workshop and practise striking the anvil with the forehammer.

He must have been very clever, as he learned to speak Latin, French, German, Flemish, Italian, and Spanish. He also spoke Gaelic, and, as far as we know, he was the last king of Scots who did so. This was the right kind of king to manage the unruly nobles, and he did manage them in a way that almost no other king did.

James was not fond only of sports and amusements : he wished to know about everything that came in his way, and to understand how things were done. For instance, he put a baby with a dumb woman on the Bass Rock, to find what language it would speak when left to itself. He also kept an alchemist, who tried to discover for him how the baser metals could be changed into gold and silver. But, as we shall see, he was interested in more important things than these, and did a great deal to improve the country and the people.

There was one thing that James blamed himself

for all his life, and that was the death of his father.
He was usually in high spirits, but every now and then
when the memory of his father came back to him, he
would become melancholy and ride off almost alone
to the shrine of some saint in some distant part
of the country.   All his life, too, he wore an iron
belt under his clothes, to remind him of his unduti-
fulness to his father.   James had, however, one great
fault—he was so rash and self-willed that he would
not listen to good advice, and this was in the end to
bring a great misfortune on his people.

In the second year of his reign, 1489, an event
happened of which James and all Scotsmen must
have been proud.   This was a great sea-fight
between English and Scots, in which the Scots
gained the victory.   There was peace at this time
between England and Scotland, but often in those
days when nations were at peace on land they were
at war on the sea.   In the year 1489, five English
ships came to the Firth of Forth and began to
plunder all the vessels they could find.   Now, at
this time there was a great sea-captain in Scotland,
called Sir Andrew Wood of Largo, who was a very skilful sailor and had fought many battles at sea.   James,
therefore, sent Sir Andrew against the English, and
though he had only two ships against their five, he
defeated them, and brought all their ships captive
into the harbour of Leith.

When this was told to Henry VII., who was then
king of England, he determined to have his revenge,
and he sent a captain, called Stephen Bull, to the
Firth of Forth with three large ships to fight Sir
Andrew and bring him to England either alive or

dead. Sir Andrew was then in Flanders, so that the English had to wait for his coming home. At length, a little after daybreak one morning, Sir Andrew was seen approaching with his two ships, *The Yellow Carvel* and *The Flower*. When the two enemies saw each other, they at once prepared for battle. They fought all through the summer's day from sunrise till sunset, and it was only the darkness that prevented them from fighting on.

When the sun rose next morning, both sides blew their trumpets, and the battle began again—the people on the shore looking on all the while. At length, near the Bell Rock, off the coast of Forfarshire, whither all the ships had drifted, the Scots "doubled their strokes" upon the Englishmen, and compelled them to surrender. Then Sir Andrew bore the English ships into the port of Dundee, and took their captain to the king. But James, who admired the brave way in which the English had fought, sent the ships back to England, and gave handsome presents to the captain and his men.

An important thing that was done during James's reign was the ending of the Lordship of the Isles and the making of peace in the Western Islands and the Western Highlands. We saw that in the reign of James III., John, Lord of the Isles, had tried, with the help of Edward IV., to make himself king of all the country to the north of the river Forth. He had not succeeded in this, and had been compelled to submit to the King of Scots. John was now a very old man, but in the year 1493 he began again to make plots with the English. This was found out, however, and his title of "Lord of the Isles" was taken from him, and that was the end of the Lordship of the Isles. For many years James had a great deal of trouble both with the Western Highlands and the Western Islands, but at last he was able to subdue them and compel the chiefs to obey the laws. And what is more, he made the chiefs like him ; and, when he fought the English in his last battle, there were no braver soldiers in his army than the chiefs and their men.

We have now to tell of a foolish action which James did, against the wishes both of his councillors and of his people. This was to help Perkin Warbeck in his attempt to become king of England. This Warbeck was really a native of Flanders, but he pretended to be Richard, Duke of York, and the true heir to the English throne. James believed him to be the Duke of York, and besides, he was offended with Henry VII. at this time, and thought that it would be a good thing for Scotland if Warbeck were king of England. He therefore invited him to come to Scotland, and in the year 1495 Warbeck did come. James treated him just as if he had been a real prince ; he gave him a pension of £1200 a year, and he married him to his own cousin, Lady Catherine Gordon, daughter of the Earl of Huntly.

But James did still more for Warbeck. He collected an army to invade England, although he had very great difficulty in raising it ; so much so that he had to make his "chains, plate, and cupboard" into money to help to pay the cost of it. Then he and Warbeck at the head of this army entered England, and took plunder wherever they went. But the people of

England did not wish Warbeck for their king, and no Englishmen came to join him as James had expected. James and Warbeck now began to blame each other, and the result was that the army had to march back to Scotland; so that all the money that had been spent in raising it was thrown away. After this the two were never good friends, and at last Perkin left Scotland in an Ayr ship, called the *Cuckoo*, which was as handsomely furnished by James as if it was to carry a king.

We have come now to one of the most important events in the history of England and Scotland. We have seen that Henry VII. and James were not good friends ; but Henry was a king who never liked to go to war when he could help it, and so he thought of a plan which would make both them and their successors live at peace ever afterwards. This plan of Henry was that his daughter, Margaret Tudor, should marry the King of Scotland. And in course of time the marriage was arranged, and in the year 1503 Margaret came to Scotland to be wedded and to become Queen of Scots. It was the grandest marriage that had ever taken place in Scotland, as James was anxious to show his bride that she had not come to a poor country.

Dressed in a jacket of crimson velvet, trimmed with cloth of gold, James met her at Dalkeith, attended by many of his nobles and bishops. Then the procession went to Edinburgh, where great preparations had been made to receive the royal pair. The houses were covered with tapestry ; a newly painted cross was set up, and near it there was a fountain that ran wine, which everyone could drink

The Marriage Procession of James IV. and Margaret Tudor, Edinburgh.

who pleased. The next day the marriage took place in the chapel of Holyrood, the Queen being magnificently dressed in a gown of white damask, with a collar of gold and pearls, and her crown, from under which her hair hung down to her feet.

The reason why this marriage was so important is that, exactly a hundred years afterwards, the great grandson of James and Margaret, James VI., became King of Scotland, England, and Ireland, and that ever since the three countries have been ruled by a single sovereign. But one thing did not happen which King Henry had expected; the Scots and the English did not live at peace for long after the marriage, and we have now to hear of one of the most terrible battles that was ever fought between them.

---

37. THE BATTLE OF FLODDEN (1513)

James IV. (1488-1513)

In the year 1509, Henry VII., King of England, died and was succeeded by his son, Henry VIII. The new king was a very different man from his father. Henry VII. never went to war when he could help it; Henry VIII., on the other hand, liked war. He was quick-tempered and quarrelsome, and wished to be lord and master of everybody. Now, James IV. had also a fiery temper, and he too was always ready to fight when he thought it necessary. Two such kings were very likely to quarrel, and, as it happened, there were several things about which they could not agree, and which at last made them great enemies.

For the first two years after Henry began to reign, he and James were quite good friends, but after that time they began to dispute with each other. Here are some of the reasons why they quarrelled. When Margaret Tudor, Henry's sister, married James, Henry VII. had promised that she should receive certain jewels as her dowry; but her brother refused to give up the jewels, which made both James and Margaret very angry. Another complaint which James had against Henry was this. In the year 1511, when Scotland and England were at peace with each other, Sir Edmund Howard, Lord High Admiral of England, attacked two Scottish ships commanded by Andrew Barton. The Scottish captain was slain, and his two ships were taken by the English. As James had been very fond of Barton, he complained to Henry, and asked that he might be paid back for the loss of the ships; but all the answer he got from Henry was that it did not become kings to quarrel about pirates. After this there was constant fighting at sea between the Scots and English, though they were not at war on land.

But the chief reason why James and Henry at last went to war has still to be mentioned. As we know, France and Scotland had long been friends, and had often fought together against England, which was the enemy of them both. Now about this time Henry VIII. and other rulers in Europe were preparing to make war on France, and James thought it right that he should stand by Scotland's old ally. He therefore told Henry that, if he made

war on France, he, James, would make war upon him.
Henry paid no attention to James's warning, and at
the end of June, 1513, he crossed to France at the
head of an army. Then James hesitated no longer,
and declared war against England.

James was more willing to fight England because
the Queen of France sent him a ring, and asked
him to advance three feet into England, and
break a lance in her honour against the English.
This was what ladies used to do in the days of
chivalry, but James should have remembered that he
was not a simple knight, but a king who was respon-
sible for the safety and happiness of his subjects.
And a sad day James's knight-errantry, as it was
called, was to bring to Scotland.

James now gave orders that a great army should
meet him on the Borough Muir of Edinburgh, where
Morningside now stands. So, in the third week of
August, 1513, the great host assembled. The men
were of all ages, from lads of sixteen to old men
of sixty, and they came from all parts of the
country, from the Lowlands and Highlands and
Western Islands. To this day the Borestone in
which the royal standard was planted, and which was
in the middle of the army, can be seen fixed in the
wall of one of the streets in Morningside, which was
then all open country.

But, though James had this great army to fight
the English, the people thought that he was making
a mistake in going to war merely because Henry had
invaded France, and they feared that he would
bring a great misfortune upon Scotland by his
rashness.

Two strange stories are told how James was warned that something terrible would happen if he did go to war with England. One evening when James, with his lords all round him, was worshipping in the church of Linlithgow, which still exists, a strange figure appeared in their midst. It was a man clad in a long blue gown, with his head bare and carrying a pikestaff in his hand. Coming forward to the king, he told him that he had been sent by his mother to warn him not to go against England. Having said this, he disappeared, so that no one could lay hands on him. The other story is that in Edinburgh, at the dead of night, a voice was heard calling aloud from the Market-cross the names of the earls and lords, barons and gentlemen who, within forty days, should be summoned to judgment.

But James was determined to have his own way, and on the 22nd of August he crossed the river Tweed with his army. He spent some days in taking English castles, and dreary days they were, as it was cold and windy and wet. At last he marched to Flodden Hill, which is on the banks of the river Till, and there waited for the English army that was coming against him. This army was not commanded by Henry VIII. himself, who was now in France, but by the Earl of Surrey—the English noble who had brought Margaret Tudor to James as his bride. Surrey was old and bent with age, so that a Scottish writer calls him "an old crooked carle lying in a chariot"; but he was what James was not—a cautious and experienced general. On the 9th of September, 1513—one of the saddest days that ever dawned for Scotland—the two armies came face to face.

About a mile off from Flodden Hill, where the Scots were encamped, there is another hill on the same ridge, called Branxton Hill, which James was afraid that the English would occupy, and thus have a better fighting-ground than himself. He therefore

Twizell Bridge, crossed by the English before the Battle.

ordered his men to set fire to their tents, and under cover of the smoke to march to Branxton Hill. By the time the smoke had cleared away, the Scots had reached their new position, and there were the English before them. The two armies were arranged in the same way. The chief part of each army was in the centre, and on its sides were two

wings or divisions.   James was in the centre of the
Scots and the Earl of Surrey in the centre of the
English ; but while James fought in the ranks just
like a common soldier, Surrey remained in his
"chariot" and directed the fighting, as James also
should have done.

It was between four and five o'clock in the after-
noon when the battle began, and, as it was the month
of September, the fighting could not last long, as the
darkness must soon put an end to it.   The battle
commenced with the firing of cannon on both sides,
but the English cannon were much better than those
of the Scots, who were soon driven from their posts,
the cannoneer who led them being killed.   Then the
Scots in all the divisions became very impatient, and
did what they should not have done ; they descended
the hill to fight the English on the level ground,
whereas they should have waited till the English
came up the hill to attack them.   As the ground was
wet from the long rains, they took off their shoes to
prevent themselves from slipping as they descended
the slope.

And now the whole armies of both English and
Scots met hand to hand.   On their left wing, the
Scots were victorious, but they followed the beaten
enemy too far instead of coming to the assistance of
other parts of the army.   On their right, however, the
Scots were beaten and thrown into great confusion,
and the English who beat them then turned back
and assisted their countrymen in other parts of the
battle.   This gave the English a great advantage,
and before long only the centre of the Scottish army
stood firm.   Then the Scots formed a circle in which

were the king and his chief nobles. With their long spears couched, just as at the battle of Falkirk, they held their ground, though they were surrounded on all sides by the enemy. The English fought with bills or battle-axes, which inflicted frightful wounds. At last it became so dark that the combatants could

no longer see to use their weapons, but the circle of the Scots was still unbroken.

When the morning came, however, Surrey saw that he had won the victory, as the Scots had left the battle-field during the night. In no battle had they suffered such heavy loss. Their brave king had fallen, slain with many wounds, and among the dead were thirteen earls, fourteen lords, an archbishop, a bishop, and two abbots. There was hardly a nobleman's or a gentleman's family in all Scotland which had not some relative among the slain.

It was a great calamity that James by his rashness had brought upon his country; but the Scottish people did not remember it against him. They had liked him for his kindly ways as a king, and he had fallen on the field of battle fighting like the bravest of his men. For many a day afterwards Scotsmen had to mourn the fatal fight at Flodden; but they remembered it also with pride, as in no field had Scottish hearts and Scottish hands been firmer and truer.

---

38. SCOTLAND IN THE DAYS OF JAMES IV.

JAMES IV. (1488-1513)

In the reign of James IV. there was a Spaniard who lived for a time at his court, and who has told us something of Scotland and its people. His name was Pedro de Ayala, and he had been sent to Scotland by Ferdinand and Isabella, who ruled over part of Spain. James showed great kindness to Ayala, who therefore wrote as pleasant things as he could of James's kingdom and subjects. Here are some of the things which he wrote about the country and its inhabitants.

The men, he says, were very brave, strong, and active; and were so fond of fighting that, when they had not an enemy to fight, they fought with each other. They were very proud, and liked to appear greater and richer than they really were, and spent more money than they should have done

S

in dress and show. They were very hospitable, and, when a foreigner came among them, every one tried to be as kind to him as possible. They had one great fault, however, and that was that they were not very industrious. As for the women, he says that they were very polite, and also graceful and handsome. They dressed much better than English-women; and Ayala especially admired their head-dress, which, he says, was the most beautiful in the world. And what was this head-dress like? On the top of the head there were two horns over which a veil was hung, and, to keep the head-dress firm, hemp and flax were mixed with the natural hair. Another thing that Ayala tells us about the Scottish women is that they ruled their households and even their husbands with a rod of iron.

The country, he also says, had greatly improved during James IV.'s reign; so much so, that it was three times richer than it had ever been before. The chief reason of this was that foreigners who had settled in Scotland had taught the people many new trades and manufactures. Though the poor had not much money, they had plenty of meat, both of large and small animals; and they had also great quantities of wool and hides. There were so many fish taken from the sea, that foreigners called the country "fishy Scotland"; and there were so many wild fruits, that the inhabitants could not use them all. There were, also, great flocks of sheep, especially in the wilder parts of the country. There was not so much corn grown as there might have been, but what there was of it was very good. When harvest-time came, only the heads of the corn were cut off, and the straw was left standing—which was indeed the custom in some parts of Scotland till not so long ago. Of the towns and villages, Ayala says that they were filled with people. The houses were built of hewn stone, and had good doors and glass windows, and a great many chimneys.

This is a very different picture of Scotland from that which was given by Æneas Sylvius in the reign of James I., and perhaps Ayala's picture is too favourable. Still, there can be no doubt that Scotland greatly improved under the rule of James IV. Let us see some of the things which James did to make his people more happy and prosperous.

The most important thing for any country is that it should be safe from its enemies. Now, in the time of James IV. the other kings in Europe were all trying to have larger navies than their neighbours, so that it was necessary that Scotland should have a navy also. James therefore determined to have a fleet of armed ships built, though this was not very easily done in Scotland, as there was so little timber in the country. However, he got timber from Denmark and France, and shipwrights also from the latter country, and at last he succeeded in getting a fleet of no fewer than sixteen large ships and ten smaller ones. There was one vessel in the building of which he took great pride. It was called the *Great St Michael*, and was the largest ship then existing; and it is said that all the woods in Fife had to be cut down to build it. After James's death, however, this large ship was sold to the king of France for a great sum of money.

A very necessary thing for the happiness of a

country is that there should be just laws, and that the people should be made to obey them. Up to this time the Courts where persons were tried for breaking the laws used to meet in different parts of the country, so that it was often difficult for people to attend them. But James set up what was called a " Daily Council," which met in Edinburgh, or wherever he happened to be staying, so that every one might know where to bring his complaint before the judges. Besides this Court there were others that met in different parts of the country, and James himself used often to attend these Courts. And there was one good reason why he should attend them : most of the fines that were imposed on persons who broke the laws went into his pocket. In this way, therefore, the laws were better obeyed in James's reign than ever they had been before.

At this time, the countries of Europe were all trying to make themselves richer by trade and commerce, and James did his best to get Scotland to follow their example. For instance, he tried to persuade the people in the seaport towns to pay more atten- tion to the catching of fish, as the fish in the seas were the chief riches of Scotland. To get them to do this, he passed a law which we should think very strange nowadays. This law commanded that every seaport should build boats and have them ready to sail by an appointed day. And how were the fishermen to be got to sail the boats? Every idle man in the town was to be compelled to become a fisherman, otherwise he was not to be allowed to live in the town.

The foreign country with which Scotland carried on most trade was Flanders, now part of Belgium and France, where there were very rich merchants. Many people from Flanders (who are called Flemings) came and settled in Scotland, and they were the foreigners who taught trades and manufactures to the Scots. For example, they taught them better ways of curing and packing fish in barrels, and also better ways of making different kinds of cloth. And what things could Scotland send to the rich merchants of Flanders? This is a list of the chief things it sent: wool, hides, skins, salmon, herrings, and other fish, coarse cloth, and pearls; for at that time many pearls, though not very large ones, were found in the rivers and seas of Scotland. And what did Flanders send in return? The chief things it sent to Scotland were: silk, velvet, satin, damask, ribbons, gold and silver thread, rings with jewels, and wine—a list which shows that there must have been rich people in Scotland who could afford to buy finery.

There was still another thing to which James paid attention, and which was also very important, and that was education. A law was passed in his reign which commanded all the barons and gentry to send their sons to school from the age of eight or nine till they became good Latin scholars, for in those days many of the best books and most documents were still written in Latin. After they had learned Latin, they were to be sent to the universities to finish their education; and it should be said that in James's reign, besides the University of St Andrews, there were now two other Universities, one at Glasgow and another at Aberdeen. It has already been mentioned that printing was introduced into Scotland during James's reign, and this, of course, also helped to make the people better educated. The two men who first printed books in Scotland were called Walter Chapman and Androw Myllar, and their names should not be forgotten, as nothing has done more for the good of any country than the printing of books.

Printer's device from books printed by Androw Myllar in 1508.

It will now be seen that during James's reign Scotland made a great step forward, and that it became a happier, a richer, and a better educated country. It was in this reign, also, that Edinburgh became the capital of Scotland. Before James's days there was no town that could be called the capital, but from this time onwards Edinburgh was always considered the chief town in the kingdom. There were several reasons why Edinburgh became so important a place. In earlier times the Parliaments met in different towns ; but now they began to meet nearly always in Edinburgh. Then the chief Law

Quhare lufe gois on forse turnis the ee
Jam expert and wo is me tharfore
Hot for a luke/my lady is forlore
Thus chydand on, with lufe our burn & bent
A wofull wedow hame wart is he went

Moralitas fabule sequitur

LD worthy folk/Poete that senature
To wryte this feynit fable tuke in cure
In his gay buke of consolacion,
For oure doctryne/and gude instructioū
Quhilk in the self suppose it senyeit be
And hid vnder the cloke of poesie
yit maister trowit doctour Nicholas
Quhilk in his tyme a noble theolog was
Applyis it to gude moralitee
Ry full of frute/and seriositee
Faire phebus is the god of sapience,
Caliopee his wyf is eloquence,
Thir twa maryit gat orpheus belyve
Quhilk callit is the part intellectiue

Specimen of Printing by Androw Myllar in 1508.

Court, as we have seen, henceforth met there. In past times, also, the kings had lived now in one place and now in another ; but from this time they lived chiefly in Holyrood Palace, which therefore became the home of the Royal Court. It was for all these reasons that the people of the country came to consider Edinburgh as the capital of the kingdom.

39. SCOTLAND AFTER FLODDEN — THE HAMILTONS AND THE DOUGLASES

JAMES V. (1513-1542)

The King of Scots and many of his nobles had fallen at Flodden, and the men who had accompanied them to the fatal field were either slain or had returned to their homes. Should the Earl of Surrey, after his great victory, invade the country, who was to defend it? In Edinburgh there was great alarm, as it was thought that, if Surrey should lead his army into Scotland, he would be certain to come against Edinburgh as being the chief town in the kingdom. The provost of Edinburgh and other magistrates had been slain at Flodden, but there were brave men in the town who determined that they would defend it to the last. They gave orders that a strong wall should be built round the town, and parts of this wall are still to be seen. All the men were commanded to have their weapons in readiness, and the women to go to the churches and pray for the safety of the country. Fortunately, Surrey did not come. Though he had gained the victory, he also had lost many men in the battle, and he thought it wisest not to try to conquer Scotland.

The question now was—Who was to govern the country, since the heir to the throne was only a year and five months old? Before James IV. marched to Flodden, he had made a will appointing Queen Margaret Regent of the kingdom. About a fortnight after the battle, therefore, the young king was crowned at Stirling, and his mother was made Regent. But

News of Flodden.

some of the chief men in the country did not wish
her to be Regent, and they determined to have
another in her place. The person they chose was
the Duke of Albany, the son of that Duke of Albany
who had been driven from Scotland by his brother,
James III. Albany was very glad to come, because,
if young James and his only brother should die, he
would be the heir to the throne.

But before Albany came, there was great trouble
in the country, as some of the nobles wished Margaret,
the queen, to remain Regent. Quarrelling and fighting
soon began, and the friends of Albany made the
queen prisoner, and got the chief power into their own
hands. There was one person who was very anxious
that Albany should not become Regent, and that
was Henry VIII. The reason of this was that
Albany was the friend of the King of France, so
that, if he became ruler of Scotland, he would be
certain to be the enemy of England. Henry, therefore, did all he could to prevent Albany's coming to
Scotland. He wrote both to his sister, the Queen
Regent, and to the King of France, to ask them to
prevent his coming; and to frighten the Scots, he sent
an army into Scotland, which burned no fewer than
five towns.

In spite of Henry, however, Albany did at length
arrive in Scotland in the year 1515, more than a
year and a half after Flodden. In many ways
he was not a suitable ruler for Scotland. He was
more of a Frenchman than a Scotsman, and he could
speak neither Scots nor English. Neither was he
a wise and prudent man. He had a very violent
temper, and when he was angry he used to throw

his bonnet into the fire, and would not allow any one to take it out. An Englishman tells us that in two years Albany burned more than twelve bonnets in this way. But Albany's chief fault as a ruler was that he thought more of France than of Scotland, and wished to go to war with England only to please the King of France.

Albany found Scotland so difficult to govern, that after two years he returned to France, and left the Scots to manage their own affairs. But the country became no quieter after he had gone, as the two following stories will show.

When Albany was in Scotland, he put to death Lord Hume, Warden of the East Marches, and his brother, William Hume, both of whom had been his enemies, and afterwards he made a Frenchman, called La Bastie, Warden. After Albany had returned to France, the relatives of the two Humes determined to have their revenge. One day, when some of them were riding out, they came upon La Bastie, and at once gave chase to him. The castle of Dunbar was his nearest place of safety, and thither he rode as fast as his horse could carry him. As he was not acquainted with the roads, however, he lost his way, and ran his horse into a marsh. His pursuers soon came up with him, slew him, and cut off his head. So savage were his enemies, that one of them tied the head to his saddle-bow by the hair, which was as long as a woman's and tied up with lace, as was the fashion in France at that time.

The other story is as follows :—After Albany had left Scotland, there were two families which were constantly at war with one another, as each of them wished to have the chief power in the country. The one family was the Red Douglases, so called to distinguish them from the Black Douglases, whom James II. had ruined; and the other was the Hamiltons. The chief man of the Douglases was the Earl of Angus, son of Archibald Bell-the-Cat, who had married the Queen Regent; and the chief of the Hamiltons was the Earl of Arran, who was the grandson of that Lord Hamilton who had married the Princess Mary, the sister of James III. These two nobles were the greatest men in Scotland, and both of them were connected with the royal family. The question, then, was which of them was to get the upper hand of the other.

At last the two nobles and their followers met in a great fight. In the year 1520, the Parliament assembled in Edinburgh, and among those who came to the town were Angus and Arran, with their men. The Hamiltons were the more numerous, and the story got abroad that they meant to take the opportunity of slaying all the Douglases in the town. To find out if this was true, Gavin Douglas, Bishop of Dunkeld, who is one of the most famous of Scottish poets, went to James Beaton, Archbishop of Glasgow, who was a chief man among the Hamiltons. " Upon my conscience," said Beaton, " I know nothing of the matter," and he struck his breast with his hand, to show that he meant what he said. But, as he did so, armour was heard to rattle under his bishop's dress. "My Lord," then said Douglas, "your conscience is not good; I heard it clatter."

Bishop Douglas at once told the Earl of Angus that the Hamiltons were preparing for fight, and

Angus, collecting his men, barricaded all the closes and lanes or vennels where the Hamiltons were lodged. Then the fighting began. The Hamiltons tried to break through the barricades, but, as they were armed only with swords, while the Douglases were armed with spears, they found this very difficult, and those of them who did break through were soon slain. Not long after the fight began, 800 horsemen, the friends of the Douglases, rode into the town, and then the Hamiltons had little hope of victory. Soon they were driven out of the town, many being slain ; and the Earl of Arran and one of his sons made their escape, both mounted on one cart-horse. This fight was called "Clear the Causeway," as the Douglases had swept the Hamiltons from the streets of the town.

When the Duke of Albany had left Scotland, he had promised to return in six months, but four years and a half passed before he actually came. On his former visit he had stayed two years, but this time he stayed only eleven months, and the reason why he left so soon was the same as before. He wished the Scots to invade England, but even the nobles who were friendly to him refused to do this, as they did not wish to run the risk of another Flodden. But if Scotland was saved from a second Flodden, Henry VIII. made her pay in another way. He sent the Earl of Surrey, son of the Surrey who won the victory at Flodden, into Scotland with an army of 9000 men, which burned both the abbey and the town of Jedburgh.

By this time we might have thought that the Scots had had enough of Albany, but he came once more, for the third time, bringing with him a band of French soldiers to make war on England. Exactly the same thing happened as before. He led an army of Scots and French to the Border, and again the Scottish nobles refused to invade England. Then Albany saw that he could not have his own way, and he left Scotland for the last time, after only about eight months' stay.

Now that the Scottish nobles were left to themselves, they again began to quarrel as to which of them was to have the chief power. At last the Earl of Angus again proved the strongest, and got the young king into his power. Then for a time the Red Douglases ruled the country. They kept the king like a prisoner, and treated him so harshly that he never forgave them, and determined that he would one day pay them back. At length he succeeded in escaping from them in a very clever way.

James was staying in Falkland Castle, in Fife, and it happened that the chiefs of the Douglases were away on business of their own. Now was the time, James thought, to try to make his escape. He told the person who was left in charge of him that he wished to hunt next morning, and that he would go to bed early. In the middle of the night, however, he slipped on his clothes and went to the stables, where a groom was waiting for him. Three swift horses were soon saddled, one for James and the others for two of his servants. As fast as their horses could carry them they rode through Fife, and reached Stirling Castle just as the day broke. James was now out of the Douglases' hands, and he was soon to make them pay for all their harshness to him.

40. "THE POOR MAN'S KING"

JAMES V. (1513-1542)

James V. was only seventeen years of age when he escaped from the Douglases, but, when he began to rule for himself, he showed that he had all the spirit of a full-grown man. When he was a child, the famous poet, Sir David Lyndsay, had charge of his education, and he could not have had a better teacher; but he was so often taken away from him that he learned very little. At the age of twelve he could not read a letter written in English, and when he grew up he could not speak French well, which most kings then did.

In many ways, however, he was the right kind of king for Scotland at this time. He was of the middle height, strong in body, and as brave as his father. It is told of him that, if he saw a face once, he never forgot it, which is a great advantage to a king. As he had red hair, his people called him the Red Tod or Fox. He was fond of going about the country in disguise, and strange stories are told of the adventures he passed through. The common people liked him so much, that they called him "The Poor Man's King." On the other hand, he did not get on so well with the nobles as his father had done, and for this reason, as we shall see, his reign had a most unhappy end.

The first thought in James's mind when he began to rule for himself was to have his revenge on the Douglases. "I vow," he said, "that Scotland will not hold us both," and he acted on his word. First

he banished them beyond the river Spey, and forbade
any of them to come within six miles of him, wherever
he happened to be. Then he got the Parliament to
pass a law taking all their estates from them and

James V.

banishing them from Scotland. It was not so easy
to carry out this law, however, as the Douglases had
so much power in the country, but at last James
succeeded in having his full revenge. The chiefs of
the Douglases were compelled to flee to England;

but they were one day to show James that he had made a mistake in treating them so sternly.

Having conquered the Douglases, James now set himself to make the laws obeyed throughout the whole country. There were two parts of the kingdom where the inhabitants behaved as if there was no law in the land; namely, the Borders and the Highlands and Western Islands. He began with the Borders first.

The people on the Borders were divided into clans, just like the Highlanders, and each clan had a chief of its own. These chiefs were constantly at war, either with each other or with the English on the other side of the Border. Unlike the Highlanders, the Borderers always rode on horseback, and their way of attacking their enemies was to come upon them suddenly, oftenest in the darkness, burn everything that would burn, and carry off cattle and sheep and whatever they thought of any value.

James's first step was to seize a number of their chiefs and put them in prison; but there was one chief and one clan who had done more mischief than all the others, and whom he determined to punish more severely. This chief was John Armstrong, the head of the clan of the Armstrongs. Within a short time, the Armstrongs had burned fifty-two churches in Scotland, and carried off much plunder from England; and they boasted that they would do what they liked, in spite of either the King of Scotland or the King of England.

An old ballad tells us how James punished Armstrong and his clan. He rode to the Borders at the head of a band of armed men, and Armstrong

T

came to meet him, grandly dressed, and attended by four-and-twenty gentlemen as gaily dressed as himself. "What lacks this knave that a king should have?" exclaimed James, and he ordered Armstrong and all his followers to be hanged on the spot.

After punishing the wild Border chiefs, James next set about quieting the Highlands and the Western

Johnnie Armstrong's Tower.

Islands. We saw that his father, James IV., had made the chiefs in these parts both respect and like him, and that many of them had followed him to Flodden at the head of their clans. After that battle, however, they again began to quarrel with each other, and made war as if there was no king in the country. But James V. showed himself as clever as his father at managing the Highlanders. He punished some of the chiefs and made friends with others, and at last he made the Highlands and Islands as quiet as they had been in the days of his father.

But James had a far more difficult task before him than the quieting of the Highlands and the Borders. We have seen that for more than two hundred years Scotland had been the friend of France and the enemy of England. But an event now happened that for a time made Scotland more than ever the enemy of England and the friend of France. In the year 1531 Henry VIII. got himself made head of the English Church, and a short time afterwards he broke away from the Church of Rome, and England became a Protestant country. As most of the other countries of Europe remained Roman Catholic, Henry was afraid that these countries would some day all unite against him and conquer England.

Henry was very anxious, therefore, to have Scotland on his side, and he did all he could to get James to be his friend. He tried to get James to marry his daughter, the Princess Mary, who was afterwards Queen Mary of England, but James would not have her. Then he tried to compel James to be friends with him, and in ways that only made the English and Scots dislike each other more than ever. One thing he did was to get many of James's nobles to take sides with England against France, which some of these nobles thought was the right thing to do for the sake of Scotland itself.

And what were the reasons why James preferred to be friendly with France rather than with England? One reason was that he was afraid that what Henry really wished was to make himself king of Scotland as well as England. And, as we know, he had good reason to fear this, as almost every king of England since Edward I. had tried in some way to be the master of Scotland. Another reason was that James did not wish to become a Protestant, and at this time most of his subjects were of the same opinion as himself and did not wish to give up the religion of Rome. There were already, however, a few Protestants in Scotland, and as it was these men who began the Reformation which was to make such a great change in the country, something must now be said of them.

---

41. THE BEGINNINGS OF THE REFORMATION—THE ROUT OF SOLWAY MOSS

James V. (1513-1542)

It was in the first years of James's reign that the Reformation began in Germany under Martin Luther, and soon Luther's opinions began to spread into other countries, and into Scotland among them. Books teaching these opinions were brought in ships to Scotland, and many people began to read them. In the year 1525 an Act of Parliament was passed forbidding the bringing in of these books; but the books still continued to be brought, as many were eager to know about the new teaching.

One of the first Scotsmen to preach Luther's doctrines was Patrick Hamilton. But, as we know, there was a law which ordered that any one who taught heresy, as it was called, should be put to death, and we have seen that it was by this law that Paul Craw and James Resby had formerly been burned. Hamilton knew quite well, therefore, that in preaching the new doctrine he ran the risk of losing his life. But he was so anxious to teach his countrymen what he believed, that he was ready to die rather than be silent. So he went on preaching, till at last he was taken and burned at St Andrews as a heretic.

As Hamilton was the first Scotsman who died for the new doctrines, he is called the "Proto-martyr of the Scottish Reformation." And he was not the only one who died for his religion in the reign of James V. After his death, no fewer than nine persons suffered the same fate, which proves that the clergy of the old Church were becoming alarmed at the spread of heresy. But, as James consented to the burning of heretics, this shows that he was determined that Scotland should remain in the Church of Rome.

The last years of James's reign became more and more unhappy. Many of his nobles thought he was wrong in being friendly with France rather than with England, and there were constant quarrels between him and them. Then, as his nobles would not support him, he had to trust more and more to the bishops, and this made the nobles angrier than ever. But James's most dangerous enemy was Henry VIII., who never gave up trying to get power over Scotland. James, however, was just as determined to remain the ally of France, and he let Henry know this by two steps which he took. In the year 1536 he went to France and married Madeleine, a daughter of Francis I. As she was very delicate in health, however, she died a short time after she came to

Scotland, and it was at her death that for the first time " doole weeds," as mourning dress was called, were worn. Of course, this marriage of James enraged Henry VIII. very much, but he was still more enraged, when two years later, in the year 1538, James married another Frenchwoman, Mary of Lorraine, who became the mother of Mary, Queen of Scots.

All this time, in spite of their constant quarrelling, there was no open war between James and Henry, though there was often fighting on the Borders. At last, in the year 1542, the two kings did go to open war with each other, and it was Henry who began it. He sent the Earl of Surrey, now the Duke of Norfolk, into Scotland, with an army which burned Roxburgh and Kelso and about twenty villages. Then James assembled an army of 36,000 men and marched to Fala Moor, about fourteen miles south-east of Edinburgh. When he wished to follow the Duke of Norfolk into England, however, his nobles told him, just as they had told the Regent Albany, that they would not allow their followers to accompany him. What they said was that James was fighting for France and not for Scotland, and that, if the army entered England, it might be defeated and the king slain or taken prisoner, and then Scotland would be in the same state as it was after Flodden. James was, of course, bitterly disappointed, but there was nothing for it but to disband the army and let the nobles have their way.

But James was determined to pay England back for Norfolk's invasion, and with the help of the rich clergy he raised another army, though not so large as the one that had met on Fala Moor. At the head of this second army James marched to the west Border, and reached the town of Lochmaben, in Dumfriesshire. While James remained in that town, the Scots crossed the river Esk one morning before daybreak and began to plunder in the usual way. But the English commanders had known that the Scots were coming, and they suddenly descended upon them when they were on ground where they had no room to move.

What is very strange is that up till this moment the Scots had no leader. However, just when the enemy appeared before them, a great favourite of James, named Sir Oliver Sinclair, announced that he had been appointed leader. But the nobles who were present were indignant that a man of lower birth than themselves should be put over them, and they refused to obey him. Then, while the Scots were quarrelling among themselves, the English came on, and though they had very few men compared with the Scots, they gained an easy victory. The Scots were driven across a ford of the river Esk into the Solway Moss. Never had Scotsmen been so disgracefully beaten by the English, and all owing to the quarrelling of the leaders. Only twenty men were slain, but many were drowned and twelve hundred were taken prisoners, among whom were two earls, five barons, and about five hundred gentlemen. This shameful defeat was called the "Rout of Solway Moss."

When James was told of the disgraceful rout of his army, he lost all heart. Of late years everything seemed to have gone against him. The conduct of his nobles had given him much trouble; for some

time he had not been in good health; and within
two years his only two lawful children had died. He
thought no more of fighting his enemies, and he
went to his palace at Falkland, where he was so ill
that he had to take to his bed. There news was
brought to him of the birth of the child who was
afterwards Mary, Queen of Scots. He asked whether

[Photo by Valentine.

Falkland Palace.

the child was a boy or a girl, and, when he was told
that the child was a girl, he said : " It cam' wi' a lass,
and it will gang wi' a lass "—meaning that the
crown had come to the Stewarts by a woman,
Marjory Bruce, the daughter of Robert I., and
that it would be lost to them through the girl that
was now born. About a week afterwards James
died. There had been many sad deaths among his

ancestors, but James's end was perhaps the saddest of them all.

The country was not so happy and prosperous in the reign of James as in that of his father, but this was not his fault. He was only an infant when he became king, and we have seen that till he grew up the great nobles quarrelled so much among themselves that there was no peace in the land. And when James did grow up, he had so many troubles with the nobles, and especially with Henry VIII., that he could not do so much for the good of his people as he would have wished. In spite of this, however, the common people all liked him, and, as has already been said, he was called " The Poor Man's King." There was one thing he did which shows that he really wished the good of his subjects. In order that everybody might get justice when they went to law, he set up in Edinburgh the Court of Session, which to this day is the great Law Court of Scotland.

---

42. THE REIGN OF MARY—BEGINNING OF A NEW TIME IN SCOTLAND

Mary, the daughter of James V., was only a week old when she succeeded to the throne. Again, therefore, as had so often happened before, there was to be a long minority, during which the country would be without a real head. And of all the minorities this was to be one of the most unhappy. Just as in former times, when the sovereign was a child, the nobles quarrelled among themselves as to who should have the chief power in the kingdom. And what made matters worse was that the King of England more than once sent armies into Scotland, which burned many towns and villages, and otherwise did much harm to the inhabitants, especially to the poorer ones. As usual, indeed, it was the poor who suffered most from the misfortunes that came upon the country. Mary's reign, therefore, had not a happy beginning, and it was to have as unhappy an end.

While Mary was queen, great changes took place, which made Scotland in many ways an entirely different country. Before beginning to tell the story of her reign, let us see what the chief of these changes were.

The greatest event of Mary's reign was what is called the Reformation. Almost from the time when Scotland became one kingdom,—more than four hundred years before the time of Mary,—its people had belonged to the Church of Rome, of which the Pope was the head. But in Mary's reign the Church of Rome came to an end in Scotland, which then became a Protestant country.

Now, in changing its religion, Scotland had to make another great change. For more than two hundred years the Scots had been the enemies of England and the friends of France. But, when Scotland became Protestant, it could no longer be the ally of France, which remained a Roman Catholic country. On the other hand, England like Scotland became Protestant; and to defend themselves against the Catholic countries, they found it necessary to become allies, though they had so long been enemies.

In the end, as we know, England and Scotland

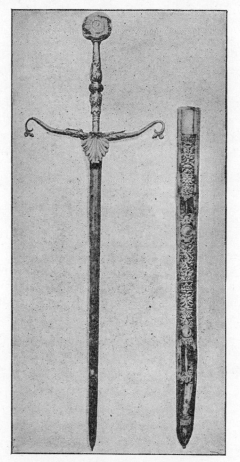

Sword of State of Scotland.
(Presented to James V. by Pope Julius II.)

were united under one ruler, James VI. of Scotland, who was also James I. of England. But, if Scotland had been a Catholic country, this union could not have taken place. We know, too, that about a hundred years after the Union of the Crowns of Scotland and England their parliaments were also united, which could not have happened either had the two countries been of different religions.

We now see how a new time in the history of Scotland began during the reign of Queen Mary, and chiefly owing to the Reformation. Had Scotland not changed its religion, it would have gone on just as it had been doing for hundreds of years. It would have continued to be the ally of France and not of England. The Crowns of England and Scotland would not have been united, and neither would their parliaments; and at the present day there might not have been a United Kingdom, ruled by one sovereign.

We saw how at the beginning Scotland was made up of four different kingdoms, and that it was only after hundreds of years that these four kingdoms were made into one. Now we are to see how Scotland became part of the United Kingdom of Great Britain and Ireland, and of the British Empire with its colonies all over the world.

----

43. A BROKEN TREATY AND ITS RESULTS
1542-1545

MARY (1542-1567)

The great question at the beginning of Mary's reign was—Which of the two parties in the country—the friends of France or the friends of England—was to get the upper hand? What the friends of England said was, that, as the Scots and the English lived in the same island and spoke the same language, it was foolish of them to go on continually fighting with each other,

Oak Cradle of Mary, Queen of Scots.

and that it would be best for both that they should be ruled by one king. If Scotland continued to be the ally of France, she would be constantly getting into trouble with England, and there would be other fatal defeats like those at Flodden and at Solway Moss. On the other hand, the friends of France thought that if England and Scotland were united under one ruler, Scotland would no longer be an independent kingdom, and would become merely a part of England. Besides, Scotland was still a

Catholic country, while England was now Protestant, and the difference of their religions would prevent them from ever becoming really friendly with each other.

At first, it seemed as if the friends of England were to win the day. The regent, or governor, who was chosen to rule the country was James, the second Earl of Arran, who was the next heir to the throne, if the infant queen should die. Arran was friendly to the Protestants and was almost a Protestant himself, and so was more inclined to England than to France. When, therefore, Henry VIII. proposed that his son, Edward, a boy five years old, should marry the Queen of Scots, Arran was quite willing that the marriage should be arranged. But most of the Scottish people did not wish for the marriage, as they thought that what Henry really wanted was to make himself master of Scotland.

Henry, however, was determined that the marriage should take place by fair means or foul. And we can easily understand why he was so anxious that the two countries should be united, for so long as Scotland was his enemy, there was always a danger that she and other enemies might combine to attack England at once. Now, at the battle of Solway Moss, as we have seen, a number of Scottish nobles and gentlemen had been taken prisoners, and what Henry did was to allow most of them to return to Scotland on the condition that they would help Arran to bring about the marriage between Edward and Mary. These persons came to be called the "English lords" or the "assured Scots," because they were known to have made promises to Henry VIII.

With the help of the "English lords," Arran did
succeed in getting the Scottish Parliament to agree

Mary of Lorraine, Mother of Queen Mary.

to a treaty of marriage, which was finally arranged
at Greenwich on the 1st of July, 1543. By this treaty

Mary was to marry Edward when she was eleven years old, and till that time there was to be peace between the two countries. Henry would have liked to have two other things put in the treaty—namely, that Mary should be placed in his keeping till the marriage took place, and that the Scots should break their alliance with France; but the Scots would not agree to either of these proposals. As the Parliament that made this treaty also passed a law which allowed the people to read the Bible in Scots or English, it seemed as if Scotland were about to ally itself with England and to become Protestant. In the end this did take place, but, as we shall see, many terrible events were to happen before that time came.

There were two persons in Scotland who were determined that it should remain Catholic and should not become the ally of England; these were Mary of Lorraine, the queen's mother, and Cardinal Beaton. Mary of Lorraine was a Frenchwoman and a Catholic, so that she was, of course, all for France; and, as Cardinal Beaton was the chief man in the Church, he also disliked England and the Protestants. Beaton was one of the cleverest men in the country and had great wealth and power, and most of the nobles and most of the people were on his side. Soon, therefore, he proved too strong for the governor Arran, who was both foolish and weak. He got the infant queen into his power, compelled Arran to do penance for having favoured the Protestants, and then had the queen crowned at Stirling (1543). But Beaton did more; he got the Scottish Parliament to break the marriage-treaty with England, and to pass severe laws against heretics, so that all Arran's work was undone.

And what did Henry VIII. think of these doings of Beaton? He was so furious at seeing his plans defeated, that he determined to make all Scotland pay for the breaking of the treaty. One Sunday morning (May, 1544) the people of Edinburgh and

Holyrood Palace, with Ruins of Chapel.

Leith saw a great fleet of ships in the Firth of Forth, just off the village of Newhaven.

It was the Earl of Hertford, with an army aboard the ships, who had been sent by Henry to take Edinburgh, the capital of the kingdom. Arran and Beaton collected an army to defend the town, but after very little fighting, they both fled to Linlithgow. Then, after taking Leith, Hertford marched against Edinburgh. Its citizens tried to defend it, but the English were too strong for them

U

and the town was soon taken, though not the Castle. As he could not take the Castle, Hertford set fire to the town and to Holyrood Palace. The burning lasted three days, and, as the poor women of the town watched the flames, they cried, "Wo worth the Cardinal! wo worth the Cardinal"—meaning that it was Beaton who had brought this calamity on the town. And not only Edinburgh, but all the surrounding country, was laid waste by Hertford's soldiers. On his march home to England, also, he burnt every village through which he passed.

Henry was not satisfied even with this terrible punishment of the Scots. Next year (1545) he sent another army to invade Scotland, but it was cleverly defeated by the Scots at Ancrum Moor, above the village of Ancrum. The very same year, however, Henry sent still another army against Scotland, this time again under the Earl of Hertford. The English earl led his troops through Berwickshire, and, as it was the time of harvest, he burnt all the crops; and before he returned to England, he had destroyed five towns and two hundred and forty villages, as well as the abbeys of Kelso, Melrose, Dryburgh, and Eccles. The Scots themselves said that no English army had ever done so much mischief before. And Henry brought all this misery on so many innocent people simply because the Scots would not have their queen married to his son, and would not have him for their ally instead of the king of France.

44. GEORGE WISHART AND CARDINAL BEATON. 1545-1547.

MARY (1542-1567)

Though Cardinal Beaton had gained the victory over Arran, there were many people in Scotland who

Cardinal Beaton.

were beginning to think that it would be better for the country if it became Protestant, and joined with

England rather than with France. Indeed, Cardinal Beaton was so alarmed at the increasing number of Protestants that he determined to stamp them out. At Perth, for example, three men and one woman were put to death as heretics, and in other ways he tried to prevent the new religious opinions from spreading in the country.

At the end of the year 1545, however, there came one to Scotland who helped greatly to make the new doctrines known to the people. This was George Wishart, afterwards known as the martyr. In the reign of James V. he had been compelled to leave the country on account of his religion, but he now thought it his duty to return and preach the truth to his fellow-countrymen. He was a very eloquent preacher, and was much liked by his friends, one of whom says that he was "courteous, lowly, lovely, glad to teach, and desirous to learn." Wishart knew quite well that he ran the risk of his life in teaching doctrines contrary to those of the Church, and when he preached there was usually with him some friend armed with a two-handed sword. It was chiefly in Dundee and in Ayrshire that he preached, as in these places there were many who wished to hear his teaching.

One time, however, Wishart came to preach at Haddington, and among his hearers there was the man who was to do more than anyone else to bring about the Reformation in Scotland. This was the famous John Knox, who was already so keen a reformer that it was he who carried the two-handed sword when Wishart preached in Haddington, Knox's native town. On the third night, after

Wishart had come to Haddington, he went to the house of a friend not far off. In the middle of the night, the house was surrounded by soldiers, and he

George Wishart.

was carried captive to St Andrews. A little more than a month afterwards, he was burned before the palace of Cardinal Beaton in that town, the Cardinal looking on all the while, for it was then considered right that the chief men in the Church and State should be present when heretics were put to death.

Cardinal Beaton had made many enemies in Scotland. Some hated him for injuries he had done to themselves; some were angry with him for having caused the death of Wishart; and others thought that it was he who had brought all the misfortunes on the country by breaking the marriage-treaty with England. Just three months after the death of Wishart, a band of Beaton's enemies broke into the Castle of St Andrews, which was his Bishop's Palace. It was early in the morning, and the cardinal was in bed. When he heard the noise, he tried to barricade the door; but his enemies soon broke it open, and, though he prayed hard that they would spare his life, they slew him on the spot. When the citizens of St Andrews awoke next morning they saw the dead body of the great cardinal hanging on the walls of the castle.

But, though Cardinal Beaton was slain, the friends of France had still the chief power in the country, and the Regent Arran and Mary of Lorraine determined to punish the murderers, who had shut themselves up in the Castle of St Andrews as their safest place of refuge. The castle was very strong, however, and the men who defended it knew that they were fighting for their lives. Besides the murderers of the cardinal, a number of other persons who were in fear of their lives also took refuge in the castle, so that there came to be as many as one hundred and twenty men to defend it. Among those who entered it was John Knox, who now for the first time began to preach the doctrines he had learned from George Wishart.

Arran at the head of an army laid siege to the castle. He had two great cannons with him, which his soldiers called Crook-mouth and Deaf Meg, but the gunners were not skilful, and they did very little harm to the strong walls. Month after month passed away and still the castle was not taken. At last, a fleet was sent from France with cannons and skilful gunners aboard. Before a month passed, the walls of the castle were so damaged by the French guns that the defenders were compelled to surrender. The arrangement made was that all their lives were to be spared, but that they were all to be taken to France. When they arrived there, those who were gentlemen were put in prison, and those who were not gentlemen were made galley-slaves. Among the last was John Knox, who was only a farmer's son, and for nineteen months the man who was to be the great reformer of Scotland was a galley-slave, and had for his companions the worst of criminals, for, as a rule, only such persons were condemned to the galleys.

---

45. A QUARREL BETWEEN OLD FRIENDS.
1547-1558.

MARY (1542-1567)

Henry VIII. died in the year 1547, and he died without seeing his son Edward married to Mary, Queen of Scots, which had been his great wish. As Edward was only a boy at the time of his father's death, the Earl of Hertford, who now became Duke of Somerset, was made Protector of England. It was Somerset, as we know, who had led the armies that had burned Edinburgh and done so much mischief in other parts of the country, and when he became Protector, he was as anxious as Henry VIII. to compel the Scots to break their alliance with France.

In the very year that Henry died, therefore, Somerset led an army into Scotland to try to force the Scots to make friends with England and to give up their alliance with France. But even the Scottish nobles who were favourable to England did not think this the right way to make friends, and they came with their followers to assist the Regent Arran in fighting the invaders. The two armies met at Pinkie, near Musselburgh, with the river Esk between them. The Scots had more men than the English, but they had not a skilful general to lead them. Instead of waiting for the enemy to attack them, as they should have done, they crossed the river, and fought on ground which hardly gave them a chance of gaining the victory. The result was that their ranks were soon broken, and they began to flee in all directions. Fifteen hundred of them were taken prisoners, and about ten thousand were slain, while the English had only very few wounded or killed. So melancholy a day was this for the Scots that they called it "Black Saturday," because it was a Saturday on which the battle was fought.

After the battle of Pinkie, the English remained in the country, and, as there was no Scottish army to resist them, they did all the mischief they could by burning and plundering towns and castles. But all this made the Scots hate England the more. They sent to France for help, and a French fleet was sent with 6000 trained soldiers. Then the Parliament met, and it decided that the young queen should be sent to France, where she would be safe from the English. When Mary landed in France, Henry II., who was

From Drawing by Clouet.]

Mary, Queen of Scots, as a Girl.

then king, was greatly pleased. "France and Scotland," he exclaimed, "are now one country"—meaning, that ever afterwards Scotland would be only a part of France. He was soon to learn that he was mistaken.

After eighteen months of fighting, the Scots and the French together drove the English out of the country. But, though the Scots and the French had fought side by side, they came more and more to dislike each other, just as they had always done when they were brought together. And events began to happen which were to make them bitter enemies.

In the year 1554, Mary of Lorraine got herself made regent in place of Arran, who was created Duke of Châtelherault, in France, to please him for the loss of his office. The Queen-regent at once began to govern Scotland just as if it were a part of France. She put Frenchmen in most of the high offices, which, of course, made the Scottish nobles very indignant. Then she wished to have a standing army like the kings of France, which meant that hired soldiers would be brought into the country, and that a tax would have to be raised to pay them. The nobles would not listen to such a proposal, and declared that they were able to defend their country with their own arms, as their ancestors had done in the past. She also wished to invade England with an army ; but the nobles told her what they had told the regent Albany and James V.—that they would not make war on England for the sake of France, and thus bring evil on their own country. By governing the country in this way the queen-regent made herself very unpopular with most of the nobles, and, as the French soldiers in the country were constantly quarrelling with the common people, the French began to be hated more and more both by high and low. Indeed, most Scotsmen were now thinking that France was a more dangerous enemy than England.

In the year 1558, however, an event happened which made it seem as if France and Scotland would one day be united under one sovereign. Mary, Queen of Scots, was married to Francis, the Dauphin of France and the heir to the French throne. At the time of the marriage two treaties were arranged, one of which was made known, and the other was kept secret. By the public treaty it was arranged that Scotland would remain an independent country. The secret treaty, however, which Mary signed, was very different. By this compact the king of France was to become king of Scotland if Mary should die without leaving an heir, and in the meantime Henry II. was to be the master of Scotland till he was paid for her board and education. If the Scottish people had known of this secret bargain, it would have made them dislike the French even more than they already did. But, as we are now to see, things turned out very differently from what Henry II. expected.

Mary of Lorraine had other enemies in Scotland besides those who hated her French ways of governing. Since the burning of George Wishart, the new religious opinions had gone on spreading more and more. In the year 1550 another heretic, named Adam Wallace, was burned on the Castle Hill of Edinburgh ; but this did more harm than good to the Church, as people began to hate seeing men put to death for their religion.

The clergy tried to stop the reading of books which taught the new doctrines, but they found this was impossible. Bibles, translated into English, were now read by persons who had not read them before. And besides the Bible there were other writings which taught people to despise and hate the old Church. In the plays of Sir David Lyndsay, James V.'s teacher when he was a boy, the clergy were mocked at for their idleness and ignorance. But the book which, after the Bible, did most to spread the new teaching was one called "Good and Godly Ballads." In this book it was taught that the Church of Rome was not the true Church, and that its clergy were so idle and vicious that they could not be worse.

In the year 1553 an event happened which greatly helped to bring on the Reformation in Scotland. In that year Mary Tudor became queen of England, and, as she was a Catholic, she drove many of the Protestants from that country, some of whom came to Scotland and went about teaching their opinions. In the year 1555, also, John Knox returned from the Continent and remained ten months, preaching in different parts of the kingdom, though at last he had to flee, as the clergy wished to have him burned like Wishart and Wallace.

At length, in the year 1557, a step was taken which brought the Reformation very near. Four nobles, the earls of Argyle, Glencairn, Morton, and Lord Lorne (son of Argyle), and a gentleman named Erskine of Dun, drew up a paper in which they stated what the Protestants wished. This paper is called the "First Covenant," as there were other covenants in later times; and those who drew it up called themselves the "Lords of the Congregation," by the Congregation being meant all the Protestants in the country. And what was written in the "Covenant"? That those who wrote it gave up the Church of Rome and would do all in their power to make the country Protestant.

We now see in what a difficult position the queen-regent was. Should the Lords of the Congregation have their way, Scotland would become a Protestant country, and the result would be that it could no longer be the ally of France, which belonged to the Church of Rome. We cannot wonder, therefore, that she did all in her power to prevent the country from changing its religion, being a Catholic and French-woman as she was. In the year 1558, still another heretic, a very old, old man, named Walter Mill, was burned at St Andrews; but he was to be the last who was to suffer for his religion in this way. For it had at length come to this—that either the Protestants or the queen-regent must rule the country. Only the sword could settle the dispute, and it was the sword that did settle it.

----

46. FALL OF THE OLD CHURCH.   1559-1560

MARY (1542-1567)

Why did John Knox and others like him wish Scotland to change its religion? The first and chief reason was that they believed that the religion of the Church of Rome was not the religion of the Bible. Another reason was that they thought the clergy were doing more harm than good to the people. In the days of King David I. and of the kings that immediately followed him, the clergy had done much good to the country, but for a long time previous to Mary's reign, they had been more and more neglect-

ing their duties as the ministers of religion.   The best
among them were quite aware of this, and saw that,
if the monks and priests and bishops did not reform
their lives, the people would some day rise against
them.

There were, indeed, many reasons why the people
should be discontented with the Church at the
time of the Reformation.   More than a third of all
the wealth in the country was in the hands of the
clergy; and the bishops and abbots lived in luxury,
while they did not give nearly so much to the poor
as they ought to have done.   The poorest people
were compelled to make gifts to the Church, otherwise
the priest would neither marry them, bury them, nor
baptize their children.   Many of the clergy, also,
lived such bad lives and were so ignorant, that
they were quite unfit to be ministers of religion,
and were the laughing-stock of the people.   Men
like Knox, therefore, said that a Church which allowed
such a state of things could not be the true Church,
and that it was their duty to try to put an end
to it.

When the Protestants and the queen-regent were
just in the middle of their quarrel, the man arrived in
Scotland whose zeal and eloquence were to do so
much to further the cause of the Reformation.   This
was John Knox, who had again returned (1559) to his
native country after his long exile on the Continent.
Knox was the very leader the reformers needed.
Though he was small of stature and not very strong
in body, he had such courage that it was said of him
that "he never feared the face of man."   He was
so eloquent, that a French Catholic said that

"he managed men's souls as he wished," and an English Protestant said that in one hour he could by his voice put more life into his hearers "than five hundred trumpets blustering" in their ears.

In the beginning of May, 1559, Knox preached a sermon in the parish church of Perth, in which he said that the worship of the Church of Rome was idolatry, and that it ought to be put an end to. Before all the congregation had left the church, a priest began to say mass, when a boy made some remark. The priest gave the boy a box on the ear; the boy threw a stone at the priest, which missed him and broke an image; and then there was a great uproar among those who were still in the church. All the pictures and images were torn down, spoiled, and broken. Next the mob rushed to the monasteries of the Franciscans and Dominicans and to the Abbey Church, and in two days there was nothing but the walls of these buildings left standing. Knox did not approve of these doings, and he called those engaged in them the "rascal multitude," but it was impossible to stop them; and in other towns, St Andrews among them, where Knox also preached, the same things were done.

When the queen-regent heard of what had taken place at Perth, she at once ordered an army of Frenchmen and Scots to be collected, and sent it against that town. But the Protestants also raised an army, and so at last war had begun. For a whole year this civil war lasted, though there was not constant fighting all the time. The chief leader of the Protestants was the Lord James Stewart, a half-brother of Queen Mary, who after Knox did more than any-

John Knox and one of his Friends.

one else to advance the cause of the Reformation ; and by his side were the earls of Argyle and Glencairn, and other nobles. If the Scots had been left to fight it out among themselves, the queen-regent would easily have been beaten, as her enemies were not only the Protestants, but all those who had come to fear and hate the French.

But the regent had trained French soldiers on her side, and more were sent to her assistance from France, so that she was likely to gain the victory in the end. Then the Protestant leaders took a step which shows how great a change had come over the country. They asked Queen Elizabeth, the Protestant sovereign of England who had succeeded the Catholic Mary, to send an army to their help. The English army came, and English and Scots together laid siege to the town of Leith, where the French had fortified themselves. This was surely a remarkable thing to have happened — the Scots fighting along with the English, who had so long been their enemies, against the French, who had so long been their friends.

The French in Leith were at last compelled to surrender, and on the 6th of July, 1560, a treaty, called the Treaty of Leith, or of Edinburgh, was arranged between the three countries—France, England, and Scotland. By this treaty it was agreed that the French soldiers were to leave Scotland, and that a Parliament was to meet on the 10th of July—four days after the treaty was signed. As Mary of Lorraine had died during the siege of Leith, it was also arranged that a council of twelve persons should govern the country till

X

Queen Mary returned from France. At the end of the civil war, therefore, the Protestants had gained almost everything they had wished.

The next thing to be done was the calling of the Parliament, which, however, did not meet on the 10th of July, but on the 3rd of August. Of all the Scottish Parliaments that ever met, this is the one which is best remembered, and for this reason, that it put an end to the Church of Rome as the national church of Scotland. In one day it passed three Acts, the first of which cast off the Pope, the second condemned all doctrines and practices contrary to those of the Protestants, and the third forbade the saying of mass. If any person broke these laws once, his property was to be taken from him ; if he broke them a second time, he was to be banished ; and if he broke them a third time, he was to be put to death. These seem very cruel laws to us, but they were not new in Scotland. In those days the law was, that if a person committed the same crime thrice, no matter how small the crime was, he was to be executed. It should be added, however, that the law was hardly ever carried out, and that no one was ever put to death in Scotland for breaking these laws against the Church of Rome.

The old Church had now been pulled down, but a new one had still to be set up. The Parliament, therefore, asked the Protestant ministers to draw up a " Confession of Faith," that is, a statement of the doctrines which the members of the new Church were to believe. This was easily done, and in three days the Confession was ready.

Next the ministers had to prepare another document to show how the Church was to be governed.

This document is called the "First Book of Discipline," and, if some things written in it had been carried out, it would have been a good thing for Scotland. For example, one thing it laid down was that there should be a school in every parish, and a more advanced school in the large towns ; and that every clever boy should pass through both of these schools, and attend the universities. But this proposal was not carried out for want of money. And one of the reasons why there was not money was that the nobles seized a great deal of the property that had belonged to the old Church, and which should have been used for the good of the country. Indeed, some of the nobles, though not all of them, helped to put an end to the old Church simply because they expected to get a share of its riches.

By Act of Parliament, Protestantism had now been made the religion of the country, and the first General Assembly of the new Church of Scotland met in 1560. But it must not be forgotten that there were even now more Catholics than Protestants in Scotland, and for many years to come it was not at all unlikely that the religion of Rome might be restored.

---

47. QUEEN MARY AND JOHN KNOX—QUEEN MARY AND ELIZABETH. 1561-1565.

In the year 1558, as we have seen, Mary, Queen of Scots, was married to Francis, the Dauphin of France. The next year, Henry II., the father of Francis, died, and Francis succeeded him, so that

Mary was now queen of France as well as of Scotland. After reigning for only about a year and a half, however, Francis died; and then Mary found

Mary, Queen of Scots.

that it was best that she should return to Scotland. On the morning of the 19th of August, 1561, the fleet that brought her home appeared in the Roads of Leith. It was not a very cheerful morning on which she arrived, as there was a thick mist on land and sea. Her subjects, however, tried to show how happy they were at her return. At night a band came to Holyrood House, where she had been taken, and played tunes on three-stringed fiddles, though her French friends thought the music very bad.

After thirteen years Mary was now in her native land and among her own subjects, but how could she look forward with any pleasure to reigning over them? She had come from the sunny land of France, where she had been accustomed to gaieties and grandeur which she could not find in Scotland. Then she was a Catholic and she loved France, and how was she to rule a people that now hated France and had set up the Protestant religion in place of the religion of Rome? It would have required the wisest and most experienced of rulers instead of a girl of eighteen, as Mary was, to rule Scotland at this time.

In some ways, however, Mary was likely to be popular with her subjects. She was one of the most beautiful women of her time, and had such winning manners that she could make both men and women of all ranks admire and love her. She was also very clever and well educated, and was as brave as the bravest knight. Her great fault was that, like her grandfather James IV., she was so passionate and self-willed that she often did things without considering what would follow.

Of course, Mary would have liked that Scotland should again make friends with France and restore the old Church; but she knew that for the present this was impossible, and that she must allow things to remain as they were. She chose as her chief advisers the Lord James Stewart and William Maitland of Lethington, who was the cleverest statesman then living in Scotland. And, as both of these men were Protestants, this meant that Protestantism was to continue as the religion of the country.

Very soon, however, it was seen how difficult it was for a Catholic sovereign to govern a Protestant kingdom. Mary agreed that the mass should not be said throughout the country, but she insisted that, as she was a Catholic, she should have the mass said in Holyrood Chapel for herself and her Catholic attendants. Lord James Stewart and Maitland thought that this ought to be allowed, and the mass was said in Holyrood Chapel as Mary had desired. John Knox, however, considered this was quite wrong, since, if the queen had her mass, her Catholic subjects would wish to have theirs also. Knox even preached sermons in the Church of St Giles against the saying of the mass in Holyrood, and Mary was so angry at this that she summoned Knox to Holyrood Palace. They had a long argument together, but, of course, they could not agree; and all through her reign Knox was Mary's chief enemy, as he thought that she would never give up trying to bring back her own religion, as was, indeed, the case.

After this quarrel about the mass, Knox and the other Protestant ministers were never such friends with the Lord James as they had been before Mary returned to Scotland. And another dispute arose between them which made the quarrel more bitter still. Though the Protestant religion had been set up, the ministers had received little or no money to maintain themselves with. They asked, therefore, that the property of the old Church should be given to them for the good of religion and education. But the Lord James and the other Protestant lords would not agree to this, and what they did was to take a third part of the property of the old Church, and give one half of it to the queen and the other half to the ministers. As this was not nearly enough to keep up ministers and churches and schools, Knox and his brother ministers were very indignant with the Protestant lords, some of whom had taken care to set aside a large share of the Church property for themselves. In these ways the Protestants came to be divided, and the result was that their cause was greatly weakened.

In the year 1562, just about twelve months after her return, Mary set out on a journey to the north of her kingdom which she had long intended to make. The journey was meant to be one of pleasure, but it turned out very differently. When she got to Inverness-shire, the Earl of Huntly, a Catholic noble, and one of the greatest men in the country, rose in rebellion. Mary now showed how brave and high-spirited she was. An Englishman who was with her said that he "never saw her merrier," and he heard her exclaim that she would like to be a man, to be out all night in the fields and carry a buckler and a broadsword. But the rebellion was soon over. The Lord James Stewart (who now became Earl of Moray) and two other earls collected an army and met the Earl of Huntly and his followers at Corrichie, about fifteen miles to the west of Aberdeen. After a short battle, Huntly was defeated, and, as he rode from the field to Aberdeen, he fell dead

Entry of Mary, Queen of Scots, into Edinburgh.

from his horse from some illness with which he was seized.

There was one thing on which Mary had set her heart, and that was to succeed Elizabeth as queen of England. Almost all Catholics, indeed, thought that Mary was the rightful queen of England, and for two reasons; because, in the first place, they held Elizabeth was not the lawful daughter of Henry VIII. and Ann Boleyn, as Henry had divorced his first wife, Catharine of Aragon, against the law of the Church of Rome; and, in the second place, because she was a heretic, and, therefore, could not be a lawful ruler. Mary's two chief advisers, the Earl of Moray and Maitland of Lethington, were also anxious that Mary should be Elizabeth's successor. What they hoped was that, if Mary became queen of England, she would become a Protestant, as England was a Protestant country, and then one Protestant sovereign would be ruler both of England and Scotland. They, therefore, sent word to persuade Elizabeth to name Mary as her successor, but Elizabeth would not agree to this. She was afraid, she said, that if her Catholic enemies were certain that Mary would be queen of England after her death, they would assassinate her to make way for Mary.

At last Mary grew tired of waiting till Elizabeth should name her as her successor, and she took a step which made Elizabeth very indignant. She married Henry Stewart, Lord Darnley, eldest son of Matthew, Earl of Lennox, in 1565. The reason why Elizabeth was angry at this marriage was that, after Mary, Darnley was the nearest heir to the English throne, as he and Mary were both the grandchildren of Margaret Tudor, Henry VIII.'s sister—Mary's grandfather being James IV., and Darnley's grand-

Lord Darnley.

father, Archibald, Earl of Angus, who was Margaret Tudor's second husband. By marrying Darnley, therefore, Mary made her claim to the English throne still stronger, and it was this that frightened Elizabeth and made her so angry with Mary.

And there were others as frightened and angry at Mary's marriage as Elizabeth ; namely, the Earl of Moray and the other Protestant lords. What made these persons dislike the marriage was that Darnley was a Catholic, and that he and Mary together would come to have the chief power in the kingdom. But if this happened, the Protestant lords would lose all their authority, and in the end the Church of Rome would be restored. Moray and his friends, therefore, did all in their power to prevent the marriage, and, after the marriage did take place, they rose in rebellion. Mary, however, at the head of a small army chased them from one part of the country to another, and at last compelled Moray to flee to England. This was called the Chase-about or Round-about Raid.

Thus it seemed at first that Mary's marriage with Darnley was to give her more power than she had ever had since she returned to Scotland. But we shall see that it was to be the chief cause of all her misfortunes.

---

48. RICCIO AND DARNLEY. 1565-1566

MARY (1542-1567)

At first, Mary and Darnley appeared to be very fond of each other. Darnley was a tall, handsome youth about twenty years of age, and therefore a few years younger than Mary. He was skilful in all manly games, and also in music and dancing, so that we need not wonder that Mary was at first greatly pleased with him. But he soon showed himself so weak and foolish and self-willed that it was impossible for any one to like or respect him. Before very long he and

Mary began to quarrel, and the longer Mary knew him she came to despise and dislike him the more.

Before their marriage Mary had promised that she

David Riccio.

would make Darnley king of Scots, as her consort; but, when she saw what kind of man he was, she drew back from her promise. That was one reason why they began to quarrel, and there was another reason which made Darnley still more angry with Mary.

Some time before the marriage there had come to Scotland an Italian, named David Riccio, the son of a musician in his native country. Riccio was himself a skilful musician, and, as Mary was very fond of music, this drew her attention to him. Soon Riccio became a great favourite with her; she gave him handsome presents, so that he was able to dress as magnificently as any courtier; and he came to have so much power that, if any one wanted a favour from Mary, he tried to have Riccio on his side. Darnley, therefore, became so jealous of Riccio that he was ready to do anything to get rid of him.

Now Riccio had many enemies besides Darnley. The Protestant lords hated him because they thought that, being a Catholic, he would help Mary to restore the old religon; and some of them had a still stronger reason for both hating and fearing him. In the month of March, 1566, there was to be a meeting of Parliament, and in that Parliament a law was to be passed for taking away the lands of the lords who had rebelled against Mary on account of her marriage with Darnley. But these lords thought that it was chiefly owing to Riccio that this law was to be passed, and that if he were out of the way, their lands would not be taken from them. So Darnley and the Protestant lords, among whom were the earls of Moray, Morton, Argyle, Glencairn, and others, formed a plot for the death of Riccio—the arrangement being that after the deed had been done, Darnley was to be made king-consort along with Mary, and that the lords were not to lose their lands.

The lords wished to try Riccio and then sentence him to death, but Darnley was too impatient to wait for this, and it was decided that he should be slain without a trial. On a Saturday night, a few days before the lords were to be deprived of their lands, Mary was at supper with a number of her friends, Riccio being among them, in her boudoir in Holyrood Palace. Suddenly there entered the room a band of armed men, the Earl of Morton, Lords Lindsay, Ruthven, and others, with Darnley at their head. In spite of the tears and prayers of the queen, Riccio was dragged out of the room and put to death with no fewer than fifty-six wounds.

What happened after the murder of Riccio shows how clever Mary was compared with Darnley. By the bargain he had made with the Protestant lords, he should have stood by their side after Riccio's death; but, only three days later, Mary persuaded him to ride secretly to Dunbar Castle, where a number of the nobles, the enemies of the Protestant lords, came to join her. And the result of Darnley's conduct was that he did not really make friends with Mary, but he made bitter enemies of the Protestant lords whom he had deserted. Before very long he was to learn how foolishly he had behaved.

Everybody in the country must now have been wondering what was to happen next. On the one side were the Protestant lords, the chief of whom was the Earl of Moray, who, along with the other barons who had been driven to England, had returned to Edinburgh the day after Riccio's murder; and on the other side was the queen, with the nobles who had gone to her at Dunbar. Was there to be another civil war between Protestants and Catholics? What happened was this. Mary could not be certain that she would win the victory if she went to war with the Protestant lords, and she therefore came to an agreement with them. The arrangement was that those of the Protestant lords who had taken part in the slaying of Riccio were to be outlawed, while the Earl of Moray and the others who had only rebelled against

Hermitage Castle, a Residence of the Earl of Bothwell.

her and had not been present at the murder, were to remain in the country, and not to be deprived c their lands.

Not long after this arrangement was made an event happened (June 19th, 1566) which was to be very important both for England and for Scotland. Mary gave birth to a son, afterwards James VI. of Scotland and James I. of England, who was to be the first sovereign to rule over Great Britain and Ireland. Had Mary not had a son, England and Scotland might never have been united, as there would have been no one to inherit the crowns of both countries. All Scotsmen were overjoyed at the birth of a prince who would be the rightful heir to the three kingdoms, and in Edinburgh no fewer than five hundred bonfires were kindled in honour of the event.

But this happy event did not bring peace to Scotland. Mary and her husband Darnley came to dislike each other more and more, and they had no pleasure in each other's company. Then Mary chose another favourite, who was to spoil her happiness for the rest of her life. This new favourite was James, Earl of Bothwell, who was a very different man from Darnley. He had lived a very wild life, and was so bold and reckless that he would let nothing stand in his way to gain his ends. Everybody saw that Bothwell had great power over Mary, and wondered what would be the end of it all.

On the 17th of December, 1566, the infant prince was baptized as a Catholic in Stirling Castle; but, though Darnley was in the castle, he was not present at his own son's baptism, while Bothwell took charge of the ceremony. A week after the baptism Mary took a step which could not but frighten Darnley. She allowed the Earl of Morton and others who had taken part in the murder of Riccio to return to Scotland, and, as we have seen, these men hated Darnley because he had betrayed them. Darnley, therefore, had good reason to fear that on their return they would seek to have their revenge upon him.

A short time after the baptism of the prince,

Darnley went to Glasgow, where he became very ill.
When Mary heard of his illness she went to Glasgow,
and persuaded him to be brought to Edinburgh,
where he would be better attended to in his sickness.
The house to which he was taken was called the Kirk
of Field, and was situated where the University of
Edinburgh now stands. It was a lonely and ruinous
place, and unhealthy besides, so that it was not suit-
able for an invalid. It now seemed as if Mary and
her husband had again become friends. She often
came to sit by his bedside, though she always left
him at night and slept at Holyrood.

One Sunday night Mary had spent some time with
him, when she suddenly remembered that she had to
go to Holyrood to be present at a festivity. A few
hours afterwards, about two o'clock the next morning,
a loud explosion was heard through the town. It
was the Kirk of Field that had been blown up with
gunpowder, which had been secretly placed in a room
on the ground-floor of the house. In a garden near
at hand the dead bodies of Darnley and his page
were found under a tree.

---

49. MARY AND BOTHWELL.   1566-1568

The persons who had hidden the gunpowder in the
Kirk of Field intended that people should think that
the house had been blown up by accident. But
everybody knew that the explosion had not taken
place by accident, and that Bothwell and others had
committed the crime in order to get rid of Darnley.
Bothwell was brought to trial, but he came attended

by so many followers that his judges were afraid to condemn him.

People in England and France as well as in Scotland believed that Mary had known of Bothwell's plot for the murder of her husband; and what she now did made them still more suspicious of her guilt. Only three months after the death of Darnley

[Photo by *Valentine.*

Ruins of Dunbar Castle.

she married Bothwell, who was known to be her husband's murderer. Then a number of the nobles joined together and determined to prevent Bothwell from reigning as king, which had been his object in slaying Darnley and marrying Mary. It seemed as if there was to be another civil war between Mary and Bothwell on the one side and the Protestant nobles on the other.

Both sides collected armies, which came face to

face on the slopes of Carberry Hill, near Mussel-burgh, but no battle was fought.   So many of Bothwell's men deserted him that he had to flee from the field, lest he should fall into the hands of his enemies.   He was to trouble Scotland no more, for soon afterwards he sailed to the Orkney Islands, of which he was the duke.   Ships were sent after him, but he escaped to Denmark ; and there he was put in prison, where, some years afterwards, he died insane.

The day of Carberry Hill was one of the saddest in Mary's life.   She was led to Edinburgh, her dress being a short red petticoat, as there had been no suit-able woman's clothes in Dunbar Castle, from which she had come to Carberry.   When she was led into the town, the crowds in the street hooted at her and called her names, so that she was almost distracted with rage and grief.   But the question was, what was now to be done with her ?   Was she to be allowed to remain queen or not ?   She was asked to give up Bothwell, but this she refused to do.   This being the case, the lords thought that it would not be safe to let her rule, as she would be certain to bring back Bothwell, and then there would be civil war once more.   What they did, therefore, was to place her in Lochleven Castle, from which, as it was in the middle of a loch, she could not easily escape.   Then a short time afterwards she was compelled to sign a paper, by which she gave the crown to her son.   Five days later the young prince was crowned at Stirling as James VI. of Scotland—John Knox preaching the coronation sermon.

As James was little more than a year old, some one

had to be chosen as Regent, and the person elected
was the Earl of Moray. As Moray was a Protestant,
his being Regent brought great joy to Knox and the
other ministers, and Moray gave them good reason
to be pleased with the way he governed. At the
end of the year (1567) in which he became Regent,
Moray held a parliament which, like the one that
had met in 1560, declared that Protestantism should
be the religion of the country. Knox and his friends

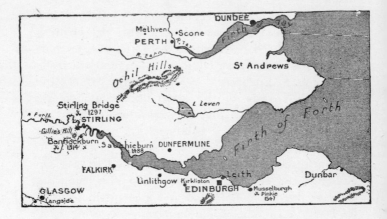

thought that all their troubles were now over, as
Moray was still young and might continue to rule
till the king was old enough to govern for himself, and
that day was still far off. They did not dream that
there were as many troubles to come as those they
had already passed through.

Moray had not been Regent for a year when news
came to him that Mary had escaped from her prison
in Loch Leven. She had managed her escape very
cleverly. One night (2nd of May, 1568) when her

keepers had gone to rest, a page named William Douglas stole the keys of the castle, and Mary and her attendants slipped out to the loch, where a boat was awaiting them. On the shore there was a band of armed men in readiness to receive them when they landed. Then, as soon as Mary was safely ashore, the whole party galloped through the night to Niddry Castle, in Linlithgowshire, and next day Mary went on to Hamilton Palace. In a few days she was surrounded by many earls and barons and bishops, who took an oath that they would give their lives to save her from her enemies, and to replace her on the throne.

The Regent Moray was in Glasgow when he heard the news of Mary's escape. He at once collected an army, not so large as that of Mary, but with better trained soldiers and more skilful officers. The two armies met at Langside, now a part of Glasgow, and Mary looked on at a distance while the battle was fought which was to decide whether she was to be queen of Scotland again or not. The battle was over in three quarters of an hour, and Mary's army was completely defeated. Then in terror lest she should fall into the hands of her enemies, she galloped from the field of battle attended by only six followers. She rode sixty miles that day, and the next she arrived at Dundrennan, on the shores of the Solway Firth. Still afraid that her enemies might overtake her, she crossed the Solway in a boat, to put herself under the protection of Queen Elizabeth.

Mary's reign was at an end, but she was to live for eighteen years longer, and all that time she was to be the prisoner of Queen Elizabeth. Why did

Elizabeth keep her a prisoner, and at last put her to death? It was because she knew that, if Mary had been set free, England would not have been safe. Had Mary been allowed to return to Scotland, there would again have been civil war ; and if she had conquered, she would have set up Roman Catholicism,

Loch Leven, from the Castle.

and this would have been a great danger to England. Had she gone to France, she would have stirred up enemies against England, and Elizabeth might have been driven from the throne. It was a cruel fate for Mary, and even those must pity her who think that Elizabeth was justified in treating her as she did.

50. SCOTLAND IN THE TIME OF QUEEN MARY.—1

All through the reign of Queen Mary there had been such constant quarrelling and fighting, that we are apt to think that people must have neglected their duties and led very unhappy lives. We know, however, that this was not the case. Of course, the English invasions did a great deal of harm, especially in the country near the Borders; and, when battles had to be fought, men had to leave their work to fight whenever they were called. But battles were not fought every day, and the English were not always invading the country, so that the farmer and the merchant and the craftsman could usually go on with their work in spite of the constant quarrelling of the great people about the Court.

About the year 1551, not long after the battle of Pinkie, there came to Scotland a French clergyman who wrote about what he saw in the country, and from what he says we may learn that, in spite of the many wars and English invasions, the people were not so badly off or so unhappy as we might have expected. One thing that struck him was that every day the country was becoming richer and more prosperous. The people had not much money, but they had plenty of provisions, which were as cheap in Scotland as in any other part of the world. There was much corn and abundance of cattle, so that both bread and meat were cheap. The chief crops he saw were barley, peas, and beans. Another thing he noticed was the great number of churches and monasteries, and he says that the clergy were richer than the nobles, which we know to have been the case. This was what a foreigner thought of Scotland, but let us see what the country looked like in the times of Queen Mary.

The surface of the country was very different then from what it is now. First of all, there was hardly a tree to be seen anywhere in the Lowlands. Round gentlemen's houses there were sometimes a few, but a traveller might walk many miles without even seeing a single bush. As there were so few trees, there could be little wood for building houses and ships, and so the Parliament passed many laws to encourage planting, and to prevent mischievous persons from injuring young trees. If any one did damage to a young tree, he was to be fined £10 (Scottish money) for the first offence and £20 for the second; and, if he broke the law a third time, he was to be put to death, though this last punishment was never really carried out. By another law, every one who had a certain amount of land was to plant three acres of wood round his dwelling. But in spite of these laws there was very little timber grown, and it was not till long after this period that Scotland became a well-wooded country.

In another way the surface of the country was different from what it is now. All over the Lowlands there were marshes and small lakes which no longer exist. The reason of this was that people then did not understand how to drain land as we do nowadays. If we could look at the country as it was in the time of Mary, another thing would strike us. We should not see any fences, whether hedges or stone walls, round the fields as there are now. All the fields lay open, so that it was necessary to have herds to keep the cattle and sheep from trampling down the crops. We see, then, that from the want of trees, from the many marshes and lakes, and from there being no hedges or walls, the country must have had a very different appearance from what it has to-day.

We must not think, however, that Scotland was a

Dundrennan Abbey.

mere wilderness in the time of Mary. In many places just as rich crops were raised as in any other country. The most fertile districts were the Lothians, Fife, the Carse of Gowrie, and Morayshire. Then on the hillsides great numbers of sheep were reared, and sheep-rearing was such a profitable business that the clergy, the nobles, and even the kings took an interest in it.

We know what a good farm was like at this time. There was the farmer's house, which contained a hall, a chamber, a pantry, and a kitchen. Near the farm was the barn for storing the corn, a byre for the cattle, and a dovecot for the pigeons, of which there were great numbers in those days. There was an orchard for the growing of fruits and vegetables, a rabbit-warren, and a fish-pond, for supplying the family with part of its food.

There was one great evil in Scotland, however, which lasted for a long time after the reign of Mary. The landlords would not let their lands for more than a few years, and at the end of that time they often turned the farmers out of their holdings. The result of this was that the farmers did not manure the land, or plant hedges, or improve their holdings in any way, as they would have done had they been certain that the landlord would not turn them off at the end of their lease. It sometimes happened, also, that the farmer who lost his farm slew the one who took his place. It will be seen, therefore, that the short leases did much harm in more ways than one. They prevented the land from being properly cultivated, and they made the landlords and the farmers bitter enemies.

---

51. SCOTLAND IN THE TIME OF QUEEN MARY.—2

In the time of Queen Mary the towns were much the same as they had been long before her reign.[1]

[1] See p. 111.

They were not surrounded with great walls with towers, like the towns on the Continent, but most of them were defended by stone-dykes, which, however, were usually in a very broken down condition. It was against the law to climb over these dykes into the town, but as they were generally full of holes it was very easy to slip through them, and this the boys in the town constantly did. If any one wished to enter the town, he had to pass through one of the ports or gates ; and, if he had any goods with him, he had to pay a toll to the gatekeeper.

The interior of the town was also much the same as it had been in the Middle Ages. The streets were no cleaner, swine went about just as they had always done, the town was no better lighted, and it was not safe to be out of doors after nightfall. In earlier times the chief public building in every town had been the parish church, but now in most of the principal towns there was another public building, called the Tolbooth, in which the courts of justice met and criminals were imprisoned.

What was an ordinary house like in the time of Mary, and how was it furnished? Here is the description of one in Stirling which belonged to a bailie in that town. This house had four rooms, the largest being the hall, which contained a counter, a form, a stool, and a place for keeping meat. In a second room, called the mid-chamber, there was a bed and a press; in the front chamber there were three beds, a chest, a form, and a little iron chimney; and in the upper chamber there were three beds, two of which, however, had no bottoms. This was all the furniture in a bailie's house in those times, and, as for utensils, here is a list of those that belonged to another bailie in the same town: three saucers, six dishes, six pewter plates, two pots, two bowls, a quart measure, and a chopin measure.

Among other changes which the Reformation brought about was a change in the amusements of the people. Before the Reformation the day when there was the greatest fun was the Feast of Fools, which took place in the month of December, and which was one of the strangest amusements that was ever invented. First, a man was dressed to look like a donkey, which was meant to represent either Balaam's ass, or the ass which stood beside Christ's manger, or the one which carried Christ and his mother to Egypt. Others were dressed like the Pope, the bishops, priests, and monks, all the dresses being turned inside out. Then the donkey braying, and the others making every kind of strange noise, the whole procession proceeded to a church, and went through the service with the books turned upside down.

This amusement, of course, came to an end at the Reformation. But there were other pastimes which the Reformers tried to stop, but which the people were very unwilling to give up. The chief of these was the frolic of Robin Hood and Little John, which took place on the first of May. Those who took part in this sport dressed themselves in green, like Robin Hood and his men, and the fun consisted in playing all kinds of jokes upon each other. By the time the sports ended, however, there was such riot and drunkenness that it led to disgraceful scenes wherever they were held. But though

Queen Mary herself wrote a letter to the magistrates of Edinburgh, commanding them to put an end to it, it was not till long afterwards that Robin Hood's Day was given up.

Of course, there were other amusements besides those that have just been mentioned. The larger towns had "playing fields," where plays were acted at different times of the year. Indoors people played cards, back-gammon, and dice, and out of doors the favourite games were golf, tennis (called *catchpully*), and football, though these games were not played in the same way as they are at the present time. Almost all the burghs, also, had a horse-race once a year, the owner of the winning horse receiving as a prize a silver ball or cup, which was given by the magistrates.

The dress of the great people was much the same as in other countries. Both the lords and the ladies wore a great ruff which rose above their ears. When the women of all ranks went out of doors, they put on a cloak or plaid, which completely covered their heads so that their faces could not be seen. Both in the town and in the country, men of the middle and lower classes wore a plaid and a blue bonnet ; though if a burgess wore a bonnet and a plaid he was liable to a fine, as this dress was not considered grand enough for a townsman. In earlier times every craftsman had to wear a particular dress, so that it might be known to what craft he belonged. By the time of Queen Mary, however, this rule was not so strictly kept. All the town officials had a livery of their own. In Aberdeen, for instance, the postman wore a blue livery, and in Edinburgh on state occasions the town servants appeared in black hose, black doublet, and black bonnets.

An Englishman who came to Scotland tells us that most of the people whom he saw ate salted mutton and geese, with cabbage, peas, and beans. He also says that it was only in the towns that wheaten bread was to be had, and that the poorer people had to be

[Photo by *Valentine.*

George Heriot's School, Edinburgh.

content with oatcakes. The chief drink of the poor was ale, but the rich drank wines brought from France. There used to be great feastings at marriages and baptisms. Crowds of people came on these occasions, and those who could afford it had on their tables all kinds of dainties, which were brought from foreign countries. Indeed, so much money was spent at marriages and christenings that the Parliament passed a law forbidding any but rich people to have anything on their tables which was not made in Scotland.

At the present day, a clever boy, if he is industrious, can rise from any rank and become rich or famous. Was this possible in the times of which we are speaking? In the reign of Mary, two of the most famous men were John Knox and George Buchanan. Knox was the son of a small farmer, and we know how he came to be a great man. He was educated in Haddington School, and after leaving school he entered the Church and became a priest. Then, as we know, he turned a Protestant, and by his zeal and eloquence came to be one of the chief men in the country. George Buchanan was also the son of a small farmer, and, like Knox, he rose to be a great man though in a different way. After being educated in Scotland, he went to the university of Paris, and made himself one of the most learned men in all Europe.

The lives of Knox and Buchanan show how a poor lad in the country could rise to be great and famous. And a boy in the town, if he were clever and attentive to his trade or business, could become a rich merchant and an important man. In the year 1563, two years after Mary's return to Scotland, a boy was born in Edinburgh who showed how this could be done. To this day most people in Scotland know his name— George Heriot. He began his life as a goldsmith, became jeweller to Queen Anne, the wife of James VI., and afterwards went to London, where he carried on business as a goldsmith and banker. When he died, he was so rich that he left money enough to found the School which bears his name to the

present day. We see, therefore, that in those times
of which we are speaking, boys could by cleverness
and industry rise from all ranks and become rich and
famous men.

---

52. THE REGENT MORAY. 1567-1570

James VI. (1567-1625)

We have seen that after the battle of Langside
Queen Mary fled from Scotland, in which she was
never again to set her foot. Was there to be no
more fighting between Catholics and Protestants now
that she was gone? The Regent Moray was now
the ruler of Scotland, and he was a Protestant, and
also one of the best and strongest rulers the country
ever had. Would he be able to put down all his
enemies, and restore peace and order after the terrible
events that had happened during the last few
years?

There were two things that had to be done if the
Reformation was to be made safe in Scotland. First,
Mary must be prevented from becoming queen again ;
and, secondly, her son James must be kept on the
throne. Though Moray was a brave and wise ruler,
he was to find it a hard task to accomplish both of
these ends.

Though the Protestants had now the chief power,
there was still a large number of Catholics in the
country who wished Mary to be restored, as she
belonged to their own religion. There were also
many of the nobles who did not wish Moray to be
regent, and were determined to have Mary brought

back. There was one noble especially who thought that he and not Moray ought to be the chief person in the country. This was the Duke of Châtelherault,

James Stewart, Earl of Moray.

once the Earl of Arran, who had been regent in the beginning of Mary's reign. If Mary and her son James died, he was the nearest heir to the throne, and that was the reason why he thought that he

Z

should be regent instead of Moray.   He was the head
of the family of the Hamiltons, which was one of the
richest and most powerful in the country, and on his
side, also, he had two great earls, both of whom were
his relatives—the Earl of Huntly, who was a Catholic,
and the Earl of Argyle, who was a Protestant.   What
gave the duke still more power was that Mary made
him her lieutenant in Scotland, so that all her friends
might gather round him.

The Regent Moray, however, was able to put down
all these enemies without even fighting a battle.
Then one of the Hamiltons, named James Hamilton
of Bothwellhaugh, thought that by slaying Moray his
family would gain the chief power, and the Duke
might be made regent.   This Hamilton of Bothwellhaugh, it should be said, had been taken prisoner at
the battle of Langside, and would have been put to
death if Moray had not ordered that his life should
be spared.

In the beginning of the year 1570, Moray travelled
from Glasgow to Stirling and thence to Linlithgow.
On the way he had been told that Hamilton was
seeking his life, and some of his friends wished to
bring Hamilton into his presence, but he would not
listen to their advice.   During the night that Moray
lodged in Linlithgow, Hamilton made all his preparations for the crime he was about to commit.   He
covered the floor of the room in which he took his
stand with a feather mattress, so that the sound
of his boots might not be heard in the room below.
He darkened the room by hanging black curtains
behind where he was to stand, so that he might not
be seen from the street, and he hung sheets round

the window to hide the smoke from his gun when he fired. The door of the house that opened on the street was barred, and at the back door a swift horse was kept ready for him when the deed was done.

As Moray's friends knew that his life was in danger, they persuaded him to ride back the way he had come the day before, thinking that he would thus avoid his intending assassin. The crowd in the street, however, was so great that this could not be done, and Moray rode slowly past the house where

Bothwellhaugh's Gun.

Hamilton was concealed. The shot was fired, and the bullet passed through Moray's body. He was able to dismount from his horse, and leaning on a friend he returned to the house he had left. Before midnight he was dead. As for Hamilton, when the shot was fired, he rushed to the horse which was in readiness for him, and escaped to his friends at Hamilton Palace, who were overjoyed to hear the news he had to tell.

All the Protestants knew that by the death of Moray they had lost their best and most powerful friend. John Knox preached his funeral sermon, in the Church of St Giles in Edinburgh, and we are told that " he made three thousand persons shed tears for the loss of such a good and godly governor." Though many of the nobles hated Moray because he had allowed Mary to be deprived of the crown, he was greatly beloved by the common people, who called him the " Good Regent." A writer who lived at the time says that " he was the defender of the widow and the fatherless," meaning that he would not allow the rich and the powerful to trample on the poor and the weak.

53. REGENCY OF LENNOX.   1570-1571

JAMES VI. (1567-1625)

Who was to fill Moray's place? This was the question that the supporters of the king had now to decide. The man whom they did choose as regent was a very different person from Moray. He was the Earl of Lennox, the father of Darnley, and it was only because he was the grandfather of the king that he was chosen. As he was both weak in health and weak of mind, he was quite unfit to rule the country at such a time.

There were still two parties in the country : the one that wished James to remain king, and the other that desired Mary to be restored. Most of the nobles were on the side of Mary ; but, on the other hand, the people in the towns, being mostly Protestants, were supporters of James. At the time of Moray's death there were two castles in the hands of the queen's party, which the king's adherents were anxious to recover. The one was Dunbarton Castle, and the other was the Castle of Edinburgh.

Dunbarton Castle was taken in a way which reminds us of the days of Wallace and Bruce. One of the sentinels in the castle told a certain Captain Thomas Crawford how the walls could be scaled. So, with the sentinel as their guide, Crawford and a band of men began the ascent at one o'clock of an

Dunbarton Castle and Rock. [*Photo by Wilson.*]

April morning (1571). They had not climbed far before they found their ladders were too short. Then Crawford and the sentinel had to climb from the highest step of their ladders to an ash-tree about twenty feet up the rock. This was safely done; the ladders were pulled up to the tree, and again firmly planted. Luckily there was a thick mist, so that the whole band reached the top of the wall without being seen. Shouting, "God save the King!" "A Darnley!

a Darnley!" they fell upon the garrison, who were only half awake, and in a few minutes the castle was taken. Among the prisoners was Hamilton, Archbishop of St Andrews, who had been one of the Regent Moray's greatest enemies. A few days afterwards he was hanged at Stirling for having been a party to the murder both of Darnley and of Moray.

The Castle of Edinburgh could not be so easily taken as that of Dunbarton. It was commanded by the best soldier in Scotland, William Kirkcaldy of Grange, who had once been the friend of the Regent Moray, but was now on the side of Mary. In the castle, also, was Maitland of Lethington, once like Kirkcaldy the friend of Moray, but now like him on Mary's side. Being a skilful soldier, Kirkcaldy knew how to strengthen all the weak parts of the castle ; and, as he received both money and ammunition from France, he was able both to pay his soldiers and to supply them with suitable arms. The siege began, but the Regent Lennox had no cannons that could do much damage to the walls of the castle, and at last he gave up the attempt to take it. Then Kirkcaldy and Maitland thought of a plan by which they might bring the war to an end, and perhaps restore Mary to the throne.

In the month of August, 1571, Lennox and many of the king's lords were assembled in Stirling, holding a great meeting. The plan of Kirkcaldy was to fall upon them by surprise, and, if possible, to take them all prisoners. So, about six o'clock one evening (3rd of September), Kirkcaldy rode out of Edinburgh at the head of a troop of mounted men. To conceal where they were going, they at first marched southwards, but they soon wheeled round in the direction of Stirling. Between three and four the next morning, when it was still dark, they were in the streets of the town.

The king's lords were all asleep, and in a few minutes, without a blow being struck, the earls of Argyle, Glencairn, Sutherland, Cassillis, Eglinton, and the Regent Lennox himself, were taken one by one from their beds. The Earl of Morton, however, was awakened by the noise in the street, and had time to barricade his door. Morton was a fierce and bold man, and he and his servants made a desperate fight; but the house was set on fire, and he was compelled to surrender. Then Kirkcaldy's band, who were mostly men from the Borders, began to plunder the town instead of making off with their prisoners.

By this time the garrison in the Castle of Stirling had been alarmed by the din in the town. The commander of the castle was the Earl of Mar, who kept the king there under his charge. At the head of his men, Mar fell upon Kirkcaldy's troops, and in a short time drove them out of the town. All the earls who had been taken prisoners broke away in safety from their captors, but the Regent Lennox was not so fortunate. He had been tied on a horse's back, but his friends had freed him and were leading him off. Then a cry arose, "Shoot the regent!" and a trooper drew his pistol and shot him through the body. A few hours afterwards he died; he had been regent only for fourteen months. Kirkcaldy, however, had failed in his bold plan. His men stole three hundred horses and much other property, but they had made none of the king's lords prisoners, which had been Kirkcaldy's chief aim.

54. REGENCY OF MAR.   1571-1572

JAMES VI. (1567-1625)

Within less than two years two regents had been
slain ; who would now be bold enough to accept such
a dangerous office? The new regent chosen was
that Earl of Mar of whom we have just heard, and
whose duty it had been to keep the king safe in
Stirling Castle. Mar was a kindly and peace-loving
man, and was liked and respected both by the King's
and the Queen's parties. But though he was made
regent, it was the Earl of Morton, the fierce and
bold earl who had defended his house so desperately
in Stirling, that had the real power.

The one thing that had to be done, if James VI.
was to be really king, was the taking of Edinburgh
Castle. Mar was made regent on the 5th of September, 1571, and the next month he entered Leith with
an army of 5000 men. Kirkcaldy was master not
only of the Castle of Edinburgh, but of the town
as well. Before Mar could get into the town, therefore, he must break down the wall which had been
built after the battle of Flodden, and this he now
tried to do. But Kirkcaldy planted his cannon in
the churchyard of St Giles, and on the high ground
where the university now stands, and thus was able
to fire down on Mar's men while they were digging
trenches before the wall. The cannon-shot was sent
even through Mar's own tent. Mar soon saw that
it was useless to try to batter down the wall, and
within a fortnight he led his men back to Leith.

Since neither the town nor the castle could be taken by storm, Mar, or rather Morton (for he was the real leader), tried another plan. This was to starve Kirkcaldy and his men, and so compel them to surrender. It was proclaimed, therefore, that if any man took provisions or coals into the town or

Edinburgh Castle, from the Grassmarket.

castle, he would be hanged on the spot; and, if any woman did so, she would be stripped and scourged. Then Kirkcaldy did a thing for which the citizens of Edinburgh never forgave him. As there was no coal to be had, he took the roofs off some of the houses and sold the rafters in the market for firewood.

There never was a sadder time in the whole history of Scotland. There had been civil war in previous reigns, but never had the contending sides

been so cruel and merciless. When prisoners were
taken, they were at once put to death. And it was
not only near Edinburgh that fighting went on, but
in other parts of the country. For instance, the
castle of Towie, in Aberdeenshire, was surrounded
by a band of Gordons who were on the side of
Mary. The castle was defended by the wife of the
owner of the castle, and she refused to surrender.
The Gordons then set fire to the castle, and slew
every person—man, woman, and child—within its
walls.

A writer, who was a boy in these times, says of
them: "You should have seen fathers [fighting]
against their sons, sons against their fathers, brother
fighting against brother . . . one professing to be the
king's man, another the queen's. The very young
ones scarce taught to speak had these words in
their mouths, and were sometimes observed to divide
and have their childish conflicts in that quarrel."
Such were the Douglas Wars, as they were called, because Douglas was the Earl of Morton's family name,
and he was the chief man in the country.

At last, in August, 1572, the two parties agreed to
cease from fighting for a time. The truce lasted
for five months, and during that time several important events happened. On the 27th of August the
Massacre of St Bartholomew took place in Paris,
when the Catholics rose one night and slaughtered
all the Protestants they could find in the city. The
result of this massacre was that the Protestants in
every country were so alarmed that they bound
themselves together more closely than ever they had
done before. In Scotland it made them more

determined than ever that Mary should not be
restored to the throne, and her friends from this time

[Photo by Inglis, Edinburgh.

Statue of John Knox.

almost gave up hope of ever seeing her in Scotland
again.

During the time of the truce, also, two of the chief
men in Scotland passed away.   The Regent Mar

died, it is said, of a broken heart, because " he loved peace and could not have it." Not long after him died John Knox, and was buried in the churchyard behind the church of St Giles, which is now the ground in front of the Parliament House. A great multitude attended his funeral, and, as the Earl of Morton looked down into the grave, he said : " Here lies one who neither flattered nor feared any flesh."

There was another event that happened during the regency of Mar, which was very important and which must not be forgotten.

When the Protestant religion was set up in Scotland in the year 1560, no bishops or archbishops were appointed. But the Earl of Morton wished to have bishops and archbishops in the Church, and he was a man to have his own way. The bishops of the old Church were dying out, and who was to get their wealth ? Morton and other nobles were eager to have a large share of it, but, as they were laymen, how was this to be done ? Morton's plan was to appoint bishops, but not to give them nearly such large incomes as those of the bishops in the old Church. And where was the rest of the money to go ? Into the pockets of Morton and other nobles, who should have it in their power to appoint the bishops. As we know, the Scots were always clever at giving nicknames, and so they called Morton's bishops *Tulchans*—a " tulchan " being a calf's skin stuffed with straw to look like a living calf, and then placed beside a cow to make it give its milk.

The making of these Tulchan bishops was the beginning of a great quarrel in Scotland which lasted for more than a hundred years, and which was to cause much unhappiness both to the Scottish kings and to their subjects. James VI. and the kings who succeeded him all wished to have bishops in the Church ; but, as many of the Scottish people did not approve of bishops, there was constant quarrelling between these kings and their subjects, and more than once civil war broke out between them.

---

55. REGENCY OF MORTON. 1572-1578

JAMES VI. (1567-1625)

On the day that John Knox died (November 24, 1572), the Earl of Morton was appointed regent. Would he be able to take the Castle of Edinburgh, which the regents Lennox and Mar had failed to do?

We have seen that there was a truce of five months between the King's and Queen's parties, and during that time there had been no fighting between them. On the first day of January, 1573, however, Kirkcaldy fired a shot from the Castle to let Morton know that the truce was at an end, and the siege of the Castle again began. One night in February a band of Kirkcaldy's men made a rush out of the Castle, and set fire to some houses covered with thatch. It was a windy night, and the fire spread rapidly from one house to another. When the citizens tried to extinguish the flames, Kirkcaldy fired on them from the Castle. It was a cruel action, and the citizens remembered it against him.

From the gate of the Castle there extends a long straight street, down which Kirkcaldy could send his shot. To prevent this, therefore, Morton made three ramparts of earth across the street, so that between these ramparts people could walk in safety from the Castle guns. As Morton had no great cannons, however, he could only try to starve the "Castilians," as they were called, till they should be compelled to surrender. He poisoned St Margaret's Well at the foot of the Castle, so that they should have no water to drink, and he took care that no provisions should reach them.

At last, there happened what Morton had long been looking for; Queen Elizabeth sent down a force of armed men to assist him in taking the Castle. As they had brought many great cannons with them, Morton could now set about battering down the Castle walls. Some of the cannons were placed where Heriot's Hospital now stands, several on the Calton Hill, and others on the ridge where George Street runs. When the batteries began to play, a loud shriek of despair was heard from the women in the Castle. First St David's Tower fell, then the Wallace Tower. Soon Kirkcaldy saw that he must yield, as his men had begun to mutiny for want of food and water.

One day, therefore, Kirkcaldy and two of his friends clambered down the Castle wall by a rope, and went to the commander of the English, as they thought that he would receive them more kindly than Morton. But the English leader would do nothing without Morton's consent, and the arrangement made was that everybody in the Castle should be allowed to go free except Kirkcaldy, Maitland, and six other persons. So at last Edinburgh Castle was taken, and from this time there was no hope that Mary would ever be restored to the throne. Many wished that Kirkcaldy's life should be spared, as he had been much loved for his brave and generous character ; but he had caused so much misery during the last years of his life that Morton and most of the Protestants were determined that he should be put to death, and he was publicly executed like a common criminal. As for Maitland, he died in prison, and so escaped the fate of his companion.

There was now no Queen's party in the country, and the civil war was at an end. What Morton had henceforth to do was to see that the laws were obeyed throughout the whole land, and this was no easy task. Morton, however, was exactly the kind of ruler who was needed at the time. He feared no man, and he was strict, stern, and even cruel. It was the Border that was the most unruly part of the country, and Morton went to the Border at the head of an army and compelled the chiefs of the clans to promise that they would live at peace.

Morton's chief fault as a ruler was his greed of money, and he was not very particular as to how he got it. Here, for example, was one way in which he sought to put money into his own coffers. The Protestant ministers grumbled that their stipends were not regularly paid, so that many of them could hardly get food or clothing. Morton told them that he would collect the stipends, and so make sure that the ministers would receive them. But what did he do with the stipends when he had collected them ? He said that there were more ministers in the country than were needed, and he made one minister do the work of three or four, so that only one stipend was paid and the others he kept to himself.

During the regency of Morton, in the year 1575, there took place the last great fight between the English and Scots on the Borders. It came about in this way. Once every month the English and Scottish Wardens used to meet at an appointed place, to settle any quarrels that had arisen between the Scots and the English. The English Warden at this time was Sir John Forster, and the Scottish Warden Sir Thomas Carmichael. Each at the head of an armed band, the two wardens met in the Reidswire, a pass leading through the Cheviot Hills. For a time everything went on smoothly, till Carmichael asked Forster to give up an Englishman who had been robbing in Scotland. Forster refused, and a quarrel arose between them. Then the English Borderers shot a flight of arrows among the Scots. As the English had more men, the Scots had to give way, but just at this moment a band of men from Jedburgh came to their assistance. It was the Scots who were now the stronger, and they soon put the enemy to flight, taking the English Warden himself a prisoner. This fight was called the " Raid of Reidswire."

Though the Regent Morton kept good order in the country, he was disliked by all classes. The common people hated him on account of the taxes he made them pay, and the ministers were opposed to him because he had kept their stipends and set up the Tulchan bishops. Most of the nobles, also, both feared and hated him, because he punished them severely whenever they broke the law. At last, so many of the nobles combined against him that he could no longer remain regent, and the end was that, greatly against his will, he had to give up his office. But the country was soon to miss his strong hand that had made both high and low obey the laws.

---

56. A FRENCH FAVOURITE—THE RUTHVEN RAID. 1578-1583

JAMES VI. (1567-1625)

When the Earl of Morton gave up the regency, James VI. was only twelve years of age, so that he was not yet able to rule for himself. The nobles who had forced Morton to resign, therefore, tried to divide the government among themselves. Soon, however, they began to quarrel, and then Morton thought that this was a chance for him to recover his power. So he came forth from his "Lion's Den," as his castle at Dalkeith was called, got the king into his hands, and again became the chief man in the kingdom, though he had not the title of regent.

But the next year (1579) there came one to Scotland who was to be the most dangerous enemy that Morton ever had. This was Esmé Stewart, Lord of Aubigny, a nephew of James's grandfather, the Earl of Lennox. Aubigny had lived all his life in France, so that, though he was a Scotsman by descent, he was a Frenchman in all his ways. And what brought Aubigny to Scotland? He had been

2 A

sent by the Catholics of France to do all in his power to have Queen Mary restored to the throne. Now Aubigny was an exceedingly smooth and clever courtier, and soon he gained such power over the boy-king, as to be able to make him do whatever he pleased. Before very long James made him Earl, and afterwards Duke of Lennox, and Keeper of Dunbarton Castle, which, after Edinburgh Castle, was the most important fortress in all Scotland.

Now, if Lennox was to succeed in bringing back Mary, there was one man who would have to be put out of the way, and that was the Earl of Morton. It was Morton, as we know, who had done more than any one else to put down the friends of Mary in Scotland, and, so long as he had the chief power in the country, she would never be restored. Lennox, therefore, at once set about trying to ruin Morton, and he did this very cleverly. He had brought money with him from France, and he gave this money in bribes to some of the chief men to assist him in bringing about the fall of Morton. But the man from whom he got the greatest help was Captain James Stewart, a brother-in-law of John Knox. This man was as fierce and strong as Morton himself, of whom he was a great enemy.

One day when the king was sitting with his Privy Council in Holyrood Palace, Captain Stewart suddenly entered, threw himself on his knees before James, and, pointing to Morton, accused him of having had a share in the murder of James's father, Darnley. Morton smiled, and haughtily said that he was ready to be tried in any court in the land. That night he was kept a prisoner in Holyrood; then he was removed to Edinburgh Castle, and afterwards to the Castle of Dunbarton, of which his enemy, Lennox was the Keeper.

Morton, as we know, had very few friends. Most of the nobles feared and hated him, and even the Reformed ministers were not his friends, though he had done more than anyone else to make Protestantism secure in Scotland. When he was brought to trial, therefore, it was his enemies who were his judges. Though he denied that he was guilty of Darnley's murder, he was condemned to death ; and the day after the trial he was executed at the Market Cross of Edinburgh, and his head was stuck on the highest point of the Tolbooth. He had been a cruel and hard man, yet, while he ruled, he had made the laws obeyed, and but for him the Protestant religion might not be the religion of Scotland to-day.

Now that Morton was got rid of, Lennox and Captain Stewart (whom James had made Earl of Arran) became the first men in the country, and Lennox went on with his great plot for bringing back Mary. But soon many enemies began to rise against him, and among these enemies were the ministers, who saw quite clearly what he was aiming at. Great was their fear, therefore, lest he should succeed in restoring Mary, which would, of course, have meant the restoring of the Catholic religion. Then to deceive the ministers, Lennox did a thing which was almost too clever. Though he was a Catholic, he publicly declared in the church of St Giles that he was a Protestant. And he did something more. He got James to have a Confession of Faith (called the "Negative Confession") drawn up, in which the errors of the Catholic Church were spoken of in very strong language. But the ministers were not taken in by all this, and they disliked Lennox more and more.

And not only the ministers, but some of the nobles were among the enemies of Lennox. There was one noble especially, the Earl of Gowrie, who had at first been friendly with him, but whom he had made his deadly enemy. With a few other nobles, Gowrie determined to put an end to Lennox's power in the country, and they did this in the usual way by getting the king into their hands. This was how they managed it.

In the month of August, 1582, James had been hunting in the district of Athole, in Perthshire, and, when the hunting was over, he went to the town of Perth. While he was there, the Earl of Gowrie and several other nobles came to him, and persuaded or compelled him to go to the castle of Ruthven or Huntingtower, which belonged to Gowrie and is about three miles from Perth. The morning after James arrived at the castle, he was about to step out of doors, but he was told that this would not be permitted. James then began to cry, but one of those present, the Master of Glamis, said: "Better bairns greet than bearded men," words which James never forgot. This seizing of James was called the "Raid of Ruthven."

As had so often happened before, the nobles who had the king in their hands were able to rule the country. Gowrie and his friends made the king write a letter to Lennox telling him that he must immediately leave Scotland. Though Lennox was very anxious to remain in order that he might carry out all his plans, it would have been at the risk of his life had he done so. He therefore returned to France, where he died a short time afterwards.

The Ruthven Raiders, as long as they had the power, did exactly the opposite of what had been done by Lennox. They made friends with England instead of with France, and they passed laws against the Catholics, of whom there was still a large number in the country. As the Protestant ministers were on their side, they treated them kindly, and paid them the stipends which the Regent Morton and others had refused to give them.

But the Raiders did not enjoy their power long. James hated them for making him a prisoner, and he did not approve of the way that they ruled, so he determined to escape from them, whenever a chance came. He was now only sixteen years of age, but he was as clever and cunning as a grown-up man. He pretended that he was quite pleased with everything and everybody, and so his keepers began to be more careless in watching him. One morning, about ten months after he had been made prisoner, he was walking in the park of Falkland Palace, where he was staying. A letter was put into his hands from his grand-uncle, the Earl of March, telling him that if he came to St Andrews, he would find friends there to defend him. At the head of a small band he at once rode to St Andrews, and that night he was safe in the town, surrounded by a number of his nobles. And so, as the Raiders had lost the king, they also lost their power in the country.

57. THE BEGINNING OF A GREAT QUARREL. 1583-1585

JAMES VI. (1567-1625)

James, on his escape from the Ruthven Raiders, was only in his eighteenth year, and, though he was very clever and very learned for his age, he was not bold and manly like some of his ancestors. All his life, also, he was fond of having favourites, who came to have great power over him. We have seen how fond he was of the Duke of Lennox, whom he had been compelled to send away from Scotland. And now he chose another favourite, who was a very different man from Lennox. The new favourite was that Captain Stewart, whom he had made Earl of Arran, and who had accused Morton of having had a share in the murder of Darnley. Lennox had been smooth and pleasant in his ways, but Arran was a man who frightened people into doing what he wished. There were few persons who dared to face him when he was angry.

Arran ruled the country quite differently from Gowrie and his friends; almost everything that they had done, he tried to undo. It was at this time, indeed, that there began in Scotland the great quarrel which was to last for more than a hundred years, and which was to end in the House of Stewart being driven from the throne. Let us see what this quarrel was about.

Even when James was a boy, he had notions of his own about what a king was and how he should rule. As a child, he had the famous scholar, George

Buchanan, for his teacher. Buchanan had taken care that his pupil should be very well educated, and, indeed, James came to be one of the most learned

George Buchanan.

kings that ever sat upon a throne. Buchanan had the same opinions about rulers as John Knox and other Protestants, and he tried to teach these opinions to James. What Knox and Buchanan thought was that the people had at first chosen kings, and that a good king was one who obeyed the laws and ruled for the good of his people.

James, however, held the opinion that this was not the right view of what a king was and should be. What he believed was that kings were not chosen at first by the people, but were appointed by God to rule over them. This being the case, it was for the king to decide what was good and what was not good for his subjects, and it was their duty to obey him. It was for the king, for example, to settle what power Parliament should have, and of what religion his subjects should be, and how the Church should be governed. The king, therefore, should be the Head, not only of the State, but also of the Church. During his whole reign James tried to be a king like this, and there can be no doubt that he did try to rule for what he thought was the good of his people. But the difficulty was that many of his subjects did not take the same view as he did of what was good for them.

Now, the Protestant ministers taught that it was in the Bible that men found the true religion, and that neither popes nor kings had a right to say what that religion was, but that each man should read the Bible for himself and find what was the truth. When, therefore, James said that he was the Head of the Church, and had the right to decide what the Church should teach and how it should be governed, many of his subjects thought that he was quite wrong, and that it was not their duty to obey him when he commanded them to do what they thought was not taught in the Bible. This, then, was the great quarrel which arose in Scotland, and the reason why it lasted so long was that all James's successors had the same opinions as himself about what was called the " Divine right of Kings."

We have seen how, during the regency of Mar, the the Earl of Morton had set up the Tulchan bishops. Both the Protestant ministers and their congregations thought that these bishops were merely sham bishops, and that they ought not to be allowed. Then a minister stood forth who, after John Knox, is the best known of all the early Protestant preachers in Scotland. This was Andrew Melville, who was one of the most learned men of his time, and as zealous as Knox, though not so clever in gaining his ends. Now, Melville disliked not only Tulchan bishops, but all kinds of bishops, and he did everything in his power to prevent bishops from being appointed in Scotland.

In the year 1581, the year that the Earl of Morton was executed, a General Assembly was held at Dundee, in which Andrew Melville took the chief part. This assembly is one of the most famous in the history of the Church of Scotland, because it was by it that Presbyterianism was set up in the country. In a Presbyterian Church all the ministers are of the same rank and order, while in an Episcopalian Church there are three orders of clergy—bishops, priests, and deacons, and various ranks and titles, such as arch-bishop, bishop, and dean. Another thing that this assembly did was to put forth what is called the Second Book of Discipline, because, as we know, a Book of Discipline had already been drawn up at the time when Protestantism was set up in the year 1560. There were two things said in this Second Book of

Discipline which have to be remembered, because it was about them that all the disputes were to arise. The one was that bishops should not be allowed in the Church, and the second was that neither the king nor the Parliament had the right to say what the Church should teach nor how it should be ruled. And now we can go back to Arran, and understand what he tried to do while he had the chief power in his hands.

We have just seen that James thought that it was his right to decide what the Church should teach and how it should be ruled. We can understand, therefore, how angry he was when the General Assembly set up Presbyterianism without his order or permission. So while Arran had the chief power, a Parliament was held, by which it was declared that the king was the Head of the Church, that there should be bishops, and that the king had the right to appoint them. It was now Andrew Melville and the other ministers who were angry, but Arran was not the man to be afraid of any person's anger. When one of the ministers said that the "Black Acts," as the Presbyterians called them, were unjust, Arran told him that, though his head were as big as a hay-stack, he would make it leap from his shoulders.

But Arran's rule did not last long. He had banished to England the lords who had taken part in the Ruthven Raid, but Queen Elizabeth, who hated Arran, determined that they should return to Scotland and rule the country in place of Arran. And an event happened which gave her an excuse for demanding that James should put away his favourite.

As we saw, the English and Scottish Wardens of

the Borders used to meet on certain days to settle any quarrels that had arisen. On one of these days, in the year 1585, a dispute arose just as had happened at the Reidswire. Fighting began, and in the battle an English lord was slain. Elizabeth then accused Arran of having caused the quarrel, and demanded that James should put him in her hands as a prisoner. James refused to do this, but, as he was afraid of offending Elizabeth too much, he shut up Arran in the Castle of St Andrews. A short time afterwards the banished lords entered Scotland, and they and their friends collected an army. Arran, who had been let out of his prison, tried also to collect a force, but this he was unable to do, and his enemies were too strong for him. From this time he lost his power in the country, though he tried hard to get it back, and he came to a sad end.

He had made many enemies, and among these enemies was one named James Douglas of Torthorwald, whose uncle he had put to death. Now it happened that many years after his fall he was travelling in a lonely part of Lanarkshire. As this was the part of the country in which his enemy Douglas lived, his friends warned him of his danger. But Arran, who never feared an enemy, proudly answered that he was not afraid of any Douglas in Scotland, and he went on his way till he came to a glen in Selkirkshire. As he and his companions were riding through the glen, he asked what its name was. They told him that it was called Catslack. "Then let us ride more quickly," he said, "for it was prophesied that I should die in a place of that name." But, before they had got out of the glen, Douglas and three of his servants were seen swiftly riding after them. Soon they were overtaken, and Arran was struck from his horse and slain while he lay on the ground. So ended the life of one who had for a time been the real king of Scotland, and who was one of the worst, but also one of the boldest and cleverest men of whom we read in all our history.

---

58. JAMES VI. AND THE ENGLISH CROWN.
1587-1593

There was one thing on which James had set his mind, and which he never lost sight of, and that was to be king of England after the death of Queen Elizabeth. And in the year 1587 an event happened which made him more anxious than ever to make sure that he should be Elizabeth's successor. In that year his mother Mary was executed in Fotheringay Castle, in England. She had been more than eighteen years a prisoner in one castle after another, and, though she had more than once tried to escape, she had never succeeded. She had also taken part in many plots against Elizabeth, who would never consent to let her go free. At last, she was accused of a plot for the assassination of Elizabeth, and, after a trial in which she defended herself with wonderful courage and skill, she was declared guilty by her judges and condemned to death. And no one ever met death more bravely than Mary, and her sad end and her long years as a prisoner make us think even more of her misfortunes than of her errors.

After his mother's death James was the true heir

Madame ma bonne soeur ayant entendu par me lord boyd
que tant sen fault que mes rebelles cessent a votre
commandement la poursuite de mes subiects qu'au contraire
ils leur ont usé & pretendent user dauantaige
de rigueur en toute haste ie vous ay voulu fayre ce
mot pour prier de donner credit a monsieur de nasse
& priene en redition pour la grand necessité en
quoy ie laissay tomber mes affayres pour vous
complayre ne ne scherschant plus secours ailleurs ze
voy les delays demora parquoy ie vous suplie ou
promptement me resouldre de votre ayde ou
moy referder car dabandre e place a trayter
avec ios mon & ce pendant qu'il se fusse moste
du tont ce ne serot mon bien ni grand hunneur
avous que vous en estant meslee ils en fassent sh
pende tempte ayant emuye les discours aulong
a mylord Ress ie ne vous importuneray plus pour
leyresant sinon vous baysant les mains priendier
vous amoy renie sernte ynardo de Winkfeldce
or su me de feullet Votre bien affectionnee bonno
soeur et cousine marie R

A la Royne dangleterre
madame ma bonne soeur

Letter of Mary, Queen of Scots, to Queen Elizabeth, Written during
her Imprisonment in England.

to the English crown, but it was still not at all certain
that he would ever wear it. First of all, Elizabeth
would not name him as her successor, though he did
all he could to persuade her to do so. Then it was
not certain that the English people would have him
as their king. But there was another danger that
threatened to prevent James from ever becoming king
of England. The Pope, and the kings of France and
Spain, who were both Catholics, were all anxious
that England also should be ruled by a Catholic
sovereign; and Philip, the Spanish king, had made
up his mind that he would try to conquer England
and bring it back to the Church of Rome.

But, if Philip did conquer England, would he give
the Crown to James, who was a Protestant? This
was a puzzle for James, but, as we know, he was
exceedingly clever, and he tried to find a way out of
it. He pretended to the Pope and the kings of
France and Spain that he was really a Catholic at
heart, and that he remained a Protestant only
because he could not help himself, as most of his
subjects were Protestants.

Now, the Protestant ministers suspected that James
was quite ready to change his religion, if he could
only make sure that he would one day be king of
England. Of course, the ministers were greatly
alarmed lest Catholicism should be brought back, and
what made them more alarmed was that nearly a
third of the Scottish nobles were Catholics, as were
also many of the people in different parts of the
country. It will be seen, therefore, that there were
two reasons why the ministers were displeased with
James; first, because he wished to set up bishops in

the Church, and secondly, because they suspected that he was ready to change his religion if it served his purpose.

As we know, Philip, king of Spain, did try to conquer England. In the year 1588, the year after Mary's death, he sent his great fleet, called the *Armada*, and we know what happened to it. Elizabeth's fleet met it in the English Channel, and a fight took place, in which the Spaniards had much the worst of it. Then terrible storms arose, which compelled the great Armada to sail round the coasts of Scotland. Several of the vessels were wrecked and cast ashore, one of them at Tobermory, in the island of Mull. The last wreck is supposed to contain a great deal of treasure, which men are now trying to fish up from the bottom of the sea.

King Philip had failed to conquer England, and the great danger had passed by. But James and the ministers did not become better friends. As was just said, there were many Scottish nobles who were still Catholics, the chief being the Earl of Huntly and the Earl of Errol. Both of these earls tried to persuade Philip to send Spanish soldiers to Scotland to assist the Scottish Catholics in putting down Protestantism, and, though the Spanish soldiers were not sent, the earls gathered an army of their own and rose in rebellion. Then the ministers demanded that James should punish these earls in such a way that they should not again be able to trouble the country. But James refused to do this, as he wished to keep on friendly terms with the Catholics not only in Scotland but in other countries.

But this constant quarrelling between James and

the ministers was not for the good of the country. What the one wished, the others opposed; and the result was that James was not able to keep order in the land, and many of his subjects came to break the the laws, as if, says an old writer, "there had been no king in Israel." Here are two stories which show how little men thought of breaking the law.

The Earl of Huntly, of whom we have just heard, had long been the enemy of the Earl of Moray, who was a relative of the Regent Moray. In the month of February, 1592, Moray was staying with a few of his servants in his House of Donnibristle, near Aberdour, on the coast of Fifeshire. One night, Huntly and a band of his followers came to the house and summoned Moray to surrender. On Moray's refusing, Huntly set fire to the house, and soon it was in flames. Then Moray rushed out sword in hand, cut his way through his enemies, and ran towards the sea-shore. But his enemies knew him from the burning tassels on his helmet, and overtook him and slew him in the water. Moray was such a handsome man that he was known as the "Bonnie Earl o' Moray," and it is said that, as Huntly gashed him in the face with his sword, Moray exclaimed, "You have spoilt a better face than your own." A beautiful ballad was written about the death of Moray, of which this is the first verse:

"Ye Highlands and ye Lowlands,
    Oh! where have you been?
They hae slain the earl o' Murray,
    And laid him on the green."

The other story is as follows. Two Border clans, the Johnstones and the Maxwells, had long been at feud with each other, and in the year 1593 they met at Dryfe Sands, near the town of Lockerbie, in Dumfriesshire. Before the battle began, the chieftain on either side offered a reward to any one who would bring the head or the hand of his enemy. Though the Johnstones had not nearly so many men as the Maxwells, they gained a complete victory.

Medal of Mary, Queen of Scots.

When the chief of the Maxwells saw that the battle had gone against him, he held out his hand and asked for quarter. Instead of sparing him, Johnstone cut off the outstretched hand, and, not satisfied with this, also cut off his enemy's head, which he hung at his saddle-bow. So many wounds in the face were given in this fight that such wounds came to be called "Lockerbie licks." This was the last great clan battle that was ever fought on the Borders.

59. PRESBYTERIANISM ABOLISHED—THE GOWRIE CONSPIRACY.   1592-1603

JAMES VI. (1567-1625)

All this time the dispute between James and the Presbyterians had never ceased. The last we heard of the dispute was the passing of the " Black Acts," which declared that the king was the Head of the Church, and that bishops should be appointed. Bishops, however, were not appointed; and in the year 1587 another Act was passed by the Parliament, which seemed to make it impossible that there should ever be bishops in Scotland again. By this last Act all the property which had belonged to the Catholic Church was given to the king ; and where was then the money to come from which would support the bishops, who, of course, would require to have much larger incomes than the ordinary ministers ?

Then, in 1592, still another Act was passed, which at last seemed to settle the long dispute. This Act declared that the Church should be Presbyterian and not Episcopalian, and James himself agreed to it. For ever afterwards the Presbyterians considered it was the most important Act that had ever been passed in their favour, and they called it the *Magna Charta* of their Church, because it did for the Church what the Great Charter did for the liberties of the people of England.

But, though James agreed to this last Act, it was only because the Presbyterians happened at the time to have great power in the country. It was one of

James's qualities, however, that, if he set his mind on anything, he would not rest till he had gained his point, and at last he did succeed in triumphing over his opponents; and this was how he managed to win the victory.

The ministers were not all so much opposed to bishops as was Andrew Melville, and in the northern parts of the country especially there were many of them who were quite willing to do James's bidding. What James did, therefore, was to summon meetings of the General Assembly, though the keen Presbyterians said that he had no right to do so, as that right belonged to the Church alone. Now, in these General Assemblies the ministers came to be so much divided in their opinions, that James was able gradually to have his way, and in the year 1600 three bishops were appointed. This was the real beginning of Episcopacy in Scotland, and we shall see that in course of time there came to be as many bishops in the Protestant Church as there had been in the Church before the Reformation.

There was another reason why James was able to put down Presbyterianism, and it is very important. We know that it was with the help of some of the nobles that the Reformation had been brought about. If nobles like the Regent Moray, the Earl of Argyle, and the Regent Morton had not been on the side of Knox and the other Reformers, it is very doubtful if the Reformation would ever have taken place. But what happened now was that all the great nobles took the side of James against the Presbyterians. And why was this? It was, in the first place, because many of the nobles preferred Episcopalianism to Presbyterianism. And there was another reason still. We have seen that by an Act of Parliament the property of the old Catholic Church was given to the king. What James, therefore, did was to give a great deal of that property to many of the nobles, and in this way to get them to take his part against the Presbyterians. We shall see that, at a later time, in the reign of James's son, the nobles went over to the other side, and the result was that Episcopacy was put down and Presbyterianism set up for a number of years.

While this long dispute was going on between James and the Presbyterians, a number of events happened which must now be told, as some of them are both strange and interesting.

One of these events was that the Catholic Earls of Huntly and Errol were at last completely conquered. In the year 1594, those earls and others raised an army to compel James to favour their religion, and they defeated a royal army at Glenlivat, in Banffshire. But James himself went against them with another army, and they were not able to stand against him. The end was that both Huntly and Errol had to surrender, and were compelled to profess themselves Protestants, though, of course, they did not at heart change their religion.

In the year 1596, all Scotland rang with a bold deed that was done on the Borders. On one of those days of truce, of which we have already heard, the English and the Scottish Wardens with their followers met by the Keirhope Water, which is just on the line between the two kingdoms. The Scottish

Warden was Sir Walter Scott of Buccleuch, and the English Warden was Lord Scrope. Among the Scots who were present at the meeting was a daring Border robber, called William Armstrong of Kinmont, but better known as "Kinmont Willie," as he is named in the ballad that tells the story. Now, it was a Border law that no one who was present on the days of truce should be harmed in any way till after the sun rose the following morning. But, as Kinmont Willie was riding home after the meeting, Lord Scrope's men made him prisoner and took him to the Castle of Carlisle, where they put him in irons.

The Scottish Warden, Buccleuch, was indignant at this breaking of the Border law, and he demanded of Lord Scrope that his prisoner should be given up. No attention was paid to Buccleuch's demand, and he determined that he would rescue Willie from his prison. So one dark night, when it was pouring torrents of rain, Buccleuch at the head of a band of horsemen rode to Carlisle. To break into the castle they carried with them ladders, crowbars, hammers, and axes. When they reached the castle walls, they found that the ladders were too short to scale them. With the help of their tools, however, they broke through a postern or back door. Kinmont Willie's cell was soon found, the door was forced, and he was borne off, all in irons as he was. So swiftly and cleverly had the deed been done, that not a single Scot or Englishman was slain.

We have now to tell of a strange adventure which befell King James himself, and which is one of the most mysterious events in all our history. It was James himself who told the story, and this is how he told it. One morning, between six and seven o'clock, in the year 1600, James was in the park of Falkland Palace, and about to mount his horse for a day's hunting, of which he was always very fond, when a man came up to him. It was the Master of Ruthven, the brother of the Earl of Gowrie, son of that earl who had planned the Ruthven Raid. Ruthven told him that the night before he had found in Perth a suspicious-looking man with a pot of gold, and that he had imprisoned the man, without telling his brother, the earl. What Ruthven had come to James for, was to ask him to ride to Perth, and try to find out who the mysterious person was.

James went off on his hunting, but after it was over he rode to Perth with a few of his attendants. When James arrived at Gowrie House, and after he had a very poor dinner, Ruthven led him up a stair and through several rooms, locking the doors of each behind him. At last they came to a room, in which there was a man with a dagger in his girdle. Ruthven seized the man's dagger and held it to the king's breast, and threatened that, if he uttered a cry or opened the window, he would stab him to the heart. Then Ruthven said that he would go and call his brother, the earl; but a short time afterwards he returned alone in a very excited state. There was no help for it, he said, and James must die. He now tried to bind James's hands, but the king dragged him to the window, which had been opened while Ruthven was out of the room, and shouted for help. Just at this moment James's attendants were leaving the house, as they had been told that their master had already gone. When they heard the king's cries, however, they rushed back to the house, made their way to the room where he was, and slew the Master of Ruthven. Then the Earl of Gowrie appeared at the head of a few followers, and in the fight that followed the earl was also slain.

Such was the adventure of James, which is

Gowrie House.

known as the Gowrie Conspiracy. Very few believed the story at the time, and to this day we do not know how much of it is true. However, the whole Gowrie family were very severely punished, as their lands were taken from them, and no one was allowed to bear their name. Also, if any one was known to throw doubts on the story, he was brought to trial and made to suffer for it; and during James's reign and the reigns of his successors, the people were commanded to keep a day of thanksgiving for the deliverance of James from his enemies.

---

60. THE UNION OF THE CROWNS OF ENGLAND AND SCOTLAND. 1603-1606

JAMES VI. (1567-1625)

James at last received the prize for which he had so eagerly wished. One Saturday night (March 24, 1603), a horseman rode up to Holyrood Palace, where James was then staying. It was an Englishman, Sir Robert Carey, who had ridden from London in less than three days to tell James that Queen Elizabeth was dead. Two days later there came a message from the Privy Council of England to say that James had been chosen as her successor. So the King of Scots was now King of England and Ireland as well.

James was at this time nearly thirty-eight years of age, and was certainly one of the queerest looking kings that ever sat upon a throne. He was of the middle height, and his legs were so weak that he could not stand long without leaning on some one's shoulders. He had what are called goggle eyes, which rolled about in such a way as to make it unpleasant to look at him. His tongue was too large for his mouth, so that he could not speak distinctly, and, when he drank out of a cup, what he was drinking ran down the sides of his mouth.   As he was always afraid of being stabbed by some one, his clothes were stuffed to protect him, so that he looked much fatter than he

James I. of England and VI. of Scotland.

really was.   He was very uncleanly in his habits, and only wet the tips of his fingers when he washed his hands.   Unlike most of his ancestors, he was not bold and manly, and he could not bear to see a sword drawn in his presence. He was also very odd in all his ways, so that, though everybody saw that he was very clever, they could hardly help laughing at him.

This was the king who came to have more power over Scotland than the bravest of his ancestors. We have seen that, even before he became king of England, he had beaten his opponents, the Presbyterians; but after he was king of England he, of course, had more influence than ever. Indeed, he became what no king of Scots had ever been, an almost absolute ruler; that is, he was able to rule Scotland almost as he pleased. How did he manage to do this?

The way he did was to govern the country through his Secret or Privy Council. Under former kings the arrangement had been that the kings and the Parliaments together should choose the members of this Council, but James got the power of choosing all the members himself. Of course, he chose only such persons as he thought would do what he told them. When James wanted anything done, therefore, he had only to write to the Council, and he had no further trouble. Here is what he himself once said to the English Parliament: "Here [in London] I sit and govern Scotland with my pen : I write, and it is done ; and by a clerk of the Council I govern Scotland now, which others could not do by the sword."

But had the Scottish Parliaments no power such as they had under previous kings? They had very little power indeed, for James held very few Parliaments; and, when he did hold them, he took care that the chief persons in them should be ready to do his bidding. In the earlier part of his reign the General Assemblies had tried to prevent him from setting up

Episcopacy; but we have seen how he had gained the power of summoning these assemblies, although the Presbyterians maintained that it was only the Church that had the right of summoning them. We can now understand how James was able to carry out all the changes in Scotland of which we are about to hear.

---

61. ESTABLISHMENT OF EPISCOPACY—THE FIVE ARTICLES OF PERTH. 1606-1625

JAMES VI. (1567-1625)

When James became king of England, he was more anxious than ever to set up bishops in Scotland, so that there might be the same kind of Church in both countries; for in England the Church was Episcopalian. Now, we have seen that most of the Scottish nobles, and even some of the ministers, were in favour of Episcopacy. Most of the ministers, however, were in favour of Presbyterianism, and before James could have his way, these ministers had to be overcome.

James, therefore, forbade them to hold General Assemblies, because he thought that, as Head of the Church, he alone had the right to summon them. Some of these ministers, however, did hold an assembly at Aberdeen; and the end was that they were brought to trial, and six of them were banished from Scotland in the year 1606. James's greatest opponent was still the famous Andrew Melville, but James soon got him out of the way also. He summoned Melville and seven others of the chief ministers to London, and kept them there for about eight months. Six of them were then allowed to return to Scotland, but James Melville, Andrew's nephew, who was one of the eight, was permitted to reside only in the north of England, and Andrew himself was banished to the Continent, where he had to remain for the rest of his life.

James had now got rid of his chief opponents, and so was able to carry out his plans. In the year 1606 a Parliament met at Perth, and passed an Act which set up Episcopacy and put an end to Presbyterianism. So now, just as in the Catholic Church before the Reformation, there were archbishops and bishops in Scotland, who had a right to sit in Parliament as the Catholic bishops and abbots had done. These bishops were not Tulchan bishops, like those whom the Regent Morton and other nobles had appointed, but were real bishops, with power over their dioceses to see that the people obeyed the laws of the Church. The chief objection to these bishops was that, as they were appointed by the king, they had to do exactly as he bade them.

James, however, was not satisfied with having set up bishops: he wished the forms of worship to be the same in the Scottish Church as in the Church of England. But, though he had so much power over his Scottish subjects, he found it very difficult to make them accept these new changes. Yet, in the end, he got his way in these also.

When James went to England, he promised that he would often come north to Scotland. He came only once, however, and stayed only for about three months (1617). Most of the time was spent in hunting and feasting, and he visited most of the chief towns, where the people showed how pleased they were to see their king once more among them. But the chief reason why he had come was to get the changes in public worship introduced into the Scottish churches. He brought with him a number of English Church clergymen, and had religious services in Holyrood Chapel such as he wished to see in all the churches in the kingdom. Then he tried to get the Parliament and a meeting of clergy to agree to have the English service, but they would not give their consent, and James had to return to England without gaining his point.

But James, as we know, was not easily beaten. The year (1618) after his visit he ordered a General Assembly to meet at Perth. Before it met, he gave bribes to some of its members and frightened others, so that it was prepared to carry out his orders. So this Assembly approved what are called the " Five Articles of Perth," which made the Church of Scotland almost exactly like the Church of England. The people did not like any of these Five Articles, but the one which they disliked most was that which ordered that worshippers should kneel when they received the bread and wine at the Communion. The reason why they objected to kneel was this. In the Roman Catholic Church it is taught that the bread and wine are changed into the real body and blood of Christ, and, when a Catholic receives the consecrated bread, he receives it on his knees. What the Protestants thought, therefore, was that if they took the Communion kneeling, it would be worshipping the bread and wine, which they considered to be idolatry.

Even the Scottish bishops warned James that he was making a mistake in forcing these changes on the people, and it was soon proved that they were right. All over the country, people refused to attend the churches where the new forms of worship were introduced, and flocked to hear the ministers who kept to the old ways. But James would not yield to please his subjects, as he really believed that he had the right to order how his subjects should worship, and that it was best to have the same kind of church in both of his kingdoms. The "Five Articles of Perth," however, were to cause great trouble in the land, and we shall see that in the reign of his son they were one of the chief causes of a great rebellion.

The chief work of James in Scotland was his setting up Episcopacy instead of Presbyterianism; but he tried to do another thing which shows how clever and far-sighted he was. He wished to unite Scotland and England, so that they should have only one Parliament and be one country as they are now. However, neither the Scots nor the English would agree to this, and it was not till a hundred years afterwards that the Parliaments were united. Yet some good came of James's attempt to unite them. In earlier times the Scots and the English had often passed laws against each other. For instance, the Scottish Parliament had forbidden any Scotsman to buy goods from an Englishman. These laws were now done away with, and the two countries traded quite freely with each other. From this time, also, every Scotsman and Englishman, born after the Union of the Crowns, became a citizen of both countries.

James died in 1625, after having reigned over Scotland for fifty-eight years. He had many faults as a king, but at least he never neglected his duties as some kings have done. His reign is one of the most important in all our history, not only because he was the first sovereign to rule over the United Kingdom, but also for the great changes he made in the

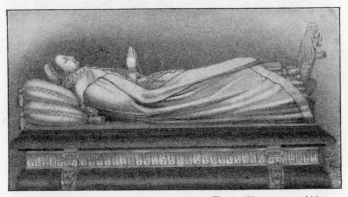

Effigy of Mary, Queen of Scots, over her Tomb, Westminster Abbey.
(Mary's remains were brought from Peterborough Cathedral to Westminster by her son, James VI.)

religion of Scotland and in the way of governing the country. But in the end it was these changes that were the cause of the House of Stewart being driven from the throne.

62. SCOTLAND IN THE REIGN OF JAMES VI.

We have seen that James VI. had more power over his subjects than any previous king of Scotland. He had shown this in putting down Presbyterianism, but he also showed it in other ways. In his reign

JAMES VI. & I.
(1566-1625).

GEORGE BUCHANAN,
Scholar and Reformer
(1506-1582).

JAMES STEWART,
Earl of Moray
(1531-1570).

JAMES DOUGLAS,
Earl of Morton
(——-1581).

SIR RICHARD MAITLAND,
of Lethington
(1496-1586).

MARY,
QUEEN OF SCOTS
(1542-1587).

MARY OF LORRAINE,
Daughter of Duke of
Guise (1515-1560).

WILLIAM DRUMMOND,
Poet,
(1585-1649).

JOHN NAPIER,
Inventor of Logarithms
(1550-1617).

JOHN KNOX,
Reformer
(1505-1572).

JAMES HEPBURN,
Earl of Bothwell
(1536-1578).

HENRY STEWART,
Lord Darnley
(1546-1567).

JAMES VI · BUCHANAN · MURRAY · MORTON · LETHINGTON · MARY · MARY OF GUISE
DRUMMOND · NAPIER · KNOX · RIZZIO · BOTHWELL · DARNLEY

the laws were better obeyed than ever they had been before. Let us see how he brought this about.

As we know, the wildest parts of the kingdom had always been the Highlands, the Western Islands, and the Borders. Kings like James IV. and James V. had done a great deal to make the people in these parts live in peace, but from the death of James V. till the Union of the Crowns they had become more and more unruly.

For example, here is one terrible affair that took place just the year before James went to England. The clan of the Macgregors, who lived in the south of Perthshire, had a quarrel with the clan of the Colquhouns in Dunbartonshire. One day a band of the Macgregors surrounded a band of the Colquhouns in a place called Glenfruin, and a fierce battle followed. The Macgregors won the victory, and carried off six hundred cattle, eight hundred sheep, two hundred horses, and other booty besides. When James heard of the " Slaughter in the Lennox," as the fight was called, he was in a furious rage, and he got an Act of Parliament passed, which took from the Macgregors all their land, and forbade any one ever afterwards to be called by their name.

But the Western Islands gave even more trouble than the Highlands, and James set himself to bring them under the law. And this was done by a very clever trick. The chiefs of the Islands were invited to come aboard a ship off the island of Mull. They came, not suspecting anything ; the ship sailed off with them, and they were all put in prison. Then next year they were compelled to sign a paper, binding themselves to obey everything that was contained in it.

2 C

This paper is called the "Band of Icolmkill," Icolm-kill being another name for Iona, and it contained nine statutes for the better government of the Western Islands. By one of the statutes every gentleman in the islands was compelled to send his eldest son to school in the Lowlands, and by another every islander was forbidden to carry firearms, which was, indeed, a law in the Lowlands also. The following year (1610) another arrangement was made, which did more than anything else to maintain peace and order in the Islands. All the great chiefs were compelled to appear before the Privy Council at certain times of the year, to make sure that none of their clansmen had broken the law. By all these arrangements, then, the Western Islands were made more peaceable and orderly than they had ever been before.

In the same way law-breakers were checked on the Borders, which had been quite as disorderly as the Highlands or Islands. The very week that James travelled to London, the clan of the Armstrongs had made a raid into Cumberland, and carried off whatever booty they could lay their hands upon. But they were never to do such a deed again, as James sent against them an armed force, which slew so many of the Armstrongs that very few of them were left.

One reason why it was so difficult to punish the Borderers was this: when any of them committed a crime, they fled to England, where they were beyond the reach of the law. But James fell upon a plan which prevented this from happening. He appointed a commission, consisting of five Englishmen and five Scotsmen, to try all the criminals on the Borders. If a Scotsman fled to England, the English commissioners sent him back to Scotland to be tried; and if an Englishman fled to Scotland, he was sent back to his own country, where he was brought before the English judges.

To make sure that no criminal would escape, a troop of twenty-five mounted police was stationed on the Borders, and were commanded to slay any one who resisted being taken. It was also ordered that no Borderer, except he were a nobleman or a gentleman, should carry any weapon, and that all persons who had iron gates to their houses should remove them and make them into ploughs or other implements. Lastly, many of the " broken men," as those who defied the law were called, were sent abroad to serve as soldiers in the German wars.

In James's reign it was made easier for the people to have justice done when they received any injury. In every county a Court was set up, which met twice a year, and to which every one could go who had suffered any injustice. It was in James's reign, also, that Justices of the Peace were introduced into Scotland. When James went to England, he saw what good these Justices did in that country, and he thought that Scotland would be the better for having Justices also. It was ordered, therefore, that in every county there should be Justices of the Peace, who should try all crimes that did not deserve death. As we know, there are still Justices of the Peace in Scotland, and this was the beginning of them.

Trade and manufactures made more progress in James's reign than they had ever done before. Glass and soap and leather, for example, were now for the first time made in Scotland. In those days there was a curious way of encouraging manufacturers and merchants. They paid a sum of money to the king, and in return they alone were allowed to make or sell certain goods, so that they could set any price upon them they pleased. This was called having a "monopoly." To this day there are "goldsmiths to the king," and "tailors to the king," which does not mean much now, but, in the times of which we are speaking, it meant a great deal, as a tradesman to the king was the only one who had the right to sell a certain kind of goods.

In James's reign Edinburgh was a more important place than it had ever been before. It was there that the Court usually stayed; and there, also, that the Privy Council and the High Courts of Justice sat. In the year 1582 the College, or, as it is now called, the University of Edinburgh, had its beginning; so that Scotland had four universities, the other three being those of St Andrews, Glasgow, and Aberdeen. The town that came next to Edinburgh in riches was Dundee, and after Dundee came Aberdeen, Perth, and St Andrews. Glasgow was as yet only a village, and was considered the prettiest place in all Scotland.

There is one question we cannot help asking, and that is—Did the Union of the Crowns do good or harm to Scotland? Most Scotsmen then living would have said that it did much more harm than good. First it took the Court away from Edinburgh, so that the tradespeople in the city lost a great deal of their business. Then from all parts of the country the nobles and gentry went to London, and spent their money there instead of at home. Before the

Union, when Scottish merchants sent their goods to France, they had to pay only small duties to the French government, but after the Union they had to pay almost as high duties as the merchants of other countries. For this reason the trade of Scotland with France became much less than it had formerly been.

But perhaps the most unpopular result of all was, that by the Union Scotland ceased to be an independent kingdom. James VI. and the kings who came after him very seldom visited their " ancient kingdom," as they called it, and Scotland became only a part of England. When England went to war, the Scots were not asked whether they approved of the war or not; yet they had to pay money and send soldiers to carry it on. All through the seventeenth century, till the Parliaments of the two countries were united, Scotland was governed from London by kings who knew very little of the country. We cannot wonder, therefore, that the Scots did not like England any better after the Union than they had done before it, and that they looked back with regret to the time when they had a king of their own and Scotland was an independent country.

---

63. CHARLES'S FIRST VISIT TO SCOTLAND.
1633

CHARLES I. (1625-1649)

The king who succeeded James was his second son, Charles; the eldest son, Prince Henry, having died while he was a young man. No son could be more unlike his father than Charles was unlike James.

James was talkative and familiar with everybody, high and low, while Charles was grave and dignified and

After Vandyck.]

Charles I.

reserved. James was odd-looking in his appearance, whereas Charles was handsome and bore himself more like a king. James, however, was a cleverer man than his son, and what is more, he understood the character of his Scottish subjects much better. It was, indeed, chiefly because Charles did not understand the Scottish people that his reign was so unfortunate.

Charles had exactly the same notions as his father had about kings and their subjects. He believed that a king was appointed by God, and that it was the duty of his people to obey him in everything. The king, he thought, was Head not only of the State but also of the Church, and it was for him to say how his people should worship and what they should believe. It was because Charles tried to carry out these notions that his subjects both in England and Scotland at last rebelled against him.

It was not till eight years after Charles succeeded to the throne that he came to Scotland to be crowned king of Scots. Just like his father James, therefore, he governed the country through the Privy Council, to which he sent down orders as to what he wished done. And during these eight years a step was taken which was to be one of the chief causes of all Charles's troubles. We have seen that a great many of the lands that had belonged to the old Catholic Church had passed into the hands of the nobles. Now, what Charles did was to take these lands from the nobles, and to pay their owners what he thought the lands were worth. But the nobles were very unwilling to give up their lands, and so they became very discontented with the king and his way of governing the country. And we shall see that a time came when most of them rose against him.

At last, in the year 1633, Charles did come to

Scotland to receive his crown, and great preparations were made to show how happy his subjects were to have their king among them. In every parish through which he and his attendants were to pass the roads were all repaired, and horses and carts were ready to convey their luggage. Holyrood Palace, where he was to stay, was fitted up to receive him, and new tapestry was hung up on the walls, because the old had been eaten away by rats. The streets of Edinburgh, which were usually in a very dirty condition, were cleaned and strewn with sand. Arches made of flowers and branches of trees spanned the streets; the houses were hung with tapestry; and at the market cross a fountain ran wine, which every one who pleased might drink. All the beggars were driven out of the town, and the heads of executed criminals, which in those days were stuck in prominent places, were ordered to be removed.

The people of Edinburgh, therefore, did all they could to show how glad they were to see their king in his northern capital. But they could not discover from Charles's looks whether he was pleased or not. When his father James appeared in public, he used to laugh and jest with those around him; but Charles looked cold and stately, so that the people said he was not so pleasant as his father.

There were some things done during his visit, also, which made him still more unpopular. When he was crowned in Holyrood Chapel, he was anointed with oil; which the Presbyterians did not like, as it was the custom in the Roman Catholic Church. Then, on the Sunday following the coronation, there was a religious service in St Giles Church, where two English Church clergymen went through the English service, and were dressed in white gowns; which the Presbyterians, whose ministers wore black gowns, thought was also Roman Catholic.

But the question about which the people were most excited was—What would the Parliament do when it met? Would it approve of all the changes that James VI. had made in the Church, or not? There was one thing certain, and that was that the Parliament would do what Charles wished, as, like his father, he had taken care that those who were on his side should have the chief power. What the Parliament did, therefore, was to approve of all the laws that James's Parliaments had passed about religion. There was to be an English service in all the churches; the bishops were to wear white gowns when they officiated; and the lower clergy were to wear surplices. So, under Charles as under James, the Church of Scotland was to be made almost exactly like the Church of England.

After staying little more than a month in Scotland, Charles returned to England. His visit had been a great disappointment to the Presbyterians, as it had shown that he was even more Episcopalian than his father. He left the country, indeed, in a very unsettled state. Most of the common people disliked the English service, and, as we have seen, the nobles were displeased with Charles for taking the church lands from them; and, besides, they did not like his giving so much power to the bishops. Everybody felt that things could not go on as they were going, and wondered what would be the end of it all.

64. THE NEW SERVICE BOOK (1637)—THE NATIONAL COVENANT (1638)

CHARLES I. (1625-1649)

Charles had let it be known that before very long he would send a Service Book to Scotland, which was to be used in all the churches, and which would show how religious worship was to be conducted. Everybody wondered what the book would be like, and eagerly expected its coming. At length, in the month of May, 1637, the Service Book or Liturgy did come, and with it there came the king's order that every minister should have two copies of it in his parish, as otherwise he would be banished from the kingdom. Then there was such excitement in the country as never had been seen in Scotland before.

People of all ranks were angry at the book for two reasons. The first reason was this. When James VI. made any changes in religion, he got the Parliament and the General Assembly to consent to them. But Charles, when he commanded the Service Book to be used by all his subjects, did not ask the consent of either the Parliament or the Assembly, and simply ordered that the book must be used because he wished it. The other reason was that people believed that what the book contained was far more Catholic than Protestant. And what made them still more indignant was that they also believed that the book had been composed by an Englishman, Archbishop Laud, a great friend of Charles: and so they called the book Laud's Liturgy.

All over the country there was great indignation at the Liturgy and at the way in which the king had acted, and nowhere was there greater anger than in Edinburgh, as was soon to appear. It was ordered

St Giles Church, Edinburgh.

that the book should be read in the church of St Giles in that town, on Sunday, the 23rd of July, about two months after Charles had sent it.

A great crowd of people came to the church to see what would happen. The archbishops of Glasgow and St Andrews were present, as well as the Lords of the Privy Council and of the Court of Session. No sooner had the Dean, who conducted the service, begun to read from the Liturgy than a great hubbub arose in the congregation. Then an old woman, who goes by the name of Jenny Geddes, started up, and calling out, "Dost thou say mass at my lug?" flung the stool on which she had been sitting at the Dean's head. When the Bishop of Edinburgh mounted the pulpit, all kinds of missiles were thrown at him, and when he and the other clergy left the church they were pelted by the mob, though none of them were seriously injured. After this no clergyman was bold enough to read the Liturgy in an Edinburgh church.

The question now was—Who would have to give way, the king or the people? From all parts of the country—from nobles, gentlemen, ministers, and townsmen—petitions were sent to the Privy Council praying that the Liturgy might be withdrawn. Great crowds of people, also, began to flock to Edinburgh, where the Privy Council held its meetings. But these crowds caused great confusion in the town, and at the request of the Council, the nobles, the gentlemen, the ministers, and the burghers each chose certain of their own number to explain to the Council what they wished. The persons thus chosen were called the "Tables," which were the same as what we now call committees. Besides these four Tables, there was one principal Table chosen from the chief men in the other four. So by means of these Tables all classes in the country—the nobles, the gentlemen, the ministers, and the townsmen—could let Charles and the Privy Council know what they wanted.

Then another step was taken which was to be the beginning of a rebellion against Charles. We saw that in the time of Mary of Lorraine, when the Reformation was beginning, the Protestant lords bound themselves by a covenant or agreement that they would not rest till religion was reformed. This is called the "First Covenant." We saw, also, that in the year 1581 a Confession of Faith, called the "Negative Confession," was drawn up and signed by King James and many of the courtiers and ministers. This came to be known as the "Second Covenant," and during the reign of James it was signed several times.

What was now done, then, was to renew this Covenant, and what did this mean? It meant that all those who signed it bound themselves to do everything in their power to prevent Roman Catholicism from being brought back to the country, and to have nothing but what they thought was the pure religion taught in the Bible. This "National Covenant," as it is called, was made up of three parts—the Negative Confession, which denounced all the errors of the Church of Rome, and of two other portions which were thought necessary at the time.

The next step was to have the National Covenant signed by as many persons as possible, so that the king might know how much his subjects disliked the Liturgy, which he was trying to impose upon them. And there was no difficulty in getting people to sign it. On the 28th of February, 1638, thousands put their names to it in Greyfriars Church and Churchyard, Edinburgh. Copies of it were sent to all parts of the country, and the people flocked to sign it. Almost all the nobles and almost all the towns did the same, so that Charles could not help seeing that he had

From Painting by]   [Wm. Hole, R.S.A.

The Signing of the Covenant in Greyfriars Churchyard.

the greater part of his subjects against him. What was to happen next? Would Charles be forced to yield, or would he be able to compel Scotland to receive his Liturgy?

---

65. THE "BISHOPS' WARS." 1639-1641

CHARLES I. (1625-1649)

Now that the Covenanters, as those who signed the Covenant were called, saw that they had so many of the people on their side, they, of course, became bolder against the king. They demanded that a free Parliament and a free General Assembly should be held, which should settle what the religion of the country was to be, how the Church was to be governed, and what forms of worship were to be followed. And what did the Covenanters mean by a *free* Parliament and a *free* Assembly? They meant a Parliament and an Assembly in which the king should not have all his own way, but in which the wishes of his subjects should also be taken into account.

At last Charles saw that there was no help for it but to consent that a free Parliament and a free General Assembly should meet. Before they met, however, he tried a plan by which he thought he might gain some of the Covenanters to his side. He got another covenant prepared which came to be called the "King's Covenant," while the National Covenant was called the "Noblemen's Covenant." The Negative Confession was also part of the King's

Covenant, but along with it there was another part which went right against the National Covenant. Charles's plan, however, did not succeed, as very few people were willing to sign his Covenant.

The General Assembly did at length meet in Glasgow in the month of November, 1638, and it is one of the most famous Assemblies that was ever held. As the leaders of the Covenanters took care, just as James and Charles had done, that as many of their friends as possible should be members of the Assembly, there was little fear that it would not do exactly as they wished. Its Moderator was the Rev. Alexander Henderson, whose name is remembered along with those of John Knox and Andrew Melville, and its Clerk was a great lawyer named Johnston of Warristoun, who was afterwards put to death in the reign of Charles II. for what he had done as a Covenanter. The Assembly sat for a month, and it did everything that the leaders of the Covenanters desired. It put an end to bishops, to the Five Articles of Perth, to the new Liturgy, and, in short, set up Presbyterianism in place of Episcopacy.

And what did Charles think of the doings of the Glasgow Assembly? He said that it was not a *lawful* Assembly because the Covenanters would not allow any of the bishops to be members of it, and Charles maintained that an Assembly without the bishops was not a real Assembly. The result was that the quarrel between the king and the Covenanters grew more and more bitter, and both sides began to see that only war could settle it.

In the beginning of the year after the Glasgow

JOHN,
Earl of Mar
(1675-1732).

JOHN, 2nd
Duke of Argyle
(1680-1743).

JOHN GRAHAM,
Viscount Dundee,
(1649-1689).

JOHN MAITLAND,
Duke of Lauder-
dale (1616-1682).

CHARLES II.
(1630-1685).

JAMES GRAHAM,
Marquis of Montrose
(1612-1650).

DAVID
LESLIE,
(——1682).

CHARLES I.
(1600-1649).

ANDREW FLETCHER,
of Salton
(1655-1716).

Sir JOHN DALRYMPLE,
Earl of Stair
(1648-1707).

JAMES
VII. & II.
(1633-1701).

ROBERT LEIGHTON,
Archbishop of Glasgow
(1611-1684).

ARCHIBALD CAMPBELL,
Earl of Argyle
(1598-1661).

GEORGE JAMESONE,
Portrait Painter
(1588-1644).

Assembly, therefore, both Charles and the Covenanters began to prepare for war. But it was not very easy for Charles to raise an army. In England as well as in Scotland, he had been quarrelling with his subjects, many of whom were more inclined to take the side of the Covenanters than the side of the king. However, he did at length succeed in raising an army, and at the end of the month of May, 1639, he led it to Berwick-on-Tweed.

By that time the Covenanters had also collected an army, and one much more ready to fight than that of Charles. The men who joined it were mostly young ploughmen from the western counties, as it was in these counties that the people were the keenest Covenanters. It happened, also, that many Scottish officers who had served in the German wars came home and joined the Covenanters' army, and they were ordered to drill the soldiers and train them how to behave in battle. The general who was chosen was Alexander Leslie, an "old, little, crooked soldier," who had been through many wars in other countries.

On the 5th of June the Covenanting army encamped on Dunse Law, about twelve miles from the Border. Tents of canvas were raised for the officers, and wooden huts, covered with turf, for the men. At the tent doors of the chief officers hung blue banners, with the words, "FOR CHRIST'S CROWN AND COVENANT," in gold letters, inscribed on them. By this time, also, Charles had marched his army to a place called the Birks, about three miles from Berwick, and on the south bank of the river Tweed.

The two armies were thus face to face. Would

2 D

there now be a great battle, to decide whether the
king or the Covenanters were to have their way?
Both sides were unwilling to begin the fight, as they

Alexander Henderson.

knew what terrible misfortunes civil war would bring
upon the country. To try to settle their quarrel
without fighting, therefore, the king and the leaders
of the Covenanters began to treat with each other,

and the end was that an arrangement was made between them. By this arrangement Charles agreed that a free General Assembly and a free Parliament should meet, but he would not admit that the Assembly which had met at Glasgow was a lawful Assembly. This treaty was called the "Pacification of Berwick," and the war was called the "First Bishops' War." Both the king and the Covenanters, however, quite understood that their quarrel was not ended, and that sooner or later the sword would have to be drawn again.

It was not long, indeed, before the sword was again drawn. In the month of August that followed the treaty made at Berwick, the General Assembly and the Parliament met in Edinburgh. As the Covenanters were most numerous in both the Assembly and the Parliament, they had no difficulty in having their wishes carried out. Just as in the Glasgow Assembly, Episcopacy was put down and Presbyterianism was set up. But the question was—Would Charles agree to do now what he had refused to do before? Charles did again refuse, and then both sides saw that there must be another war to settle the quarrel.

This time, however, the Covenanters determined that they would invade England and prevent Charles from entering Scotland. So in the month of August, 1640, their army, commanded by Alexander Leslie, crossed the river Tweed into England. A force was sent by Charles to prevent the Scots from crossing the Tyne, but it was easily defeated, and then the Scots marched into Newcastle, where they took up their quarters.

And what was Charles doing all this time? He had found it even more difficult than before to raise an army. He had quarrelled with his English Parliament, which refused to give him money to pay for maintaining soldiers. He did succeed, however, in collecting an army; but it was an army that was unwilling to fight in his cause, and the common soldiers even mutinied against their officers. With such a force Charles could not dare to fight the Scots, and, just as in the case of the first Bishops' War, the leaders of the Covenanters told Charles that they would become his loyal subjects if he would agree to approve of the National Covenant and to put down Episcopacy.

But by this time Charles's English Parliament had become so rebellious that he had very little power in the country. In the end, therefore, it was with the English Parliament and not with the king that the Covenanters had to make a treaty. It was a long time before the arrangement was made, and the Scottish army remained a whole year in Newcastle. At last a treaty was made at Westminster (August, 1641), and by this treaty all the demands of the Covenanters were granted, and what is more, they were to receive a large sum of money to pay the expenses of supporting their army in England. And so ended what is called the "Second Bishops' War." The Covenanters had for the time gained their end; but they knew that, if Charles should ever recover his power, he would never allow Presbyterianism to be the religion of Scotland.

66. THE SOLEMN LEAGUE AND COVENANT.
1643

CHARLES I. (1625-1649)

Charles was now in a most unhappy position. His English Parliament had rebelled against him, and his Scottish subjects had also risen against him. Where was he to look for friends and supporters? He seems to have thought that he would find them in Scotland rather than in England, for only a week after the Westminster Treaty he came to Edinburgh. But how different was this visit from his first one in 1633! Then he had come as the lord and master of his subjects, who must submit to whatever he commanded. Now, as he himself said, he had come to "give content and satisfaction" to all his people.

When Charles arrived in Edinburgh, the Parliament was sitting there, and, if he was to gain friends, he would have to agree to the Acts which it passed. And, indeed, he had to consent to many things which must have been against both his will and his conscience. He had to approve of the Westminster Treaty, which settled that Presbyterianism and not Episcopacy was to be the religion of Scotland. He had also to give up much of the power which he and his father James had claimed to be their right. For example, both he and his father had appointed the members of the Privy Council and other high officials without asking the consent of the Parliament, but Charles now agreed that in future neither he nor his successors would appoint them without the

Parliament's approval. Of course, the reason why Charles assented to all these things was that he wished to have the Scots on his side if his English Parliament should go to war with him.

And now that the Covenanters had got all they wished, were they satisfied and happy? They were not, and for two reasons. The first reason was that they knew that Charles had yielded only because he could not help himself, and that, if ever he got back his power, he would be sure to restore Episcopacy.

The second reason was that they had begun to be divided among themselves. There were two nobles who had taken an important part in supporting the National Covenant—the Earl of Montrose and the Earl of Argyle, both of whom were made marquises by Charles. At first, Montrose had been one of the keenest of all the Covenanters, but he had now gone over to the side of the king. He was a bold and dashing man, and greater in war than in peace. Argyle was also a keen Covenanter, and remained one all his life. He was the most powerful noble in all Scotland, and, as he was a wise and prudent counsellor, he came to be the chief of the Covenanting leaders.

Montrose being now on the king's side, he, of course, tried to gain friends for him; and he did succeed in gaining a few whom the Covenanters called the "Plotters." Just before Charles had come to Edinburgh, however, Montrose and others of the Plotters had been imprisoned in the Castle to prevent them from going on with their plots. While Charles was in Edinburgh, also, a mysterious thing happened which we cannot explain, and which went by the name of "The Incident." The story is that there was a plot to slay Argyle and another noble, the Marquis of Hamilton, and, when they were put out of the way, to have Charles restored to power. How much is true in this story we cannot tell, but we see, at least, that the Covenanters were not now such a united body as they had been at first. And, indeed, from this time onwards more and more of the nobles who had once been Covenanters went over to the side of the king.

Charles left Edinburgh in the month of November (1641), to return to London; and there great troubles awaited him. He and his English Parliament went on quarrelling more bitterly than ever, and, at last, just as had been the case in Scotland, both sides found that only the sword could settle their dispute. So, in the year 1642, civil war broke out between the supporters of the king and the supporters of the Parliament. In the first battles that were fought Charles was victorious, and it seemed as if in the end the Parliament would be defeated.

Now, both Charles and the English Parliament were very anxious to have the Scots on their side, as a Scottish army would be of great assistance to them. Both, therefore, did all they could to persuade the Scots to join them. But the Scots were divided among themselves as to whether they should assist the king or the Parliament. By far the greater number, however, thought that they should support the Parliament and not the king, and for this reason: if Charles should be victorious, he would be sure to lead an army into Scotland and restore Episcopacy, which he believed to be the best form of Church government both for king and for people.

In the end, therefore, the Covenanters agreed to assist the English Parliament against the king, and a treaty was made between them. This treaty is called the "Solemn League and Covenant," by which both parties agreed that they would try to set up Presbyterianism in England as well as in Scotland. The Covenanters really meant that this should be tried; but the English Parliament agreed to the arrangement only because it was so anxious to have the Scots on its side against the king. In Scotland the Covenanters did all they could to make every person in the country accept the Solemn League and Covenant, and they even passed a law compelling both ministers and their congregations to agree to it, which was exactly what James VI. and Charles had done in favour of Episcopacy.

Having made this treaty with the English Parliament, the Scots had now to raise an army to assist it in its war against the king. An army was soon raised, and under the command of David Leslie, the nephew of Alexander Leslie, it marched into England, where it remained for three years. It helped to win the battle of Marston Moor, in which Charles was defeated, and in other ways it assisted the Parliament to conquer him completely in the end. But we shall see that the Scots afterwards found that they had made a great mistake in ever sending an army into England.

67. THE DEEDS OF MONTROSE. 1644-1645

CHARLES I. (1625-1649)

While the army of the Covenanters was in England, a great danger arose in Scotland. We have seen how the Marquis of Montrose, who was at first a Covenanter, had gone over to the side of the king. Now that the army of the Covenanters was in England, therefore, he determined to try to conquer Scotland for Charles; and, if any one was likely to succeed in doing this, he was the man, as he was now to show.

In the year 1644, the year after the Scottish army went across the Border, Montrose came from England disguised as a groom and with only two companions. If he had been caught, he would have been imprisoned, as he was known to be plotting for Charles. However, he travelled safely through the Lowlands, and reached the house of a friend near Perth. It had been arranged beforehand that a band of soldiers was to come from Ireland, and that Montrose was to be their leader. The Irish soldiers came, and a wild and savage set of men they were. But Montrose expected that many of the Highlanders would also join him, and he had the king's order to summon them to fight in his cause.

Now, the way in which an army was raised in the Highlands was this. A cross was made of two sticks, and the ends of it were burned in the fire and then dipped in goat's blood. Then this Fiery Cross, as it was called, was given to a clansman, who ran at full speed through glen and over mountain, holding the cross aloft so that it might be seen by every one. When he had run a certain

Marquis of Montrose.

distance, he handed it on to another clansman, and so it was passed from hand to hand till the whole country knew that the chiefs were about to go to war. If any Highlander did not obey the summons, he was no longer one of his clan, and this was the greatest punishment that could happen to him. So the Fiery Cross was sent round to summon the clansmen to join the standard of Montrose, and many did obey the summons, not so much, however, because they cared for King Charles, as because they hated the Marquis of Argyle, the chief of the Covenanters, who had offended most of the Highlanders in that part of the country where Montrose now was.

Now that Montrose had an army around him, he was not the man to lose time before he led it to battle. The Covenanters were, of course, greatly alarmed when they heard that so bold a leader as Montrose was at the head of this wild army of Irish and Highlanders, and they at once sent a force against him. The two armies met at Tippermuir, near the town of Perth. The Covenanters had far more men than Montrose, but most of them had never seen a battle in their lives, and did not know how to use their weapons. The Highlanders, on the other hand, by their ways of living were used to fighting, and they were trained in handling their swords and dirks. When the battle began, they, as they always did, made a furious rush on the enemy. Only well-trained soldiers could have stood against such an onset; but, as we have seen, the men in the Covenanting army were not trained soldiers, and their ranks were broken at once, and they fled in all directions. The battle was over in less than ten minutes, and, while very few of Montrose's men fell, the greater number of the enemy were either slain or made prisoners.

Having gained this easy victory, Montrose now marched into the town of Perth; but he could not remain long there, as the Marquis of Argyle was approaching with an army much larger than his own. Then he marched to Aberdeen, and now it was seen of what kind of men his army was composed. The town was taken and plundered, and his Irish soldiers, whom he could not control, robbed and slew every one who came in their way. Before they killed their victims, they made them take off their clothes, so that these should not be soiled with blood.

It was in the month of September, 1644, that Montrose had taken Aberdeen, and during the rest of the winter and on into the next summer he kept marching from one part of the country to another. He fought no fewer than four battles, and in every one of these he was victorious. He plundered the lands of his great enemy, Argyle, and afterwards completely defeated him at Inverlochy, near Fort William, in Inverness-shire.

But Montrose's greatest victory was the last one which he was to gain. This battle was fought at Kilsyth, in Stirlingshire, on the 15th of August, 1645, just a year from the time when he had raised his standard. As usual, the Covenanters had most men; and on this occasion they were led by an experienced general, named Baillie. Very foolishly, however, the chiefs of the Covenanters would not allow him to act as he thought best. Before the battle began, Montrose ordered his men to strip to their shirts, as the weather was very hot. Then, as in his previous battles, his whole army threw themselves on the enemy. Baillie fought like a brave soldier and general, and Montrose did not gain so easy a victory as he had done at Tippermuir, but in the end the Covenanters were completely defeated. Almost all their foot-soldiers were slain or taken prisoners, and so savage were Montrose's followers in the pursuit, that they killed many of the unarmed inhabitants of the surrounding country.

After Montrose's victory at Kilsyth there was not another army in Scotland to meet him in the field. So he now marched to Glasgow, which surrendered to him without his requiring to strike a blow. Indeed, he now thought himself so much master of the whole country that, in the name of the king, he summoned a Parliament to meet in Glasgow on the 20th of October. But before that day came he was to be in a very different position. From this time onwards, indeed, everything went against him, and he was now near the end of all his triumphs.

Up till now the Highlanders had followed him, not so much because they loved King Charles, as because they got plenty of plunder. But Montrose would not permit them to plunder in Glasgow, and the result was that they were so angry that most of them deserted him and returned to their homes among the mountains. Then Montrose led his men through the Lowlands as far as the Borders, hoping that the friends of the king would flock to his standard. Very few did join him, however, as most of the people of the Lowlands were on the side of the Covenanters.

In the meantime the Covenanters had got another army to meet their victorious enemy. David Leslie, their best general, came from England at the head of a body of trained soldiers, who would be more difficult to defeat than the untrained troops whom Montrose had hitherto had to face. The two armies met at

Archibald, First Marquis of Argyle.

Philiphaugh, on the banks of the Ettrick, near the town of Selkirk. As we have seen, most of the Highlanders, Montrose's best fighting men, had deserted him and returned to their homes. On this occasion, also, he had opposed to him a skilful general, and troops that had been accustomed to fighting. The result was that he was completely defeated, and with a few friends he fled from the field of battle to the Highlands, as he would certainly have been put to death if he had been captured.

After the battle the victors took a terrible revenge for all that had happened during the past year. They slew not only the men who were taken prisoners, but even their wives. Most of those who were put to death were Irish and not Scots ; and at this time, both in England and Scotland, the Irish were looked upon rather as beasts than as human beings. Only a few years before, the Irish had massacred great numbers of Scots and English—men, women, and children—in Ireland. In the battles of Montrose, also, it had been his Irish soldiers who had behaved with the greatest cruelty. The victors at Philiphaugh, therefore, had good reasons for fearing and hating the Irish, though this does not excuse their putting captive women to death. It should not be forgotten, however, that in the wars carried on in other countries at that time far more cruel deeds were done than any that happened in Scotland.

---

68. THE SCOTS AND OLIVER CROMWELL.
1645-1647

CHARLES I. (1625-1649)

Montrose had hoped that, after conquering Scotland for Charles, he would be able to assist him in conquering his enemies in England. But this was not to happen. Montrose had been completely defeated at Philiphaugh, and was not able to raise another army sufficiently strong to fight General Leslie. A few months before the battle of Philiphaugh, also, the army of the English Parliament had gained a great victory over Charles at Naseby, and after that defeat there was very little hope that he would ever be an independent king again.

And now that the English Parliament had conquered the king, would it keep the treaty it had made with the Scots in the Solemn League and Covenant? The Covenanters had hoped that, should the Parliament be victorious, it would establish Presbyterianism in England as well as in Scotland. They were now to find that they had been greatly mistaken.

In the English Parliament the party that came to have the greatest power was the party called the Independents. The chief lead r of this body was the famous Oliver Cromwell, who by his skill as a general had done more than any one else to win the victory over the Royalists, as Charles's supporters were called. Now, the Independents had notions of their own as to how the Church should be governed, and these notions were entirely different from those of the Presbyterians. The Independents, therefore, could never agree that Presbyterianism should be set up in England. The result was that a bitter quarrel broke out between them and the Scots.

When the Scots consented to send an army into England, the agreement made was that the English Parliament should pay all its expenses. But after the king was defeated at Naseby, the Parliament thought that it had no longer any need of the Scottish army,

and it refused to pay any more money for its support.
The English Parliament, however, was very much
afraid of one thing, and that was lest Charles should

Oliver Cromwell.

make friends with the Scots; for, if this were to
happen, it would have to fight both the Covenanters
and the Royalists. Great, therefore, was the fear
and indignation of the Parliamentarians when they

2 E

were told that Charles had gone to the Scottish army, which was then encamped near Newark, in Nottinghamshire. Still greater was their alarm when they learned that, as soon as the king was in the hands of the Scots, they had marched to Newcastle, where they could keep him in greater safety.

The Scots were greatly puzzled when Charles appeared in their camp. They would have been quite willing to have him as their king, if he would only agree to accept the two Covenants and to maintain Presbyterianism in Scotland. When they asked Charles to consent to this, however, he would not give his word. Then the English Parliament sent a stern message to the Scots to say that, if they did not give up the king, there must be war between them. What were the Scots to do? They could not fight for a king who would not rule them as they wished. They consented, therefore, to give up the king, but on the condition that no harm should be done to him. It was now no longer necessary that the Scots should remain in England, so after they had received a sum of money (though not nearly so much as they demanded) in payment of all their expenses, they returned to Scotland, greatly to the relief of the English Parliamentary party.

What had the Covenanters gained by making the Solemn League and Covenant with the Parliament of England? The chief thing they had hoped for was that, if the Parliament were victorious over the king, Presbyterianism would be set up both in England and Scotland. As we have seen, however, that did not happen, and in this the Covenanters were greatly disappointed. But there was one thing that did take place, which was the result of the Solemn League and Covenant. In the year 1643 there met at Westminster an assembly of divines and laymen, a few being Scotsmen, who tried to settle all their difficulties about religion. They continued to meet for six years, but on many points they could not agree. It was, however, from this Westminster Assembly, as it is called, that Scotland got the Confession of Faith, the Version of the Psalms still sung in our churches, and the Longer and Shorter Catechisms, which have all remained in use down to the present day.

---

69. THE "ENGAGEMENT" (1647)—EXECUTION OF CHARLES (1649)

By this time a great change had taken place in Scotland. When the rebellion against Charles first began, most of the nobles and most of the common people were united against him. Now, however, many of the nobles as well as many of the people were anxious to have their king restored, more especially as he was a prisoner in the hands of the Independents, whom all Scotsmen disliked for their religious opinions. So, near the end of the year 1647, three Scottish nobles—the Earls of Loudoun, Lanark, and Lauderdale—went to Charles, who was then a prisoner in Carisbrooke Castle, in the Isle of Wight, and made a secret treaty with him. By this treaty Charles agreed that he would consent to the Solemn League and Covenant if people were not compelled to sign it against their will, and the three nobles promised that, if it should be necessary, the Scots would assist Charles with an army against the English Parliament. This treaty was called the "Engagement"; and so afraid were Charles and the Scottish lords that it should become known to Cromwell and the other Independents, that they put it in a leaden box and buried it in the garden of the Castle.

When the Engagement became known in Scotland there arose a great quarrel, which was to bring many misfortunes on the country. All the keen Covenanters thought that the Engagement should never have been made, as they believed that every one should be compelled to sign the Solemn League and Covenant. So there came to be two parties bitterly opposed to each other—those in favour of the Engagement, who were called "Engagers," and those against it, who were called "Anti-Engagers." And now the Engagers, whose chief leader was the Marquis of Hamilton, determined to invade England with a Scottish army to free Charles from the Independents, and to restore him to the throne. Hamilton had great difficulty in raising an army, but he did succeed in raising one, though it was quite unfit to stand against the English soldiers who had been trained by Cromwell. However, Hamilton did invade England; but when he was marching through Lancashire he was met by the troops of Cromwell, and after three days' fighting his army was almost completely destroyed, he himself being taken prisoner a few days later.

This great defeat of the Engagers now gave the chief power in Scotland to the Anti-Engagers.

From Painting by Sir John Gilbert, R.A.]   *[By Permission of the Corporation of Sheffield.*

Charles I. leaving Westminster Hall after Sentence of Death had been passed.

About 6000 men from Ayrshire, Lanarkshire, and Renfrewshire, where the Covenanters were strongest, marched all the way to Edinburgh, where they were joyfully received by the citizens. This march of the western Covenanters was called the "Whiggamores' Raid," from the word "whiggam," which was used in the west country to make horses quicken their pace.

The Anti-Engagers being now at the head of affairs, the Marquis of Argyle, who had always been opposed to the Engagement, and Johnston of Warristoun, the great lawyer, became the most influential men in the country. They had a very difficult task before them, as they were soon to see. Cromwell and the Independents had been greatly enraged when the Scottish army under Hamilton had invaded England, and they determined that this should not happen again. So Cromwell at the head of an army came to Edinburgh and compelled Argyle and Warristoun to make a treaty, by which it was agreed that the Anti-Engagers and the Independents would never make peace with the "Malignants," as they called the Royalists or supporters of the king.

The Scottish Presbyterians and the Independents had such different opinions about both the Church and the State that they could never have agreed; but an event now happened which was to make them deadly enemies, and was to cause great bloodshed and misery to Scotland. On the 30th of January, 1649, King Charles was executed by the order of the Independents.

When the news was brought to Scotland, almost every Scotsman, whatever were his opinions, was indignant at the deed. Many of them had thought that Charles had not ruled wisely and they had rebelled against him, but still, he and his ancestors had been their kings for centuries past, and they were indignant that he had been put to death by the Independents whom all Scotsmen hated and feared. And the next step taken by Argyle and his supporters was to show that they had always regarded Charles as their lawful king, and to show, also, that they were prepared to do battle with the Independents as enemies to religion and the State.

---

70. CHARLES II. PROCLAIMED KING (1649) —DUNBAR DROVE (1650)

Both Scotland and England were now without a king, but there was this difference between the two countries: the party that had the chief power in England did not wish to have a king, whereas most people in Scotland did desire to have one. The only king whom the Scots could choose was, of course, Charles, the eldest son of Charles I., now eighteen years of age. Only six days after the execution of Charles I., therefore, young Charles was proclaimed at the market-cross of Edinburgh as King of Great Britain and Ireland (5th of February, 1649).

But the question was—Would young Charles be the kind of king whom the Covenanters desired? We have seen that Charles I. lost the crown of Scotland because he would not accept the National Covenant and the Solemn League and Covenant. Would his son be willing to accept them? This was what had now to be found out before the crown could be set on his head.

At this time Charles was living at The Hague, in Holland, as, of course, his life would not have been safe in England. So Commissioners were sent to him there with this message—that if he would agree to the Covenants, he would be made King of Scotland ; but that if he would not agree to them, he could not be king. Now Charles hated the Covenants quite as much as his father had done. But Charles I. was a religious man, and would not accept the Covenants even to regain his crown. His son, on the other hand, cared nothing for religion, and was quite willing to agree to anything if he could gain his end. However, he would have much preferred to be King of Scots without taking the Covenants, and this he determined to try before giving his answer to the Commissioners.

What Charles did was to send the Marquis of Montrose to Scotland to attempt to conquer the country, and so win the crown for him. A braver and truer man than Charles would have gone with Montrose and shared all dangers with him. Montrose soon found how difficult and dangerous his enterprise was. He landed in the Orkney Islands, then passed over to Caithness, and marched with his little army into Sutherland. But he was not to gain such victories as those he had won for Charles I. In Carbisdale, on the south side of the Kyle of Sutherland, he was defeated in his first battle.

To escape from his enemies he disguised himself as a countryman, but he was discovered and made prisoner and sent to Edinburgh. He knew what his end must be, as the Covenanters had already con-demned him to death on account of his rebelling against them in the reign of Charles I. So he was executed as a traitor to the Covenant, just as some years later his rival, the Marquis of Argyle, was to be executed as a traitor to the king.

After Montrose's death, Charles had no choice but to accept the Covenants if he was to be king of Scotland. So he did take an oath that he would agree to the Covenants ; and then he came to Scot-land, where the people received him with great joy as their lawful king. But what did Cromwell and the Independents think of the Scots setting up Charles as their ruler ? They were both indignant and afraid. They were indignant because the Cove-nanters had broken their treaty with them, and they were afraid lest a Scottish army should invade England to make Charles king of that country also. Only a month after Charles had landed in Scotland, therefore, Cromwell came north with an army to compel the Scots to give up Charles. The Scots knew quite well when they made Charles king that they would have to fight Cromwell, and they had made preparations to receive him. Just as in former days when the English invaded Scotland, they laid waste all the country north of the river Tweed. When Cromwell crossed that river, therefore, he found nothing that either his men or his horses could eat, and not a soul was to be seen except a few old women. On he marched, however, till he came to Edinburgh, where at last he found a Scottish army to face him. The Scots were lucky in having a very skilful general to lead them—David Leslie, who had defeated Montrose at Philiphaugh. As Leslie was anxious that Cromwell should get neither into Edinburgh nor into Leith, he stationed his army between these towns, and in such a way that it would have been very dangerous for Cromwell to attack him.

Now, there were two things which Cromwell wished to bring about. The one was to get his army into Leith, as then his ships with provisions aboard could anchor safely in the harbour. But, as we have seen, Leslie had taken care that he should not succeed in getting to Leith. The other thing that Cromwell desired very much was to have a pitched battle with the Scots, as he was quite confident that his trained soldiers would gain the victory. But Leslie knew that his men were not trained to war like those of Cromwell, and he determined not to fight if he could help it. Leslie's plan, indeed, was to starve the English, and compel them to retreat to their own country.

Cromwell soon began to find himself in a very uncomfortable position. Though it was the month of August, it was very windy and wet. It was so windy, indeed, that his ships in the Firth of Forth could not land provisions for his army. From cold and wet and want of food, sickness broke out among his men, and many of them died. Still he tried to get Leslie to fight. He led his army to the Braid Hills, and he tried to reach Queensferry, but Leslie marched some of his men to Corstorphine Hill and stopped him.

At last, Cromwell saw that there was no help for it but to retreat, and he marched back to Dunbar. Then Leslie broke up his camp, and led his army along the high ground overlooking the Firth of Forth; and on the very day that Cromwell entered Dunbar, Leslie encamped on Doon Hill, which lies above that town. Cromwell was fairly caught in a trap. There were only two things he could do if Leslie would not fight. He could embark his men aboard his ships; but this would have been very dangerous, because the ships could not take in the whole army, and those left behind would be at the mercy of the Scots. The other thing he might have done was to continue his march to England. But in this march he would have had to go through a narrow pass at a place called the Pease Bridge, and Leslie had stationed a force there to prevent him. Cromwell had never been in such a difficult position before, and it seemed as if he would soon have to surrender to the Scots.

But now the Scots did the same foolish thing which they had often done before in their battles with the English. They left their safe ground on the Doon Hill, and took up their position in a place where Cromwell could attack them. When Cromwell saw them descend from the hill, he could hardly contain himself for joy, as he knew that his army was far more than a match for that of the Scots. When the sun rose next morning (3rd of September, 1650), the English began the attack, and soon it was seen what poor soldiers most of the Scots were. Only two regiments "fought it out manfully," and "were all killed as they stood." As for the rest of the army, many of the men surrendered without striking a blow, and others flung away their weapons and tried to escape. Between three and four thousand were slain while fleeing from the field, and nearly ten thousand were taken prisoners. The Scots themselves called the battle " Dunbar Drove," as they had been driven from the field like a drove of cattle.

---

71. CORONATION OF CHARLES II. (1651)— BATTLE OF WORCESTER (1651)

The army of the Covenanters was almost completely destroyed at Dunbar. Would they give in and agree to send Charles out of the country, or hand him over to Cromwell? Cromwell hoped that this was what would happen, but he was greatly mistaken. As we know, all the Covenanters hated Cromwell and the Independents, and most of them wished to have Charles as king, if he would only agree that the Church should remain Presbyterian as they had made it. The leaders of the Covenanters, therefore, determined that they would go on fighting rather than give up Charles, as Cromwell demanded.

But never was Scotland more unfit than now to defend itself against a foreign enemy. We have seen that there was already a great division among the Covenanters. There were the Engagers and the Anti-Engagers, but now another division took place among them. Some of them would not have Charles to rule over them, as they believed that in his heart he mocked at the Covenants, and that, if he were made king, he would do all he could to put an end to them. These Covenanters came to be known as the " Protesters " or " Remonstrants."

Most of the Covenanters, however, thought that the wisest thing to do was to accept Charles as their king, believing that in his own interest he would not try to restore Episcopacy, and so run the risk of the same fate as his father. These last Covenanters were called " Resolutioners." But besides the Protesters and the Resolutioners, there was still another party in the country who were equally hated by both of them. These were the Royalists, or, as the Covenanters called them, the Malignants, who jeered at the Covenanters and all their ways. How could the country, divided in this manner, hope to overcome such a terrible enemy as Cromwell?

Of the three parties, the Resolutioners were the most numerous, and it was they who had the chief power in the country. If Charles was to be king, therefore, it was with them that he would have to make friends. But before the Resolutioners would agree to crown him king, Charles had to make a hard bargain. No Malignant, that is, none whom he really liked, was allowed to hold any public office, or even to serve in his household. He had to give up pleasures which the Covenanters thought sinful, and to listen to sermons of which he made a joke when alone with his friends.

Once, when he was in Perth, he suddenly rode off, meaning to join some friends who had promised to raise an army for him. After a ride of forty-two miles he found no army, but only a few Highlanders. When the leaders of the Covenanters at Perth found that Charles had taken flight, they sent a party to search for him. And where was he found? " In a nasty room, on an old bolster above a mat of sedges and rushes, overwearied and very fearful." As this was not a very comfortable condition for a king to be in, Charles agreed to ride back to Perth, though he knew he would not be much happier there. This adventure of Charles was called the "Start."

Though, as we saw, Charles had been proclaimed king, he had not yet been crowned. At last, the Resolutioners, in spite of the Protesters, determined that he should receive the crown, and on the 1st of January, 1651, at Scone, the Marquis of Argyle placed it upon his head. In many ways it was the most unhappy coronation that had ever taken place in Scotland; and for this reason, that neither the king nor those who crowned him had any confidence in each other. Charles hated and despised the very things that the Covenanters loved and honoured most. Then Charles liked a merry life, so that he came to be called the "Merrie Monarch," and took pleasure in doing things which were not a good example to his subjects. On the other hand, the Covenanters were severe and stern in their lives, and could not understand how any one who had a soul to save could live as Charles did. How could a king and subjects, who were so different, hope to live happily with each other?

And what was Cromwell doing all this time? He had not been idle. Since the battle of Dunbar he had conquered almost the whole of Scotland to the south of the river Forth, so that Charles was king only of the country to the north of that river. It had now to be settled, therefore, whether Charles or Cromwell was to be master of Scotland. So a new army was raised for Charles, and was placed under the command of David Leslie, the skilful general who had given Cromwell so much trouble.

Now, what Leslie had to do was to prevent Cromwell from getting across the Forth and subduing the north country. So he stationed the chief part of his army at the Tor Wood, near Falkirk, where he was so surrounded by bogs and waters that Cromwell did not dare to attack him. Then he placed another part of his army at Inverkeithing, on the north side of the Forth, where the English might attempt to cross the river from Queensferry.

As Cromwell could not get Leslie out of the Tor Wood, he determined to try if the Forth could not be crossed at Queensferry. He therefore ordered one of his best generals, named Lambert, to ferry his men across, and attack the Scots, who were encamped at Inverkeithing. There were both Highlanders and Lowlanders in the Scottish army. The Scots fought much more bravely than they did at Dunbar, but were at last beaten with the loss of most of their men, who were either slain or taken prisoners. The Scots who fought most gallantly were the men of the clan Maclean, who were led by their chief, Sir Hector Maclean. As Sir Hector slew one Englishman after another, he shouted "Another for Hector"; but at length he was cut down, and almost all his clansmen perished by his side on the field.

It was now easy for Cromwell to cross the Forth, and he lost no time in marching to Perth. What were Charles and Leslie now to do? Cromwell was master of the country both to the north and to the south of the Forth, and they dared not meet him in open battle as they would certainly have been defeated.

They determined to do a desperate thing. They led the Scottish army into England, in the hope that many Englishmen, who hated the Independents, would join the king's standard.

As soon as Cromwell heard that the Scots had marched into England, he at once pursued them with the greater part of his army, and overtook them at the town of Worcester. On the 3rd of September, 1651, exactly a year since Cromwell's victory at Dunbar, another great battle was fought between the Scots and English. The battle began outside the town, but the Scots were driven within the walls, and their cannon were taken. Then a frightful slaughter took place, and General Leslie was made prisoner. Cromwell called this victory his "crowning Mercy," as there was no longer any army left to fight for Charles. As for Charles himself, he succeeded in escaping; and, after many adventures in which his life was often in danger, he sailed to the Continent, where for nine years he was to be an exiled king.

---

72. SCOTLAND UNDER CROMWELL. 1651-1660

Scotland was now still more helpless than she had been after the battle of Dunbar. Her last army had been destroyed at Worcester; her best general had been taken prisoner; and the king was gone. What made things still worse was, that the three parties in the country—the Royalists, the Resolutioners, and the Protesters—could never agree to combine for the defence of their country. There never was a time, therefore, when Scotland could be more easily conquered than now.

And Cromwell was determined to subdue Scotland and make it part of England, as so many English kings had tried to do and failed.   When he marched after Charles to Worcester, he left behind him a part of his army under the command of one of his best generals, General Monk.   Monk at once set about subduing the country, Highlands and Lowlands.   As there was no Scottish army to prevent him, he had very little difficulty in taking town after town, and placing English garrisons in them.   The only town that offered him any resistance was Dundee; but there was such a massacre of the inhabitants after it was taken that no other town dared to oppose him. It was in August of the year 1651 that Cromwell had marched after Charles, and by the end of that year Monk had subdued the whole country from the Tweed to the Pentland Firth.   So the English under Cromwell had done what no king of England had succeeded in doing.   Edward I., indeed, had conquered Scotland; but he held it only for a short time, whereas the English under Cromwell held it for nine years.

To show that Scotland was no longer an independent kingdom, Monk did exactly what Edward I. had done.   Edward had carried off the Stone of Destiny on which the kings of Scots had been crowned, as well as the Holy Cross of St Margaret and all the public records.   So Monk sent off to England the Chair of State in which the Scottish kings had sat, the robes they had worn, and all the documents which showed that Scotland had been a

Hiding the Honours of Scotland.

(At the Restoration the Honours were conveyed to the Crown Room of Edinburgh Castle, where they were on view till the Union, 1707. From this date they remained locked away in a strong chest in the Crown Room till 1818, when Sir Walter Scott was instrumental in bringing them once more to light.)

free kingdom. Monk was also very anxious to get hold of the " Honours of Scotland," that is, the crown, sceptre, and sword of state ; but, owing to the boldness and cleverness of a woman, he was disappointed.

After the battle of Dunbar the Honours had been placed for safety in the Castle of Dunnottar, a very strong castle on the coast of Kincardineshire. The English knew that they were there, and laid siege to the castle. Fearing that the stronghold would be taken, Mr Granger, a minister in the neighbour-hood, devised a plan for getting them out safely. First he spread a report that they had been taken abroad. Then he got his wife to ask leave of the English general to enter the castle to bring out some bundles of lint. The general granted permission, and Mrs Granger brought out the Honours covered up with the lint. At night they were safely buried under the pulpit of her husband's church. At this day the Honours, which Mrs Granger so cleverly rescued, may be seen in the Castle of Edinburgh.

Scotland having now been conquered, it had next to be made part of England, for this was the plan of Cromwell and the Independents. How was that to be done? As we know, there was no king in England. After the death of Charles I. in 1649, what was called the Commonwealth was set up ; and this government lasted till the year 1653, when Cromwell was made the chief person in the country, with the title not of King but of Protector. So it was first under the Commonwealth and afterwards under the Protectorate that Scotland was ruled by the English for nine years.

The first thing done by the Commonwealth was to

send down Commissioners to Scotland, who were to see that the laws were obeyed throughout the whole country.   And the Scottish people, though they hated the English, admitt.d that the laws were never better obeyed than under these Commissioners. Everyone got justice, and the country was so completely freed from robbers that it was said that a man with a hundred pounds in his pocket might ride through all Scotland with only a switch in his hand, and no one would dare to touch him.   This had never been the case before in Scotland, and other new things besides were now seen.   For example, every one was allowed to worship as he pleased, which had not been the case either under the Covenanters or under the kings.   General Assemblies, however, were not permitted to meet, because the Protesters and the Resolutioners quarrelled so much that they disturbed the peace of the country.

Another thing done both by the Commonwealth and the Protectorate was to make one Parliament for Scotland, England, and Ireland, just as there is now.   Scotland was to send thirty members to this United Parliament, and she did send twenty-one members.   But the United Parliament pleased neither the Scots nor the English, because the time had not yet come when the two peoples were prepared to unite their Parliaments as they afterwards did.

How was it that the Scottish people did not rise against their English conquerors as they had done in the days of Wallace and Bruce?   One reason, of course, was that they were so divided among themselves that they could not unite against their common enemy.   Another reason was that there were English soldiers in all the chief towns, and that strong forts had been built at Leith, Perth, Inverness, Inverlochy, and Ayr. If any body of Scots had attempted to rise in rebellion, therefore, English soldiers from the towns and forts would have fallen upon them at once.

There was, indeed, one attempt made to drive out the English. In the Highlands, the Earl of Glencairn and others raised a number of the clansmen to fight for Charles, but the leaders quarrelled so much among themselves that they were not able to do great things. Charles, however, sent General Middleton, of whom we shall hear again, to command the Royalist forces. But Middleton had not been long in the country before one of Monk's officers completely defeated him at Dalnaspidal, at the head of Loch Garry, and after that defeat there was peace all the time the English remained in Scotland.

At last the time came when the Scots got rid of the English, though not by conquering them. Oliver Cromwell died in the year 1658, and his son Richard was made Protector in his place. But Richard was not a great man, and could not rule the country as his father had done. The people of England also began to be discontented with the way they were being governed, and to long for their lawful king. When General Monk saw this, he marched from Scotland to London at the head of his army, and then declared that the time had come for Charles II. to be restored to his throne. So on the 25th of May, 1660, Charles landed at Dover, and became really king of Great Britain and Ireland, as his father and grandfather had been before him.

In this way, therefore, Scotland was freed from the English usurpers, as they were called, and almost every Scotsman was glad to see the last of them. They had, indeed, ruled more justly than any of the Scottish kings, and in many ways the country was more prosperous under them than it had ever been. But still they were invaders and had no right to govern Scotland. The Covenanters disliked them because they were Independents and not Presbyterians, and the Royalists disliked them quite as much because they kept the lawful king from his throne. Yet a time was coming when many people in Scotland were to look back with regret to the days of Oliver Cromwell.

---

73. EPISCOPACY RE-ESTABLISHED. 1660-1662

CHARLES II. (1660-1685)

There was great rejoicing both in England and in Scotland at the restoration of Charles to the throne of his fathers. In Edinburgh there was such feasting and revelry as had never been seen before. Bells were rung, trumpets sounded, cannons fired, and at night bonfires blazed everywhere. At the market-cross there was again a fountain of wine, from which every one could drink who pleased. In the High Street there was a long table laden with sweetmeats and wine. The healths of the king and his brother, the Duke of York, were drunk ; and it is said that three hundred glasses, out of which the wine had been quaffed, were broken, that they might never be used again on ordinary occasions. Yet, though Charles's reign began with such rejoicings, it was to be the saddest in the whole history of Scotland.

Charles II.

It would have required the wisest of kings to have ruled Scotland at that time, and Charles, though he was very clever, was more taken up with his own pleasures than with the good of his subjects. Though he reigned for twenty-five years, he never once came to visit Scotland. How then was the country governed? Exactly in the same way as under James VI. and Charles I. Soon after Charles was restored he appointed a Privy Council, and it was by this Privy Council that Scotland was governed. We saw that in the year 1641, Charles I. had agreed that ever afterwards he and his successors should not appoint the Privy Council without consulting the Parliament; but Charles II. chose **his** own Privy Councillors, and, of course, he chose only such persons as would do his bidding.

And how did Charles let the Council know what he wished? It was in this way. The Secretary of the Council always stayed in London, and all that Charles had to do was to command the Secretary to write to the Council and say what he wanted to be done. Now the Secretary whom Charles appointed is one of the best known men in Scottish history. We have already heard of him as one of the nobles who made the Engagement. He was the Earl of Lauderdale, a descendant of Maitland of Lethington, who had been the Secretary of Queen Mary.

Lauderdale had begun by being a keen Covenanter, but he had gone over to the side of the king, and he was now to be the chief enemy of those who had once been his friends. He was a huge, fat man, with a swollen face and red hair, and with a tongue too big for his mouth. He was also very debauched in his way of living, though he used to read the Bible in Hebrew. Though he had so many faults, he was the cleverest Scottish statesman then living, and he came to have so much influence over Charles that he was called the "King of Scotland." In all that has to be told of Charles's reign, therefore, we have always to think of Lauderdale behind it.

When Charles's reign began, the great question to be settled was whether Presbyterianism or Episcopacy was to be established in the country; and it was not long before it was settled. On the 1st of January, 1661, less than a year after Charles had been restored, a Parliament met in Edinburgh. Just as James VI. and Charles I. had done, Charles II. took care that most of its members should be his friends and supporters. As Charles did not come himself, he appointed a royal Commissioner to represent him, and this Commissioner was a man of whom we have heard before—General Middleton, now Earl of Middleton. Like Lauderdale, Middleton had once been a Covenanter, but had become a keen Royalist. He was quite an unfit person to hold such a great office, as he was only a rough soldier, and besides was very dissolute in his habits.

The Parliament did everything that Charles and Lauderdale wished. It passed what was called the "Rescissory Act," which declared that all the Acts passed by the Parliaments of the Covenanters were no longer the law. It also declared that the king was Head of the Church as well as of the State. So at one stroke all that the Covenanters had fought for was put an end to.

The Parliament had done its work, and now the Privy Council put the finishing touches to it. As the king had been declared to be the Head of the Church, it was of course in his power to say whether Presbyterianism or Episcopacy should be established. The

Privy Council, therefore, issued a proclamation to
say that it was the king's will that Episcopacy should
be the form of Church government in Scotland.

But there were then no bishops in Scotland, and
how were they to be got? Four men were sent up
to England to be consecrated to the office of bishop,
so that they might consecrate others to the office in
Scotland. Now among the four persons who were
sent to England, there were two whose names ought
to be remembered. The one was Robert Leighton,
a pious and peace-loving man, who had once been a
Covenanter, but who afterwards became Archbishop
of Glasgow. The other person was James Sharp, who
had also been a Covenanting minister. Of all the
bishops, it was Sharp whom the Presbyterians came
to hate most. About the time that Charles was
restored he had been sent to London to do what
he could in favour of the Presbyterians, but instead of
doing so he had become an Episcopalian. He was
made Archbishop of St Andrews, and therefore the
chief person in the Church ; and he did all in his
power to put down Presbyterianism. As we shall
see, he was to come to a terrible end.

There was still another thing done while Middleton
was Commissioner, which was the beginning of the
sad times that were to follow. In the reigns of
James VI. and Charles I. ministers were given to
the congregations by the owners of the Church lands,
who were called the " patrons " of the churches. The
Covenanters thought that this was wrong, and they
got an Act passed by Parliament which declared
that congregations should choose their own ministers.
That Act, however, was now declared to be unlawful,

and from this time ministers had to be appointed by the patrons and not by the congregations.

But what was to be done with those ministers who had not been appointed by patrons? It was ordered that by a certain date every minister should go to the patron and ask his consent to be the minister of his particular congregation. It was expected, of course, that all the ministers would do this rather than lose their daily bread. But this was not the case, as many ministers chose rather to lose their livelihood than go against their consciences. As we shall see, these new laws were the cause of all the "troubles," as they were called, that were to follow both during Charles's reign and the reign of his successor.

There is one person whose name has not been mentioned, of whom we should certainly have expected to hear—namely, the Marquis of Argyle. As we know, he had been the chief leader of the Covenanters, but had lost his power while Cromwell ruled Scotland. Argyle, as we know, had done his utmost to have Charles II. made king, and it was he who had placed the crown on Charles's head at Scone. Thinking, therefore, that Charles would receive him with favour, he went to London to pay his homage to him. Charles, however, received him coldly, and sent him down to Edinburgh to be tried for his past conduct. The charge brought against him was that he had recognised the government of Cromwell as a lawful government. This charge could not be proved against him, but almost all his judges were his enemies, and they were especially angry with him for having allowed the execution of Montrose. So he was found guilty, and sentenced to death. And thus the two great rivals and enemies had come to the same end: Montrose suffered as a traitor to the Covenants, and Argyle as a traitor to the king.

---

74. THE PENTLAND RISING. 1663-1667

Charles II. (1660-1685)

The Earl of Middleton had been Commissioner only for about two years, when he quarrelled with Lauderdale and was deprived of his office. The Earl of Rothes, a friend of Lauderdale, was put in his place (1663), but he did not act any more wisely than Middleton had done. He was, indeed, quite an unsuitable person to be the chief official in any country, as he was not educated and was frequently intoxicated.

Two changes had to be brought about before Episcopacy was established all over the country. All the ministers must be Episcopalians, and the people must be compelled to attend the parish churches. But in many parts of the country, especially in Ayrshire, Wigtownshire, and Kirkcudbrightshire, most of the people were Covenanters and hated Episcopalianism. What was done with these people who would not attend the parish churches? An Act of Parliament was passed which imposed heavy fines on all who did not attend church as they were commanded. This Act of course got a nickname; it was called the "Bishops' Drag-net," because it dragged the people to church as a drag-net drags fishes out of the sea.

We have seen that many of the ministers left their churches rather than hold their charges from a patron, as the law now commanded. How were their places filled? It was, of course, very difficult to fill them, as ministers cannot be trained in a day. What was done, therefore, was to take any one that offered himself, no matter how ignorant he was, and place him over a congregation whose minister had been deposed. These strange ministers were nicknamed the "King's Curates," and were the laughing-stock of everybody. Often foolish tricks were played upon them by the people: the tongue of the church bell would be carried off, the church door barricaded, or even the curate stoned.

But what gave the Government most trouble was that the congregations would insist on going to hear the "outed ministers," as they were called, wherever they chose to preach. To put a stop to this a law was passed which forbade these ministers to go within twenty miles of their former parishes, so that their congregations could not have the opportunity of hearing them.

Now it was easy to pass all these laws; but it was not so easy to carry them out, for, as has just been said, most of the people in many parts of the country thought it wrong to do anything that was against the Covenants. So the Government was compelled to do what was usually done in Scotland in those times. When any one would not pay his debts, soldiers were sent to live in his house till all the debt was paid, or till he was "eaten up." And this was what was done now. Soldiers were sent to the places where the people would not attend the parish churches, and were quartered on every one who would not obey the law. As these soldiers were the roughest of men, they behaved in the most insolent way, and made themselves greatly hated by those among whom they lived.

At last, an event happened which had long been expected. One of the commanders of the soldiers was Sir James Turner, who had been thrice sent out to the south-western counties to enforce the law. In November, 1666, Turner was in Dumfries, when suddenly a band of men entered the town and made him a prisoner. Then they marched into Ayrshire, where many others joined them. Next they went to Lanark, and thence they determined to go on to Edinburgh, where they hoped the people would take their side and help them to put down Episcopacy.

About three thousand of them started on their long journey to Edinburgh, and a dreary journey it was. It rained torrents all the way, and the roads were so bad that at every step they sank deep in the mud. But what was still more discouraging was that, as they came near Edinburgh, they found the people were enemies instead of friends. They got the length of Colinton, three miles west of Edinburgh, and then they saw it was useless to go any further. How to get home was now their care. They set off across the Pentland Hills, but when they came to a place called Rullion Green, the king's troops, commanded by Sir Thomas Dalziel, fell upon them. They made a brave fight under their leader, Colonel Wallace; but they were completely beaten, and about fifty of them were slain and fifty taken prisoners. This was the end of what was called the Pentland Rising.

It was not quite the end, however, for the prisoners had to be punished as rebels against the king. And cruel the punishment was. Fifteen were hanged in Edinburgh, and at Glasgow and Ayr others suffered the same fate. Before being executed, also, some were cruelly tortured to make them acknowledge the king as the Head of the Church. The instrument by which they were tortured was called the Boot, which was a wooden frame made to fit over the leg. Wedges were then driven in between the leg and the " boot," so as to crush the limb and cause great agony. Among those who were tortured and executed was a youth named Hugh M'Kail, who was greatly esteemed for his zeal and learning; and it is said that, when he stood on the scaffold, there was not one in the crowd of onlookers who was not in tears.

---

75. BATTLES OF DRUMCLOG AND BOTH-WELL BRIDGE. 1679

CHARLES II. (1660-1685)

The Earl of Rothes quarrelled with Lauderdale just as Middleton had done, and at the end of four years the commissionership was taken from him (1668). Lauderdale had thought that neither Middleton nor Rothes had ruled wisely, so he determined to try if he himself could not put an end to all the troubles in the country. Accordingly he got himself made Commissioner, and for the next eleven years (1668-1679) it was he who governed Scotland.

At first he began by ruling more gently than Rothes and Middleton. He put out what was called a Letter of Indulgence, allowing the "outed ministers" who had lived peaceably to be restored to their churches. About forty ministers accepted the Indulgence, but the others remained as stubborn as ever. What was to be done with those ministers and their congregations who refused to become Episcopalians, and who would not acknowledge Charles as their king because he had not signed the Covenants? What Lauderdale was afraid of was that there might be a rebellion against Charles II., just as there had been against Charles I. Soon, therefore, he began to pass even stricter laws against the Covenanters than either Middleton or Rothes had done. Before passing these laws, however, he put out another Letter of Indulgence; but though a few more ministers returned to their churches, the greater number still remained unyielding.

Here are the laws that were passed to compel the Covenanters to submit to what the Goverment commanded. Every master was to be fined if those he employed did not attend the parish church, and he had to sign a bond that every person living on his lands should live peacefully and obey the law. Another strange Act was this. There were over a hundred persons in the country who had made themselves very conspicuous by disobeying the law, and against these persons were issued what were called Letters of Intercommuning. What these letters meant was that nobody was to be allowed to speak to these persons or to give them food or lodging.

It was, of course, very difficult to carry out these

laws; but Lauderdale thought of a plan which would make them obeyed. It was in Ayrshire that the Covenanters were most numerous, and where they offered most resistance to the law. What Lauderdale did, therefore, was to order 6000 armed Highlanders and 3000 armed Lowlanders to march to Ayrshire and remain there for a month.

Lauderdale hoped that the people would rise against this army, and that he would then have an excuse for treating them as rebels. But the people did not rise, and no fighting took place. The army, however, did a great deal of mischief through the whole of the countryside. They prevented the inhabitants from going about their daily work; and they took food and lodging wherever they pleased, so that many persons were reduced to poverty and misery. At the end of the month, also, the Highlanders made off with everything that was not too heavy to carry—plate, wool, linen, clothes, and furniture, together with many horses to convey the plunder. But we shall see that this visit of the "Highland Host," as it was called, only made the Covenanters of the West more bitter than ever against the Government.

The year (1679) after the visit of the Highland Host was the most unhappy year in Scotland during the whole reign of Charles II. We already know that the man whom the Covenanters hated most bitterly was Archbishop Sharp. Since the beginning of Charles's reign, Sharp, though he had once been a Presbyterian, had done all he could to compel the Covenanters to submit to the laws. Now, in Fife where he lived, there were many Covenanters, and a

2 G

servant of his named Carmichael had treated them
very harshly. At last twelve men, the chief of whom
were David Hackston of Rathillet and John Balfour
of Kinloch, bound themselves together to slay
Carmichael.

On the 3rd of May, 1679, the twelve set out to
seek for Carmichael, to carry out their purpose.
Carmichael, however, had heard of their intention, and
kept himself concealed. But just as Hackston and
his companions were beginning to weary of waiting
for him, they were told that Sharp himself was
approaching in his carriage. They at once said to
each other that God had put their chief enemy into
their hands. The carriage drew near, and in it were
Sharp and his daughter. The murderers fired
several shots into the carriage, but in their excitement
they missed their aim. Sharp and his daughter
prayed hard that his life might be spared, but the
murderers dragged him forth and slew him on the
spot with their swords. This bloody deed took place
at Magus Muir, about two miles from St Andrews.

Other terrible events were to happen during the
same year (1679). The Government, as we have seen,
had done its utmost to prevent the people from
attending the preaching of the outed ministers.
Though it was at the risk of being fined and imprisoned, however, the most zealous of the Covenanters insisted on hearing these preachers. At
first they met in barns and other buildings, carrying
only their Bibles with them. But, as they were
watched by the king's soldiers, they had to give
up meeting in such places. Now, therefore, they
were compelled to hold their meetings in out-of-

the-way spots among the hills and moors in the neighbouring country. Now, also, they carried guns and swords and other weapons with them to resist the king's troops if they should come upon them. To make sure that they would not be surprised, watchers were placed round about to give a signal if the enemy was at hand. Many battles took place between these congregations and the dragoons, and in the wild districts of the south and west of Scotland we often come upon stones which mark the spot where some noted Covenanter was slain.

Now the Government was very much afraid of these *conventicles*, as they were called, because they might lead to a general rebellion such as had happened in the reign of Charles I. In the parts of the country, therefore, where conventicles were held, soldiers were stationed to break them up, and to take as many prisoners as possible. On a Sabbath morning in May, one of these conventicles was held on Loudoun Hill, near the borders of Ayrshire and Lanarkshire. When the religious service was going on, the watchers announced that the king's troops were approaching. The Covenanters had about forty horsemen and two hundred footmen, so they determined to fight. About two miles off there is a boggy moor, called Drumclog, where they could fight at greater advantage, and thither they marched. The king's troops came on, led by John Graham of Claverhouse, who was a great hunter of the Covenanters, and was much feared and hated by them. There was a short and sharp battle, and Claverhouse and his men were completely routed.

The Covenanters were now rebels, and they knew

Covenanters' Preaching.

that they would be punished as such.   They determined, therefore, to try if they could not get others to join them and make open war on the Government. The day after their victory they marched to Glasgow, where they had many friends; but there was a strong garrison in the town and they could not gain entrance.   Then they marched back to Hamilton, and by this time so many had joined them that they had a large army.

The Government was greatly alarmed, for it seemed that the rebellion that had long been dreaded had at last broken out.   A large army was at once collected, and the Duke of Monmouth, a son of the king, was brought down from England to command it.   The two armies met at Bothwell Bridge, on the river Clyde, the river being between them.   Before the battle began the Covenanters told Monmouth, just as their fathers had told Charles I., that they would lay down their arms if the king would grant a free Parliament and a free General Assembly.

As Monmouth would not agree to this, the Covenanters determined to fight for their cause.   But though they had a large army, they were not in a condition to give battle.   Their leaders had such different opinions about religion that they could not agree, and we are told that even when the battle was about to begin they "preached and prayed against each other."   How could an army make a brave fight when its leaders were all quarrelling with one another? Though some of the Covenanters fought like brave men, therefore, the whole army was soon in disorder and fleeing in all directions.   Monmouth, who was a humane man, had given orders that the fugitives should be spared; but the order was not obeyed, and about 400 were slain and 1200 taken prisoners.

After the battle, the prisoners were tied two and two together and led to Edinburgh. But the question was—where were they to be put, as there was no prison in the town large enough to hold them? They were placed in Greyfriars Churchyard, and there for nearly five months, half-clad, ill-fed, and exposed to the weather, most of them were kept. Four hundred of them took an oath to submit to the Government, and were allowed to go home. Two hundred and fifty of them, however, would not yield, and they were shipped off to Barbados, in the West Indies, to work as slaves. But the ship did not reach its destination; it was wrecked off the Orkney Islands, and almost all of them perished.

After the battle of Bothwell Bridge, Lauderdale had to give up the commissionership. He had failed to make the country quiet, just as Middleton and Rothes had failed before him.

---

76. THE CAMERONIANS. 1679-1685

Charles II. (1660-1685)

Most of the ministers who had been driven from their churches at the beginning of Charles's reign were now either banished or had agreed to accept Episcopacy. Even in the West, also, most of the people had been compelled to attend the parish churches, though it was so much against their will. But there were still many persons in different parts of the country who would not yield, because to do so would have been against their consciences. Neither fines, nor imprisonment, nor the fear of death prevented these persons from attending conventicles and listening to the ministers who were courageous enough to preach to them.

There were two ministers who still went about the country and preached wherever they could find a congregation. The one was Donald Cargill and the other was Richard Cameron (from whom some of the Covenanters got the name of " Cameronians "). It was, of course, at the risk of their lives that Cargill and Cameron went on preaching, and they had to hide in the mountains and the moors to escape the soldiers who were in search of them.

In the year 1680 some of the Covenanters took a step which showed that they were determined never to yield. About twenty of them entered the town of Sanquhar, in Dumfriesshire, and affixed a paper to the town-cross. This paper was called the " Sanquhar Declaration." It declared that those who had put it there disowned Charles as their king because he had broken the Covenant, to which he had sworn when the crown was offered to him. This was an act of rebellion, and death was its punishment. The Government was therefore more anxious than ever to get hold of Cameron and Cargill, and the soldiers were everywhere in search of them.

About a month after the Sanquhar Declaration, a band of Covenanters had met near Auchinleck, in Ayrshire. Their leaders were Cameron and Hackston of Rathillet (who had taken part in the murder of Archbishop Sharp). They had been all

night on the moorside, when about ten o'clock in
the morning a party of dragoons came in sight. The
"Wanderers," as the Covenanters were called, determined to do battle. Behind them was a bog called
Airds Moss, but there were passages through it by
which they might escape if they were beaten. Before
the battle began Cameron exclaimed three times:
"Lord spare the green and take the ripe." Though
the Wanderers fought like desperate men, they
were soon overcome by the greater numbers of the
enemy. Cameron was slain, and his head and hands
were cut off and carried to Edinburgh, where they
were stuck up in conspicuous places. Hackston rode
off from the field of battle, but his horse sank in the
bog, and he was made prisoner. Led to Edinburgh,
he was there put to death with dreadful tortures,
which he bore without flinching.

The year (1681) after Cameron was slain, Cargill
also met his fate. One evening he had preached at
Dunsyre, in Lanarkshire, and after the sermon he hid
in a mill not far off. There was a prize of more than
£300 offered to any one who either slew him or took
him prisoner. Before the morning he was taken,
and along with four of his followers he was executed
in Edinburgh. Just before his death he wrote: "This
is the most joyful day ever I saw in my pilgrimage
on earth."

About the same time as Cargill was executed, the
new royal Commissioner came to Scotland. He was
James, Duke of York, the brother of King Charles,
and afterwards James VII. Neither Episcopalians
nor Presbyterians could be pleased at his being
made Commissioner, as he was a Roman Catholic,

From Painting by R. Herdman, R.S.A.]

[National Gallery of Scotland.

After the Battle.

and might try to set up his own religion in Scotland. And that was exactly what he did try to do, as was soon to be seen.

No Parliament had met in Scotland for nine years; but James now assembled one, and got it to pass two Acts which frightened everybody, Episcopalians as well as Presbyterians. One of these Acts declared that the lawful heir, whatever his religion might be, should succeed to the throne, which, of course, meant that, though James was a Catholic, he should succeed his brother Charles. The other Act was called the Test Act, which everyone who held any office in the Church or the State was to sign. Nobody could understand the meaning of this Act, and it became a general laughing-stock. The boys of Heriot's Hospital got a copy of the Act, smeared it with butter, and put it in their watch-dog's mouth. The dog would not swallow it, and was hanged.

But the Test Act was no laughing matter, as one person was to find. The Earl of Argyle, son of the Marquis of Argyle who was executed in the beginning of Charles's reign, said he was willing to sign the Act, though he did not understand it. This did not satisfy James, however, and Argyle was imprisoned in Edinburgh Castle, and tried for high treason. What would have been the end of the trial we cannot say, but Argyle cleverly made his escape from his prison. Disguised as a page, and holding up the train of his daughter, he passed his guards, made his way out of the Castle, and got safely to Holland. At a later time, as we shall see, he came to an unhappy end.

To the very close of Charles's reign the struggle

went on between the Government and the Covenanters who still held out. A new preacher arose who was as bold and zealous as Cameron and Cargill, and kept up the courage of his followers. This was James Renwick, who was only a little over twenty years of age. Renwick wrote a document called the "Apologetical Declaration," in which it was said that the Covenanters would not spare the lives of those who sought theirs. After this Declaration the Covenanters were hunted down by the soldiers more than ever.

There were two officers of the king's troops who were especially hated and feared. One of them has already been mentioned; namely, John Graham of Claverhouse. Claverhouse had no mercy for those who would not submit to the law of the land, and he came to be known as "bluidy Clavers." The other commander was Sir Thomas Dalziel, usually called Tom Dalziel. He was so keen a Royalist that after Charles I.'s death he never cut his beard, which reached down to his waist; and as he never wore boots and dressed very oddly, he drew people's attention wherever he went. He had been a soldier in Russia, which was then a barbarous country, and he had learned rough and cruel ways of treating his enemies.

When Claverhouse and Dalziel caught any Covenanter, this was what they now did. They asked him if he approved of the Apologetical Declaration which Renwick had drawn up. If he said "yes," they ordered him to be shot on the spot. If he said "no," he was taken to Edinburgh and tried before a judge. And at this time there was a judge who was as much feared as either Claverhouse or Dalziel; namely, the Lord Advocate, Sir George Mackenzie, who was the cause of so many Covenanters being sentenced to death that he was called the "bluidy Mackenzie."

This was the state of the country when, on the 2nd of February, 1685, Charles II. died, after an actual reign of twenty-five years. It had been the most unhappy reign in the whole history of Scotland. And what had been the cause of all the unhappiness? It was because neither the Covenanters nor the Royalists thought, as we now do, that men should be allowed to be of what religion they please. When the Covenanters were in power, they would not allow any minister who did not sign the Covenant to remain in his church; and after the Restoration the Royalists drove out every minister who would not admit that the king was the Head of the Church as well as of the State. What made matters worse was that the men who carried out the laws, both the soldiers and the judges, were so thoughtless and cruel, and, besides, were often men of such dissolute lives and bad character.

---

77. THE "KILLING TIME." 1685-1687

JAMES VII. (1685-1688)

We have seen that when James, Duke of York, was Commissioner, he got a law passed declaring that the lawful heir should become king of Scotland, even though he was of a different religion from his subjects. Although James was a Catholic, therefore, he succeeded his brother Charles as king of Scotland as well as of England and Ireland. Presbyterians and Episcopalians were equally alarmed when

James VII.

they saw a Catholic king ascend the throne, as they knew that James would do his utmost to make Scotland a Catholic country. And it was, indeed, in trying to make England and Scotland alike Catholic that in the end he was driven from the thrones of both countries.

The Covenanters had never been more severely treated than when James was Commissioner, and now, when he had become king, they were hunted down as they had never been before. The first year of his reign (1685-6), indeed, was called the "black year," the "killing time." There were two classes of persons among the Covenanters who received different punishments according to the crimes charged against them. The one class consisted of those who showed in some way that they were not loyal subjects, and their punishment was to have one ear cut off and then to be sent to America to work as slaves. Hundreds of Covenanters were punished in this way. The other class were those who approved of the Apologetical Declaration of which we have heard. Whenever any one of this class was caught by the king's troops, he was shot on the spot.

In a letter which Claverhouse himself wrote, he tells us how he acted when a Covenanter fell into his hands. He was very anxious to catch a certain Covenanter, named John Brown of Priesthill, and his nephew. After a long march through the moors and mosses of Lanarkshire and Ayrshire, he did succeed in taking them both. They were at once asked if they approved of the Apologetical Declaration. The nephew said that he did not, and his life was spared. Brown's answer was that "he knew no king." "Whereupon," says Claverhouse, "I caused shoot him dead, which he suffered very unconcernedly." But the cruellest thing done in the "black year"

was the drowning at Wigtown of two women—
the one called Margaret Lauchleson, over sixty
years of age, and the other Margaret Wilson, who
was under twenty. They both refused to give up
the Covenant, and their punishment was, to be tied
to stakes till the sea came in and drowned them.
These women are known as the "Wigtownshire
Martyrs."

Both in England and Scotland there were many
persons who thought that a Catholic should not be
king, and in the very first year of James's reign
attempts were made in both countries to drive him
from the throne. These attempts were made by two
leaders, one an Englishman, the Duke of Monmouth,
who had gained the victory at Bothwell Bridge, and
the other a Scotsman, the Earl of Argyle, who, as we
saw, had to flee from Scotland when James was
Commissioner. As for the Duke of Monmouth, he
landed in England with an army, but was defeated
and taken prisoner, and afterwards executed by
James's order.

Argyle was equally unfortunate. He sailed from
Holland with a few companions and landed on the
west coast of Scotland. He hoped that his clansmen
in Argyleshire would rise and join him, but the
Government took care to prevent this. He also
hoped that the Covenanters of the West would
be eager to assist him, but in this also he was
disappointed. Then Argyle and the other leaders
quarrelled, so that they separated and had to think
only of saving their lives. But Argyle was not to
escape. He was caught at Inchinnan, near the town
of Renfrew, and was taken to Edinburgh. As he

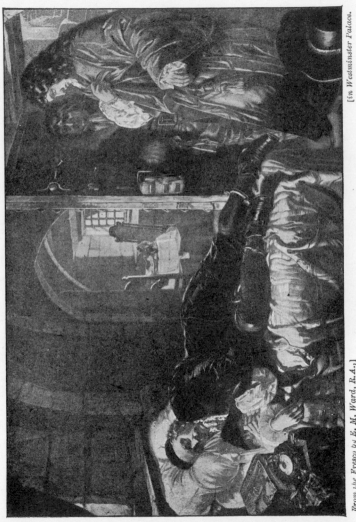

The Last Sleep of Argyle.

had been condemned as a traitor in the previous reign, it was not thought necessary to try him again, and he was executed like his father, the Marquis of Argyle, before him.

At the time of Argyle's invasion a horrible thing was done, for which the Government was greatly to blame. When the news of Argyle's coming was known, all the Covenanters who were in prison were taken to Dunnottar Castle, where, as we have seen, the Honours of Scotland were placed for safety in the time of Cromwell. There were about two hundred of them, both men and women, and of these a hundred were shut up in a vault of the castle, still called the "Whigs' Vault." The floor was ankle-deep with mud, and there was only one window to let in the air. For two months the prisoners were kept in the castle. Many died and many became ill for want of food and air. At last, the survivors were brought to Leith, and got the choice of acknowledging James as their king, or of being sent as slaves to America. Rather than acknowledge a king who had not accepted the Covenants, most of them preferred to be slaves in a distant land for the rest of their lives.

---

78. THE REVOLUTION. 1688-1689

James VII. (1685-1688)

We have now to see how James tried to make Scotland a Roman Catholic country, and what was the end of his attempt. His first step was this. There were cruel laws in Scotland against Roman

Catholics as well as against Covenanters. James, therefore, asked the Scottish Parliament to abolish these laws, but, to his great indignation, the Parliament refused to do so. Then he determined to have nothing more to do with Parliaments. But it was what he did next that was to be the cause of his ruin, both in Scotland and in England. He wrote to the Privy Council to say that as king he had power to do away with any laws whenever he pleased. This was what was called the Dispensing Power, and in England he had got the judges to declare that the king possessed such a power. But James's subjects both in England and Scotland thought that a ruler who could do as he pleased was not a king, but a tyrant.

Other things that happened showed what James was aiming at. The highest offices in the kingdom were given to Catholics. The Lord Chancellor, the Earl of Perth, became a Catholic, and so did his brother Viscount Melfort, and the Earl of Moray, who were the two Secretaries of State. In Holyrood Chapel the Catholics conducted their religious services, and Catholic books began to be printed in Edinburgh, a thing that had hitherto been forbidden by the law. So indignant were the people of Edinburgh, that one Sunday a mob attacked the Catholic priests and insulted the Lord Chancellor Perth.

James now thought of a plan by which he hoped in the end to make Scotland a Catholic country. He issued a Letter of Indulgence, which allowed both Catholics and Presbyterians to conduct their worship in their own way. What James hoped was that, when the Catholics became strong enough, he would then be able to put down both Presbyterians and Episcopalians. This, however, was not to happen, though many Presbyterian ministers who were exiles in Holland were now permitted to return to their native country. The Covenanters who followed Renwick, however, could not accept the Indulgence, because they would not acknowledge James as their lawful king.

Though it was at the risk of his life, Renwick still continued to preach in different parts of the country; but at last he was taken. In the month of January, 1688, he came secretly to Edinburgh, where he stayed in a friend's house. The morning after he arrived, some officials entered the house. Renwick knew who they were, and presented his pistol at them, but missed his shot. He made his way out of the house, however, and rushed down the street; but he was known to be a fugitive by his bare head, and was immediately surrounded and seized. Some members of the Privy Council would have liked to spare his life, as they were weary of so much bloodshed, and Renwick was so young, being only in his twenty-sixth year. But he would not consent to acknowledge James as his lawful king, and by the law he must suffer death. On the scaffold he sang the 103rd Psalm, and read a chapter from the Book of Revelations; and among his last words he said, "Lord, I die in the faith that Thou wilt not leave Scotland."

Renwick was the last Covenanter to be put to death for his religion, for the year (1688) in which he was executed was the last that James was to be allowed to reign. In England, just as in Scotland, James had tried to set up Roman Catholicism, and the English hated that religion as much as did the Scots. At length seven of the chief men in England sent a message to William of Orange, who had married James's daughter, Mary, inviting him to come and rule over them as a Protestant king. William accepted the invitation, and in November, 1688, he sailed from Holland with a fleet and army, and landed in England. James led an army against William, but his officers deserted him, and he was compelled to flee to France lest he should fall into the hands of his enemies.

Of course, William was anxious to become king of Scotland as well as of England, and he sent an address to the Scottish people, in which he promised to rule them justly if they would receive him as their king. All the Presbyterians, though not the Episcopalians, were overjoyed at the thought of being ruled by a Protestant, and many of the nobles were also in favour of William. It was soon to be seen that the supporters of William were the stronger party in the country. When James had heard of William's coming, he had ordered the greater part of the army in Scotland to march to his assistance in England. But, when these troops were gone, all the enemies of James in Scotland were free to do what they pleased, and for a time there was great disorder in the country.

Great crowds of those who wished William to be king flocked to Edinburgh to be ready to fight for him if it should be necessary. A mob rose in the town and attacked Holyrood Chapel, where the Roman Catholic service had been conducted. Holyrood was guarded by a few soldiers, but they were put to rout by the mob, who rushed into the chapel and destroyed everything Catholic which they found in it. James's Lord Chancellor, the Catholic Earl of Perth, was so terrified that he fled from the town, and only the Castle was held by the friends of James.

In the west country, also, where the Covenanters had suffered so much, the people took the law into their own hands. On Christmas Day, 1688, they began to drive the "King's Curates" from their churches and manses without any warning, and often with great roughness and violence. More than two hundred curates were turned out of their homes and left without a livelihood, and, as it was the dead of winter, many of them suffered great hardships. This was called the "rabbling" of the curates.

In January, 1689, the English Parliament had offered the crown of England to William and Mary, and he had now to be offered the crown of Scotland. But before this could be done, a Parliament had to meet, and William was asked to summon one. The Parliament did meet, though it was not called a Parliament but a Convention, because William was not yet a lawful king. The Convention, when it met, declared that it had the right to dethrone a king who had broken the laws as James had done. This was called the "Claim of Right." It also declared that there was now no king, and appointed certain persons to go to London and offer the crown to William and Mary. So on the 11th of May the Scottish crown was offered to them, and both took the coronation oath that they would govern Scotland according to the laws of the kingdom.

This dethroning of James and setting up of William and Mary is called the " Revolution," and it is one of the most important events in the history either of England or of Scotland. It put an end to the House of Stewart, which had ruled over Scotland for more than three hundred years, and over England, Scotland, and Ireland for eighty-six years. The Revolution also made other great changes in all the three countries. Since the time of James VI. the kings of the House of Stewart had maintained that they had been appointed kings by God and not by the people; but in dethroning James VII. the people had claimed the right of appointing their own kings. From this time onwards, therefore, it came to be understood that kings would be allowed to remain on the throne only if they governed according to the laws of the land. In Scotland the Stewart kings had tried to make themselves masters both of the Church and of the State, but after the Revolution the kings could make no changes in the laws without the consent of their Parliaments. It will be seen, therefore, that after James was dethroned a new time began both in England and Scotland.

79. SCOTLAND IN THE SEVENTEENTH CENTURY

Owing to the long quarrels between the Scottish kings and their subjects, the country could not make so much progress as it otherwise might have done. At the time of the Revolution the country districts looked very much the same as in the time of Queen

Mary, more than a hundred years before. There were still hardly any fences, whether dykes or hedges, round the fields. Great parts of the country where there are now fertile fields were covered with lochs and marshes, and very few trees were to be seen anywhere, except round gentlemen's country-seats. When foreigners came to the country they were

Part of Old Edinburgh showing Seventeenth-Century Houses.
(Looking north towards St Giles.)

greatly surprised to see the sides of the hills, up to their very summits, covered with crops of barley and other grain. The reason of this was that the flat ground was not drained, and crops had to be grown on the dry slopes of the hills.

In the beginning of the reign of Charles II., a famous Englishman made a journey into Scotland, and afterwards wrote a book about his travels in the country. His name was John Ray, and he was the son of a blacksmith, but he had been sent to the University of Cambridge, and afterwards became a great naturalist. He entered Scotland from Berwick-on-Tweed, and rode from that town to Edinburgh, so that he passed through the most fertile parts of the country. Here are some of the things which he says about the people and their way of living.

The poorer men in the country districts, he says, mostly wore blue bonnets, while the women wore white linen on their heads, which hung down their backs "as if a napkin had been pinned on them." When the women went out of doors, they wore coloured plaids, which covered both their heads and their shoulders. The houses in which the country people lived were built of stone, with roofs of turf, and had only one room. They had no chimneys, and for windows they had only holes in the wall, which in stormy weather were stopped up with cloths. The chief food of the people was broth made with vegetables and barley, and oatmeal cakes and butter. In the fields there were good crops of barley and oats, but very little wheat or grass was grown anywhere.

The "Tirling Pin," the old style of door-knocker in Scotland.

Another Englishman who visited Scotland tells us what Edinburgh was like in those days. Though it was the capital of the country, it had only one street, called the High Street, which stretched from the Castle to Holyrood Palace. This street, he says, was better paved than any other street he had ever seen. It was raised in the middle, so that in wet weather the water ran down the slopes. In those days, therefore, the people walked, not on side paths as they do now, but in the centre of the street. The houses were six and seven storeys high, and were all faced with wood. Very few of them had glass in their windows, which opened and shut like doors. Just as in the country, the women, when they went out of doors, wore plaids over their heads and shoulders, though the unmarried ones went bareheaded. The great fault our

Old Street Lamps formerly used in Stirling.

Englishman had to find against the town was its dirtiness, both in the streets and in the houses. Another nuisance was, that there were so many beggars that no one could walk in the streets without being annoyed by them.

In other ways the country was not much changed from what it had been in the days of Queen Mary. For instance, no one could be a blacksmith, or a mason, or any kind of artisan, unless he belonged to the craft. If any one who did not belong to a craft ventured to practise it, he was brought before the magistrate and fined. And no artisan dared to sell his goods anywhere except in the town where he lived. Once some glovemakers came from Perth to Edinburgh to sell their gloves, but they were ordered home and their gloves were taken from them.

It was the same with tradespeople as with the craftsmen. In the year 1682, near the end of Charles II.'s reign, the Merchants' Company of Edinburgh was founded. Before the Company could be started it had, of course, to get what was called a patent

from the king. Now this patent seems a very curious thing to us at the present day. For what did the patent declare? It forbade any one to sell or make cloth unless he belonged to the new Merchants' Company. Of course, it was very difficult to prevent other people from making and selling cloth, and the Company had a great deal of trouble in finding the offenders out and having them punished. But there was one class of persons against whom the Company were especially indignant.

Church Sand-glass used to measure length of Sermon. (Height of glass, from 7 to 9 inches.)

Numbers of women set up shops in the town and sold cloth. The Company did all they could to stop them, but they never quite succeeded.

These strange laws about trade and manufactures show how different the country was then from what it is now; but a stranger thing still has to be mentioned, and that is the belief in what was called Witchcraft. It was believed that certain persons, chiefly old and ugly women, had sold themselves to Satan, who gave them power to do all kinds of mischief to their fellow-creatures. There was hardly a town or village in Scotland in which there were not one or more of these so-called witches. It was believed that on certain nights of the year they used to meet Satan in out-of-the-way places, and behave like demons and not like human beings. If any mischief happened, it was supposed that a witch had caused it. If there was a bad harvest, if there was a plague among the cattle or sheep, if any one was taken ill with

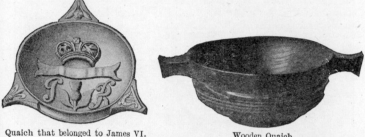

Quaich that belonged to James VI.   Wooden Quaich.

Old Scottish Drinking-vessels.

an unusual disease, a witch was sure to be blamed.

We can easily understand how witches were hated and feared by everybody, high and low. Now in the Bible there is a verse which says, "Thou shalt not suffer a witch to live." All Christians, therefore, both Protestants and Catholics, thought it right that persons proved guilty of witchcraft should be put to death. In the reign of Mary, a law was passed which condemned to death all who were proved to be witches, and the law was so strictly carried out that thousands of persons were executed on this charge.

What was done was this. If any person was

suspected, he or she was reported to the minister and the Kirk Session. If they appeared to be guilty, the minister and Session asked the Privy Council to appoint certain persons to try them. Then the trial took place, and things were done during the trial which it is difficult to believe. To make the accused confess their guilt, they were put to terrible tortures.

Holyrood Gate and Wing of Palace containing Queen Mary's Apartments. (The Gate is not now in existence.)

Sometimes they were prevented from sleeping for several days, until they were distracted and were willing to confess anything. There were also persons called "witchfinders," who used to prick the poor wretches with pins till they found what was called the "devil's mark." What is strange, however, is that many of those accused quite freely confessed that they had sold themselves to Satan.

It was not only ignorant people who believed in witchcraft. Ministers, judges, and the most learned men believed in it, and thought that it was right that witches should suffer death. Both Presbyterians and Episcopalians did all they could to stamp them out of the country, but quite in vain; and it was only by slow degrees that the belief in witchcraft died out. It was in the year 1727 that the last witch was executed in Scotland.

It will be seen that many things remained in Scotland just as they had been during the Middle Ages. There was one change that took place, however, which shows that the country was becoming more civilised. In the Middle Ages every man carried weapons to defend himself if he were attacked, but in the seventeenth century, of which we have been speaking, this was no longer allowed. It was now against the law for any one to carry weapons, unless he had received a licence from the Government. This was a great change for the good of the country. When men did not carry weapons they were less likely to quarrel, and they began to prefer peace to war. More and more, therefore, the people of Scotland, like those of other countries, sought to improve their modes of living in the peaceful ways of trade and commerce.

80. WILLIAM AND MARY

<small>BATTLE OF KILLIECRANKIE (1689)—PRESBYTERIANISM
RESTORED (1690)</small>

William, Prince of Orange, was now king of Scotland, but would he be able to remain its king? There were many persons in the country who were his enemies, and they were ready to do all they could to drive him from the throne. Only a few of the nobles were friendly to him, and even on some of these he could not depend. Almost all the Episcopalians disliked him, because they held that he was not the lawful king, and because they feared that he would not support their Church.

And there was another enemy against whom William would have to be on his guard. When James, the exiled king, fled from England, he had gone to France, where Louis XIV. was then reigning. What if Louis should give James an army to assist him in regaining his crown? Indeed, before William received the Scottish Crown, James had landed in Ireland with some French officers to try to conquer that country. We see, therefore, that William was surrounded by enemies on all sides, so that it was very doubtful if he would be able to remain king either of Scotland or of England. All through his reign, and, indeed, for a long time afterwards, there was always a fear lest the Stewarts should recover the kingdoms they had lost.

It was not long before an attempt was made to bring James back to Scotland. Only a month after William had been crowned king of Scotland, a

rebellion broke out against him in the Highlands.
The leader of the rebellion was one of whom we have
already heard—the great enemy of the Covenanters,

"Bonnie Dundee."

John Graham of Claverhouse, whom James had made
Viscount Dundee. As Dundee had been one of
James's chief men in Scotland, he could not, of course,
be a supporter of William, and now he determined

to try if he could not do for James what his relative Montrose had done for Charles I. Like Montrose, therefore, he went to the Highlands and raised an army of the clansmen, who were always ready for fighting when they found a leader.

As soon as it was known that the Highlanders had risen, an army was sent against them under General Mackay, who had seen a great deal of war in foreign countries. Most of the soldiers under him, however, were quite untrained, and had never been in a battle in their lives. The two armies met at the Pass of Killiecrankie, not far from Pitlochry, in Perthshire (July 27, 1689). Mackay's men were on the flat ground at the head of the Pass, and those of Dundee on the hills rising above it.

As usual, the Highlanders came on with a furious rush. Mackay's troops had been armed with bayonets, which were then a new invention; but the bayonet was not fixed on the muzzle of the gun as it is now, and it had to be screwed on after the shot was fired. While Mackay's soldiers were fumbling with their bayonets, therefore, the Highlanders had a great advantage, and they broke through the enemy's ranks at the first onset. Soon the king's troops were in complete rout, and Mackay was able to save only a small part of his army. Dundee had won a splendid victory, but he did not live to see it, as he was shot at the very beginning of the battle. As for the victorious clansmen, they at once set about plundering the deserted camp of Mackay, and then made off to their homes laden with booty.

About three weeks after the battle of Killiecrankie, the Highlanders met an enemy whom they found more than their match. After the death of Dundee, an army of 5000 Highlanders was brought together under another commander, named Colonel Cannon. This army laid siege to the town of Dunkeld, where

[*Photo by Valentine.*

Pass of Killiecrankie.

there was a force of 1200 Cameronians, commanded by a young officer, Lieutenant Cleland. As the town had no walls round it, the Highlanders made their way into the streets, and the Cameronians had to take refuge in the Cathedral and mansion-

2 I

house near at hand. The Highlanders then concealed themselves in the houses of the town, and kept up a constant fire on the enemy.

But the Cameronians had no thought of giving in. When their musket-balls were exhausted, they tore the lead from the roof of the cathedral. At last, with burning faggots at the ends of their pikes, they rushed out on the houses where the Highlanders were concealed, set fire to them, and locked the doors. Many Highlanders perished ; in one house as many as sixteen ; and in the end, after a fight that had lasted four hours, the survivors made off across the neighbouring hills, the Cameronians singing a psalm of triumph as they saw them retreat. This was a fiercer battle on both sides than that of Killiecrankie, as it lasted much longer and the combatants were more equally matched in courage. Like Dundee, however, Cleland did not live to see his victory, as he was killed by two gunshots while giving orders to his men. After this defeat of the Highlanders at Dunkeld, they did not rise again during the remainder of William's reign.

William's most dangerous enemies had now been conquered, but the country was still in a very excited state. The chief cause of the excitement was the question, what Church would be set up in Scotland? Would it be Episcopacy or Presbyterianism? For a time William was in doubt as to which of the two it would be wiser to prefer. There was a Scotsman, however, to whose opinion William gave great weight. This was William Carstares, a Presbyterian minister, who had been banished during the reign of Charles II., and had become a friend of William in Holland. Carstares persuaded William that he could not depend on the Episcopalians, as they were almost all the friends of James, and that the Presbyterians were his only true supporters in Scotland. Carstares' advice was that it would be William's wisest step to establish Presbyterianism, and William determined to follow it.

In the year 1690, therefore, the Parliament met, and passed an Act which established Presbyterianism in Scotland, and to this day the Church of Scotland is a Presbyterian Church. The same Parliament passed another very important Act in connection with the Church. It will be remembered that, when the Covenanters were in power, they had made it the law that congregations should choose their own ministers. When Charles II. came to the throne, however, this law was set aside, and it was enacted that the patrons should present ministers to their congregations. As we saw, it was this Act of Charles which had caused so many ministers to leave their churches, and which had given rise to all the troubles during the reigns of Charles and James. What William's Parliament now did, therefore, was to put an end to patronage, and to make it the law that ministers should not be appointed without the approval of the congregations. In the next reign, we shall see that patronage was once more restored, and that it was the cause of a great deal of trouble in the country.

From Painting by G. Ogilvy Reid, R.S.A.]   [By Permission of Royal Scottish Academy.

After Killiecrankie.

81. MASSACRE OF GLENCOE (1692)—THE DARIEN EXPEDITION (1698)

Though the Highlanders had been defeated at Dunkeld by the Cameronians, they were still in a very restless state, and it was feared that another rebellion might break out. It was in the West Highlands, and especially in Argyleshire, where it seemed most likely that the rebellion would take place. The reason of this was that almost all the clans in that part of the country hated the Earl of Argyle, and, as he was a supporter of William, this made the chiefs, who were his enemies, take the side of James. What the Government feared was that a French force would land in the Highlands, and then many of the clans would be certain to join it, and there would be another civil war. General Mackay, therefore, was sent to the West Highlands with a body of soldiers, and, to overawe the chiefs, he built a fort at Inverlochy, which he called Fort William, after the name of the king.

But the Government was anxious to make sure that the chiefs would not again rise as they had done under Dundee. The first plan that was tried was one which had often been tried before. A sum of money, amounting to £12,000, was distributed among the chiefs, to bribe them to be loyal to William. This did very little good, however. Some of the chiefs refused to take the bribe, and others accepted it, but became no more loyal than before.

Then, in the year 1691, the Government took a step which was to lead to a frightful crime. It proclaimed that, if the chiefs did not take the oath of allegiance to William by the 1st of January, 1692, they would be treated as outlaws, and their lands would become the property of the king. By the appointed day all the chiefs had taken the oath except one—Alexander Macdonald, chief of the clan of Macdonald, that inhabited the valley of Glencoe, in the north of Argyleshire. He meant to take the

Glencoe.   [Photo by Valentine.

oath, but he foolishly put off till it was too late. On the appointed day he went to Fort William, but the officer there told him that he could not receive his oath, and that the nearest place where it could be taken was Inveraray. Inveraray was at the other end of Argyleshire; the roads were deep in snow; and Macdonald was an old man and unable to travel swiftly. When he arrived at Inveraray, it was five days after the appointed time. However, he did take the oath, and that should have saved him and his clan.

Now, the person who had most power in Scotland at this time was Sir John Dalrymple, the Secretary of State, and he was determined to teach the Highland chiefs such a lesson as would keep them quiet ever afterwards. He got William, therefore, to sign what were called " Letters of Fire and Sword " against the clan Macdonald, without telling him that the chief had taken the oath. These " letters of fire and sword " had been quite common in Scotland, and what they meant was that the persons against whom they were directed should be treated as rebels, and hunted down till they were either slain or taken prisoners.

One day, not a month after Macdonald had taken the oath, a troop of 120 soldiers appeared in the valley of Glencoe. Most of them were Highlanders, and they were commanded by two men, Major Duncanson and Captain Glenlyon, both of whom belonged to the clan of the Campbells, who were the deadly enemies of the Macdonalds. The soldiers were hospitably received by the Macdonalds, and for about a fortnight the strangers and their hosts lived in the friendliest way together. At last, when their plans were ready, the officers gave the orders which they had received from Dalrymple. One morning about five o'clock, the old chief was shot as he was getting out of bed, and his wife immediately met the same fate. The plan had been that every Macdonald should be massacred, but, as it was a dark winter morning, many escaped among the neighbouring hills. Thirty-eight, however, were slain, and among

From Painting by J. B. M'Donald.] [By Permission of Royal Scottish Academy.

Glencoe.

them were two children, two women, and an old man of eighty. This was the " Massacre of Glencoe," one of the most frightful crimes in the history of Scotland. Instead of helping William, as Dalrymple had intended, it made his enemies still more bitter against him, though, of course, William had never thought that the letters of fire and sword would be carried out in such a cruel and treacherous way.

Another event that happened a few years later made William very unpopular in the Lowlands as well as in the West Highlands. At this time all the nations of Europe were trying to enrich themselves by trading in foreign countries, and a Scotsman, named William Paterson, came forward with a plan to make Scotland as rich as her neighbours. This Paterson was one of the cleverest Scotsmen then living. He was born in Dumfriesshire, but left his native country, and travelled in all parts of the world. He made a fortune in the West Indies, and it was he who started the Bank of England.

Paterson's plan was to found a colony on the Isthmus of Darien or Panama, which is the narrow neck of land between North and South America, and across which a canal has now been constructed. This place, Paterson thought, was the best in the whole world for carrying on trade in. The Pacific Ocean was on its west side, and the Atlantic Ocean on the east, so that ships could sail from it both to Europe and Asia. The plan was so much thought of that the Scottish Parliament passed an Act to set up a company, called " The Company of Scotland trading to Africa and the Indies." Of course, before the company could be started, the king had to give his consent to it, and William did give his consent by granting a charter that was asked.

The next step was to get money to start the company. Paterson asked not only the Scots but also the English and the Dutch to take shares, and at first the English were so eager that in a short time they promised to pay in the sum of £300,000. Soon, however, the English merchants became alarmed lest the new company should spoil their own trade, and they got the English Parliament to do all in its power to suppress it. In the end, therefore, it was only the Scots who paid money into the company. So certain, indeed, were the Scots that Paterson's plan would be successful, that almost everyone who had money to spare took shares in the company—some even paying in their last penny.

At length, on the 26th of July, 1698, three ships sailed from Leith, carrying the colonists who were to settle in the Isthmus. They sailed in the high hope that before many years had passed they would all return rich men to their native country. They were to be wofully disappointed. Before they had been long in the Isthmus, one misfortune after another befell them. Disease broke out among them, as many as twelve dying in a single day. They ran short of provisions, and they began to quarrel among themselves. They were attacked by the Spaniards, who said that the Isthmus belonged to them ; and the English in the West Indies and North America refused to give them any assistance. At the end of a year only a few of the colonists survived, and they sailed away from the unhappy place. Twice afterwards ships were sent from Scotland to the Isthmus, but only to find it deserted. Such was the melancholy end of the Darien scheme. Of about four thousand men who had gone out to the colony, only some thirty ever returned to their native country, and thousands of people in Scotland were reduced to poverty for the rest of their lives.

The Scots believed that it was chiefly owing to William and the English merchants that the Darien scheme had failed, and so indignant were they that during the last years of William's reign it sometimes seemed as if there would be a rebellion against him. One night a mob arose in Edinburgh, broke all the windows of those who were friendly to the Government, and rang the city bells to the tune of "Wilful Willie, wilt thou be wilful still?" But there was one thought in the people's minds that prevented them from rebelling against William. They knew that, bad as William's rule might be, it was not so bad as that of the king who had been dethroned. When William died in 1702, therefore, he was still ruler of the United Kingdom, and the friends of the exiled James had no hope that he would be William's successor.

---

82. THE ACT OF SECURITY. 1704

Queen Anne (1702-1714)

William was succeeded by Queen Anne, the daughter of the exiled king, James VII. of Scotland and II. of England. Queen Anne's reign is one of the most famous in the history of England, as it was a time when many great writers lived, and

when English soldiers gained the most brilliant
victories that England ever won.   In the case of
Scotland, however, the one great event for which
Anne's reign is chiefly remembered is the union
of the Parliaments of England and Scotland.

When Anne became queen in 1702, almost exactly
a hundred years had passed since the crowns of
England and Scotland had been united.   During
that time the Scots and the English had not grown
more friendly to each other than they had been
before the union took place.   There were two chief
reasons why the Scots were discontented with
England.   The first reason was, that all the kings
after James VI. lived in London, and governed
Scotland as if they were only kings of England and
not of Scotland also.   The second reason was, that
the English would not allow the Scots to trade with
their colonies in America ; and we have just seen
how the English merchants did all they could to
prevent the Scots from founding a trading colony on
the Isthmus of Darien.

Now, as the English disliked the Scots as much as
the Scots disliked them, it seemed very unlikely that
they would agree to unite their Parliaments, and so
become one people.   Both in England and in
Scotland, however, some of the wisest statesmen
thought that it would be best for both countries
if the union could be brought about.   In the first
place, it would put an end to their constant quarrelling ; and in the second place, it would make them
better able to hold their own against all foreign
countries.

It is somewhat strange that it was a great quarrel

between the Scottish and the English Parliaments
that led to their being made one. In the year 1701,
the year before Anne came to the throne, the
English Parliament had passed an Act called the Act
of Settlement. By this Act it was declared that on
Anne's death the crown should go to Sophia, Electress of Hanover, the granddaughter of James VI.
This meant, of course, that Sophia would be queen
of Scotland as well as of England, and yet the Scots
were not asked if they would agree to the Act.

Great was the indignation in Scotland at what
was considered an insult to the whole Scottish nation,
and the Scottish Parliament determined to let
England know that Scotland was an independent
kingdom. As an answer to the English Parliament,
therefore, it passed (1704) an Act called the Act of
Security. By this Act, a successor to Anne was to
be chosen twenty days after she died, if she left no
heirs. This successor must be a Protestant, and also
a descendant of the House of Stewart; but he or she
was not to be the person chosen by the English
unless they would agree that Scotland should have
free religion, free government, and free trade.

The English Parliament was greatly alarmed at
the Act of Security, for what it meant was that after
Anne's death Scotland might choose a different
sovereign from England, and become a separate
kingdom. For a time it seemed as if there might
be war between the two countries, and, indeed, both
began to prepare for it. Then the English Parliament, as an answer to the Scots, passed another Act
which made the two peoples still more bitter against
one another. It was called the Alien Act, and it

declared that, if by Christmas Day of 1705 the Scots would not agree to have the same sovereign as England after Anne's death, no Scottish merchandise would be admitted into England.

Just at this time, when the two nations seemed on the point of going to war, an event happened which made them greater enemies than ever. In the year 1705 a Scottish ship was seized in the river Thames, because an English Company declared that the captain had interfered with its privileges. The Scots demanded that the ship should be given up, but no attention was paid to them. While the quarrel was going on, an English ship, called the *Worcester*, and commanded by a certain Captain Green, came into the Firth of Forth, and it was immediately seized. The captain and the crew were accused of being pirates, and of having taken a Scottish ship that was missing. This was known afterwards not to be true, and there was no real proof that Green and his men were guilty. But so furious were the Scots against England that they were ready to believe anything against any Englishman, and Captain Green and two of his officers were hanged, though quite innocent of the crime with which they were charged.

83. UNION OF THE PARLIAMENTS OF SCOTLAND AND ENGLAND. 1707

QUEEN ANNE (1702-1714)

The English and Scots had hardly ever been such bitter enemies as they were now, but this was the very reason why certain statesmen in each country thought that the only way to make them live at peace was to have one Parliament to look after the interests of both. First the English Parliament, therefore, and then the Scottish Parliament, asked the queen to appoint commissioners from the two countries to draw up a Treaty of Union. So, in the year 1706, thirty-two commissioners from Scotland and thirty-two from England were appointed, and they met in a room called the Cockpit, in the Palace of Whitehall, London. After meeting for nine weeks, they agreed upon a treaty, and the next step was to get the Parliaments of the two countries to pass it into law.

It was arranged that the Treaty should be first brought before the Scottish Parliament, because in Scotland there was far greater opposition to the Union than in England. Before the Parliament met there was the greatest excitement all over Scotland. Would the Treaty be passed or not? This was the question which everybody was asking, and which nobody could answer.

The Parliament met on the 3rd of October, 1706, and it was the last Scottish Parliament that was to meet. When the Scottish Parliaments assembled, there used to be a magnificent procession, which was called the "Riding of the Parliament"; and, as the spectacle was to be seen no more, let us look at the procession as it made its way from Holyrood Palace, where the Royal Commissioner stayed, to the Parliament House, where the Court of Session now sits.

To prevent any crowding, the streets were railed on both sides, and inside the railings were stationed

[*Photo by Wilson.*

Palace of Whitehall, in front of which Charles I. was executed.

soldiers on foot and on horseback, to keep the passage clear. At the head of the procession came the heralds, in the strange dress which they still wear when the Lord High Commissioner comes to open the General Assembly. Next came the members of Parliament, riding two and two, in the order of their rank, and all attended by lackeys. These were followed by the Lyon King-of-Arms, in his wonderful costume, with heralds and trumpeters preceding him. Immediately before the Commissioner himself, the crown, the sceptre, the purse, and the Royal Commission were carried by four earls. The coach of the Commissioner was drawn by six white horses, and was attended by his pages and footmen. Behind him came the dukes and marquises, and the officers of state, with their lackeys ; and a troop of Horse Guards, mounted on horses of all colours, closed the long procession.

The Parliament sat for more than three months before it could be decided whether the Treaty of Union was to pass or not, and never was Scotland in a greater state of excitement than during that time. Some of the members of Parliament were in favour of the Treaty and others were against it, and so angrily did they debate that at times it seemed as if swords would be drawn. Outside the Parliament, also, the people were divided as to whether the Union would be for the good of the country or not. By far the greater number, however, were against it, because they thought it would put an end to Scotland as an independent kingdom. The mob in Edinburgh was furious against the Union. They stoned the Duke of Queensberry, the Lord High Commissioner, as he drove to the Parliament House, which they tried to break into, but failed. In other parts of the country people were equally excited. At Dumfries the Treaty was burned, and in Glasgow there was a rebellion which had to be put down by the royal troops.

At last the Treaty was passed by the Parliament, and on January 16, 1707, the Commissioner

2 K

touched it with the royal sceptre, which was the
sign that the Treaty became law. At the same
time he touched an Act which should not be forgotten,
and which was part of the Treaty of Union. This
Act is also called the Act of Security, and it declared
that the Church of Scotland was to remain a Presbyterian Church for ever afterwards.

As the English Parliament also agreed to the

Parliament House, Edinburgh.

Treaty of Union, it was now the law in both
kingdoms. What did the Treaty contain? First, it
declared that England and Scotland were henceforth
to be one kingdom, which was to be called Great
Britain. They were to have one flag, on which the
Cross of St Andrew, the patron saint of Scotland, and
the Cross of St George, the patron saint of England,
were to be placed. The two countries were to be taxed

in the same way, and they were to have equal rights in trade—the same coins, weights, and measures to be used in both England and Scotland. The laws and Law Courts were to remain just as they had been in both kingdoms before the Union. Lastly, there was to be one Parliament—the arrangement being that Scotland was to send sixteen peers to the House of Lords and forty-five members to the House of Commons.

---

84. DISCONTENT WITH THE UNION, 1707-1714

QUEEN ANNE (1702-1714)

When the Treaty of Union was passed, the arrangement was that it should come into force on the 1st of May, 1707. From that day, therefore, there began a new time both for England and Scotland. They now made one kingdom, named Great Britain. One Parliament made laws for both, and, when war was declared against a foreign country, both had to assist in raising and maintaining soldiers to carry it on. If colonies were founded in any part of the world, they belonged equally to Scotsmen and Englishmen. All this means that Scotland and England had now the same *political* history. But besides the political history of a country, there are many other things which have to be told about it. We like to know what great events happened in it ; who were its chief men, and what they did ; how it became richer and more civilised. There is therefore much to tell about Scotland after it became a part of Great Britain.

We have seen that most people in Scotland did not wish the Union to take place, as they thought they would lose more than they would gain by it. And for a long time after it did take place, many Scotsmen continued to think that it had been a mistake. Indeed, the Treaty had no sooner become law than the Scots began to grumble at the way in which they were treated by England.

Here, for example, were some of the things of which they complained. By the Treaty a new way of raising the taxes was introduced into Scotland, and, as Scotsmen did not understand how it was done, Englishmen were sent down to act as tax-collectors. Now, as these collectors were very strict in insisting that the taxes should be paid, they came to be hated all over the country, and thus helped to make the Union more and more disliked.

Another thing that made the Scots very indignant was this. It was part of the Treaty that about £400,000 should be paid to them by the English to encourage their trade, and to make up for the losses connected with the Darien Expedition. This sum of money was called the Equivalent, but the Scots who were opposed to the Union called it a bribe. Now, the money was to have been given immediately after the Union was completed, but week after week passed, and still it did not come. People then began to jest about it and to say that it had been sent to Spain, or that the bridge at Berwick had broken down under its weight. At length it did arrive, in twelve waggons, guarded by 120 dragoons. But so angry were the Edinburgh mob at the delay, and also because they thought it was an English bribe, that they stoned the soldiers as they rode through the town.

There was one class of persons in Scotland who were delighted to see the people so discontented with the Union. These were the friends of the exiled King James, who were known as the Jacobites—so called from *Jacobus*, the Latin name for *James*. The Jacobites had done all in their power to prevent the Union, because it cut off James and his heirs from ever regaining the throne. It was with great rejoicing, therefore, that they saw it to be so unpopular, as they hoped that most Scotsmen would come to wish for the restoration of James.

As we have seen, the great hope of the Jacobites was that Louis XIV., the King of France, would send an army to Scotland to restore James to the throne; and in the year 1708 this did actually happen. For some time before the Union Louis had been at war with England, and he thought that it would be a great blow to that country if Scotland could be conquered. In the month of March, therefore, he sent to Scotland a fleet consisting of five great ships and twenty-one frigates, with 4000 men aboard. It was commanded by the best admiral in France, and with him sailed James's eldest son, whom his enemies called the Pretender, and his friends the Chevalier de St George.

The plan was that by a certain day the fleet should reach Leith, and lay siege to Edinburgh. In the darkness of the night, however, the French sailed past the Firth of Forth, and not long after they entered it, the British fleet under Admiral Byng appeared

in sight. It was now impossible for the invaders
to land, as the British admiral would have seized
their ships. As they were not a match for the
British fleet, they steered past it and made the best
of their way home to France. They encountered
such stormy weather, however, that many of their
vessels were wrecked, and most of their men were
lost. This was a great disappointment to the
Jacobites; as they had been confident that, if the
French had landed, they would have conquered the
country. And this was not at all unlikely, as there
were many Jacobites both in the Highlands and Lowlands, and there was only a small army of royal troops
to fight Jacobites and French combined.

Queen Anne reigned for six years after this
attempted invasion, and each succeeding year of her
reign the Scots became more and more dissatisfied
with the Union. All classes of the people had some
complaint to make against it. The Scottish nobles
were enraged, because they thought that the English
peers in the House of Lords treated them unjustly,
and that the nobility of Scotland had not the same
privileges as the nobility of England.

In the year 1712, also, the ministers of the Church
of Scotland were made both afraid and angry by
an Act which was passed by the united Parliament.
We have seen how, immediately after the Revolution,
patronage was abolished by the Scottish Parliament.
The new Act, however, restored patronage; that is,
it took away from the congregations the right of
choosing their ministers. Now the ministers said
that this Act was contrary to the Act of Security,
which declared that the Church of Scotland should

not be changed in any way after the Union. It was that Act which had made the ministers indignant; and what frightened them was that, if this change were made, other still greater changes might follow. We shall see that the restoration of patronage was afterwards to be the cause of a great deal of trouble to the Church of Scotland.

But it was another Act (1713) that raised the greatest indignation in Scotland against the Union. This Act imposed a tax on malt, which was to be the same in England, Scotland, and Ireland. The Scots, however, protested that this tax was against the Treaty of Union, and that it was unjust that Scotland, where not nearly so much barley was grown, should pay the same duty as England. What made the Scots so angry at this tax was that ale, which is made from malted barley, was the drink of the common people, who would thus have to pay a higher price for it. The Scottish members of Parliament, however, managed so cleverly that, though the Act was passed, it did not become law in Scotland. Queen Anne died in the year after the passing of the Malt Tax, but a short time before her death the Union was very nearly brought to an end. It is curious that even some of the statesmen who had carried it through had come to be opposed to it, because, they said, it had done more harm than good, and the two nations had become more unfriendly to each other than ever. So in the House of Lords it was proposed that each country should again have its own Parliament; and it was only by four votes that the proposal was not carried. And that it was not, was very fortunate for both countries, as almost certainly there would have been civil war in Scotland if it had been agreed to dissolve the Union. For, however much the Scots might grumble against the Union, the majority of them knew that it had made the Protestant religion secure, and that, if it were abolished, the House of Stewart might be restored and Roman Catholicism along with it.

85. THE 'FIFTEEN

George I. (1714-1727)

The Treaty of Union had declared that on Queen Anne's death, Sophia, Electress of Hanover, the granddaughter of James VI., should succeed her on the throne. As Sophia, however, died a short time before Anne, her son George became king under the title of George I. Neither the Scots nor the English knew much of their new sovereign, and it was not in his favour that he could not speak English and never learned to do so. However, he was a Protestant, and was descended from the House of Stewart, and this was enough to make him welcome to most of the people of Scotland. When, on August 5, 1714, he was proclaimed king in Edinburgh, there was great rejoicing in the town, and the following night the Duchess of Argyle gave a grand ball at Holyrood to celebrate the occasion.

Great was the disappointment of the Jacobites, however, when George succeeded to the crown, as they had hoped that on Anne's death the House of Stewart would be restored. In many parts of the country, therefore, both in the Highlands and in the

Lowlands, they began to arm themselves and to plot in secret for the restoration of James or his heir, the Pretender. George had only been a year on the throne when the Jacobites found a leader. This was John, Earl of Mar, who had been one of the chief men in carrying through the Union, but who had afterwards changed his mind and had voted against it. Indeed, Mar had changed his mind so often that he went by the name of " Bobbing John." He had at first tried to gain the favour of George, but, as the king treated him coldly, he determined to raise a rebellion against him in Scotland in the hope of bringing back the Stewarts.

In the beginning of August, 1715, Mar, disguised as a workman, went aboard a coal-sloop in the Thames, and sailed to Fife, where he endeavoured to rouse the Jacobites to rebel. Then he went on to Aberdeenshire, where his own lands lay, and arranged a great hunting of the deer, to which he invited the Highland chiefs who were friendly to the Stewarts. The hunting (which the Highlanders called a *Tinchel*) was only a pretext for bringing the chiefs together, and, when the day came, it was arranged that on the 7th of September the standard should be raised for King James VIII.

On the appointed day, Mar, with about sixty men around him, raised the standard at Castleton, in Braemar. The rebellion had begun, but the Highlanders considered it a bad omen that the gilt ball on the top of the standard pole fell to the ground. Mar then marched southwards, and was soon joined by many nobles and chiefs with their followers. He gave orders that the town of Perth should be seized, and when this had been done, he proceeded there with his army, whose numbers soon amounted to 9000 men.

Perth was a very important place to have taken, and the Jacobites nearly took a still more important one. Some of them in Edinburgh laid a plan for capturing the Castle, the arrangement being that they were to climb the rock on a dark night. At the appointed hour a few of them met at the spot where they were to begin their climb, but the rest were drinking at a tavern, and came late. When the laggards appeared, it was found that the rope-ladder was too short, and they were discovered by a sentinel in the Castle. The watch at once came upon them, and in the fight that took place four Jacobites were wounded and made prisoners. It was very fortunate for the Government that the Castle was not captured, as the Equivalent, which, as we know, amounted to nearly £400,000, was stored there, and would have fallen into the hands of the rebels.

What was the Government doing in the midst of this danger? In all Scotland there were only about 3000 royal troops, and these were scattered up and down the country. However, the Government was wise in the choice of the general who was appointed to command them. This was the Duke of Argyle, who had learned the art of war under the famous Duke of Marlborough, and who was considered the third best British general then living. As soon as Argyle came to Scotland, he did a very prudent thing. He stationed his army at Stirling, to prevent Mar from leading his troops across the river Forth.

Now, the Earl of Mar, if he had been a commander like Montrose or Viscount Dundee, would at once have led his army into the Lowlands. Instead of doing this, however, he let week after week pass, and did nothing. At last, however, he put part of his army under the command of one of his best officers, named Mackintosh of Borlum, and ordered him to try to transport it across the Firth of Forth. Mackintosh managed this very cleverly. He seized all the boats on the north side of the Forth, and one dark night conveyed half of his men across to the coast of Haddingtonshire. Then he marched on Edinburgh, expecting that the Jacobites in the town would help him to take it. But Argyle, who had been told of his coming, was too quick for him. Mounting two men on each horse, he marched rapidly from Stirling to Edinburgh, which he reached before the enemy.

As Mackintosh was thus prevented from entering Edinburgh, he led his men to the Fort of Leith, which had been built in the time of Cromwell. But it was not safe for him to remain there, and he was compelled to march south, as he was not strong enough to fight Argyle. Where was he to lead his men next? That was now the question. Just about the same time as Mar had raised his standard, a rebellion had broken out in Dumfriesshire and in Northumberland, and so it was arranged that Mackintosh should join those rebels. The junction took place, and the combined forces marched into England through Cumberland, Westmorland, and Lancashire till they reached the town of Preston. They got no further, however, as in that town they were surrounded by the royal troops, and were compelled to surrender.

On the very day (November 13) that the rebels surrendered at Preston, a battle was fought between

Chevalier de St George.
("The Old Pretender.")

Mar and Argyle. Mar had at last led his army from Perth, and marched to Sheriffmuir near the town of Dunblane, and there Argyle met him. Mar had much the larger army, but he was not a leader like Montrose or Dundee, and could not put spirit into his men. The battle that took place was one of the strangest ever fought. When night fell and the fight was over, neither side knew which had won. Next morning, however, Mar's army was not to be seen, so that Argyle was master of the field.

The battle of Sheriffmuir put an end to the rebellion. Mar marched back to Perth, but his men began to desert him, and he had not the spirit for another battle. From the beginning of the rebellion Mar had expected that Prince James, the Pretender, would come over from France and put himself at the head of the Jacobite army. At length, in January, 1716, he did come, but it was too late for him to be of any use. Great numbers of the soldiers had deserted and returned to their homes, and those that remained were cast down and dispirited. And James himself was not the man to lead troops to victory. Indeed, he went about among the men with such a stony look, that they wondered if he was able to speak.

The question for the rebels now was—should they remain in Perth till Argyle, who had now a much larger army than he had had at Sheriffmuir, should come to attack them? It was decided not to wait for Argyle, and on the 30th of January the army left Perth. Before it left the town, however, the cruellest thing in the whole civil war was done. Five villages in the neighbourhood were burnt to the ground to prevent Argyle's army from finding provisions on its march from Stirling to Perth. The prince and his army then marched to Dundee, and thence to

Montrose. At Montrose, the friends of the prince persuaded him that it was no longer safe for him to remain in Scotland, and so, without the army knowing of it, he and Mar and some others slipped at night into a vessel in the harbour and sailed for France. And this was the end of the 'Fifteen, for the army, being thus deserted by its leaders, soon broke up, each man "taking the road that pleased him best."

86. THE HIGHLANDS—THE MALT TAX— THE "DYKE-BREAKERS"

George I. (1714-1727)

The rebellion of 1715 had caused much bloodshed and misery, both in England and in Scotland. The Government had therefore to try to prevent such a rebellion from happening again. First, it had to punish the leaders who had taken part in the Rising, as the Jacobites called the rebellion. In London, an English nobleman, the Earl of Derwentwater, and a Scottish nobleman, Lord Kenmure, were executed. In Scotland several hundred prisoners were taken, but there was so much sympathy with them that they had to be conveyed to Carlisle to be tried by an English jury. This, of course, greatly enraged the Scots, as they thought it was shameful that Scotsmen should be tried by Englishmen. However, in the end even the Jacobites admitted that the prisoners had a fair trial, for not one of them was put to death.

More had to be done, however, if another rising

was to be prevented. In 1725, therefore, an Act was passed which commanded that all their arms should be taken from the Highland clans who were known to be the friends of the Stewarts. To carry out this law an English general, named General Wade, was sent to the Highlands with a body of troops. But the Highlanders were too clever for him. They gave up arms, indeed, but only old and useless ones, and they kept those that were really useful hidden away, to be in readiness if they were ever needed.

General Wade, however, did one thing which will make his name always remembered in the Highlands. In past times the great difficulty in punishing the Highlanders when they broke the laws was that there were no roads by which troops could march quickly from one place to another. General Wade, therefore, was ordered to construct great roads, crossing the Highlands and connecting the garrisons at Fort George, Fort Augustus, and Fort William, and also Crieff with Inverness. The work was begun in 1726, and went on every summer for eleven years. The total length of the roads is 250 miles, their average breadth 16 feet; and no fewer than forty bridges had to be made at different places. Two rhyming lines, which were stuck up near Fort William, are well known—

"Had you seen these roads before they were made,
  You would hold up your hands and bless General Wade."

Were the Scots better pleased with the Union under George I. than they had been under Queen Anne? It cannot be said that they were. They still complained that the United Parliament was not fair to Scotland, and that it always thought of England first. During the reign of George there was one great disturbance, which showed how difficult it was for a single Parliament to make laws for the two countries.

We saw how, in the reign of Anne, Scotland had escaped paying the Malt Tax. In the year 1725, however, a famous English statesman, Sir Robert Walpole, proposed that, instead of a tax on malt, the Scots should pay on every barrel of beer sixpence more of duty than they had hitherto paid. Such an outcry arose in Scotland, however, that he was compelled to give up this plan and to adopt another. The new arrangement was that threepence of duty should be paid on every bushel of malt. The Scots liked this arrangement no better than the other. The people of Edinburgh and Glasgow, where most malt was made, were furious against the new tax. The Edinburgh brewers refused to brew any ale, which was the chief drink of the inhabitants of the town; but the Court of Session threatened to imprison them, and they were compelled to give in. In Glasgow things went much further. There was a great riot in the town, and soldiers had to be sent to put down the rioters.

There was another occasion when soldiers had to be sent to enforce the law in a different part of the country. On this occasion, however, the disturbance was not caused by laws passed by the Government. In the year 1723 the landlords in Wigtownshire, Kirkcudbrightshire, and Dumfriesshire began suddenly to drive their tenants out of

ADAM DUNCAN,
Admiral
(1731-1804).

WILLIAM CULLEN,
Physician
(1710-1790).

ADAM SMITH,
Political
Economist
(1723-1790).

DUNCAN FORBES,
of Culloden
(1685-1747).

EWEN MACPHERSON,
of Cluny
(——-1756).

CHARLES EDWARD,
"Bonnie
Prince Charlie"
(1720-1788).

ALLAN RAMSAY,
Poet
(1686-1758).

WILLIAM ROBERTSON,
Historian
(1721-1793).

DAVID HUME,
Philosopher & Historian
(1711-1776).

LORD GEORGE MURRAY,
Son of Duke of Athole
(1700-1760).

FLORA
MACDONALD
(1722-1790).

DONALD CAMERON,
The "Gentle Lochiel"
(1695-1748).

their farms, and to turn most of their lands into pasture. The reasons they gave for doing this were that the tenants did not pay their rents, and that they were lazy, and did not farm their fields properly. The landlords also did what we know was a new thing in Scotland; they began to enclose the fields with stone walls.

Now, these proceedings of the landlords were very hard on the tenants who were turned out of their farms, and had no other means of supporting themselves and their families. The result was that as many as five hundred farmers and others bound themselves to have their revenge on the landlords, and the revenge they took was this. Whenever a wall was begun to be built, men, women, and children went in the dead of night, armed with crowbars and other implements, and destroyed all the parts of the wall that had been finished during the day. This went on for more than a year, and the landlords were unable to stop the "Dyke-breakers" or "Levellers," as they were called. At last they applied to the Government to send a regiment of soldiers to put an end to the dyke-breaking. The regiment of the Scots Fusiliers was sent, and a fight took place, in which the Levellers were beaten and sixteen of them taken prisoners. Some of them were fined, and others were banished, and the end was that the dyke-breaking was stopped. It should be added that some of the landlords were really sorry for the evicted families, and tried to have woollen manufactures set up in the towns to supply them with employment.

87. THE PORTEOUS MOB. 1736

George II. (1727-1760)

George I. died in 1727, and was succeeded by his son, George II. Prince James, the Pretender, hoped that at the death of George I. there might be a chance of another rising in his favour like the 'Fifteen. But neither the Jacobites in Scotland nor those in England were willing to risk their lives at this time, and so the new king succeeded peacefully to the throne. There was, indeed, to be a Jacobite rebellion in George II.'s reign, and a much more formidable one than the 'Fifteen, but it did not take place till he had been many years on the throne.

We have seen how, during the reigns of Anne and George I., the people of Scotland had often been discontented with the laws passed by the United Parliament. Now, there was one law against which most of the people of Scotland of all ranks had been very indignant since the day the Union had taken place. This was the law against smuggling, which forbade tea or brandy or wine to be brought into the country without the payment of a duty to the Government.

It was not only the poor people who thought this an unjust law; the farmers, the country gentlemen, and even some of the ministers were of the same opinion. The result was that smuggling went on in all parts of the country. In dark nights and out-of-the-way places, ships would appear off the coast, and boats would be sent ashore laden with tea or brandy or wine, which would be bought by the people of the neighbourhood without having to pay the duty. Often desperate fights took place between the smugglers and the custom-house officers, but the smuggling still went on, as there were always people ready to buy the smuggled goods, and the smugglers themselves grew rich by their trade. One of the most famous stories in the history of Scotland, the story of the Porteous Mob, shows us how ready the people were to take the side of the smugglers in their breaking the law.

There were two smugglers, called Robertson and Wilson, from whom the custom-house officers had more than once taken their smuggled goods. These two determined to pay themselves back, and they broke into the custom-house of Pittenweem, in Fife, and stole about £200. Soon afterwards they were caught, imprisoned in the Tolbooth of Edinburgh, and condemned to death. Before the day of execution came, however, they made an attempt to escape. They removed the grating of their prison window, but Wilson, who was a man of large size, stuck in attempting to get through the opening, and the gaoler came in and caught him in this position. Wilson, it is said, was very angry with himself for having prevented Robertson from escaping, as the latter, being a smaller man, could easily have got through the opening if he had gone first.

In those times it was the custom to have condemned criminals led to church on the Sunday before their execution. Our two smugglers, therefore, were taken to church according to the usual custom; but, while the bell was ringing and the congregation were still entering, they suddenly fell upon the men who were guarding them. Robertson succeeded in getting free, and, as none of the congregation tried to stop him, he made his way into the street and escaped. Wilson, however, was not so fortunate, as his guards held him firmly. Then, seeing he could not escape himself, he determined to prevent the guards from following his comrade.

The Old Tolbooth, which formerly stood near St Giles.

He seized one with each hand, and a third with his teeth, and, as he was a man of great strength, he pinned them fast till Robertson had time to escape.

Wilson was led back to his prison, and the day came for his execution. In the Grassmarket, where the execution was to take place, a great crowd assembled, as was usual on such occasions. The City Guard, commanded by Captain Porteous, was there, as was also usual at public executions. Till the hangman had done his work, the crowd had remained perfectly quiet ; but no sooner had Wilson's body been taken down from the gallows, than they began to pelt the guards with stones. Then Porteous lost his temper, and ordered his men to fire. They fired over the heads of the crowd, but unfortunately shot several persons who were looking on from the neighbouring windows.

Almost all the people of Edinburgh had sympathised with Wilson, and they were now beside themselves with rage at Porteous. They demanded that he should be brought to trial, and he was actually tried and condemned to death. There were, however, some persons who thought that Porteous had only done his duty when he ordered his men to fire on the riotous mob, and at their request Queen Caroline, the wife of George II., granted a respite of six weeks to the condemned man.

The night before the day which had been fixed for his execution, Porteous was making merry with some of his friends whom he had invited to his prison in the Tolbooth. He had heard of the respite, and knew that he was safe for the morrow. Suddenly a loud noise was heard in the street ; it was an immense crowd that had assembled before the door of the Tolbooth. Tar-barrels were set ablaze and applied to the door ; an opening was soon made, and the leaders of the crowd rushed into Porteous's cell.

At first, Porteous was not to be seen. When he heard the noise of the mob, he had tried to escape by the chimney, but an iron grating stopped his way. He was soon discovered, and sternly told that he must

prepare for death. He refused to walk, and so he had
to be carried to the place of execution in the Grassmarket. As there were no gallows on the spot, one
of the rioters bought a rope on the way, and a dyer's
pole served for the beam.

As the person who acted as hangman was unskil-
ful at his work, it was pitiful to see the last struggles
of the unhappy victim. When the execution was
over, the crowd dispersed and did no more mischief.
What, indeed, was remarkable about the whole affair
was the orderliness with which the mob carried
through the work of the night; and it was believed
that certain persons of rank, who were never discovered, had carefully arranged all that had taken
place, and had acted as the leaders of the crowd.

---

88. THE 'FORTY-FIVE.—1

GEORGE II. (1727-1760)

The Jacobites had never lost hope that the House
of Stewart would one day be restored to the throne.
If Britain should go to war with a foreign country
and most of her soldiers be abroad, there might
then be the chance of a more successful rising than
the 'Fifteen. As we have seen, the great hope of
the Jacobites was that Britain would go to war with
France, as then the French king might send an army
to some part of the British Isles. At last, in the
year 1743, a war did break out between Britain and
France, and in the following year a French fleet was
despatched to invade the south of England. Before

the French could land, however, the British fleet
appeared, and the French admiral was afraid to
risk a battle. Then, as the French fleet sailed back

Prince Charles Edward.

to France, a great storm overtook it and did great
damage to many of the ships.

This was a grievous disappointment to the
Jacobites, as it was not likely that the French king

would spend money in fitting out another fleet to invade Britain. Two years had not passed, however, before it seemed for a while as if their hopes were at length to be fulfilled.

Prince James, the son of James VII., was now too old to think of himself fighting for the throne of Great Britain, but he had a son who the Jacobites thought would prove a greater hero than his father. This was Prince Charles Edward, who was now about twenty-five years of age. He was an entirely different man from his father James; he was bold, stirring, and adventurous, and he determined to make an attempt to recover the throne of his ancestors.

At first he tried to persuade the French king to give him troops to invade Britain, but when he found this was useless, he resolved to go alone. "I will go," he said, "if I have only a single footman," and he wrote to his father that he was determined "to conquer or die." As it was in the Highlands of Scotland he had his most eager supporters, it was in the Highlands he decided to raise his standard. So in the month of July, he sailed from France with only two ships, and having seven companions on board, who came to be known as the "Seven Men of Moidart." The beginning of his expedition, however, was unlucky, as one of his ships was attacked by a British man-of-war, and was so damaged that it had to sail back to France.

With his one vessel he sailed to the little island of Eriskay, in the Outer Hebrides, and two days afterwards he landed at Arisaig, in the south of Inverness-shire. Would the Highland chieftains flock to his standard, as he had expected? At first it seemed as if they were unwilling to obey his summons. They knew what a risk they ran by taking part in the rebellion in which Charles wished them to join. If they were defeated, the end would be the loss of their lands and even of their lives. But Charles showed that he had a wonderful power in winning men to his cause, and at this time he looked like a young hero who could lead to victory. He was tall and strong and active, and no Highland chief could endure more fatigue than he. With his fair hair and dark eyes he was also handsome to look upon, and his admirers called him " Bonnie Prince Charlie."

It was not long before he persuaded one chief after another to join him. Among them were two whom he was specially glad to have on his side — young Lochiel, son of the chief of the Camerons, and young Macdonald, son of the chief of Clanranald. Soon Charles had so many followers around him, that he determined to raise his standard and begin his attempt to win the crown of Great Britain for his father. On the 19th of August, less than a month after the Prince had landed in Scotland, the standard was raised in Glenfinnan amid the cheering of his followers, who tossed their bonnets in the air to show their delight. The standard was a beautiful banner of red silk with white in the middle.

By this time the Government knew that Charles was in Scotland, and that the rebellion had begun. To put it down as swiftly as possible, therefore, a small army was sent into the Highlands, under the command of Sir John Cope. As Cope marched through Perthshire, however, he found that the inhabitants were more friendly to Charles than to

himself. They stole his baggage-horses, and mis-
directed him when he inquired regarding the road
which he wished to follow to Fort Augustus. At
length he reached a place called Dalnacardoch, in the
Forest of Atholl, and there he was told that Charles,
at the head of 3000 men, was approaching. Cope
was not a great general, and for a time he was in
doubt whether he should risk a battle or not. At
last, he decided that it would be safer not to fight
the enemy, and he marched to Inverness instead of
to Fort Augustus, as he had intended.

There was now no army to prevent Charles from
leading his men into the Lowlands, and this he
resolved to do. First he marched to Perth, then
crossed the Forth near Stirling, and he was at
Corstorphine, three miles to the west of Edinburgh,
in less than a month after the standard had been
raised at Glenfinnan.

Great was the alarm of the people of Edinburgh.
At first, they thought of defending the town against
the enemy, and they tried to raise men for this
purpose; but they soon found it was of no use, and
they sent a deputation to Charles. Charles's answer
was that, if the town were not immediately surrendered, he would at once attack it. But there was
no need of an attack, as Lochiel and two other
officers cleverly contrived to get 900 Highlanders
into the city by the Netherbow. A few hours
afterwards Charles rode through the King's Park to
Holyrood Palace; at noon his father was proclaimed
king, under the title of James VIII., and at night
there was a grand ball at Holyrood in honour of
the occasion.

"Bonnie Prince Charlie."

And where was Sir John Cope all this time? He had left Inverness and marched to Aberdeen, where he embarked his troops, reaching Dunbar on the very day that Charles entered Edinburgh. Cope's next movement was to march towards Edinburgh, but Charles went to meet him; and the two armies came face to face near Prestonpans, nine miles to the east of Edinburgh. On the night of the 20th of September both armies lay down on the field, expecting battle on the morrow. Before daylight, however, a native of the district undertook to guide Charles's army by a narrow path through a bog, so that it might come suddenly on the army of Cope, which would be taken completely by surprise. This was exactly what happened.

Just as the sun rose, the Highlanders fell upon Cope's men, who had little time to prepare to meet their enemy. The battle was over in less than ten minutes; Cope's foot-soldiers were almost all either captured, wounded, or slain; and the horsemen escaped only by riding as fast as they could from the field. Among those who fell was the brave Colonel Gardiner, whose monument may be seen on the field of battle.

---

89. THE 'FORTY-FIVE.—2

After his victory at Prestonpans, Charles with his army returned to Edinburgh, where he remained for over a month, living like a king. It was a great disappointment to him, however, that so few men from the Lowlands came to join him. The truth was that the people of the Lowlands did not wish the Stewarts to be restored, as they knew that that would mean the bringing back of Roman Catholicism. As for Charles's Highlanders, the Lowlanders regarded most of them as mere savages, whom it was a disgrace to Charles to have brought among civilised people.

Would the people of England be more willing to

Doune Castle, with Prince Charles Edward and Prisoners.

join him than the Scots of the Lowlands? This was what Charles now resolved to try to discover, and he marched to Carlisle, where, on the 9th of November, he found himself at the head of his army. Carlisle was soon taken, and the army continued its march through Cumberland, Westmorland, and Lancashire. But every day it became clearer that the inhabitants were not favourable to his cause. Very few joined him, and his officers, who had expected that great numbers of Englishmen would flock to his standard, began to lose heart, and to wish they were at home among their native mountains.

When the army reached Derby, Charles's officers told him that they would go no farther. The royal troops were gathering round them, and it was plain that the people of England were not willing to rise against George II. Yet, as the Prince's army marched farther and farther south, the people of London were greatly alarmed, and many persons thought that, if it had reached the city, it would at once have surrendered, and George II. might have been driven from the throne.

The retreat from Derby was a terrible disappointment to Charles, and he was never the same man afterwards. During the march southwards he had been in the highest spirits, and, clad in his Highland dress, he had usually walked at the head of the army. In the retreat to Scotland, he was gloomy and fretful, and was generally the last to begin each day's march. His Highland followers, also, behaved very differently during the retreat from the way in which they had behaved on the march southwards. Then they had been as orderly as regular soldiers, but, on the march homewards, they were like a band of robbers, and stole everything which they thought was worth carrying off.

As the royal troops were in pursuit of them, the rebels had to make all haste to reach Scotland. When they at length crossed the river Esk, which divides the two countries, they were so overjoyed that they struck up the bagpipes and danced to the music.

Map showing route taken by Prince Charles Edward in his advance into England and retreat to Culloden.

Now safe in Scotland, where were they to march next? They could not return to Edinburgh, as it was now occupied by the royal troops. They chose, therefore, to march to Glasgow, which they reached in the last week of December. But, as the Highlanders drew near their native mountains, they began to desert in great numbers. The people of Glasgow also showed that they had no liking for Charles, and he had to compel them to supply his men with shirts, coats, bonnets, and shoes, of which they were sadly in need after their long march to England.

After remaining about a week in Glasgow, the rebels proceeded to Stirling, which they soon took, though the commander of the Castle refused to surrender. Then the news came that a royal army was approaching. It was commanded by General John Hawley, who was hated by his men for the cruel way in which he treated them, and who boasted that he would drive the Highlanders before him. He was to find that he was greatly mistaken. The two armies met at Falkirk, and Hawley was as completely beaten as Cope had been at Prestonpans.

But Charles's victory did not do much good to his cause. Shortly after the battle, his chief officers told him that it was unsafe for his army to remain in the Lowlands, and that they must at once march into the Highlands. When Charles heard this proposal, he felt that it was the deathblow to all his hopes. "Have I lived to see this?" he exclaimed, and in his rage and disappointment he dashed his hand against the wall. Greatly against his will, therefore, his army left Stirling, crossed the river Forth, and marched to Inverness, which he easily took.

SIR RALPH
ABERCROMBIE,
Soldier
(1734-1801).

SIR JOHN MOORE,
Soldier
(1761-1809).

Lord
JEFFREY,
Writer & Critic
(1773-1850).

SIR WALTER
SCOTT,
Poet & Novelist
(1771-1832).

ROBERT BURNS,
Poet
(1759-1796).

THOMAS TELFORD,
Engineer
(1757-1834).

ROBERT ADAM,
Architect
(1728-1792).

MUNGO PARK,
African Traveller
(1771-1805).

THOMAS GRAHAM,
Lord Lynedoch
(1748-1843).

SIR HENRY RAEBURN,
Portrait Painter
(1756-1823).

WILLIAM HUNTER,
Anatomist
(1718-1783).

JAMES HUTTON,
Geologist
(1726-1797).

JAMES WATT,
Inventor

JAMES BRUCE,
"The Abyssinian."

DAVID LIVINGSTONE, Sir RODERICK J. Sir CHARLES THOMAS Sir COLIN THOMAS HENRY, LORD Sir DAVID JOHN THOMSON,
Missionary and MURCHISON, LYELL, CAMPBELL, BABINGTON, Brougham, Orator WILKIE, Landscape
Traveller MURCHISON, Geologist Lord Clyde Lord Macaulay and Law Reformer Painter Painter
(1813-1873). Geologist (1797-1875). (1792-1863). (1800-1859). (1778-1868). (1799-1841). (1778-1840).
(1792-1871).

THOMAS CARLYLE, Sir JAMES Y. SIMPSON, Sir DAVID BREWSTER, JAS. A. BROUN-RAMSAY, Sir WM. HAMILTON, THOMAS CHALMERS,
Writer Physician Physicist Marquis of Dalhousie Philosopher, Founder of Free
(1795-1881). (1811-1870). (1781-1868). (1812-1860). (1788-1856). Church (1780-1847).

2 M

It was in February, 1746, that Charles reached Inverness, and there he remained for nearly two months. His men were not idle during that time, and they gained several victories in different parts of the Highlands. But Charles had now to face the strongest army that had yet been sent against him. The Duke of Cumberland, the brother of George II., at the head of the royal troops, had crossed the Forth, with the intention of giving battle to Charles. After spending some time in Aberdeen, he marched westwards towards Inverness, near which the Highlanders

Pistol of Prince Charles Edward.

lay. Charles had now to decide whether he would fight Cumberland or not. His army was not in a very fit state for battle, as for some time there had been a great lack of provisions for the men. Many of the Highlanders also were in other parts of the country, and could not return in time for the fight. What made things still worse for Charles was that he was not on friendly terms with several of his officers, who had also quarrelled among themselves.

However, it was decided to fight Cumberland, and Charles assembled his men on Culloden Muir, about five miles from Inverness. In the course of the day a bold plan was formed. When night came on, the whole army marched from the Muir with the intention of surprising Cumberland, who was encamped at Nairn, about twelve miles distant. But when the foremost men were within three miles of the enemy's camp, the day broke, and, as Cumberland could not now be taken by surprise, Charles's army had to march wearily back to Culloden Muir.

The men had hardly lain down to rest when they were roused by the news that Cumberland was close at hand. Never was an army less fit for battle than that which Charles had now to lead. His men were famished for want of food; they were weary with their long march; and they had lost their night's sleep. Charles had only about 5000 men, while Cumberland had 9000, most of whom were trained soldiers, and Cumberland had also taken care to prepare his men for the Highland way of fighting.

Both armies now made ready for battle (April 16). Cumberland drew up his men in two lines, with a considerable space between them. The battle began with the firing of cannon from both sides, but Cumberland's fire was far more deadly, as he had both more and better guns than Charles. For about an hour the clansmen stood the deadly fire, but at last they could endure it no longer, and they made a furious rush on Cumberland's front rank. So terrible was their onset that they broke through the first line. But Cumberland had been prepared for this. In his second line, the men were arranged three deep—the first rank kneeling, the second stooping, and the third standing upright, all with their guns ready pointed. When the Highlanders broke through the first line, therefore, they were received by the fire of these three ranks, and almost every man of them was shot dead, so that they lay in great heaps on the field. This decided the battle, and soon the remnant of Charles's army was in flight.

Cumberland's victory at Culloden put an end to the rebellion. Charles fled from the field of battle,

The Cairn, Culloden Moor.

and for nearly five months he had to hide in the Highlands and Western Islands, till he escaped in a ship to France. The story of his adventures, of the faithfulness of the Highlanders, who had his life in their hands, of the devotion of Flora Macdonald, who saved him in the time of his greatest danger, would fill a book by itself, but the story cannot be told here; nor can we tell the pitiful tale of his life as an exile in France and Italy, and of its miserable end.

After his victory at Culloden, Cumberland had to teach the Highland chiefs and their clansmen such a lesson as would prevent them from rising again in rebellion. So cruelly did he do his work that in Scotland he was called the " Butcher Cumberland," and his only excuse is that the rebellions of the '15 and the '45 had made Englishmen think that the Highlanders were a kind of savages who could not be treated like a civilised people. Only six of the leaders of the rebellion were taken prisoners, and five of these were executed; but nearly eighty others suffered death, all of them bravely maintaining to the end that they died in a just cause.

---

90. PROGRESS OF SCOTLAND AFTER THE UNION—THE " FIRST SECESSION " (1740)

We have seen how the people of Scotland continued to complain against the Union long after it had taken place. For a time, indeed, it really did seem as if it had done more harm than good to the country. When the Treaty of Union was arranged, England was at war with France, and the war went on for some years longer. But, as Scotland was now part of the United Kingdom, she as well as England became the enemy of France, and so her trade with that country was stopped for a time, which was a great loss to Scottish merchants. That was one unfortunate result of the Union. After the Union, also, the Scots had to pay heavier taxes, and higher duties on goods imported from foreign countries ; and this, of course, kept back trade instead of improving it.

It was not, indeed, till about the middle of the eighteenth century that Scotsmen began to see that the Union was likely to prove a good thing in the end. Let us look at some of the things which showed that the country was then growing more prosperous.

First of all, new manufactures were introduced into Scotland, and old ones began to be improved. The industry that did most good was the manufacture of linen. Linen had been made for a long time past, but only in small quantities and of a very coarse kind. Now, however, more of it began to be made and of much finer quality. Hitherto it had been made only by the spinning-wheel, but about the time of which we are speaking what is called the "rock and reel" was introduced, so that the cloth was manufactured much more quickly and was of a much finer sort. Linen, indeed, became so plentiful in Scotland that an English traveller tells us that "he found good linen everywhere, especially in the Lowlands." And we are also told that between the years 1728 and 1738 the quantity of linen exported from Scotland to foreign countries was more than doubled. Now, this increase in the manufacture of linen did good in two ways : it gave employment to more people, and it brought more money into the country.

Another sign that the country was becoming more prosperous was that trade began to increase year by year. After the Union the trade with England became much greater than it had ever been. What the English chiefly bought from the Scots was Highland cattle. Every year hundreds of Englishmen came to Crieff Fair to buy these cattle, which were driven to England by Highland drovers, who were paid at the rate of a shilling a day. At the Fair of Crieff, in the year 1723, the Highlanders sold 30,000 cattle, for which they received 30,000 guineas.

But it was the trade with the North American colonies that brought most riches to Scotland. Before the Union, as we know, England did not allow the Scots to do business with those colonies ; but now the towns in the west of Scotland, such as Paisley, Greenock, and Glasgow, began to carry on a great trade with America. The merchants of these towns exported linen to the colonists, and their ships brought home cargoes of tobacco in return. It was Glasgow especially that carried on this trade, and the "tobacco merchants" of that town became the richest men in the country.

Of course, as trade and manufactures increased, the towns also grew in size and wealth. It was the towns in the West especially that grew most quickly, because it was they that carried on the trade with the colonies. Greenock, for example, began to be a very busy place. Till some time after the Union, it had only a pier, where ships could land their cargoes, but it now built a large harbour where many vessels could anchor. Paisley was another town that became very prosperous, chiefly owing to the manufacture of linen yarn, which was introduced from Holland. But Glasgow was the place which grew most rapidly. At the time of the

Union Glasgow had no trading-vessels of its own, and had to hire them from English seaports; but by the year 1740 it possessed sixty-seven vessels, and by 1792 it had seven hundred and eighteen. At the beginning of the eighteenth century it had only about 12,000 inhabitants, but, by the end of it, it had more than 40,000.

Not only did trade and manufactures increase, but agriculture also began to be greatly improved. As we know, there had been very little timber in Scotland, and very few fences of any kind round the fields. Now, however, forests were planted in different parts of the country, and fences of stone or hedges began to be made by the landlords. Things were grown in the country which had not been seen before. For the first time cabbages and turnips, which had been grown only in gardens, were planted in open fields. English travellers in Scotland had always complained that they could get no hay to feed their horses, but hay also now began to be made. It was at this time, too, that potatoes began to be grown in fields, and to be used as food by the Scottish people; though at first, like the people in England and France, they thought that potatoes were only fit to be eaten by cattle.

We now see that Scotland had begun to make such progress as she had never made in previous times, and no doubt this was largely owing to the Union; and we shall see, also, that she went on prospering more and more, and that, in proportion to her size and the number of her inhabitants she became as rich as other countries.

Before this chapter is finished, there is another

PLAN OF THE
CITY OF
GLASGOW
from actual survey
1790.

subject that must be mentioned. Since the Revolution in 1689, when James VII. was driven from the throne, we have heard very little of the Church and of religion, whereas in the time before the Revolution we heard of almost nothing else. From the Reformation to the Revolution, a period of more than a hundred years, the history of Scotland is almost wholly taken up with the quarrels about religion between the kings and their subjects. After the Revolution, on the other hand, there were no wars and battles about religion, as there had been in the reigns of Charles I., Charles II., and James VII.

But, if there were no religious wars, there were many disputes and quarrels about religion, even after the Revolution. As we know, during the reign of William, Presbyterianism was set up in Scotland in place of Episcopalianism. There were, however, many Episcopalians in the country, especially in the North, and the Presbyterians were indignant that they would not join what was now the Church of Scotland, and they tried, often very harshly, to compel them to do so. And the Episcopalians had an unhappy time for another reason. They thought that James VII. and his descendants were the rightful kings, and during the rebellion of 1715 they did all in their power to assist the rebels. The result was that the Government passed very severe laws against them, which made it almost impossible for them to have religious services of their own.

But, besides their quarrels with the Episcopalians, the Presbyterians came to have great disputes among themselves; and the greatest dispute of all was about patronage, of which we have heard more than once.

We have seen that during the reign of Queen Anne, an Act was passed which directed that congregations should no longer choose their own ministers, but that the patrons should appoint them. Now, most of the ministers and most of the congregations did not approve of this Act, and for a long time it was not obeyed.

At last, however, about the year 1730, a number of ministers were forced upon congregations against their will, and then a great quarrel arose in the Church. One minister, the Rev. Ebenezer Erskine of Stirling, stood forth and declared that a Church could not be the true Church which permitted ministers to be forced on unwilling congregations. For a number of years the dispute went on in the General Assemblies, and at last, in the year 1740, Erskine and seven other ministers were put out of the Church. This is called the first " Secession " from the Established Church of Scotland, and there were to be several others, of which the last and most important was the Disruption in the year 1843, when the Free Church of Scotland began.

---

91. PROGRESS IN THE HIGHLANDS

Before the rebellion of 1745 there had been few, if any, reigns in which battles had not been fought in some part of Scotland, but since the '45, war has been unknown within her borders. Of course, Scottish soldiers have fought in many countries in defence of the British Empire. On the Continent of Europe, in America, in India, and Africa, they have fought side by side with English and Irish soldiers against the enemies of Great Britain, but in Scotland herself the sword has never been drawn by Scot against Scot since Charles Edward was overthrown at Culloden. From the year 1745 onwards, therefore, the history of Scotland in itself is a history of peaceful progress in trade and commerce and manufactures,

View of Caledonian Canal.   [*Photo by Valentine.*

and in everything that makes a people happier and more civilised. It is of this progress that we have to hear in the concluding chapters of our history.

As we know, the most backward part of Scotland had always been the Highlands, and we have only to look at a map to understand the reason of this. Had the country of the Highlanders been a flat plain, it would have been easy for the kings of Scotland to compel its inhabitants to obey the law like their

other subjects, and the result would have been
that they would have come to live the same
kind of life as other Scotsmen, and to make as
much progress as the Lowlanders. But we have seen
how, owing to the wild country of the Highlands,
the kings of Scots had always found it difficult to
make its inhabitants obey the laws.

At the beginning of the eighteenth century the
Highlanders remained in much the same condition as
they had been in for hundreds of years before. They
were still divided into clans with chiefs over them,
whose orders they were compelled to obey. If the
chief went to war, every clansman had to follow him,
as otherwise he would have been cast out of the
clan. Most of the Highlanders, when they were not
at war, tried to make a living by their own industry;
but, owing to the nature of their country, this was
not very easy. There was not much ground on
which they could grow crops, and the soil was
usually so stony that it had to be dug up with a
spade, as ploughs would have been of no use.

But, as we have seen, it was chiefly by the rearing
of cattle that the Highlanders sought to earn their
livelihood, and even this industry was carried on
under great difficulties. The best soil was taken up
with crops, and the cattle had to graze on the mosses
and mountains, where the pasture was often very
poor. In winter, when the hills were covered with
snow, the beasts were kept under the same roof as
the families of their owners, and were fed with whatever could be spared from the food of the household.
In bad seasons the poorest Highlanders used a
strange diet. The cattle were bled, and the

CLAN MAP
OF
SCOTLAND

English Miles

1. Macleods.
2. Glengarry.
3. Chisholms.
4. Macleods of Lewis.
5. Clan Donald (N. and S.), Macdonalds.
6. Macgilliechallum.
7. Clan Quhele or Shaws.
8. Clan Ranald of Lochaber.
9. Macdonalds of Keppoch.
10. Macintoshes of Glentilt.
11. Clan Donachaidh or Robertsons.
12. Earl of Atholl.
13. Macthomas.
14. Fergusons.
15. Spaldings.
16. Clan Macian or Macdonalds of Ardnamurchan and Sunnart.

17. Clan Gillian or Macleans.
18. Stewarts of Appin.
19. Macdonalds.
20. Clan Gregor or Macgregor.
21. Macdougalls.
22. Glenorchy Campbell.
23. Macnaughton.
24. Clan Lauren, Maclarens.
25. Macgregors.
26. Macfarlanes.
27. Colquhouns.
28. Galbraiths.
29. Macaulays.
30. Stewarts.
31. Campbells.
32. Macallisters.

W. & A. K. Johnston, Limited, Edinburgh & London.

blood was mixed with milk and oatmeal to make cakes.

We can hardly wonder, therefore, that the wilder Highlanders tried to earn their livelihood in other ways. And one of these ways was to plunder the Lowlanders who lived in the country near the Highlands. They robbed their corn in time of harvest,

Shield of Rob Roy, a noted Highland Freebooter of the early Eighteenth Century.

and they robbed their cattle whenever they had the opportunity. Another means by which the wilder Highlanders enriched themselves was this. They would promise not to steal the property of any Lowlander who would pay them a certain sum of money, which went by the name of *blackmail*. Both blackmailing and cattle-lifting went on till as late as the year 1745, and it is said that in that year the Lowlanders who lived near the Highlands lost as much as £37,000, owing to the plundering habits of their neighbours among the hills.

After the rebellion of 1745, however, great changes took place in the Highlands, whose inhabitants began gradually to adopt the Lowland ways of living. A law was passed which forbade them to carry arms under a heavy fine. To their great indignation,

From Photo by Valentine.

General Wade's Bridge across the Tay at Aberfeldy.

also, they were prohibited from wearing the tartan, plaid, and kilt, which was their national dress, though, in the year 1782, this law was set aside. By another law the power of raising their clans for war was taken from the chiefs, and after this the Highlanders were tried in the same Courts of Justice as the other subjects of the king.

These laws, of course, made great changes both in the Highland country and in its inhabitants. There

CALEDONIA.

was no more cattle-lifting, and there were no more clan fights. As the Highlanders had shown themselves such brave soldiers, however, a great statesman, the Earl of Chatham, thought that some of them might be used in fighting the battles of Britain against its enemies in different parts of the world. And we know that there have been no braver soldiers in the British army than those of the Highland regiments.

As the Highland chiefs had no longer any power over their clansmen, they also began to change their ways of living. They became landlords instead of chiefs. In order to make money, they took to rearing herds of cattle, which they could sell in the Lowland towns. At a later time they also began to turn their lands into sheep-farms, which were rented by sheep-farmers from the Lowlands. The result of this was that thousands of Highlanders were driven from their homes, and had to emigrate to Canada and other parts of the British Empire.

As we know, the great difficulty in civilising the Highlands had always been the want of roads. We have seen how General Wade had constructed his great military roads, but these were not sufficient to open up all the Highland country. In the beginning of the nineteenth century, therefore, the Government commissioned a famous engineer, Thomas Telford, to superintend the making of roads all through the Highlands. The work went on for about twenty years, and in that time 920 miles of good roads were made, and 1200 bridges were built of stone or iron. In the year 1803, also, was begun the Caledonian Canal, which extends from the Moray Firth to the head of Loch Linnhe.

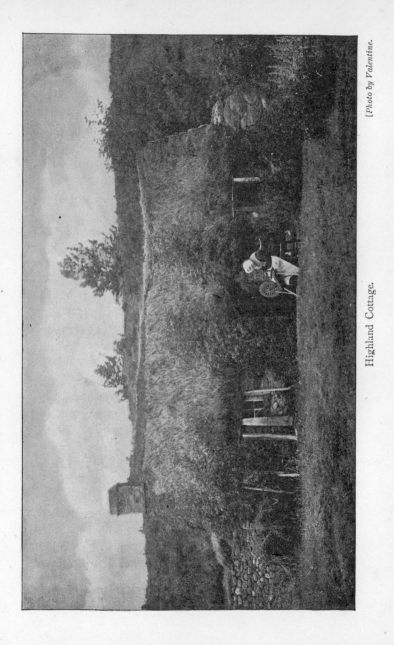

Highland Cottage.

[Photo by Valentine.

The making of these works did great good to the Highlands in many ways. It gave employment to hundreds of Highlanders, who were thus trained to labour with their hands as they had never been before. Then, as new roads were made every year, it became easier to go from one part of the country to another, and to carry on trade with the Lowland towns.

From this time onwards, indeed, the Highlanders began to live more and more like their old enemies, the Lowlanders. Ploughs and other implements were now seen in the Highlands as well as in the Lowlands. Mud cabins were changed into stone cottages, and cattle and pigs no longer lived under the same roofs as their owners. In remote parts of the country and in the Western and the Orkney Islands there is still great room for improvement among the people, both in their abodes and in their manner of living, but it is to be hoped that they also before long will share in the prosperity and in the comforts of their fellow-countrymen.

92. PROGRESS IN THE LOWLANDS

We have seen that a great improvement took place in the Highlands after the year 1745, but the advancement in the Lowlands was still more marked. There now began, indeed, a new Age in all civilised countries—the Age of Machinery. So many new tools, implements, and machines came to be invented that the old ways of living were completely changed, and more progress was made in fifty years than had formerly been made in many centuries. Let us see some of the changes that took place in the time of which we are speaking.

Vast improvements were made in agriculture. In former days farmers had to make their own implements, which were very unsuitable for their purpose. For example, ploughs were huge, clumsy implements, constructed chiefly of wood, and requiring as many as ten or twelve oxen to draw them. Now, however, they began to be made of iron by

Old Style of Plough.

trained workmen, who went on improving them till they became what they are at the present day. Hitherto, flails, of which we read in the Bible, had been used for separating the corn from the chaff; but in the year 1787, a Scotsman, named Andrew Meikle, invented the threshing-machine, which did the work far more thoroughly and in a much shorter time. In the beginning of the eighteenth century Scotland was far behind England in agriculture, but by the end of it Englishmen came to Scotland to learn the best methods of farming.

Great advance was also made in all kinds of manufactures. Till the beginning of the Age of Machinery people had used homespun cloth, made with the hand-loom; but machines were now invented for the manufacture of different kinds of cloth. In the year 1767 the spinning-jenny was invented by a Lancashire weaver, named Hargreaves, and shortly afterwards the power-loom, invented by Cartwright,

Sedan Chair.
(Style of conveyance common in the eighteenth century.)

also came into use. As all the new inventions were quickly introduced into Scotland, manufactories were set up in different parts of the country. In Hawick and other towns on the Borders, woollen cloth began to be made; carpets were woven at Kilmarnock, and cotton cloth in Rothesay. In these manufactories, of course, many persons got employment who had hitherto found it difficult to earn a livelihood.

Nothing, however, did more to enrich Scotland than the discovery how to turn to account the iron, of which there is such abundance in the country. In past times articles made of iron, even such things as horse-bits, had to be imported from Flanders; but in the year 1760, ironworks were set up on the banks of the river Carron, near Falkirk, and these still exist at the present day. The manufacture of iron

"Coach and Pair" of the Eighteenth Century.

led to many improvements. It was found that coal was the best fuel for smelting the iron, and coal-mines, therefore, began to be worked in different parts of the country. Owing to one invention after another, it was also found that iron could be put to many uses which had not been dreamt of at first. Steam-engines of iron came to be made through James Watt's discovery of the power of steam, and in course of time bridges and even ships were constructed of it.

It was fortunate for Scotland, therefore, that she possessed so many rich mines of iron and coal, as the iron manufacture became one of the most important of all her industries.

When manufactures of all kinds grew so rapidly, it became more and more necessary that it should be made easy to convey goods from one part of the country to another, and this, also, was gradually accomplished. In the year 1768 the Forth and Clyde Canal, between Edinburgh and Glasgow, was begun, and it was opened for traffic in 1790. In past times the roads in every country had been so bad that it was almost impossible to convey goods for any considerable distance. About the year 1815, however, a Scotsman, named Macadam, devised the way of making roads which is still in use, and which we call by his name to-day. Another great difficulty in the way of transporting goods was the want of safe bridges where they were needed. Now, as we know, bridges are to be found everywhere in Scotland—the two most wonderful being those over the firths of Tay and Forth. We have, indeed, only to remember the great steamers that cross the Atlantic and Pacific oceans, the electric telegraph and the telephone, to realise how, not merely the different parts of one country, but all countries in the world, have been brought together in a way that could not have been dreamt of in past times.

These various improvements made great and radical changes in the ways of living among all classes of the people. Both rich and poor came to wear better clothes, to live in better houses, and to have better food. Perhaps the greatest change of all was that the people

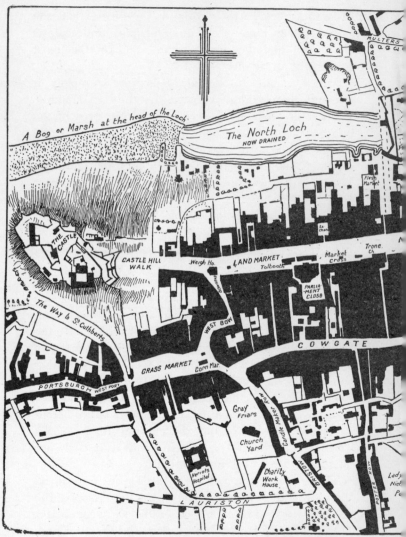

A Bog or Marsh at the head of the Loch.

The North Loch
NOW DRAINED

THE CASTLE

CASTLE HILL WALK

Weigh Ho.

LAND MARKET
Tolbooth

Market Cross

Trone Ch.

Ex Chan

PARLIAMENT CLOSE

The Way to St Cuthberts

WEST BOW

COWGATE

GRASS MARKET
Corn Mar.

PORTSBURGH   WEST PORT

Gray Friars
Church Yard

Candle Maker Row

BRISTO

Heriots Hospital

Charity Work House

POTTER ROW

Lady Nich

LAURISTON

MULTERS

Flesh Market

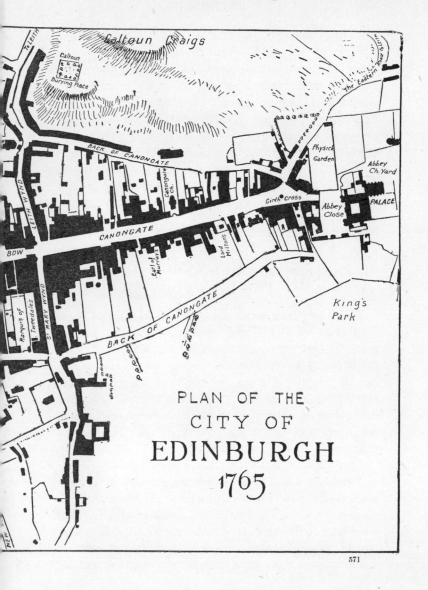

PLAN OF THE
CITY OF
EDINBURGH
1765

from the country began to flock into the towns, where they could find employment in the manufactories and other works which had been set agoing. The result of this was that many of the towns grew rapidly in size and in the number of their inhabitants. At the beginning of the eighteenth century, as we have seen, Glasgow was little more than a village, but it is now the largest city in Scotland and the second in Great Britain. And other towns, also, such as Edinburgh, Dundee, Aberdeen, Paisley, and Greenock, greatly increased in population, though none of them grew so much as Glasgow.

---

93. THE REFORM BILL (1832)—THE DISRUPTION (1843)—THE EDUCATION BILL (1872)

The most important thing in the history of Scotland after the '45 is the great advance the country made in agriculture and manufactures, and in all other industries. There were, however, two events which caused great excitement at the time they happened, and of which every Scotsman has heard. The one event was the introduction of the Reform Bill, which was passed in 1832; and the other was the Disruption, which took place in 1843.

The Reform Bill was passed because the people of England and Scotland were determined to have more to do with the government of the country. As we saw, when the Parliaments of Scotland and England were united in 1707, it was arranged that Scotland should send forty-five members to the House of Commons. Of these forty-five the counties sent up thirty, and the towns fifteen—Edinburgh being the only town that had a member to itself. Now, as the population of Scotland had greatly increased since the Union, forty-five members were not nearly sufficient to represent its people in Parliament. What made matters worse, however, was that only about 2000 persons in all Scotland had the right to vote for a member of Parliament. What the Reform Bill did, then, was to increase the number both of Scottish and English members, and to give the franchise, or right of voting, to a much larger body of persons.

To understand how the Disruption was brought about, we have to go as far back as the reign of Queen Anne. In her reign, as we saw, the right of choosing ministers was taken from the congregations and given to the patrons. We have heard, also, how in the year 1740, eight ministers left the Established Church because they thought that patronage was wrong. · After this First Secession, as it is called, there were several others, but the greatest secession of all was that which took place at the Disruption, and this was due to exactly the same cause. At Auchterarder and a few other places, ministers were placed over congregations against the will of the people, and the end was that nearly four hundred and fifty ministers, headed by the great Dr Chalmers, left their churches and manses rather than accept patronage. This was the beginning of the Free Church of Scotland, most of whose members in the year 1900 joined with the United Presbyterians to form the United Free Church.

Since the Disruption there has been one other

event in which the whole Scottish nation is greatly
interested—namely, the passing of the Education
Act of 1872. We saw how, at the time of the
Reformation, John Knox and his fellow-reformers
tried to have a school set up in every parish. In
this, however, they did not succeed, and it was not
till nearly the end of the eighteenth century that their
wish was completely carried out. When the Disruption took place, both the Established Church and
the Free Church came to have schools in the same
parish, which were kept up partly by the congregations and partly by money given by the Government.
By the Education Act, however, the schools were
given up by the churches and became public schools,
supported by taxes paid by the people, and managed
by school boards, chosen by those who pay rates.
The same Act compelled parents to send their children
to school when they reach a certain age, and to keep
them there for a certain time. In the year 1889
education was made free.

94. SCOTLAND AND THE BRITISH EMPIRE

By the union of the English and Scottish Parliaments in 1707, Scotland was made part of the United
Kingdom of Great Britain and Ireland, and it thus
became her duty to do all in her power to make that
Kingdom great and prosperous. Has she contributed
as much to its greatness and prosperity as could be
expected of her ?

For long after the Union, as we have seen, the
English and Scots did not work well together. Most

people in Scotland believed that the Union had been a mistake, and that the country would have been more prosperous had it never taken place. In the second half of the eighteenth century, however, Scotland began to make such progress that all but a few persons became convinced that the Union had been a good thing after all. They began to see that England and Scotland were really one country, and that the more prosperous the one grew the better it was for the other, and from this time onwards both Scotsmen and Englishmen realised that they were like partners in the same business and had both the same interests.

In the last chapter it has been told how, after 1745, Scotland went forward in her trade and manufactures and in her industries. This was well for herself, but it was also well for the United Kingdom, as it helped Great Britain to hold its own with other great countries, which were also striving to be rich and powerful. By her industry and enterprise, therefore, Scotland did her part in making the United Kingdom what it now is.

In many other ways, too, Scotsmen have done much to add to the greatness and prosperity of the British Empire. Some of the most useful inventions have been the work of Scotsmen. To mention only a few, it was a Scotsman, James Watt, who first showed how the steam-engine could be worked; a Scotsman, James Nasmyth, invented the steam-hammer; two Scotsmen, John Rennie and Thomas Telford, were the great bridge-builders of their time; and a Scotsman, Henry Bell, was the first to introduce steam-boats into navigation. In modern times it has

been the discoveries of science that have done most
to advance civilisation, and not a few of these dis-

Robert Burns in his Cottage.

coveries have been made by Scotsmen, but their
names are too numerous to be mentioned here.

Every nation is proud of its great writers, because they do good, and give pleasure not only to the people

Sir Walter Scott in his Study.

who produced them, but to all mankind. A nation that has not produced great writers, indeed, can

hardly itself be called great.   In Scotland since the
Union there have been many writers whose works are
read all over the world.   One of the most famous and
most useful books that ever was written is *The
Wealth of Nations*, by the Scotsman, Adam Smith,
who lived in the eighteenth century.   Every educated
man in the most remote countries has heard of the
poems of Robert Burns, the national poet of Scotland.
Of the writings of Sir Walter Scott, it has been said
that they have given pleasure to a greater number of
people in all lands than the writings of any other
author.   And nearer our own time, the works of
Thomas Carlyle have been read by thousands of
persons in all countries, who have been influenced by
them to the end of their lives.

There is still another way in which Scotland has
helped to make the United Kingdom great and
powerful as it is at the present time.   By its colonies
in all parts of the world, Great Britain has become a
mighty empire, the like of which has never been
seen before.   Now, Scotland has done even more than
might have been expected of her in helping to build up
this great Empire.   In proportion to her population,
she has sent out more of her people to the colonies
than England has done, and more great men to govern
them.   It will be seen, therefore, that since the union
of her Parliament with that of England, Scotland has
not only grown rich and prosperous for her own good,
but also for the good of the whole British Empire.

We began this history by asking the question how
there came to be a country called Scotland, and a
people called the Scottish people.   And that is the
question this book has tried to answer.   It commenced

with the cave-dwellers in the Bay of Oban, and it ends with the Scotland we see at the present day. What would the Oban cave-dweller think, could he look out on the Bay and see the steamers bringing hundreds of travellers from all parts of the world to admire the beautiful scenery of the country, where, with his few tools and weapons, he with difficulty gained a livelihood for himself and those who belonged to him? It has taken thousands of years to bring about the wonderful change, and we may be sure that as wonderful changes must happen in the days to come. At some future time the Scotland of to-day will no doubt appear as strange to the men then living as the Scotland of the cave-dwellers appears to us.

CHIEF EVENTS

PERIOD OF THE ROMAN INVASION

	A.D.
Agricola invades North Britain	80
Battle of Mons Graupius.	
Invasion of Severus	208
Departure of the Romans from Britain . . .	412

PERIOD DURING WHICH THE FOUR KINGDOMS BECAME UNITED

St Columba lands in Iona	563
Irish Christianity established in Pictland . .	565
Roman Christianity established in Northumbria .	664
Battle of Nectan's Mere (Dunnichen) . . .	685
Roman Christianity established in Pictland . .	710
Northmen plunder Iona	802
Kenneth MacAlpin becomes king of Picts and Scots .	844
Battle of Carham	1018
Strathclyde annexed by the King of Scots . .	1018
Duncan I. defeated and slain by Macbeth . .	1040

PERIOD OF THE ANGLO-CELTIC KINGS

Marriage of Malcolm Canmore and Margaret . .	1069
Magnus Barefoot acquires the Western Islands .	1102
Battle of the Standard	1138
The Treaty of Falaise, by which William the Lion surrenders the Independence of Scotland to Henry II.	1174
Richard I. acknowledges the Independence of Scotland	1189
Alexander II. conquers Argyle	1222
Battle of Largs	1263
Western Islands acquired by Scotland . . .	1266
Accidental death of Alexander III. at Kinghorn .	1286
Death of the Maid of Norway	1290

Period of the War of Independence

A D.

Edward I. awards the Scottish Crown to John Balliol.	1292
John Balliol dethroned by Edward I.	1296
Revolt of William Wallace	1296
Battle of Stirling Bridge	1297
Battle of Falkirk	1298
Execution of Wallace	1305
Coronation of Robert Bruce	1306
Battle of Bannockburn	1314
Meeting of the First Scottish Parliament	1326
Treaty of Northampton	1328
Death of Robert Bruce	1329
Accession of David II.	1329
Edward Balliol invades Scotland	1332
Battle of Halidon Hill	1333
Battle of Neville's Cross	1346

Period of the Stewart Kings

Accession of Robert II., the first of the Stewart Kings	1371
Battle of Otterburn (Chevy Chase)	1388
The Clan Fight at Perth	1396
Death of the Duke of Rothesay	1402
Burning of the Lollard, James Resby	1407
Battle of Harlaw	1411
Foundation of the University of St Andrews	1412
Burning of Paul Craw	1433
Assassination of James I. at Perth	1437
Fall of the Black Douglases	1455
Foundation of the University of Glasgow	1451
Accidental death of James II. at Kelso	1460
Orkney and Shetland Islands acquired by Scotland	1468
St Andrews made an Archbishopric	1472
Execution of James III.'s Favourites at Lauder Bridge	1482
Battle of Sauchieburn and Assassination of James III.	1488
End of the Lordship of the Isles	1493

A.D.

Foundation of the University of Aberdeen	1495
Marriage of James IV. and Margaret Tudor	1503
Battle of Flodden and Death of James IV.	1513
Burning of Patrick Hamilton	1528
Foundation of the Court of Session	1532
The Rout of Solway Moss and Death of James V	1542

MARY (1542-1567)

Burning of George Wishart	1545
Murder of Cardinal Beaton	1545
Battle of Pinkie	1547
The First Covenant	1557
Return of John Knox from the Continent	1559
Establishment of Protestantism	1560
Return of Mary from France	1561
Marriage of Mary and Darnley	1565
Murder of Riccio	1566
Murder of Darnley	1567
Marriage of Mary and Bothwell	1567
Battle of Langside	1568
Mary's flight to England	1568

JAMES VI. (1567-1625)

Murder of the Regent Moray	1570
Regent Lennox slain	1571
Death of John Knox	1572
Death of the Regent Mar	1572
Raid of Ruthven	1581
Execution of Mary	1587
Gowrie Conspiracy	1600
Union of the Crowns of England and Scotland	1603
Episcopacy established	1606
The Five Articles of Perth	1618
Death of James VI.	1625

CHARLES I. (1625-1649)

A.D.

Charles's visit to Scotland	1633
Laud's Liturgy	1637
Riot in the Church of St Giles	1637
The National Covenant	1638
Episcopacy abolished by the General Assembly at Glasgow	1638
First Bishops' War	1639
Second Bishops' War	1640
Solemn League and Covenant	1643
Battle of Philiphaugh	1645
The Engagement	1647
Execution of Charles I.	1649

CHARLES II. (1649-1651)

Charles II. proclaimed King	1649
Execution of Montrose	1650
Battle of Dunbar	1650
Battle of Worcester	1651

INTERREGNUM (1651-1660)

Scotland under the Commonwealth	1651
Scotland under the Protectorate	1653
Restoration of Charles II.	1660

CHARLES II. (1660-1685)

Restoration of Episcopacy	1661
The Pentland Rising	1666
First Letter of Indulgence	1669
Murder of Archbishop Sharp	1679
Battle of Drumclog	1679
Battle of Bothwell Bridge	1679
Sanquhar Declaration	1680
Test Act	1681
Death of Charles II.	1685

James VII. (1685-1689)

William II. and Mary II. (1689-1694)
William II. (alone) (1694-1702)

Anne (1702-1714)

George I. (1714-1727)

George II. (1727-1760)

SUBSEQUENT EVENTS

	A.D.
First Steamboat .	1788
Colliers and Salters freed	1799
Reform Bill passed	1832
The Disruption .	1843
Education Act passed .	1872
Patronage abolished .	1874
Elementary Education made free	1889
Union of the Free and the United Presbyterian Churches	1900

LIST OF SOVEREIGNS

	A.D.
Malcolm II.	1005-1034
Duncan I., grandson	1034-1040
Macbeth	1040-1057
Malcolm III. (Canmore), son of Duncan I.	1057-1093
Donald Bane, brother	1093-1094
Duncan II., son of Canmore	1094-1094
Donald Bane (Second Reign), brother	1094-1097
Edgar, son of Canmore	1097-1107
Alexander I., brother	1107-1124
David I., brother	1124-1153
Malcolm IV., grandson	1153-1165
William the Lion, brother	1165-1214
Alexander II., son	1214-1249
Alexander III., son	1249-1286
Margaret (The Maid of Norway), grand-daughter	1286-1290
First Interregnum	1290-1292
John Balliol, descendant of David I.	1292-1296
Second Interregnum	1296-1306
Robert I., descendant of David I.	1306-1329
David II., son	1329-1371
Robert II., nephew	1371-1390
Robert III., son	1390-1406
James I., son	1406-1437
James II, son	1437-1460
James III., son	1460-1488
James IV, son	1488-1513
James V., son	1513-1542
Mary, daughter	1542-1567
James VI., son	1567-1625
Charles I., son	1625-1649
Charles II., son	1649-1651
Commonwealth and Protectorate	1651-1660

	A.D.
Charles II.	1660-1685
James VII., brother	1685-1689
William II. and Mary II., nephew and daughter	1689-1694
William II. (alone)	1694-1702
Anne, daughter of James VII.	1702-1714
George I., great-grandson of James VI.	1714-1727
George II., son	1727-1760
George III., grandson	1760-1820
George IV., son	1820-1830
William III., brother	1830-1837
Victoria, niece	1837-1901
Edward I., son	1901-1910
George V., son	1910

GENEALOGY OF THE FAMILY OF DUNCAN I.

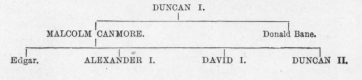

DUNCAN I.
|
MALCOLM CANMORE.   Donald Bane.
|
Edgar.   ALEXANDER I.   DAVID I.   DUNCAN II.

GENEALOGY OF ROBERT BRUCE AND JOHN BALLIOL

DAVID I.
|
Prince Henry.
|
David, Earl of Huntingdon.
|
Margaret.   Isabel.
| |
Devorguilla.   Robert Bruce, Lord of Annandale.
| (Rival of John Balliol.)
JOHN BALLIOL (King). |
                          Robert Bruce, Earl of Carrick.
                                              |
                             ROBERT BRUCE (King).

THE STEWART LINE

ROBERT I. (The Bruce).
|
Marjory, married to Walter the High Steward.
|
ROBERT II.
|
Robert, Duke   ROBERT III.
of Albany. |
                  David,   JAMES I.
                  Duke of |
                  Rothesay.   JAMES II.
                                        |
                                      JAMES III.
                                        |
                                      JAMES IV.,
                       married Margaret Tudor, daughter of Henry VII.
                                        |
                                      JAMES V.
                                        |
                               MARY, QUEEN OF SCOTS.
                                        |
                                      JAMES VI.

TABLE SHOWING HOW THE CROWNS OF SCOTLAND AND ENGLAND WERE UNITED

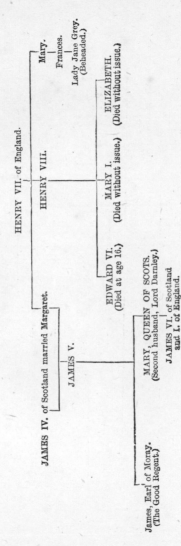

HENRY VII. of England.

JAMES IV. of Scotland married Margaret.

HENRY VIII.

Mary.
Frances.
Lady Jane Grey. (Beheaded.)

ELIZABETH. (Died without issue.)

MARY I. (Died without issue.)

EDWARD VI. (Died at age 16.)

JAMES V.

MARY, QUEEN OF SCOTS. (Second husband, Lord Darnley.)

JAMES VI. of Scotland and I. of England.

James, Earl of Moray. (The Good Regent.)

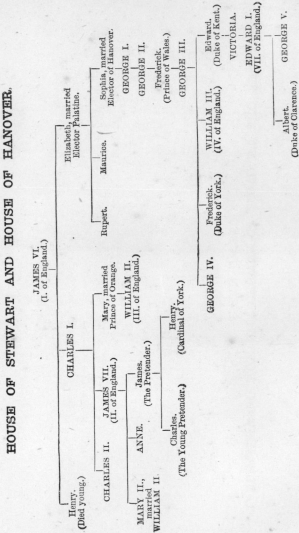

HOUSE OF STEWART AND HOUSE OF HANOVER.